INSIGHT GUIDES

GREEK
ISLANDS

Discovery CHANNEL

APA PUBLICATIONS L
Part of the Langenscheidt Publishing Group

GREEK
ISLANDS

ABOUT THIS BOOK

Editorial
Project Editor
Jeffery Pike
Editorial Director
Brian Bell

Distribution

United States
Langenscheidt Publishers, Inc.
36–36 33rd Street 4th Floor
Long Island City, NY 11106
Fax: 1 (718) 784 0640

UK & Ireland
GeoCenter International Ltd
Meridian House, Churchill Way West
Basingstoke, Hants RG21 6YR
Fax: (44) 1256 817988

Australia
Universal Publishers
1 Waterloo Road
Macquarie Park, NSW 2113
Fax: (61) 2 9888 9074

New Zealand
Hema Maps New Zealand Ltd (HNZ)
Unit D, 24 Ra ORA Drive
East Tamaki, Auckland
Fax: (64) 9 273 6479

Worldwide
Apa Publications GmbH & Co.
Verlag KG (Singapore branch)
38 Joo Koon Road, Singapore 628990
Tel: (65) 6865 1600. Fax: (65) 6861 6438

Printing

Insight Print Services (Pte) Ltd
38 Joo Koon Road, Singapore 628990
Tel: (65) 6865 1600. Fax: (65) 6861 6438

©2008 Apa Publications GmbH & Co.
Verlag KG (Singapore branch)
All Rights Reserved
First Edition 1990
Third Edition 1999
Updated 2008

CONTACTING THE EDITORS
We would appreciate it if readers
would alert us to errors or out-
dated information by writing to:
**Insight Guides, P.O. Box 7910,
London SE1 1WE, England.**
Fax: (44) 20 7403 0290.
insight@apaguide.co.uk
NO part of this book may be reproduced,
stored in a retrieval system or transmitted
in any form or means electronic, mechanical, photocopying, recording or otherwise, without prior written permission of
Apa Publications. Brief text quotations
with use of photographs are exempted
for book review purposes only. Information has been obtained from sources
believed to be reliable, but its accuracy
and completeness, and the opinions
based thereon, are not guaranteed.

www.insightguides.com

The first Insight Guide pio-
neered the use of creative full-
colour photography in travel
guides in 1970. Since then, we
have expanded our range to cater
for our readers' need, not only for
reliable information about their
chosen destination but also a
real understanding of the culture
and workings of that destination.
Now, when the internet can supply inexhaustible facts, our books
marry text and pictures to provide
those much more elusive quali-
ties: knowledge and discernment.
To achieve this, they rely heavily
on the authority of locally based
writers and photographers.

How to use the book

To understand Greece today, you
need to know something of its
turbulent past. The **History** and
Features section, with a yellow colour
bar, covers the country's history from
ancient times to the struggle for
independence and the formation of
the modern state. The culture and
everyday life of the islands are
explored in lively essays by experts.

The central **Places** section, with a
blue bar, provides a detailed run-

grapher. He has drawn on the last edition of *Insight Guide: Greek Islands*, which was edited by **Martha Ellen Zenfell**.

John Chapple, who has lived in Greece since 1969, revised the chapters on Athens, the Saronic Gulf, Ionian islands and Sporades, and the essays on Greek life.

Marc Dubin, a well-travelled resident of London who has a house on Sámos, has updated the chapters on the Dodecanese and the Northeast Aegean islands, as well as writing on Greek music and attempts to cope with tourism.

Lance Chilton has published numerous guide books on Greece and Cyprus. He updated the Crete chapter, as well as supplying new material on island wildlife, wild flowers and the Palace of Knossós. Journalist **Stephanie Ferguson** brought her story of an island family up to date, and contributed new pages on religious festivals and food and drink. **Jeffrey Carson**, who has lived on Páros since 1970, has revised the chapter on the Cyclades.

This edition builds on previous editions of the guide, whose contributors also included **Rowlinson Carter** (history and Island Elections), **Mark Mazower** (history), **Marcus Brooke** (Ancient Delos, Lindos and Crete), **Rhoda Nottridge** (Corfu), **David Glenn** (Sailing), **Kerin Hope** (Athens), **Carol Reed**, **John Carr** (Cruising), **Anthony Wood** (Working the Land), **Jane Cocking**, **Nile Stanton**, **Anita Peltonen** (Cyclades and Northeast Aegean) and **Diana Farr Louis** and **Nikos Stavroualakis**.

The current update was carried out by **Pam Barrett** and edited in-house by **Alexia Georgiou**.

down of just about every island that it's possible to visit. The main places of interest are coordinated by number with full-colour maps.

The **Travel Tips** listings section, with an orange bar, provides all the information you need on travel, accommodation, eating and drinking, sports and language. You can locate information quickly by referring to the index on the back cover flap – and the flaps are designed to double as bookmarks.

The contributors

This new edition was edited by **Jeffery Pike**, a London-based freelance journalist and photo-

Map Legend

▬ ▪▪	International Boundary
▬ ▬ ▬	Province
⊖	Border Crossing
▬▪▬	National Park/Reserve
▬ ▬ ▬	Ferry Route
Ⓜ	Metro
✈ ✈	Airport International / Regional
🚌	Bus Station
Ⓟ	Parking
❶	Tourist Information
✉	Post Office
🏛 † ✝	Church / Ruins
✝	Monastery
☪	Mosque
✡	Synagogue
🏰 ⌂	Castle / Ruins
∴	Archaeological Site
∩	Cave
🏛	Statue / Monument
★	Place of Interest

The main places of interest in the Places section are coordinated by number with a full-colour map (e.g. ❶), and a symbol at the top of every right-hand page tells you where to find the map.

CONTENTS

Pátmos, the
Dodecanese

Insight on ...

Information panels

Travel Tips

Places

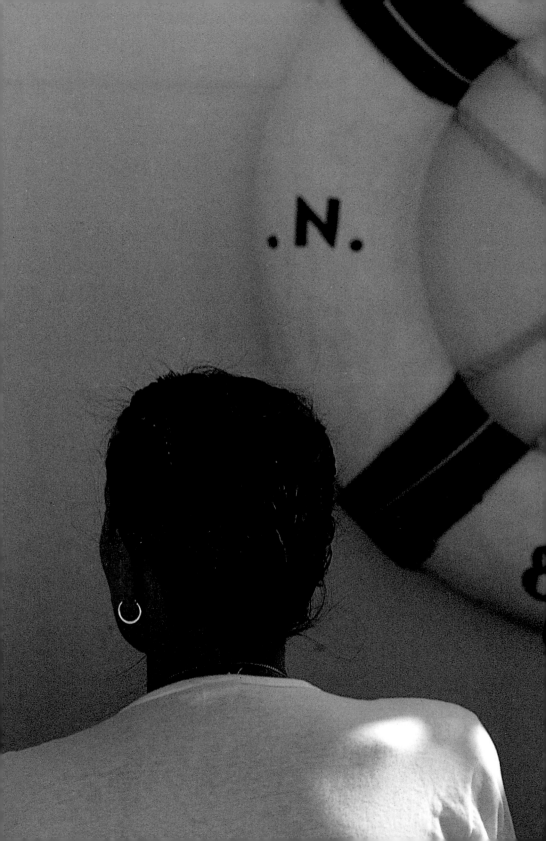

ISLAND MENTALITY

Greece has about 2,000 islands altogether. Despite their superficial similarities, each has a distinct identity and often an idiosyncratic history

It is one of those words that psychiatrists might use to trigger an automatic response from a patient stretched on the couch. Say "island" and childhood recollections of Robinson Crusoe may spring to mind. Often, islands are associated with the escape from a complex universe into a private, more manageable world that offers individuals control over their own destiny. Crusoe becomes comfortable in his reconstructed womb, and it's a surprise, when rescue is at hand, that he doesn't tell his saviours to push off.

"Greek island" would probably add some specific touches to the imagery: a cluster of blisteringly white buildings against a shimmering sea, donkeys slowly carrying their burdens against a backdrop of olive groves, small circles of weather-beaten fishermen bent over their nets, and jolly tavernas full of *retsína, moussaká*, shattered plates and background music from *Never on Sunday* and *Zorba the Greek*. Accurate as far as it goes, perhaps, but any generalisation about the Greek islands – anything, that is, more ambitious than the staringly obvious – would almost certainly be wrong.

Inter-island relations

Although the islands are classified as members of one group or another, each has a strong sense of separate identity and invariably an idiosyncratic history to back it up. Often, the feeling between neighbouring islands is mutual suspicion bordering on loathing, although this is something visitors would seldom be aware of unless they made a point of going down to the local *ouzerí* and chatting to the men entrenched there. Conditioned by long winter nights when nothing much happens, the men have developed the knack of waffling on about

any subject under the sun, and a new face in the audience is welcome.

As an example of inter-island relations, Skiáthos and Skópelos in the Sporades have never been able to see eye to eye on the matter of ice. The origins of the dispute are buried in history, but it may spring from days when making ice depended on clanking contraptions which were partly home-made and therefore the focus of parochial pride. Neither side in the respective *ouzerís* will volunteer what is wrong with the other island's ice. Uncharacteristically, questions are turned aside, but hopeless shaking of grey heads hints at a truth so awful that they cannot bring themselves to utter it.

The telephone directories on Skiáthos and Skópelos reveal some of the same surnames. Could the families be related? The inquiry hits a nerve as painful as the ice business.

Only in one area, if the old boys are to be believed, are the two islands in full agreement, and that concerns Skýros, the largest island in

PRECEDING PAGES: a fishing boat in Mýkonos; a little blue-domed church in the Cyclades; an Orthodox priest on his way to work; ferry passengers in the Saronic Gulf. **LEFT:** birds, cats and villager. **RIGHT:** *Óhi* Day celebrations on Skópelos.

the chain. Skiáthos and Skópelos are within full view of one another, a distasteful but undeniable fact, whereas Skýros lies below the horizon. According to the miraculously united old boys, that means that Skýros may not exist.

Such theories are expounded with twinkling eyes and guffaws. Even if they should not be taken too literally, they are great fun, and the opportunity to move between neighbouring islands in order to compare notes should not be missed. It is sometimes said that if, against the odds, two islands struck the curious visitor as being practically identical, those islands would necessarily be at opposite ends of the Aegean.

with the skills which developed into the Minoan civilisation.

Intruders

To look at the history of Corfu, for instance, merely from the 11th century is to pick up that particular story a long way down the line. Nevertheless, the record from that date reveals an amazing cavalcade of intruders to the island *(see panel below)*. All of them must have left a mark, even if the traces today would require more diligent research than most visitors would care to conduct while staying there on holiday. Dedicated scholars could probably assemble a

Apart from the natural tendency for small island communities to be staunchly independent, there is a historical basis for their individualism. From the time of the Phoenicians, the islands have been tossed around like loose pebbles in the cultural tides that have surged backwards and forwards through the eastern Mediterranean, and none has emerged from that experience quite like any other.

Momentous events were taking place on Crete and some of the Cyclades as early as 3000BC. The golden age of Athens under Pericles lay as far in the future then as, for us, it now lies in the past – more than two millennia either way. Settlers from Mesopotamia landed

FOREIGN OCCUPIERS

The history of Corfu is a typical saga of occupation by foreign powers, each of whom left some mark. From the 11th century, the island was ruled successively by Greeks (the Byzantine Empire), Normans, Sicilians, Venetians, Greek Orthodox once more ("the despotate of Epirus"), more Sicilians, Neapolitans and then the Venetians again – this time for 400 years. Then the procession of foreign rulers resumed: France, Russia, Britain, and then Greece. Italy occupied Corfu briefly in the 1920s and again during World War II. After Italy collapsed in 1943, Germany became the last foreign occupier, until the German surrender in 1944.

jigsaw, with pieces extant in Corfu, that would reflect each and every one of these waves.

The evidence does not necessarily consist of archeological ruins or excavated objects. Corfu extrapolated from one small chapter of its convoluted history an abiding passion for cricket. It is still played on the square in the middle of the town, albeit with local variations which would raise the eyebrows of traditionalists in England.

Other islands got almost as much unwanted outside attention as Corfu. Piracy was a perennial problem, hence the number of citadels *(kástra)* on high ground to which the island population retreated when danger threatened.

isn't mapped. A good tip for amateur archeologists would be to ask themselves where, taking into account security, prevailing winds, terrain, water supply etc, they themselves would have chosen to build something – and then start looking for evidence of past peoples.

The topographical differences among the islands are worth considering. If some of the islands look like mountain peaks, it is because much of the area now covered by the Aegean was once a solid land bridge between Greece and Asia Minor, which eventually fractured and "sank". These islands are the tips of what used to be ranges encroaching from either side.

Determined pirates

The defences did not always keep determined pirates like Khair-ed-din Barbarossa out, but they did mean that the pirates had to make an effort instead of lazily helping themselves to everything of value when they happened to be cruising by.

Crete and Rhodes have by far the richest and most thoroughly documented sites for historically-minded visitors, but on any island there is bound to be something to pick over, even if it

LEFT: traditional music provided a focus for the development of island identity. **ABOVE:** café life is very much a part of island social interaction.

The largest mountain ranges in mainland Greece caused famous military bottlenecks at places like Thermopylae where, in Xerxes' time, there was only the narrowest of passages between the mountains and the sea. Since then the sea has receded, so what used to be a death trap, where Spartan defenders calmly bathed and combed their hair (according to Herodotus) while waiting for the Persian onslaught, is now a coastal plain 5 km (3 miles) wide.

The contours of submerged mountains and valleys extending from the area around Thermopylae caused the seabed around the islands to drop precipitously to 1,800 metres (6,000 ft). On the Turkish side, the sea is generally much shallower, and it is the shallows which can cause the Aegean, quiet and bather-friendly one moment, to be transformed into a lethal cauldron within the space of an hour or two.

Anyone hiring a boat on holiday should never leave port without consulting the islanders. For thousands of years, lives have depended on accurate weather predictions, and local knowledge handed down is often more reliable than official forecasts carried on the radio or in newspapers.

If the purpose of a visit to the islands is nothing more than to settle on a stretch of agreeable beach and live cheaply, visitors

should be lucky on both counts. Greece has about 2,000 islands altogether and these, plus the mainland, add up to technically the longest coastline of any country in Europe. Basic commodities, including restaurant meals and ferry tickets, are price-controlled. While the adoption of the euro in early 2002 was an opportunity for some initial "rounding up", in the long run inflation should slow down to past European norms.

The pink pound

One expensive exception is Mýkonos, which has cashed in on its reputation as a centre of gay tourism. Whatever the local business people may think in private of the antics of many of its visitors (probably oblique references to their need for the island's vast number of churches), they tend to be stoical about them in public and continue to pocket the money.

Mýkonos would not have been allowed to develop its reputation under the puritanical military junta, when even topless sunbathing was discouraged. Since the overthrow of the glum colonels, what bathers choose to wear or discard has been a matter of personal choice, and there is usually at least one beach on an island where nudity is tolerated, even if it is not official.

The best way to enjoy the islands is to arrive with a certain attitude of mind. By all means, begin by uncritically enjoying the cluster of blisteringly white buildings against a shimmering sea, donkeys with a backdrop of olive groves, and so on – the vista, indeed, seared into the senses by island holiday brochures.

When the novelty wears off, or perhaps earlier, examine each island as if it were an onion, and start stripping off the skins. If not a longstanding dispute about ice, some other unexpected aspect is certain to be revealed.

How to strip the onion is a large part of what this book is about. It hopes to show by example. The book will never be written that says everything about 2,000 islands. The learned Helidorius once tried to set out all he had learned about the monuments of Athens, as they existed in the second century BC. Fifteen volumes later... ❑

ILLEGAL SUBSTANCES

The apparently tolerant attitude towards tourist behaviour in Greece does not extend to the use of drugs, and the more popular islands are subject to close undercover surveillance. Some humdrum medicines sold without prescription elsewhere may be illegal in Greece, and as the legal system seems to rest on the principle that the slightest suspicion warrants a spell in prison before the proceedings proper begin, it is wise to err on the side of extreme caution and leave nothing to chance. There are random drug searches at customs, and the minimum sentence for possessing even a small quantity of cannabis is three to four years.

LEFT: fishing in local waters supplies tourists and villagers alike. **RIGHT:** preparing the evening meal of *hórta* – wild greens.

Settentrio

DALMATIÆ PARS

ALBANIA PARS ILLYRIDIS

MACEDONIA

Orbeli

Sintica

Migdonia

Bisaltica

Odo mantica

Iori

Pelagonia

Paeonia

Lincheste

Amphaxitis

Astrei

Ematia

Golfo di Saloichi olin Thermaicus Sinus

Tamoriza

Eordei

Comenolitari

Deuriopes

Macedonia

Pieria

Dassaretti

Elymiotæ

Parthini

Stymphalis

Penestæ

Pelasgiotus

Pelagonia Tripolitis

Magnesia

Oresti æ

Atintan

TESSALIA

Estiæotis

Camina Elyma

Chimera et Chaonia

Tymphæa

Iannalia

Parorei

EPIRO

Thesproti

Pindus M.

Thessaliotis

Pindus M.

Phtiotis

Hellopes

Dolopes

Larta

Dryopes

Cassopaei

Molossi

Athamanes

Perrhæb

Amphilochi

Doris

Phocis

Aetoli

Agræi

LIVADIA

Beotia

Despotato

Acarnania

ACHAIA

Aetolia

Locri Ozolæ

Ducato di At

Santa Maura I. et Leucas Insula

Golfo di Lepanto ol. Cirræus et Corinthiacus sinus

Engia I.

Cefalonia I. et Cephalenia

Achaia

Clarenza

Arcadia

MORE A

Zante I. et Zacynthus

PELOPONNESVS

Elis

Laconia

Tzacconia Braccio di Maina

Messenia

LA GRECIA
VNIVERSALE ANTICA
Paragonata con la Moderna da
Giacomo Cantelli da Vignola
Con le direttioni delle Carte Migliori e de piu accre=
ditati Scrittori di Geografia. data in luce da Gio=
Giacomo Rossi in Roma alla Pace l'anno 1683.
con Priu. del S. Pont.

MARE IONIO O DI GRECIA

MARE DEL GOLFO DI VENETIA

Ponente

MARE DI SAPIENZA

Sapienza. I. ol. Sphagia

Giorgio Widman Sculp.

THRACIÆ PARS oggi ROMANIA

Bistones

MARE DI MARMARA olim PROPONTIS

CONSTANTINOPOLI

ARCIPELAGO oggi MAR BIANCO anticamente ÆGÆVM MARE

Mysia Minor

Mysia Maior

ANATOLIA

Stalimene I. et Lemnos

Metelino I. olim Lesbos

ICARIVM MARE

Scio I. et Chiar et Chies

Nicaria I. et Icaria

Samo I. et Samos

CARAMANIA et LYDIA

ASIA MINOR

Andro I. et Andros

Tino I. et Tenos

Rocho I.

Delos grande et Pheneo

Micolo I. et Miconus

Insulæ Cyclades

Nicsia I. et Naxos

Parul et Paros

Morgo I. et Amorgos

Caria

MARE MIRTOVM

Doris

Lango I. et Cos

Sporades Insulæ

MARE MIRTOVM

Santorini o S. Erini olim Thera Insula

MARE DI CANDIA ol CRETICVM Mare

Scarpanto I. et Carpathus

Isola di Rodi et Rhodus

MARE DI SCARPANTO olim Carpathium Mare

CANDIA olim CRETA

Decisive Dates

3200BC: Beginnings of Bronze Age cultures in Crete and the Cyclades.

2600–1450BC: Minoan civilisation in Crete.

c1500BC: Huge volcanic eruption on Santorini produces tidal waves that cause devastation. Major sites in central and southern Crete destroyed by fire.

c1450BC: Mycenaeans (originally from the northern Peloponnese) occupy Crete and Rhodes; establish a trading empire; adapt Minoan script into Linear B – the first written Greek.

1184BC: Traditional date for the fall of Troy.

11TH CENTURY BC: Dorians from the north invade the islands, destroying Mycenaean civilisation and bringing Iron Age technology and new "geometric" pottery.

1150–750BC: The "Dark Ages". Cultural and economic development stagnates, the art of writing is forgotten. Refugee Mycenaeans (known as Ionians) settle on Aegean islands, in Asia Minor and in Attica.

900–750BC: The growth of city states. Athens becomes the foremost Ionian city.

776BC: Probable date of the first Olympic Games.

c770BC: Contact with Etruscans, Phoenicians and Egyptians spurs a revival of Greek cultural life. Greeks adopt the Phoenician alphabet.

750–700BC: The Homeric epics *The Odyssey* and *The Iliad* are written down for the first time.

c715BC: Archilochus, the first lyric poet, born on Paros.

c650BC: Poetess Sappho born on Lesbos (Lésvos).

c570BC: Pythagoras born on Sámos.

546BC: The Persian empire expands to control Ionian Greek cities on west coast of Anatolia (now Turkey).

520–500BC: Persians, under Darius the Great, systematically conquer many Aegean islands. Revolts are ruthlessly put down.

499–479BC: Persian invasions of Greek mainland repulsed by united Greek front, led by Spartan army and Athenian navy. Ionian states freed from Persian rule.

THE CLASSICAL AGE

477BC: Athens establishes Delian League, comprising many islands and cities in Asia Minor; the treasury and nominal headquarters is on Delos.

471–465BC: Islands that attempt to secede from the League are brutally quashed by Athens.

460BC: Hippocrates, the "father of medicine", born on Kos.

454BC: The League's treasury is removed from Delos to Athens. Effectively, the island states are now part of an Athenian Empire.

431–404BC: Peloponnesian War between Athens (and her allies) and Sparta (and other Peloponnesian states) leaves Athens defeated and weakened.

338BC: Greeks defeated by Philip II of Macedon.

336–323BC: Philip succeeded by his son Alexander, who extends his empire as far as India and Egypt.

323BC: On Alexander's death, the empire is divided between his generals. Greek islands are controlled by Ptolemy and his successors.

c300BC: Thíra on Santoríni becomes capital of the Ptolemaic Aegean.

227BC: Earthquake destroys Colossus of Rhodes.

ROMANS AND BYZANTINES

146BC: Romans annex Macedonia and Greece.

AD58: St Paul on Rhodes.

AD95: St John writes the Apocalypse on Pátmos.

3RD CENTURY: Christianity spreads; Goths threaten Greece's northen frontier.

323: Constantine becomes sole ruler of the Roman Empire; establishes his capital at Constantinople.

391: Paganism outlawed in the Roman Empire.

393: Olympic Games banned as a pagan festival.

395: Goths under Alaric devastate Athens and the Peloponnese.

395: Roman Empire splits into two: Latin west and Byzantine east.

653–658: Arabs occupy Rhodes; sell the remains of the Colossus as scrap metal.

747–843: Icons are banned in the Eastern Church.

827: Arabs establish themselves in Crete, proceed to plunder the rest of the Aegean for over 100 years.
961: Byzantines retake Crete.
1081: Normans from Sicily invade Greek islands.
1088: Monastery of St John founded on Pátmos.
1096: The First Crusade.
1204: The Fourth Crusade: Constantinople taken. Break-up of the Byzantine Empire. Venetians claim the right to the Ionians and other islands.
1210: Venetians take Crete.
1309: Knights Hospitallers of St John arrive on Rhodes, take over and fortify the Dodecanese.
1389: Venetians gain control of much of Greece and the islands.
1453: Ottoman Turks capture Constantinople, rename it Istanbul and make it capital of Ottoman Empire.
1522–37: Rhodes and the other Dodecanese islands invaded and taken over by Ottoman Turks.
1541: El Greco born in Crete.
1649–69: Venetian-Turkish War; ends with Iráklion falling to Turkish forces. Crete is under Ottoman rule.
1797: Napoleon takes the Ionian Islands.
1799: Ionian Republic declared.
1815–64: British rule in the Ionian Islands.

THE STRUGGLE FOR INDEPENDENCE

1821–27: War of Independence against Turkey.
1823: Solomós writes the *Hymn to Liberty*.
1827–29: Aigina (Éghina) the capital of Greece.
1830: Turks cede Euboea (Évvia) to Greeks, but keep control of the Dodecanese, east Aegean and north mainland.
1834: Athens becomes capital of Greece.
1854–57: Piraeus (Piréas) blockaded by British and French fleets.
1864: Ionian islands, relinquished by Britain, become part of the Greek state.
1896: First modern Olympics held in Athens.
1897: Greece goes to war with Turkey again, but is heavily defeated.
1898: Crete becomes an independent principality within the Ottoman Empire.
1909: Army officers revolt against political establishment in Athens, invite Cretan lawyer Elefthérios Venizélos to form a new government.
1910: Venizélos becomes Prime Minister; his Liberal Party dominates Greek politics for 25 years.
1912–13: Balkan Wars: Greece takes from Turkey

Crete, Northern and Eastern Aegean islands, and Macedonia. Italy occupies Dodecanese.
1913: King George I is murdered, succeeded by his son, Constantine I.
1924: Greece becomes a republic.
1940: Greece is neutral in World War II until Mussolini's Italy attacks; Greece aligns with the Allies.
1941: Greece invaded by Nazi Germany.
1943-44: Greece is liberated by Allies, who keep control of the Dodecanese until 1947.
1946–9: Civil War between Greek government and Communists opposed to restoring the monarchy.
1947: Dodecanese become part of Greece.
1947–67: Constitutional monarchy in Greece.

1953: Earthquake causes great damage in Ionian Islands: large-scale emigration.
1967–74: Greece ruled by junta of right-wing colonels; King Constantine in exile.
1974: Colonels overthrown; republic established.
1981: Andréas Papandréou's left-wing PASOK party forms first Greek Socialist government.
1981: Greece becomes member of EEC (now EU).
1989: PASOK brought down by corruption scandals.
1996: Papandréou dies; suceeded by Kóstas Simítis.
1999: Severe earthquake hits northern Athens.
2002: Greece adopts the euro.
2004: Centre-right New Democracy wins elections; Athens hosts the Olympic Games.
2007: New Democracy re-elected in September. ❑

PRECEDING PAGES: 17th-century map of ancient Greece. **LEFT:** the owl, symbol of goddess Athene's wisdom, appeared on early Athenian coins.
RIGHT: British troops liberate Athens in 1944.

WAVES OF INVADERS

The history of Greece, and especially its islands, is inextricably linked to the sea. It is a history full of foreign conquerors and occupiers

What distinguishes the course of Greek history from that of her Balkan neighbours is the impact of the sea. The sea diffuses cultures, transfers peoples and encourages trade – and until our own times it was invariably a swifter means of transmission than overland. Nowhere in Greece is the sea as inescapable as on the islands.

The poverty of the arid island soil has forced inhabitants to venture far afield for their livelihood. At the same time, the islands have been vulnerable to foreign incursions, whether by Arab pirates, Italian colonists or modern tourists. All have played their part in transforming local conditions; some have had an even wider impact. Phoenician traders, for example, appear to have brought their alphabet to Crete in the early Archaic period, which the Greeks then adopted and changed. At the same time, Egyptian influence was leading island sculptors to work in stone. It is no coincidence that the earliest examples of monumental Greek sculpture are all to be found on the islands.

On Crete, the Bronze Age had produced the first urban civilisation in the Aegean: this was the age of the Knossós and Festós palaces, erected in the centuries after 2000 BC. Other islands such as Santoríni also flourished at this time. Thucydides' account of how King Minos of Crete established his sons as governors in the Cyclades and cleared the sea of pirates certainly suggests considerable Cretan control of the Aegean. The Aegean was not to be dominated by a single sea power for another millennium until the rise of the Athenian empire.

Economic growth

Before this, however, communities of Greeks had begun to flourish on most of the islands, exploiting local quarries and mines, and developing indigenous political systems. Some communities achieved considerable wealth, notably

LEFT: a marble figure from the Early Cycladic era.
RIGHT: an inaccurate artist's impression of the Colossus of Rhodes.

on Sífnos, whose gold and silver mines had made her inhabitants reputedly the richest citizens in the Cyclades by the 6th century BC. Some reflection of this wealth can be seen in the ruins of the marble treasury which Sifniots dedicated to Apollo at Delphi.

It was in the 6th century, too, that the inhab-

itants of Santoríni began to mint their own coinage, a physical manifestation of the island's powerful status in the Aegean. At one point Santoríni's influence was to extend not only to Crete, Mílos, Páros and Rhodes, but as far west as Corinth and as far east as Asia Minor.

During the 5th century BC, the islands' independence was curtailed as Athens used anti-Persian fears to manipulate the Delian League. This had been formed in 478 BC as an alliance between equal partners to form a strong naval power in the Aegean. But Athens soon controlled the League and used its resources in a series of wars against rivals such as the naval power of Aegina (Éghina).

It was Athenian intrigues with the Corinthian colony on Corfu, however, that led to the Peloponnesian War which was ultimately to cripple – and break – Athens forever.

In the Hellenistic period the islands remained turbulent backwaters, prone to internecine struggles which made them easy prey for their more powerful neighbours. By the middle of the 1st century BC, Rome had established herself in the Aegean; Crete became the centre of a province which included a part of North Africa.

Under Roman guidance roads were laid, aqueducts constructed, new towns and grand buildings erected. Despite this prosperity, the

Aegean as a whole remained in the background in Roman times. Little is known of conditions of life in the islands either then or after AD 395, when they passed into the control of the eastern Roman Empire. Only with the onset of the Arab raids in the 7th century does the historical record become more complete.

With the decline of Roman power in the Mediterranean, the islands faced a long period of instability: for more than a millennium they were attacked by invaders from all points of the compass. From the north, briefly, came the Vandals and Goths; from the south, the Arabs, who established themselves on Crete in 827 and proceeded to plunder the rest of the Aegean

for over a century. From the west came Normans in the 11th century, followed by the Genoese and Venetians; finally, from the east came the Ottoman Turks, who succeeded in dominating almost all of the islands in the Aegean between the 15th and 18th centuries.

Other groups, too, played minor roles – quite apart from powers such as the English, French and Russians, who all shared an interest in the Greek islands. The impact of these various peoples on the islands was complex and tangled, making it awkward to generalise about the historical experiences of the islands themselves. Only by considering the main island groups individually may things fall into place.

The Ionian islands

On the eve of the 1821 Greek uprising, an English traveller to Corfu noted: "The natural weakness and position of the Ionian islands, and all their past history, demonstrate that they must ever be an appendage of some more powerful state; powerful at sea and able to protect them as well as to command." Close to the Greek mainland, vital staging-posts on the voyage from western Europe to the Levant, it was inevitable that the Ionian islands should be a source of constant conflict.

Corfu had suffered brief attacks during the 5th century from Vandals and Goths, the destroyers of the Roman Empire in the West, but it was not until the eastern Empire lost its possessions in southern Italy that the Ionian islands again became vulnerable to invasion. This time the predators were the Normans. At the time when William the Conqueror was establishing Norman control over England, Robert Guiscard, Duke of Apulia, defeated the Byzantine army and its emperor, before dying of a fever at Kefalloniá. His nephew Roger, King of Sicily, occupied Corfu in 1146 and held it for six years. As the Byzantine hold over the islands weakened, the Venetians came in as reluctant allies.

These allies soon proved to have territorial ambitions of their own. The islands were situated on important trade routes to the eastern Mediterranean, and commercial interests led to the desire for political control. After the sack of Constantinople in 1204 during the Fourth Crusade, the islands were divided into fiefdoms among noble Venetian families. Not until 1387, however, were the islands brought under direct

Venetian rule, which continued through a succession of Ottoman attacks down to 1797, when under the new order created by Napoleon's conquests, the islands went to France.

During these four centuries, the Ionian islands were ruled by local nobility and by administrators sent out from Venice. The influence of the Republic was felt in the introduction of cash crops such as olives and currants, in the repressive regime under which the peasants worked and in the Italian language which the nobility affected to speak. At first Venetian rule was energetic – so that, for example, after Ottoman raids had left Zákynthos virtually

and political assassination made life precarious.

The end of Venetian rule was bloodless: when the French invaders arrived, they discovered the fortress guns rusting and the garrison without any gunpowder. Napoleon himself had written in 1797 that "the great maxim of the Republic ought henceforth to be never to abandon Corfu, Zante…" However, British troops managed to establish a foothold in the minor islands in 1809. After Napoleon's defeat this was extended and the new Septinsular Republic was placed under British protection.

Sir Thomas Maitland, the first Lord High Commissioner, in the words of a Victorian

uninhabited in the late 15th century, vigorous resettlement policies soon created the basis for new prosperity. Zákynthos had only 36 families in 1485, but 752 families by 1516, and her revenues increased forty-fold in 30 years thanks to the introduction of these valuable crops.

By the 18th century Venice had lost her possessions in the Aegean and the Peloponnese; in the Ionian Sea, the Venetian-held islands were ravaged by pirates operating from Paxos (Paxí) and the Albanian coast; internally, blood feuds

LEFT: Dionýsios Solomós, the Ionian poet whose *Hymn to Freedom* was adopted as the national anthem after Independence. **ABOVE:** a watercolour of Itháki harbour.

BRIBERY AND CORRUPTION

By the end of the 18th century, the Venetians' last remaining stronghold in the Ionians was corrupt. In 1812, the British Whig politician Henry Holland wrote of the Venetian rulers of Corfu: "The governors and other officers sent to the island were usually of noble family and often of decayed fortune; men who undertook the office as a speculation of interest and executed it accordingly. Bribery and every mode of illegal practice were carried on openly; toleration for a crime might easily be purchased; and the laws, in many respects imperfect themselves, were rendered wholly null by the corruption of the judges."

historian, "established a Constitution which, possessing every appearance of freedom, in reality left the whole power in his hands". But it could not satisfy the islanders' desire for freedom from foreign rule, a desire which intensified after the creation of the Kingdom of Greece in 1832. In 1864 Britain relinquished control and the Ionian Islands became part of the modern Greek state, a condition stipulated by the new King George I for taking the throne.

The Cyclades, Sporades and Saronic Gulf islands

The Cyclades, unlike the Ionian islands, were a commercial backwater: main trade routes passed through Crete and the eastern Aegean islands to Smyrna and Aleppo. While they remained a lure to pirates, they were never of comparable interest to major powers. Until the rise of the seafaring Italian city-states in the 11th century, most trade in the Aegean was in the hands of Greeks.

However, the weakness of the Byzantine navy was underlined by a series of Arab raids against the islands and the Greek mainland. By the 12th century a British chronicler noted that piracy had become the curse of the Aegean: many of the islands were abandoned, while others – Skýros in the Sporades, for example – became pirate lairs.

The sack of Constantinople in 1204, which brought the Ionian islands under Venetian control, also brought new masters to the Aegean. The unimportance of this group of islands to them meant that the Venetians were content to leave the task of occupying them to private citizens. Of these, the most successful was Marco Sanudo, a nephew of the Doge Dandolo, who equipped eight galleys at his own expense and sailed to the Aegean where he founded the Duchy of Náxos in 1207.

Náxos itself became the capital of a fiefdom of some islands, and on it Sanudo built a castle, erected a Catholic cathedral and provided solid fortifications for the town. Other adventurers helped themselves to islands such as Ándhros and Santoríni. The Ghisi family obtained Tínos and Mýkonos, as well as the islands in the Sporades, establishing a dynasty which clashed with the Sanudi until both were overwhelmed by the Ottoman navy in the 16th century.

Traces of the Venetian presence are to be found in the Catholic communities which survive on both Sýros and Tínos. The Duchy of Náxos lasted over 350 years, and only ended with the death of Joseph Nasi, the Sephardic Jewish favourite of Selim II, upon whom the sultan had bestowed the islands after their capture from the Sanudi.

But the exceptional longevity of the Duchy of Náxos should not be allowed to obscure the turbulence of life in the Aegean in these centuries. Piracy had increased in the late 13th century, with Greek corsairs from Monemvasiá or Santoríni, Sicilians and Genoese – and had led, for example, the inhabitants of the island of Amorgós to emigrating en masse to Náxos whose fertile interior was relatively inaccessible.

PRIESTS AND BAD ROADS

When the British took control of the Ionian islands in 1815, they found a society very different to their own. Wheeled transport was virtually unknown on several islands owing to the appalling roads, and the priests opposed the introduction of the potato to the islands on the grounds that this was the apple with which the serpent had tempted Eve in the Garden of Eden. At the same time, the inhabitants of the islands were demanding the amenities of western Europe. The British obliged by bringing improved roads, drainage schemes and, with a touch of the public-school love of team sports, the game of cricket.

In the 14th century, Catalan mercenaries, brought in for the conflict between Venice and Genoa, ravaged some of the islands and raided others. Ottoman troops landed on Náxos and took 6,000 captives. The Ottoman forces often consisted of recent converts to Islam, and were led by renegade Aegean Greeks such as the notorious brothers from the island of Lésvos, Khair-ed-din and Amrudj Barbarossa.

Local rulers began to complain of depopulation: Ándhros had to be resettled by Alban-

ian mainlanders; Íos, virtually uninhabited, was replenished by families from the Peloponnese. Astypálea was repopulated in 1413, abandoned in 1473 and only inhabited once more after 1570. In the 16th century, the islands suffered a series of attacks by the Turkish navy and by mid-century Venetian influence was on the wane. Within 50 years, most of the islands had been brought under Ottoman rule, though the last, Tínos, only succumbed as late as 1712.

LEFT: detail of an embroidery from Skýros, probably from the 17th century. **ABOVE:** a 1795 watercolour showing the unfinished Temple of Apollo, Náxos.

> ### VENETIAN REMAINS
>
> There is still linguistic evidence of the Venetian occupation of the Cyclades, in local family names derived from Italian.

Conditions of life did not improve under Ottoman rule. Piracy, famine and fatal disease remained the perennial problems. In the 18th century, the plague decimated the islands on four separate occasions, continuing into the next century, well after the disease had died out in most of Europe. Thus the Ottomans, like their predecessors, were forced to repopulate.

Often the new colonists were not Greeks. Tournefort reported in the early 18th century that most of the inhabitants of Andíparos were descended from French and Maltese corsairs. He also noted that villages on Ándhros were "peopled only by Albanians, dressed still in their traditional style and living their own way, that is to say with neither creed nor law".

It was the Albanians who were to play a major role in the struggle for Greek independence. Waves of Albanians had been colonising the islands of the Aegean since the 14th century. They were concentrated on the Saronic islands – the eminent Koundouriotis family, for example, moved from Epiros to Hydra around the year 1580. By the late 18th century, Hydra, with a largely Albanian population, possessed one of the largest and most powerful shipping fleets in the Aegean, which played no small part in defeating the Ottoman Turks after 1821.

The importance of these islands was underlined by the choice of Aegina (Éghina), for a short time, as the first capital of the new Greek state. Refugees flocked here when it was the seat of government, only to leave again when it was replaced by Náfplion, on the mainland. When Edouard About visited the town in 1839 he reported it "abandoned – the homes that had been built tumbled into ruins, the town once more became a village; its life and activity fled with the government".

The Northeast Aegean islands

Although the east Aegean islands shared the experience of Arab raids with the Cyclades, the two areas developed differently as the rivalry between Venice and Genoa increased after the Fourth Crusade. As allies of the resurgent Byzantine Empire against her Latin enemies, the Genoese were given trading rights in the Black Sea and granted permission to colonise the eastern Aegean.

A Genoese trading company controlled the mastic plantations of Híos from the beginning of the 14th century. In 1333 Lésvos passed into the hands of the Gatteluso family, who eventually extended their control to Thássos, Límnos and Samothráki. However, as in the west Aegean, the power of the Ottoman navies simply overwhelmed these local potentates, and with the fall of Híos in 1566 all the islands of the east Aegean passed into Ottoman hands.

Lésvos had been conquered by the Ottoman Turks as early as 1462, and most of the inhabitants emigrated. In 1472 the inhabitants of Sámos fled to Híos, but their descendants

then spread to Híos where, in 1822, the Ottomans brutally suppressed a rather uncertain revolt. Fustel de Coulanges wrote in 1856: "Any person aged more than 32 years whom one meets today on Híos was enslaved and saw his father slaughtered".

It was little consolation to know that the massacre on Híos had aroused the attention of European liberals, and strengthened philhellenic sentiment. Refugees fled westwards, transporting the island's traditional *loukoúmi* industry (the making and selling of Turkish delight) to Sýros in the Cyclades, whose port of Ermoúpolis became the busiest port in the new Greek

returned to the deserted island in the 16th century. Belon du Mans, who visited the island around 1546, wrote: "It is striking that an island like Sámos must remain deserted. The fear of pirates has rendered her uninhabited so that now there is not a single village there, nor any animals". Despite the islands' proximity to the mainland, they attracted only a small number of Muslim colonisers, and the bulk of the population remained Greek, supplemented by the inevitable Albanian immigrants. Only on Lésvos were Muslim settlers to be found farming the land; elsewhere they stayed close to the towns.

The 1821 insurrection sent shock waves through the islands. Sámos was first; the unrest

state. Other refugees settled in Alexandria, Trieste, Marseilles and as far north as Amsterdam.

Elsewhere in the east Aegean, the changes were just as great. The Ottoman authorities were only able to suppress the uprising with the aid of Mehmet Ali and his Egyptian mercenaries, who had as little respect for the local Muslim notables as they had for the Greeks: many Turkish landowners sold up and emigrated to Anatolia, while their properties were bought by middle-class Greeks who became an increasingly powerful force in the aging Ottoman Empire.

By the end of the century the Ottoman hold had become tenuous: Sámos, for example, had acquired an autonomous regime under an appointed Christian "prince". And on Thássos the Oxford don Henry Tozer found in 1884 that there were no Muslims there apart from the governor himself and a few soldiers. Since the people had to pay neither the "head tax" – universal elsewhere in the Ottoman Empire – nor Ottoman trade duties, it is not surprising that they appeared content with their system of government.

The Muslim islanders, on the other hand, continued to leave for the mainland. Even before the Greco-Turkish population exchange in 1923, the Turkish communities on Híos and Lésvos had dwindled considerably. Their place was filled by a mass of Greek refugees from Anatolia.

The Dodecanese

The 14 or more islands, misleadingly known as the "Dodecanese" (*dhódheka* means "12"), suffered as elsewhere from the collapse of Roman authority. They were repeatedly attacked and plundered. The Byzantine hold remained firmer here than it did in the west, but after 1204 many of the islands were ceded to Frankish adventurers in return for nominal acknowledgement of Byzantine sovereignty.

By the beginning of the 14th century, Venice had helped herself to those two crucial stepping stones to the East, Kássos and Kárpathos. At the same time, Rhodes was captured from the Genoese by the Knights of St John, a military order which, after the loss of Jerusalem in 1187, had been based in Cyprus since 1291. Foulques de Villaret, the first Grand Master of Rhodes, reconstructed the city.

Although the Knights of St John were able to withstand a siege by the Ottomans in 1480, they could not hold off the Ottoman threat indefinitely. In 1521 they were outnumbered by a massive Ottoman force nearly 200,000 strong, and after a siege lasting five months the starving defenders were forced to capitulate. With the fall of Rhodes, the position of the neighbouring islands became untenable, and by 1537 they had all been incorporated into the formidable Ottoman Empire.

The island's Orthodox inhabitants were

> ### SCRAP MERCHANTS
>
> When the Arabs occupied Rhodes from AD 653–658, they broke up the remains of the famous 3rd-century BC Colossus and sold the bronze for scrap.

compelled to leave the town of Rhodes and settle outside. But because the Ottomans never made up more than one-third of the Rhodian population, their overall influence was never that strong. Since the land on many islands was difficult to farm, the islanders looked elsewhere for their livelihoods.

Many became seamen, while on Kálymnos and Sými the tradition of sponge fishing prospered. In 1521, the islanders of Kálymnos paid homage to Suleiman II with sponges and white bread to

demonstrate that "sponge fishers do not cultivate corn, but buy flour – and only of the best quality". During the 19th century, the sponge fishers went international, opening agencies in London, Frankfurt and Basle.

But these developments, typical of the growing Greek middle class, did not lead to union with Greece until late in the day. The islands had been intended for the new Greek state in 1830, but were retained at the last minute by Turkey in return for the mainland island Euboea (Évvia). Liberation from the Ottoman Empire came unexpectedly through the occupation of the islands by the Italians during their war with the Turks in 1912.

LEFT: the sea battle of Sámos, one of the first clashes in the War of Independence; watercolour from 1824.
RIGHT: 19th-century drawing of a Kássos woman.

At first, the islanders welcomed the Italians. A congress on Pátmos passed a resolution thanking the Italian nation for delivering them from the Turkish yoke. However, another resolution at the same congress calling for unification of the islands with Greece was less satisfactory to the local Italian commander who broke up the congress and forbade such public meetings.

The Italians did not intend to hold the islands permanently but, with the dismemberment of the Ottoman Empire, their dreams of establishing a foothold in Asia Minor led them to renege on a promise made in 1920 to return the islands to Greece. Mussolini sent groups

Strategic Crete

The "Great Island" has had the most violent history of all, thanks to its strategic position, agricultural riches and, not least, its inhabitants' fierce tradition of resistance to foreign oppression. From AD 823, when it was conquered by Arab freebooters out of Alexandria, who made it the centre of the slave trade and a base for pirate raids throughout the Aegean, the strategic importance of Crete has been obvious.

Around 3000 BC, a prosperous civilisation spread its influence throughout the Aegean. The Minoans left proof of their architectural genius in the ruined palaces of Knossós and Festós.

ΣΚΗΝΗ ΕΝ ΚΡΗΤΗ ΚΑΤΑ ΤΟ 1866.

of zealous administrators to turn the islands into a Fascist colony. But the process was brought to an abrupt halt by World War II. Once Italy surrendered in 1943, the islands were taken over by the Germans who managed, in the course of their brief and very brutal occupation, to exterminate the ancient Jewish population, against the evident wishes of the islanders, the Italians and even some of their own soldiers.

Of the 1,800 Jews from Kos and Rhodes, only about 20 returned from Auschwitz. Just a few months after the Jews had been deported, the islands were occupied by the Allies, who finally handed them over to Greece in 1947.

DICTATORSHIP IN ACTION

The Italian occupation of the Dodecanese under Mussolini imposed on the islanders the farcical prohibitions of a totalitarian regime, intent on "Italianising" the islands. An extensive secret police network guarded against nationalist activity; the practice of Orthodox religion was outlawed; the blue and white colours of the Greek flag were prohibited in public; all shop signs had to be worded in Italian – and slogans such as "*Viva il Duce, viva la nuova Italia imperiale!*" were daubed on the walls of recalcitrant shopkeepers. In the 1930s, many islanders emigrated to the Greek mainland, to Egypt and to Australia.

Though they were daring soldiers, they appear to have preferred commerce to agriculture. They established outposts in the Peloponnese and made contact with the Egyptians.

By 1500 BC, Minoan civilisation had reached its zenith. But then Crete was shaken by a series of disasters: a stupendous volcanic eruption on the island of Santoríni (Thíra) unleashed a tidal wave that damaged settlements along the north coast. Then, barely a generation later, most of the important sites in central and southern Crete were destroyed by fire. But the causes of the wider disintegration of Minoan control remain a mystery. Only Knossós continued to be inhab-

centre of a renaissance of Byzantine culture: Cretan artists such as Domínikos Theotokópoulos, otherwise known as El Greco, helped to enrich the Renaissance in western Europe.

Though the Venetians developed the towns and fortresses on the north coast, they knew how little they were loved by the Cretans. In 1615 a certain Fra Paolo Serpi had warned that "the Greek faith is never to be trusted," and he had recommended that the people "must be watched with more attention lest, like the wild beasts they are, they should find an occasion to use their teeth and claws. The surest way is to keep good garrisons to awe them." Under such

ited as Cretan dominance in the Aegean ended.

In the early 13th century AD, Venice and Genoa tussled to wrest the island away from the waning Byzantine Empire. Although Venice ultimately turned Crete into a prize possession, Byzantine influence remained strong. The old Greek noble families survived, while ties with Constantinople were reflected everywhere in church art and secular literature.

This strong Byzantine tradition became crucial after 1453 when the island gave refuge to exiles fleeing the Turks, and briefly became the

LEFT: oil painting of the 1866 Cretan Revolt.
ABOVE: Iráklion at the turn of the century.

a regime the peasants were probably worse off than under the Turks on the mainland.

Occasionally, as in 1263 and 1571, there were major uprisings which the Venetians harshly put down. After one such revolt, 300 people were executed and many exiled, their villages were burned and razed, their property confiscated and other severe penalties exacted. In 1538 the coasts were laid waste by the pirate Khair-ed-din Barbarossa. On top of all this, the inhabitants faced other – natural – terrors such as the famine which in 1626 reduced the population of the island by one-fifth. In these circumstances it is not surprising that the Venetian presence on the island remained small and that

Roman Catholicism never became widespread.

Venice kept its hold on Crete long after most of her other Aegean possessions had been surrendered. But, in 1645, the town of Haniá fell to the Turks and, in 1669, after a siege lasting two years, Iráklion fell too and the entire island came under Ottoman rule. By this time, the Ottoman administration had lost much of its early vigour: in the early 18th century one commentator described Iráklion as "the carcass of a large city... little better than a desert".

In an effort to escape the burdens of Ottoman rule many Cretan families converted to Islam, especially during the 18th century, on a scale

unknown elsewhere in the Aegean. But these converts continued to speak Greek, drink alcohol and had names such as Effendakis and Mehmedakis, which were linguistic hybrids of Greek and Turkish elements. Villages continued to be called by their Greek names even after all their inhabitants had converted.

From 1770, a series of revolts broke out against Ottoman rule. But it was to take more than a century to bring about independence; nevertheless, these insurrections altered the balance of power on the island as many Muslim farmers sold out to Christians before moving, first to the coastal towns, and then, at the turn of the century, away from the island altogether.

These revolts also had a catastrophic effect on the island's economy. Passing through the interior shortly after the 1866–69 insurrection, Tozer noted: "Every village that we passed through, and all that we could see along the hillsides, had been plundered, gutted and burnt." Even today, abandoned villages are not an uncommon sight in the countryside inland.

In 1896, when the next major revolt broke out, the inadequacies of Ottoman rule were so evident that the European powers stepped in. For example, on the whole of the island there was just one short stretch of carriage road which went from from Haniá to Suda Bay; and as William Miller reported in 1897, in Iráklion, the largest town on the island, there were no carriages at all "for the two that used to exist were last employed for the conveyance of the admirals on the Queen's Jubilee last year, on which occasion the bottom of both vehicles fell out, and the distinguished officers had to walk inside the bottomless machines". Troubles in Ottoman Crete in 1897 provoked a wave of sympathy on the mainland. Greek naval forces were sent to the island while the army marched northwards – only to be checked by the Ottoman forces who pushed back down into Greece. This defeat was humiliating for the Greeks, but it proved only to delay the future enlargement of the kingdom for a while.

The following year the island of Crete was made an independent principality under Ottoman sovereignty. The new prince was, significantly, a member of the Greek royal house. The writing was on the wall and within a few years union with Greece had finally been achieved.

A new revolt

In 1909, political change was once again forced through by military means. Junior army officers staged a revolt against the political establishment in Athens and, at their invitation, a new politician with a radical reputation, Elefthérios Venizélos, came to Athens from Crete to form a new government. A consummate diplomat and a man of great personal charm, Venizélos channelled the untapped energies of the Greek middle class into his own Liberal Party, which governed Greece for 13 of the next 25 years. ❑

LEFT: watercolour of urban Cretan costume.
RIGHT: a naïve painting of Elefthérios Venizélos.

THE ISLANDS TODAY

The 20th century was a political roller-coaster for Greece and its islands,
veering between monarchy, military dictatorship and socialist republicanism

The islands did not all become part of independent Greece at the same time. Only the Cyclades, the Sporades and Évvia (Euboea) formed part of the original state in 1830. At the insistence of about-to-be King George I, a Danish prince. and, more to the point, because they were no longer considered of strategic value, the Ionian islands were ceded by Britain to Greece in 1864.

The other major additions came from war. Crete and the Northeast Aegean islands became part of Greece in 1913 after the First Balkan War. The Dodecanese islands were freed from Italian occupation by World War II and formally incorporated into Greece in 1948. Since several of the islands were wealthy ports at a time when Athens was still a village, it is scarcely surprising that their influence on developments in the new state was enormous.

In politics, the Hydriot families of Voúlgaris and Koundouriótis, the Metaxás dynasty in the Ionians, not to mention the Cretan Elefthérios Venizélos – in many ways the founder of the modern Greek state – all typified the vigour which the islanders brought to the political scene. And their influence did not stop here: Greek literature and music was marked by the Ionian islands' close links with Italy, while Lésvos has produced both the Nobel Prize-winning poet Odysseus Elytis and the naïve painter Theóphilos.

The islands' economic influence has also been profound, especially before the Balkan Wars of 1912–13 added the fertile regions of northern Greece to the impoverished state, and again in recent decades with the increasing flow of tourists. The shipping fleets of the Aegean islands, exports of currants and olive oil from Zákynthos and Kefalloniá, and emigrant remittances from islanders scattered across the globe – from Romania to Australia to Florida – have all helped to bolster the country's economy.

LEFT: a Cretan peasant in traditional dress, around 1950. **RIGHT:** a pelican once started an inter-island feud between Mýkonos and Tínos.

Islands for outcasts

But islands had other uses, too. Límnos, under Ottoman rule, was used as a place of exile for political offenders. Henry Tozer, who visited the island in 1884, learned that a former grand vizier had been living on the island for eight years and was "almost forgotten at the capital".

The fortress islet of Spinalónga, off the northeast coast of Crete, after a long career as Venetian outpost and Turkish village, was used as a leper colony until the late 1950s.

The Greek central government also found the islands useful for prisons, both for regular criminals in the large compounds on Aegina (Éghina) and Corfu and, more ominously, at certain times for political opponents. On Aegina, what was built as a mint for the new Kapodístrias government in the late 1820s long served as a prison (its most recent use has been to house wounded wild birds until they are well enough to be released) and the prison on Corfu is still used.

In the 1930s the dictator Metaxás sent his opponents to forbidding islands. During the civil war (1947–49), in which the left-wing forces that had formed a strong resistance to the occupying Nazis were suppressed, the uninhabited island of Makroníssos just off the southeastern coast of Attica was extensively used as a prison camp for political detainees.

The colonels, who ruled Greece with a heavy, sometimes brutal, hand from 21 April 1967 until 24 July 1974, continued the tradition, incarcerating their political opponents in Makroníssos, Yioúra, Léros, and Amorgós as well as the regular prisons on Aegina and Corfu. On occasions, particularly on Amorgós and Corfu, the islanders managed to circumvent military security and give the political prisoners some support.

Incoming and outgoing

Since the late 1950s the islands have experienced the erratic but inexorable growth of tourism, a trend initiated when Greek shipowners began to acquire islands for their private use. When Stavros Niarchos and Aristotle Onassis continued their competition by buying the islands of Spetsopoúla just off Spétses in the Saronic Gulf and Skórpios just off Lefkádha in the Ionian Sea, they set an ideal which innumerable tourists have tried to follow in finding their own island paradise.

Mýkonos and Corfu were the first to bring in large numbers of summer visitors, but the trend has spread to virtually all the inhabited islands. If there is a ship going there, then there will be tourists, and the luxury of what they will find is more or less according to the island's accessibility. For both visitors and the islanders themselves, the big change in recent years has been the increasing availability of hydrofoils and catamarans, more expensive but far faster vessels introduced since 1970 and 1990 respectively.

The counter to this influx has been a steady flow of emigration from the islands. In the early years of this century most of the emigrants were from the mainland; large numbers of islanders didn't follow until the 1960s. Several reasons lie behind this failure to emigrate until the latter half of the 20th century. In the first place, would-be emigrants were constrained by the availability of transport and their own awareness of the wider world.

An extreme case of such isolation was to be found in Gávdhos, an islet off Crete. According to Spratt, who visited there in 1865, the inhabitants did not see a boat approach for months on end, and he himself disembarked among naked swimmers who, to his Victorian eye, were "primitive in their habits and ideas... a mixed and degenerate race". Thus, to some extent, the opportunities for emigration depended upon improvements in transport and communications.

In the second place, several islands prospered after they incorporated into the Greek state. Sýros, for example, became the most important port and manufacturing centre in Greece in the first few decades after 1830. Even after

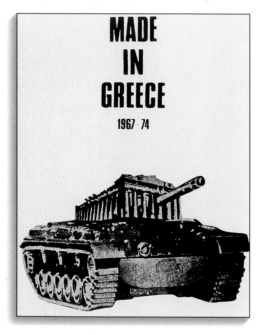

MADE IN GREECE

1967-74

BACKWARD-LOOKING COLONELS

The military junta that ruled Greece from 1967 to 1974, under the leadership of Colonel George Papadópoulos, was driven by a mixture of self-interest and hazy nationalism. In their attitudes, the colonels – from peasant or lower middle-class backgrounds – drew on earlier traditions, and symbolised a provincial reaction to a new world of urban consumers. They laid great stress on a return to traditional morality and religion, censored the press and suppressed intellectual debate, and closed the frontiers to bearded, long-haired or miniskirted foreigners – at least until they realised the implications for Greece's tourist trade.

the rise of Piraeus (Pireás) it remained an important centre where the standing may be gauged by the fine 19th-century villas and warehouses of its capital Ermoúpolis. On other islands, such as Ándhros and Náxos, the late 19th century was a period of rapid exploitation of mineral resources.

By World War I, however, much of this activity had slowed down, and emigration both to Athens and abroad was increasing. In Athens and Piraeus newcomers from islands formed closely-knit communities, each with its own clubs and cafés – islands of familiarity in the urban sprawl. With the collapse of international trade between the wars, the trend was slowed for several decades, but it gathered pace once more with the European "miracle" of the postwar years. Many islanders moved to Italy and West Germany.

Improved communications

By now, the road and rail links between Greece and western Europe had been modernised. So too had links between the islands and the mainland: the first air connection with Athens had been established as far back as 1927 by the Italians, but it was only in the 1960s that aerial links with the Aegean were extended. In the same period, car ferries were introduced. These developments opened up the closed societies of the islands, and the opening continues at speed. The major islands all have airports, and hydrofoil or catamaran service has spread to all the major island groups.

Improved communications also opened up the closed island economies – which had survived World War II mostly by subsistence farming – to a new world of export and import. Trucks now can be loaded with agricultural produce on Crete, say, or Pátmos, and then be driven directly up from Piraeus to the sun-starved markets of northwestern Europe. The return flow is consumer delights, clothes, plastic, motorbikes, electronics.

A new balance is slowly being established. In the warm months, at least, the islands are thriving, as you can see in the crowded boats and new construction. The islands are less remote, able to deal with the world at large

while still keeping the attraction of being off the beaten track. The bright and ambitious young islanders can now go to work abroad, or study in European and American universities, but more of them return to Greece. They can settle in Athens and visit their island homes, retaining a tie to their village, or, increasingly, they can settle down to live and work on the island of their birth. A sure sign that the tide has changed is that a fair share of the new buildings you may see are being constructed by Albanians, who have spread even to the islands to find work, just as previous generations of islanders emigrated to work abroad.❑

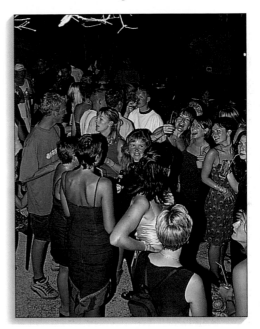

LEFT: a poster protesting at the military regime.
RIGHT: partying at an an outdoor club in Líndhos on Rhodes.

PORTRAIT OF AN ISLAND FAMILY

The modest tourist boom on Hálki has boosted the island's economy,
but life is still simple and hard for most islanders

Early evening on Hálki in the Dodecanese and the sun sets behind the crusader castle, high above the village, turning the sands of Póndamos Beach a deep rose colour.

As the tourists enjoy a sundowner in the harbour, or sit out on the newly restored balconies of their holiday villas, Mihalis Perakis leads his family's donkeys down to drink from the trough in the rocks as he has done for as long as he can remember. He fills his plastic containers from the watering hole for the stock – no taps or easy-fill troughs for them.

Hálki has no rivers or springs, and relies on the water boat to bring supplies for the island families. Daily life revolves around stocking up cans, filling cisterns, known as *stérnes*, and making sure the animals – for many families the only form of transport or wealth – are properly watered. Low-key tourism has grown steadily since 1987 and now, with all those extra bodies to shower, shave and refresh, the water system has been improved, but water still has to be treated with great respect.

Ambitious plans

Mihalis, is a plumber working for Hálki council. His mother, Lefkosia, one of the island's best cooks, has always been in great demand among taverna owners and is now planning to open her own restaurant in the harbour, if the rent is right. Lefkosia's daughter Katholiki (Kiki), helps her mother when she can. But she has just finished her nursing training at the hospital in Rhodes and hopes to work at the local surgery on Hálki. Mihalis is kept busy with the vagaries of the Greek plumbing system while his brother, Metaxas, has just completed his army service, and also works for the municipality when he's not chilling out in the cafés.

Their father Stavros, known to everyone as Fanos, has his own fishing-boat. When he's not out laying his nets or bringing in the catch he

prepares food and helps his wife in the harbourside taverna. These days EU subsidies for his goats and sheep have helped lighten the financial load, and he still sells meat and wool on Rhodes. But life remains hard on this dry little rock.

Once fertile, the island became barren when seawater seeped into the boreholes. Now the

islanders grow nothing except olives, and goats nibble where a dairy herd once grazed. As the sponge industry declined, Halkians left in droves to seek their fortunes in Florida. Horió became deserted as people moved down to Emborió, the harbour, when the grand old sea captains' houses crumbled. The island's population dwindled from around 3,000 in its heyday to a paltry 300.

In 1987 the Greek government stepped in to bring work to Hálki and under a UNESCO scheme declared it the Island of Peace and Friendship. A hotel was built for foreign tourists in the derelict sponge factory and local people were given jobs restoring the houses. These

---

PRECEDING PAGES: a festive gathering at Ólymbos, Kárpathos; *kafenéon* society. **LEFT:** an island family. **RIGHT:** weaving carpets in Santoríni.

days there are two bakeries and "supermarkets" as well as the marvellous old *pantopolíon* or grocer's shop run by Petros. The harbour front has been smartened up with new paving and ornate lights thanks to the efforts of the mayor. The islanders have been encouraged to renovate their properties and cultivate gardens. Where there was once scrubby wasteland with rabbits bred for the pot hopping among old tin cans and rubbish, now bougainvillea and geraniums bloom.

The island's income has been given a boost

When she's cooking for a taverna she might get two hours' sleep in the afternoon. Some people grab a siesta, but it's often impossible for islanders involved in the busy tourist trade.

Home for the Perakis family is basic by western European standards, quite comfortable by theirs. The kitchen has fitted units and a modern stove – Lefkosia's pride and joy – and there is a simple living room and giant colour TV. The phone is on a digital exchange but they still have an outside lavatory and shower.

by its steady influx of visitors throughout the season. There are more bars, more tavernas, a handicraft shop, but nothing wild. Trucks and cars replace donkeys, jitneys and mopeds. Teenagers have got gutsy motorbikes to rev up.

Traditional routine

The Perakis family have large flocks now and in summer Lefkosia rises at 4am. She does the housework while it's cool, then feeds the sheep near the house, a traditional Neoclassical villa at the back of the village. She gives milk to the lambs, feeds the chickens, ducks and rabbits, then might go up the mountainside to pick *hórta* (wild greens) before going to the taverna.

Although the houses done up for the tourists have en suite shower rooms and loos, many of the islanders still have al fresco arrangements.

Like many islanders, the family work night and day in summer and spend little time at home. In autumn and winter it's different. With no tourists around, it's time to pick olives and make the oil, or go fishing for the local equivalent of whitebait. Fanos catches fish for the family and is part of the island's co-operative, but other fishermen sell their wares from loudspeaker vans around the Rhodes suburbs.

In winter Lefkosia and other island women still bake the family's bread outside in the wood-fuelled oven. Lambs, too, are spit-roasted outdoors. It's a lot of work. They have to gather sticks for the fire. It takes an hour to get the oven hot and an hour to cook the bread, but they say it tastes marvellous.

Sometimes the storms are so bad the sea fills the tavernas, so boats are anchored out of the harbour in case they get smashed up. Winters are hard for the young people who don't escape to Rhodes, so they watch videos, play cards or work the machines in the coffee bars. Mihalis prefers traditional Greek music and dance, particularly Hálki's own fast and furious *soustá*. He is the island's champion dancer, and often leads the circles at village festivals. The *kafeníon* tends to be a men-only domain in winter where fishermen, shepherds and soldiers spin out the hours with blue videos and card schools.

As more tourists visit the island, the local boys and soldiers serving at the barracks have more chance to play *kamáki*, chatting up the visiting foreign women. In summer you'll see the more liberated Hálki girls in the cafeteria. Greek girls have more freedom these days, but parents still keep a watchful eye on them and you'll see fathers whisking protesting daughters home like Cinderella.

In winter, some island girls remain indoors and do embroidery or lace-making and learn to run the home. Others might go to college to train for a career. Some local girls fraternise with the soldiers, usually to the horror of the villagers who would prefer them to have husbands from families they know. The girls often see the soldiers as escape routes from a humdrum island life, especially with few Hálki suitors around. The island barracks has national service conscripts from all over Greece, and village girls often think if they can land a husband from Athens or another big city, life will be rosy. Dressed in army uniform one girl stole off with a soldier on the early morning ferry. The boatman's son noticed the "soldier" was wearing women's shoes, but didn't give them away. They telephoned her parents from Rhodes who insisted the couple should be married immediately because of the family shame. She was 14. And pregnant.

Tourism may bring work to the island, but the influx of foreigners with Western ideas can lead to problems. The old ways and the new clash head on and young Greeks are the victims in the middle. It may be accepted that boys chase after female tourists but, if their intentions become more serious, family and neighbourhood close ranks. Parents want their young to marry other Greeks. Not just because of religion: they know the rules and traditions.

"Life is still difficult for women in Greece," says Katholiki Perakis. "My generation wants modern things like bikes and personal stereos, and we want to mix with other people. But our parents and grandparents are years behind and don't understand. I think the gulf will narrow in time and the next generation will be free." ❑

LEFT: an island woman bakes bread in a wood-fuelled oven. **RIGHT:** autumn is olive-picking time.

WEATHER PERMITTING...

On Hálki the islanders, and tourists, rely on the island's single 3-car ferry to reach Kámiros Skála on Rhodes. In the past if the boats weren't running they were stranded. These days more big inter-island ferries call into Hálki and there's an occasional hydrofoil from Rhodes Town. But if the wind whips up they may not call into the harbour. The islanders are still governed by the weather. In the past if anyone fell ill and needed hospital treatment they had to suffer until it was safe to leave harbour. "One girl had a miscarriage because she couldn't get to hospital on time," recalls Lefkosia Perakis. These days a helicopter airlifts patients.

ISLAND ELECTIONS

A tale of passion and intrigue, family strife and private feuds… Island municipal elections usually provoke drama – and often involve drains

The time was clearly ripe when an island shopkeeper, an amiable old soul who liked poetry and had spoken warmly of his son's help in running the business, had the son by the throat and was spluttering with rage. The son, roughly twice his size, managed to break away and retreated into the road, howling. "The election," the old man explained, staring after him, "he just told me who he's voting for."

The candidates' posters had been going up for several days – as soon as the last of the season's charter flights had left. They showed the incumbent mayor wearing a benign and statesmanlike expression. The potential usurper was younger, had a large moustache, and affected the pose of a visionary. Gossip in the *ouzeri* revealed that "hate" would not cover what they thought of one another. The young pretender had once been hounded off the island – a suitcase literally thrown after him into a departing boat – for reasons that were never clear. He was back, they said in the *ouzeri*, for his revenge.

Unruly passions

It would be difficult to exaggerate the passions aroused by island municipal elections. They are run on national party political lines, a passionate matter in its own right in Greece, but are wonderfully exacerbated by real as well as somewhat enigmatic local issues, the power of future patronage, and private feuds. Almost anything is capable of convulsing small, compressed communities of people who, at the time of the year when elections come round, have nothing else to do, are irascible after the strain of the tourist season, and are looking forward to a state-sanctioned opportunity to get cross.

The elections cannot be totally avoided, however much some islanders might wish to distance themselves from the flying fur. Voting is compulsory unless a voter can prove to have been more than 180 km (112 miles) from home

on polling day. Failure to vote may lead to bureaucratic difficulties in, for example, acquiring a passport or having an old one renewed.

A previous election on a neighbouring island had given a foretaste of what might be in store. It had been predicted that the result of that previous election would be extremely close, and

one of the candidates had arranged a secret weapon – 30 registered voters who were living on the mainland but were willing to come back and vote for him. His opponent uncovered the plot and, in collusion with supporters at the mainland port where the returning voters had assembled, managed to have the ferry services to the island cancelled until after voting.

The Englishman telling this tale had been persuaded to fetch the stranded voters, an operation which involved sneaking away in his boat and collecting them under cover of darkness. After numerous complications of an appropriately Byzantine nature, the small boat returned to the island top-heavy with voters and their

---

LEFT: the Communist party has considerable support in some Aegean islands, such as Lésvos. **RIGHT:** a rally in support of PASOK.

baggage with minutes to spare. It tottered into the fishing port to the cheers of supporters and the speechless fury of the opposition. The election result was tipped by the imported voters, who supplied a majority of just one vote.

With this incident to draw on, the election committee of the present challenger was approached. "What are the issues?" they were asked through an interpreter, a girl who worked in the shop next door. They went into conference and emerged with a verdict: "Drains." So drains were discussed and, in particular, the mayor's failure to live up to his promises about new ones.

The interpreter became restless and, if her

"No!" The opposition candidate held up an admonishing finger. A lorry had come to a halt outside the campaign office. A gang of workmen climbed down and attacked the cobbles with pick-axes under the noses of the committee. "You see, no problem with drains. New ones."

Two days before voting, the candidates made their speeches – the challenger down on the quay, the incumbent afterwards outside the church. The general idea was that the audience would move on from one to hear the other. A hugely amplified fanfare announced the start. "Ladies and gentlemen," a voice boomed from behind the as-yet empty balcony, "I give you...

translations were to be taken literally, all the committee's replies ended with statements like "...and if you believe that, sir, you are an idiot." When the interpreter stormed out, saying that she could stand no more of their lies, she confirmed the suspicion that she might support the other candidate.

Down the road, the opposition was asked what they thought the election was about. Their spokesman reeled off a list which concerned democracy, a caring society, organised crime, human rights. "But what about drains?" he was prompted by a bystander.

"What about drains?" he echoed.

"Well, the other party says..."

NATIONAL POLITICS

Since 1975, following the overthrow of the military dictatorship, Greece has been a parliamentary democracy headed by a president, elected for a five-year term. The single-chamber parliament has 300 deputies, elected for four years. Andréas Papandréou's Panhellenic Socialist Movement (PASOK) ruled with a large majority from 1981 until 1989, when it was brought down by a series of scandals. Its major opponent, the right-wing New Democracy party under Konstantínos Mitsotakis, was in power for only four years. PASOK then held a comfortable majority until 2004 when New Democracy returned to power, led by Costas Karamanlis.

Dimitris Prevezanos!" Four small boys let off compressed-air hooters to herald the grand entrance.

Dimitris Prevezanos, however, failed to materialise. Another fanfare, another introduction, further hooting – and still no Dimitris. Instead, a water pipe chose that moment to detach itself from a tank above the balcony. Prevezanos supporters, wearing Sunday suits, leapt out of the way.

An enquiry regarding his non-appearance received a simple explanation: "His speech was about drains. Now he must talk about something else. Maybe he can't think of something else."

The mayor did not mention drains, presumably because by then most of the main street and the quay had been dug up, as no one on the island could have failed to notice. Instead, he concentrated on broader issues and emphasised his record.

An army contingent arrived on the island for polling day. A man was running a book on the results, with a plastic bag stuffed with bank notes to cover all bets. When asked how much, he winked: twelve thousand euros. It says something about the island that he felt able to wander off from time to time and leave the bag unattended on a table.

It was a partisan opinion; however when, third time lucky, the candidate did appear, he did have something to say about drains. He may have had other topics but the time taken to repair the pipe had to be subtracted from the time available before the incumbent went into action. When he finished speaking, the audience duly filed up the hill to listen to Kostas Papadoulis, the incumbent. The small boys passed their hooters to another set of small boys who would apply them to the task of getting Papadoulis re-elected.

LEFT: the whole village discusses the burning issues of the election. RIGHT: an election banner in Réthymnon.

The bets were settled at 8pm when red flares announced that the result was known: Papadoulis was back in office for four years. He was carried shoulder-high around the village while a disappointed Dimitris Prevezanos was said to be packing for a further spell of exile, this time self-imposed, on the mainland.

The following morning, father and son resumed normal relations and – to almost nobody's surprise – the work on the drains ran into "technical difficulties" and ceased. They were not completed for the next big event on the calendar, Easter, and only just in time for the second, the charter flights which signalled the beginning of the tourist season. ❑

DEBUNKING THE BOUZOÚKI

Like the islands themselves, Greek music has been influenced by many other cultures, which gives it a richness and complexity that's worth seeking out

The visitor is ambling along some majestic harbour at sunset, with the sea breeze between the masts of the yachts and caiques, and looking forward to a meal of fried octopus, washed down perhaps with a little *oúzo*. What better way to complete the image than with background music on the *bouzoúki*? After all, isn't *bouzoúki* music the quintessence of all things Greek?

Well, no. Those familiar soundtracks for Manos Hatzidhakis' *Never on Sunday* and Mikis Theodhorakis' *Zorba the Greek*, sold ad nauseam in cover versions from resort souvenir stalls, have effectively closed foreign minds to the possibility of anything else of value in Greek music.

What the big record companies push on inexperienced foreigners, in catalogue sections cynically labelled *"Touristiká"*, is merely the tip of the iceberg, a snapshot of a brief period in the early 1960s which coincided with Greece's arrival as a mass-tourism destination. While the original compositions, arrangements and recordings skilfully distilled elements of Greek music into a form suitable for the cinema, the offcut remixes – watered down for western tastes and sporting such titles as *Disco Bouzouki My Love* (*sic*) – are another matter.

Diverse influences

Greece amply deserves the cliché image of a musical crossroads and collecting-basket, with a range of cosmopolitan influences inside a deceptively small country. Many of the different genres of music have been recorded, and even a small selection of CDs will give some idea of Greece's rich musical traditions.

The great *bouzoúki* myth has overshadowed the Aegean music hidden away behind *skyládhika* (roadhouse-type venues) with their heavy amplification. This has an altogether cleaner

PRECEDING PAGES: the lights of a fishing boat, Sýros; musicians on Kárpathos playing *lýra* and lute. **LEFT:** a music shop selling both traditional instruments and amplifiers. **RIGHT:** the ubiquitous *bouzoúki*.

sound – gentler than the commercialised musics. Acoustic *nisiotiká* or island music, especially in the Cyclades (of all Greek territories the least affected by the waves of invaders that have periodically swept over Greece), is very much *sui generis*, displaying only some influence of Italian songs.

The rhythms, often in unconventional time-signatures, are lilting and hypnotic; the melodies, traditionally executed on violin, bagpipes and some sort of fretted lute, are exquisite. The lyrics, tokens of a more innocent time, grapple with eternal island concerns – the sea that took a loved one, the island mother who wonders if her sons will ever return from foreign exile, the precious days when the endless fishing can be laid aside and clean clothes can be donned for the festival of the Panaghía – but occasionally verge on the poetically surreal, as in the popular *Mes Sto Egeou ta Nisia*.

These days, the various artists of the Náxos-born Konitopoulos clan are the best you'll hear, but particularly prized are 1950s and 1960s recordings of the mother-daughter team from the Dodecanese, Anna and Emilia Hatzidhaki. In the Ionian islands, the Italian heritage is evident in Neapolitan-style *kantádhes*, sung by choirs, and often accompanied by mandolin, violin and guitar tuned to a western temperament and using seven-tone scales.

SCALE MODEL

Some Greek modes do not start with do–re–mi (C–D–E), like the western major scale, but do–do sharp–mi (C–C#–E).

Compositions and instrumentation of Asia Minor and the northern mainland (the *sandoúri* or hammer dulcimer, or brass bands on Lésvos) enrich the repertoire of the northeast Aegean

islands and the Dodecanese. Meanwhile traces of North African and Arab music can be discerned in the long vocal introductions to Cretan songs. Across the mainland, the Gypsies' contribution to instrumental music – especially the clarinet – has been pervasive if unacknowledged, and especially in the mountainous spine of the north Píndhos, much is shared musically with southern Albania (historically northern Epirus).

Earliest influences

Ancient Greek music was monophonic – without harmonies – and its scales were probably much like those of contemporary ecclesiastical chant. A lot of traditional Greek music is either pentatonic (five notes make up the scale) or based on a modal system which has much in common with musics of the Middle East, and is possibly influenced by Byzantine chant.

Greece's lyrics were never divorced from music, as they were in the West, where tunes were composed for existing stanzas or opera librettos commissioned separately. Since antiquity, when poetry was sung, both have been inseparable. Instrumental music remains a relative rarity, while the solo voice is still used for mourning songs, "table" songs and the singing of epics.

Rhythms – and blues?

Western metre generally was limited to units of, or compounds of, two, three or four beats. The Greeks, on the other hand, seem to have matched their musical rhythms to the cadences of their poetry, from the age of the Homeric hexameter onwards. Western musicians have only recently begun to appreciate and use the catchy 5/8, 7/8, 9/8 and even 11/8 time signatures, common in Greek traditional music.

The composer Mimis Plessas, a former jazzman who now accounts for a fair portion of Greek movie soundtrack music, relates an interesting account of a jam session with the American jazz trumpeter Dizzy Gillespie in 1953. Being Greek, Plessas had no trouble fingering a nimble 7/8 rhythm on the piano – and promptly lost Dizzy. "I can't do it – something's missing," said the great jazzman. Less convincingly, Plessas has said: "Imagine the field cry of the black man transported to Greece – that's what Greek music is."

Plessas was not the first individual to have simplistically found similarities between the American blues and Greek song – especially *rembétika*, the genre foreigners are most likely to be exposed to, and gravitate towards. In its original form, this was the clandestine music of a particular segment of the Anatolian refugee population who flooded into Athens, Piraeus and Thessaloníki after the disastrous 1919–22 Graeco-Turkish war, and the subsequent compulsory exchange of religious minorities between the two nations.

It is superficially similar to the blues in its origins and preoccupations – poverty and social exclusion, disease, the allure of drugs and idleness, faithless women, thwarted love – and its practitioners and lyrics were similarly persecuted and censored throughout the 1920s and 1930s.

Westernising Greeks despised, and still despise, its "Oriental" roots, but one can safely say that *rembétika* existed in some form around the east Aegean coast and the Black Sea for decades before that. On one occasion, an expatriate Soviet novelist, on exposure to the music, delightedly exclaimed that a nearly identical style, played on *balalaïka*, had flourished in the harbour dives of Odessa's Moldvanka quarter before (and after) the 1917 Revolution.

By the 1950s, however, *rembétika* became "domesticated" and incorporated into the canon of mainstream Greek music; in 1953 Manolis Hiotis marked the demise of the "pure" rembetic style by adding a fourth string to the *bouzoúki*, allowing it to be tuned tonally rather than modally – and giving rise to *laïkó* and *elafrá*, the urban "popular" music you hear on the radio today.

This can be seen as one aspect of the on-going post-war westernisation of Greece, now under American tutelage, with the Greek musical scene arrayed in two opposing camps: adherents of traditionally-derived styles opposed to those who spurn these roots in favour of imported jazz/cabaret, symphonic and rock models.

The state of the art

Former communist Theodhorákis himself, after his *Zorba* outing of 1965, shunned Byzantine/rembetic/traditional bases completely in favour of western quasi-symphonic works and film music. In general, the political Left has historically condemned "decadent", apolitical, escapist styles such as *rembétika* and *laïkó*, attempting at one point to "raise mass consciousness" with recycled *andártika*, wartime resistance songs.

More thoughtful musicians have attempted to bridge the high-low culture gap with hybrid styles: the strongly rooted *éntekhno* of Yannis Markopoulos, where traditional instruments and themes are used within large-scale compositions of great emotive power; a whole

LEFT: music ensemble, the Ionian islands.
ABOVE: a concert in Zákynthos, where choirs sing Neapolitan-style *kantádhes*.

succession of guitarist singer-songwriters, led by Dionysis Savvopoulos, who challenged the supremacy of the ubiquitous *bouzoúki* with modern lyrics as well, giving rise to Greek folk-rock; and numerous revivalists, such as Haïnidhes and Loudhovikos ton Anoghion, who countered the fashionable rock-drum-kit-and-electrification of live traditional performances with updated and rearranged standards which acknowledged instrumental debts to surrounding cultures.

Rembétika enjoyed a brief revival after the fall of the junta, which had tried to ban it like much else, but the fad – most pronounced

among urban intellectuals – has now waned, and the flood of well-produced re-issue recordings is now principally aimed at a foreign audience, many first primed to the music by Stavros Xarhakos' soundtrack to the 1983 film, *Rembétiko*.

But "pure" *laïkó* and *nisiotiká*, despite being looked down on by educated Greeks (especially overseas students), refuses to die. It's a tale often repeated in Greece, where the westernised, cultural elite keep busy attempting unsuccessfully to banish "low-class" habits. Unruly multiculturalism continues to be the the the nemesis of nationalists and reformers in search of an illusory "purity". ❑

PERILS OF THE CATERING TRADE

Many people from abroad have dreamed of opening a restaurant or bar in
Greece – but the dream is often shattered by labyrinthine legislation

A few years ago the British popular press revelled in the case of a London grand-mother who invested her £30,000 life savings in a restaurant on Rhodes and looked forward to a happy and prosperous retirement. Instead, she found herself locked up in a police cell with the prospect of spending the next five months there unless she bought off the sentence for the equivalent of £1,000.

The first lesson for any foreigner wishing to follow Mrs Molly Huddleston's example by starting a business on a Greek island is that the Greek legal process can all too easily begin rather than end with a spell in prison. Detailed prosecution, defence, litigation and so forth take place later, often much later. A knowledge of the law and the resolve to remain meticulously on the right side of it are therefore desirable starting points – although the process can often feel like shadow-boxing with an opponent of stupefying complexity.

False assumptions

So where had Mrs Huddleston gone wrong? It was her belief that visitors to the island might occasionally enjoy "traditional British food" after so much Greek, and that is what she provided. Cucumbers and tomatoes are optional ingredients in a British salad, but she had forgotten (or perhaps never known) that in Greece the contents of a salad are defined by law. Mrs Huddleston's salads were either light on the cucumbers and tomatoes, or omitted them altogether – a serious matter.

Furthermore, while Mrs Huddleston was aware of the fixed price for a baked potato, she rashly assumed that she could charge a little more if she filled them with chilli sauce, a dish popular with her more discerning customers. That, too, went into the policeman's notebook.

Mrs Huddleston's misfortune was not a flash in the pan – the work of a bad-tempered police-man with a grudge or a hangover. At the same

time, at the other end of the Aegean, Fat Ronnie, a young American chef, had given up his job at a prestigious New York hotel to pursue the ambition of opening his own restaurant. He had never seen a Greek island, but the enthusiastic description by a Greek friend who knew the islands – and of a restaurant that happened to be

for sale on one of them – made up his mind.

The friend was a lawyer, so Ronnie, by nature a cautious fellow, avoided some of the pitfalls into which naïve foreign investors might plunge. The sale of bars and discos, in particular, is seldom cut and dried. The owner will probably open negotiations asking for a large lump sum for "goodwill", a percentage of turnover in perpetuity, and "rent". Buyers anxious to secure a place in paradise should not accept that all property transactions are concluded along such lines and should seek legal advice.

But this may not be cut and dried either. On the smaller islands, there are probably no more than a couple of local lawyers and they will

---

LEFT: taverna tables await the tourists. **RIGHT:** the classic Greek salad is strictly regulated by law.

each act for one half of the population against the other. Being lawyers, they will be at or near the top of ferociously polarised municipal politics and the make-or-break powers of patronage flowing from them. The foreign buyer ought to find out who the vendor's lawyer is (anyone would be able to tell them!) and proceed forthwith to the other one.

Lobster tale

Fat Ronnie had astutely, if unknowingly, overcome potential difficulties in that direction, but he was nevertheless faring no better (and possibly rather worse) than Mrs Huddleston in

ONE LAW FOR ALL

The apparently vindictive regulations concerning cucumber and tomato in salads, or the definition of fresh lobster, were designed to give visitors a fair deal and to prevent profiteering. Although foreign caterers are more likely to be caught out, the laws apply to everyone. One Greek restaurateur was prosecuted because he had charged more than the stipulated price for a fixed portion of chicken – even though what he was serving was an authentic chicken curry with expensive extra ingredients. The fact that he was prominent in local politics, and his party was in power, could not prevent the charges being taken through the courts.

Rhodes. Within a fortnight of opening, he had logged no fewer than 107 separate offences which, in addition to violation of the notoriously demanding cucumber legislation, included the extraordinary business of a consignment of lobsters which, although still alive and kicking, were deemed by the inspectors to be "not fresh".

A bemused Ronnie tried to find out what it all meant. The 107 offences? Prison, undoubtedly, until and unless he bought off the sentence or, as Mrs Huddleston was proposing, appealed quickly to the European Court of Human Rights. The "not fresh" lobsters? If he couldn't produce a suitable receipt showing the precise date when he bought them, it was assumed that they were not within the prescribed definition of "fresh" and therefore his menu lied when it said they were.

The condemned lobsters were actually still alive when Ronnie had to destroy them under official supervision. At that point, Ronnie was seriously reconsidering the wisdom of starting his own business in Greece.

Another couple, a Greek man and English woman, tried twice to set up restaurants on islands. Their first attempt involved fixing up rented premises at considerable expense which, as soon as the restaurant opened, were found to have been in violation of the building code for restaurants. The owner knew this, but was happy to have his premises refurbished. As soon as the couple left, he rented them to a fellow-islander for an *ouzeri*.

They tried again on another island, this time with a pizzeria. They made it through the bureaucratic hassle, acquired all the necessary papers – but when they opened, they discovered that the islanders wouldn't sell them provisions. They stayed the season, buying their supplies in Piraeus, but then returned to Athens where they now operate, quite successfully, a very good restaurant.

The wisdom of business

One quickly concludes from these horror stories that the Greeks don't want foreigners working their turf – but reconsider what "foreigner" means and where the term is used. These stories are all based on the fact that the islands are small, close-knit communities which consider anyone not born on their island (including Greeks) as foreigners. They earn most of their annual income in the few summer months and are threatened by the idea that someone, anyone, from outside is going to take away their livelihood.

So potential competitors, wherever they come from, are likely to feel the full weight of the Greek mountain of legislation. Even if all the legalities are surmounted, potential competitors may well suffer from local non-cooperation, if nothing else. Before catatonic paranoia sets in they ought to remind themselves that the laws were drawn up by Greeks for Greeks. The fact that foreigners become entangled is nothing more than incidental.

Fat Ronnie had originally planned to serve French and Italian food, but the inspectors rejected his draft menu because, without special dispensation, restaurants must have a preponderance of Greek dishes on the menu in the interest of cultural integrity. The law was brought in, commendably, to inhibit the fast-food, sausage-and-chips blight that has ruined so many places pandering to the tastes of mass tourism.

The government's good intentions in both respects – making sure that visitors are not overcharged and that the tourist areas are not reduced to anonymous cultural slag heaps – do unfortunately have a tendency to backfire.

Learning the rules

If you are not Greek and want to set up a restaurant on a Greek island you need a good island lawyer. In fact, no foreigner should attempt to do business anywhere in Greece without high-calibre legal support. With good legal advice it is possible for you as a foreigner to set up shop on the more level playing field now at least theoretically established by the European Union.

One of the many things the lawyer will do is explain that the regulations which can be misused locally against potential competition were, in fact, drawn up to protect the customer. Greek salads, for example, were defined by law because some restaurants served tourists supposed Greek salads either short on or missing tomatoes, cucumbers, feta or olives, all basic ingredients for a Greek salad.

In 1997 there was much publicity when the Minister of Development, Vaso Papandreou, was eating in an island restaurant and noticed

that the waiting staff issuing strange orders to the kitchen. The waiters were saying the equivalent of "meatballs f" and meatballs g", which turned out to mean a smaller serving for the foreigners and a larger serving for the Greeks. Legal protection for the foreign tourist is a very good idea.

Even before finding a lawyer, however, you should know very well where you are going. If you want to conduct any kind of business on a Greek island it would be a sensible idea for you first to spend a few years living there getting to know your neighbours. Even better, marry one of the islanders. ❑

LEFT: a cafeteria on Hydra. **RIGHT:** tile style.

EATING YOUR WAY ROUND THE ISLANDS

Traditional Greek food is better than its reputation, especially if you ignore what's offered for tourists and seek out traditional local dishes

Anyone who has experienced tourist menus of chicken and chips, microwaved *moussakás* and "ros-beef" can be excused for believing that Greece isn't the place for culinary delights. So for a taste of real Greek cooking follow the locals down to the back-street tavernas. The food at traditional family-run places with plastic tablecloths more than compensates for lack of fancy décor. If communication is a problem, go in, take a look at what's cooking and point at what you want. Ordering this way is accepted practice.

You'll soon find there's more to Greek cuisine than kebabs and *taramosaláta*. Vegetables like fresh green beans, okra or butter beans, cooked in olive oil and tomato; hearty fish soups; cheese and spinach pies with a feather-light filo pastry; rich casseroles of octopus and snails; courgette flowers stuffed with rice and fried in batter – the islands offer dishes for all tastes. There are plenty of options for vegetarians because of the many fast days in the Orthodox calendar. But fish is very expensive (and sold by weight, not per portion).

Regional variations reflect island history and many dishes have strong Italian and Turkish influences from past occupations. You'll find pastas and pilafs, plus vegetable recipes like *briam* and *imam baïldi*, their Turkish names absorbed into Greek menus.

From the cabbage *dolmádhes* of Kálymnos, the *sofríto* casseroles of Corfu to the *froutála* omelettes of Ándhros, every island has its speciality. Some may seem strange – sea urchins or boiled sheep's heads are not for the faint-hearted – but most island food is delicious. If all else fails, *horiátiki,* the classic Greek village salad *(above),* with feta, olives, chunky cucumber and tomato, takes some beating.

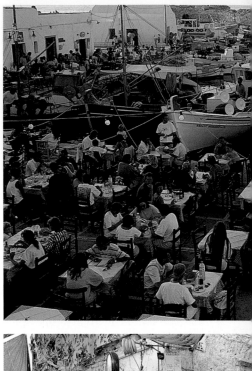

▷ **APPETISERS**
A selection of *mezédhes* or starters (clockwise from top left): Cretan potatoes baked with herbs; *taramosaláta*; *dolmádhes* stuffed with mince and savoury rice; pickled octopus.

◁ **HARD CHEESE**
Besides salty feta, Greece has a wide range of cheeses, both soft and hard, creamy and sharp, made from goats' and sheep's milk. Crete in particular supplies a wide variety.

△ **TEMPTING TENTACLES**
Charcoal-grilled octopus is a common sight and a perfect appetiser with an ouzo.

◁ **EATING AL FRESCO**
The informal taverna is the most common form of eatery, often with tables outside and music at night. For a wider menu, with more oven-baked dishes, look for an *estiatório*, or a *psistariá*, which specialises in spit-roasts and grills.

◁ **PICK YOUR PRODUCE**
Some islands have to import fresh fruit and veg because they can't grow their own, while others have rich market gardens.

▷ **MORE *MEZEDHES***
Clockwise from top centre: *tyropittákia*, triangular cheese pies; *loukánika*, home-made sausages with olives; bean and sausage casserole; *bourekákia*, filo rolls stuffed with spinach.

◁ **TURKISH DELIGHT**
Special *souvlákia* sold in Drapetsona, Piraeus, are made to recipes brought by refugees from Asia Minor in the 1920s. Skewered meat and tomatoes are served on a bed of pitta bread.

▷ **STRONG STUFF**
Ouzo, the national drink, is flavoured with aniseed and turns milky when water is added. It's usually drunk with olives or other starters *(mezédhes)*.

AND SOMETHING TO DRINK?

You can drink anything in Greece from cocktails to local firewater. If you prefer wine, retsina (white wine flavoured with pine resin, *above*) is an acquired taste, ranging from lightly to heavily scented. It's usually better from the barrel, but brands like Cambas and Rhodian CAIR are fine.

Popular inexpensive wines include Cambas, Boutari and Lac des Roches, available in reds, whites and rosés, but if you want something better try Emery's crisp white Villare, Tsantalí Agiorítiko in white and red, Boutari Grand Reserve or the Carras label. Try local wines from the barrel or Greek boutique labels such as Papaïoannou or Skouras. Amstel and Heineken beers are widely available, bottled and draught.

After dinner try Greek brandy, Metaxa, which comes in three starred grades. The *kafenéon* (coffee bar) or *zaharoplastío* (pastry shop) will serve up Greek coffee – *skéto* (without sugar), *glykó* (sweet) or *métrio* (medium). If you want instant, ask for "Nescafe" which has become the generic term.

CRUISING ROUND THE ISLANDS

Greeks have sailed between the islands for thousands of years. Today it is possible

to follow in their wake, on anything from day-trips to all-inclusive luxury cruises

Having more than 50 inhabited islands means having ships to serve them, and Greece has a long shipping tradition. Anyone who has ridden over the Aegean, with the prows of the white ships rivalling the dazzling sun itself, knows the affinity Greeks have for their ships. The giants of the past, such as Aristotle Onassis and Stavros Niarchos, are no longer with us, and their successors keep a much lower profile.

They are here, though, hundreds of Greek shipping companies operating out of one square kilometre of office blocks clustered together in the port city of Piraeus. They are centred on the seafront of Aktí Miaoúli, where international bankers in pinstriped suits rub shoulders with burly crewmen and banana vendors.

The owners remain emotionally, even mystically, committed to their business. Few satisfactions can equal that of gazing out of one's air-conditioned headquarters seven floors above Aktí Miaoúli and watching one's ship come in, slowly coming to moor along the quay. The same feeling must have prompted the great 18th-century captains of Hydra and Spétses to build their *arhondiká* facing out to sea.

The transporting of goods to and from the Greek islands is fundamental to the economies of all the Greek islands. For visitors to the country, however, the most interesting aspect is the pleasure of being cargo, the joys of cruising.

Which cruise to choose?

The most frequent voyages in Greece are one-day cruises, most of them operating out of Piraeus or the Flísvos harbour in Fáliron just outside Athens, and taking you to the islands of Aegina, Hydra and Póros, with a guide and a packed lunch.

There are also three, four, seven and 14-day cruises, most of them operating out of Piraeus but some one- to- three-day cruises visit Santoríni and some of the eastern Cyclades islands from Iráklion. Small companies such as Pleasure Cruises Shipping operate one-day cruises to Póros, Hydra and Aegina, while slightly larger companies such as Golden Sun Cruises operate one-, three-, four- and seven-day cruises.

The longer cruises are dominated by Royal Olympic Cruises, whose liners are the jewels in the Greek passenger shipping fleet. They are floating hotels, with swimming pools, boutiques, and a choice of restaurants and enter-

ONE-DAY WONDERS

A typical one-day cruise from Piraeus or Fáliron is an excellent introduction to the Greek islands, combined with a relaxing day on board ship. You will visit the 5th-century BC Temple of Aphaia *(Aféa)* in Aegina, one of the finest in all Greece; in Póros you will pass through the narrow straits with the town's white houses towering above the ship on one side and the extensive expanse of lemon-tree forest on the other; in Hydra you will visit that beautiful little town ringed around the harbour. There are also one-day cruises from Iráklion, Crete, to Santoríni. Sailing into that remarkable crater is one of the highlights of Aegean travel.

tainment. Royal Olympic's three-day cruises start from Piraeus, taking in Mýkonos, Rhodes, Kuşadası (Ephesus) in Turkey, Pátmos, and back to Piraeus. The four-day cruises go to Piraeus, Mýkonos, Kusadasi, Turkey, Pátmos, Rhodes, Iráklion, Santoríni, Piraeus. All these are on either Royal Olympic's *Triton* or the new *World Renaissance*.

> **MARITIME HQ**
>
> In the 19th century the centre of Greece's shipping industry was the island of Sýros. Now it is Piraeus, which is home to more than 600 shipping firms.

Six seven-day cruises are available on the *Stella Solaris*, the *Stella Oceanis*, the *Odysseus*, the *Orpheus* or the new *Olympic Countess*. The focus varies between the Aegean islands, the Ionian Sea, Egypt, Israel, Turkey, and they also visit Yalta and Odessa in the Black Sea.

Three 14-day cruises are available on the *Stella Solaris* covering more of the eastern Mediterranean and the Black Sea. The 21-day cruise on the *Stella Solaris* is in fact three of the seven-day trips end to end, covering all the territory more thoroughly

This is far and away the best way to see the most interesting ports in the eastern Mediterranean and Black Sea in full comfort with good food to excess.

Politics at sea

As with all things Greek, there is a political dimension, hinging on the word *cabotage*. Cabotage is an international legal term meaning, as far as the Greek shipping companies are concerned, that they have the monopoly of carrying goods and passengers between Greek ports. Many foreign ships cruise Greek waters with passengers they bring from outside, and return to some port outside Greece, but cabotage has protected the Greek shipping companies from foreign competition in Greek waters for years.

This nautical monopoly was supposed to cease when the European Union decreed that cabotage, for EU ships at least, would end on the last day of 1998. In the end it did not happen, the day of reckoning postponed – as with many Aegean idiosyncrasies – until 2005. From then on, in theory, the market is wide open, which should mean that, as is already happening, existing Greek ships are improved and

brand-new ships will be brought into service to stave off competition.

Royal Olympic Cruises – created by the merger of Epirotiki and Sun Lines – is a major result of this trend. The company has already introduced two new ships designed to carry about 1,000 passengers, just the size needed for cruising the Greek islands.

Greek governments are fond of imposing regulations, often impenetrable, usually expensive, upon every aspect of life they can dream of, and this certainly includes Greek ship-

ping. Many Greek ship-owners have responded to this by registering their ships in another country. This was fine for international routes but, with cabotage in force, foreign-registered ships could not cruise between the Greek islands. Now, with the end of cabotage approaching, the Greek ship-owners can threaten their government with flags of convenience if maritime legislation is not adjusted in their favour.

Much of the problem has to do with labour relations, a major issue as Greece imposed austerity measures in the years before it joined the single European currency. It will be interesting to see how supportive of Greek cruise companies the political powers will be. ❑

PRECEDING PAGES: Kastellórizo harbour at dawn; yacht and cruise ship at anchor in Rhodes. **LEFT:** *Stella Solaris* off Santoríni. **RIGHT:** cruising into Pátmos.

THE SAILING SCENE

Sailing is a rewarding way of exploring this country of islands, whether in your own yacht, in a chartered boat or as part of a flotilla

While the package holidaymaker and the ubiquitous backpacker are forced to rely on the ferries and their often impenetrable timetables in order to travel among the islands, the yachtsman can enjoy a remarkable degree of independence – except, of course, from the winds. Sailing around

Greece is not over-complicated by bureaucracy, but some paperwork, unfortunately, is unavoidable.

To sail into Greek waters in your own yacht, you need customs clearance in one of 28 designated entry ports (the list can be obtained from tourist boards or your country's national sailing authority) to obtain a Transit Log for yachts over 12 metres (39 ft), or a Temporary Duty-Free Admission booklet for smaller yachts. Usually, both these documents are valid for six months and enable a crew to sail freely throughout the country.

A visiting yacht should be officially registered in its country of origin and its skipper should make sure that each member of the crew has a valid passport. It's worth writing out a crew list with passport numbers so that any official check can be made easier.

Chartering, now a fundamental part of the sailing scene in Greece, began throughout the islands in the mid-1970s; it was the idea of an enterprising group of British boat-owners who decided that they had had enough of miserable English summers and wanted holidays in the sun. This type of sailing is increasingly prevalent and has done much to encourage the development of marinas and improved facilities. At the same time, the increase in numbers in recent years has seen a spread of poorer quality boats.

But most reputable charter companies supply yachts that are renewed every five years or so. They are designed for holidays in the sun and equipped to a luxurious standard with deep freezes, deck showers, snorkeling equipment and even a pair of gardening gloves to handle the anchor chain.

Making the right choice

It's important to match experience with the correct type of charter. Inexperienced sailors should select a flotilla holiday where a group of yachts cruise as a fleet, under the instructive eye of a lead boat crew. If you are an experienced sailor, you may want to arrange a "bare boat" charter, in which you act as your own skipper. If you can afford a crewed charter, you can simply relax on deck and leave all the sailing, boat handling, cooking and bureaucracy to paid hands.

Whether you're taking your own yacht to Greece or chartering, the choice of sailing areas is large and your choice should take account of varying local weather conditions.

The recognised sailing season is from April to October when the skies are clear, and temperatures are between 25° and 35°C (80s and 90s Fahrenheit) in July and August. Winds throughout the Aegean Sea tend to be from the north. The most talked-about weather phenomenon is the *meltémi*, which can affect the entire

Aegean and Ionian, and can reach Beaufort Force 7 to 8 in mid-summer. It is an unpredictable wind. Usually it rises just before or after noon and calms with sunset, but it can arrive without warning and blow for as little as one hour or for as long as one week. Yachtsmen must take care not to be caught on a lee shore, and should be aware that the *meltémi* can cause an extremely uncomfortable steep, short sea.

In the northern Aegean the *meltémi* blows from the northeast and, further south towards the Cyclades, predominantly from the north. Recently, the strong midsummer northerlies that blow down the Turkish coast have per-

up-to-date information whenever you need it, as you also can from VHF channels 16 and 25. Virtually every Greek evening newscast is followed by a weather report which someone can translate for you, and the port authorities will be well informed. If you have a laptop and phone socket, log onto www.poseidon.ncmr.gr, the wind-and-waves profiler run by the National Centre for Marine Research.

The Saronic Gulf and the Ionian Sea offer the gentlest sailing conditions, mainly because the islands are relatively close to each other and because the *meltémi* in the Ionian is usually far weaker than it can be in the open Aegean.

suaded some charter companies to classify the Dodecanese as the most difficult waters in which to sail.

Sailing in the Dodecanese has the additional problem of the nearby Turkish border. The Turks insist that anyone sailing in their waters must clear customs at one of their ports of entry. The border is policed at sea and it is therefore unwise to enter Turkish waters unless you intend to enter Turkey officially.

Weather reporting in Greece is generally good. If you have a weather fax you can get

LEFT: running repairs aloft. **ABOVE:** a flotilla of yachts moored at Póthia in Kálymnos.

FLY THE FLAG

All charter vessels must sail under the Greek flag, even if the yacht is hired from, say, a British-based company. It is wiser to charter from one of the larger companies, which will prepare the charter agreement and is better organised at helping you through the process of leaving the marina. Keep the boat's papers, including the crew list, accessible: you may have to present them to the port authorities when you dock in a new harbour. If you are going to "bareboat" charter, at least two of the crew must have sailing qualifications, and you will need to take them with you to satisfy the authorities that you can be trusted in Greek waters.

The Ionian is blessed with a northwest wind called the *maéstros*, nowhere near as strong as the *meltémi*. The *maéstros* tends to blow only in the afternoon when the heat of the Greek mainland accelerates the wind off the sea. Occasionally a hot, southerly *sirócco* wind, sometimes carrying red dust from North Africa, will blow hard but it doesn't last long.

Despite this variety of local winds, Greek seas are often quite windless and yachtsmen should be prepared to motor. Whatever the conditions, you should always protect yourself against the sun and the increased glare off the water – which can produce temporary blindness.

But the greatest appeal of the Greek islands is the solitude offered by their remoteness. The green islands of the Ionian are, perhaps, the yachtsman's first choice for a number of reasons. The shelter among the many islands offers safe cruising, but if you want more lively conditions, a trip in the open waters to the west of Lefkádha (Léfkas) and Kefalloniá will provide marvellous sailing. Easy anchorages and safe village moorings are within a few hours' sail of each other throughout the Ionian islands. The time to sail the Ionian is definitely during spring and autumn months: August sees Italian yachtsmen pouring over from Italy, clogging up the numerous but small harbours.

The Saronic Gulf is a favourite haunt of cruising yachts because it is so close to Piraeus. The little island of Angístri, off Aegina, has some lovely beaches; Póros, Hydra and Spétses have attractive town harbours as well as quieter coves; and the east coast of the Peloponnese is unjustly underrated. In mid-season it will be difficult to find a berth at the town quays where, almost without exception, mooring is stern or bow to the quay and as close as possible to the quayside tavernas.

Moving east from the Saronic Gulf, the influence of the *meltémi* becomes stronger, and it is not until you travel north of the Sporades that you find less travelled cruising grounds, among the great inlets and peninsulas to the east of the deep bay which has Thessalóniki at its head. There are fewer villages and towns along this coast and you should be prepared to anchor offshore, sometimes in depths of 30 metres (100 ft) or more. (For further information, see the *Travel Tips* listings section at the end of this book.)❑

MARINAS AROUND THE ISLANDS

The biggest concentration of marinas in Greece is on the coast of Attica near Athens and Piraeus. But because of the commercial shipping and general traffic in and out of the capital, it is not an area of peace and beauty. Zéa Marina, in Piraeus, is large and crowded; Mikrolímano, the home of the Greek deep-water racing fleet, is cleaner and prettier; and Kalamáki, 8 km (5 miles) away from central Athens, is the largest.

Other major marinas among or near Greek islands are at Thessalóniki, where there is an excellent development at Kalamariá; at Gouvía, about an hour's sail north from Corfu town; and at Corfu itself. Corfu's own marina is more convenient than Gouvía, ideal for a city tour and for bunkering water and fuel. The recently enlarged marina at Lefkádha is right in town, just off the canal. And there's a large marina at Mandhráki in Rhodes, which is more suited to larger yachts, plus a smaller one on Kálymnos.

All these marinas make excellent staging posts for yachts which need to re-stock with food and water. There are, of course, charter bases in all these locations, which normally means there are repair and chandlery facilities on hand.

There's more about marinas in the Greek National Tourist Office's free booklet, *Sailing the Greek Seas*.

Island Hopping

The pleasures of travelling from one island to another using Greece's interlinking ferry routes are numerous. There is the never-ceasing view – a bas-relief pattern in blue of low, mysterious mountains. A chance to mingle with the Greeks themselves who pile on board with food, children and, as often as not, a *bouzoúki* or two. Plus, a unique opportunity to visit other islands not on the itinerary – 15 minutes closely observing a port from the top deck can reveal much about a place and its people. A bustle of activity takes place within view – reunions, farewells and the redistribution of a virtual warehouse of goods. Is that a piano being loaded on board? Is that crate of chickens really being exchanged for blankets?

Without thorough checking, however, it is easy to fall prey to the worst aspects of island-hopping in the form of missed connections, being stranded, or – a particularly Greek pastime – sailing straight past a chosen island and then having to make a two-day journey to reach it again.

To travel the ferries wisely, it helps to remember three basic facts. First, ferry journeys can be long. Second, they can be frustrating. If your ship reaches the small remote island you are trying to reach in the middle of the night, it is your responsibility to wake up and get off. For this reason, seasoned island-hoppers travel with an alarm clock. However, a hasty departure in darkness has deposited more than one independent traveller on the wrong island altogether.

Third, weather is a factor. The wind called the *meltémi* is a fact of Greek life, although recent reports indicate that *el Niño* has weakened it somewhat. Don't bank on it. When the winds are too strong the ships are delayed or kept in port. If you are depending upon the ferries to take you back to Athens for your international flight, leave at least one full day's leeway. Athens has its pleasures; missing your flight home does not.

The best known ferry routes are the main Cyclades circuit (Santoríni, Íos, Náxos, Páros and Mýkonos) and the Argo Saronic Gulf route (Aegina, Hydra, Póros). Another route is to the major Dodecanese islands; travelling between Rhodes, Kós, Kálymnos, Léros and Pátmos is easy. Less well known, and therefore more satisfying, are the western Cyclades islands (Kýthnos, Sérifos, Sífnos and

Mílos) and three of the four Sporades islands (Skiáthos, Skópelos, Alónissos). These routes exist as much to serve domestic needs as they do to serve tourists and they operate all year round, albeit at a reduced level. Both Rhodes and Kós in the Dodecanese are hubs for several satellite islands. And there are also the Ionian islands, where it is easy to travel between Lefkádha, Itháki and Kefalloniá.

After June each year, Greek tourist offices stock the free booklet *Greek Travel Routes: Domestic Sea Schedules*, produced by Greek Travel Pages. A map is useful when studying it, for some of the listings give the name of the port where

the ferry docks, rather than the name of the island.

In recent years hydrofoils, and larger catamarans which carry cars, have been playing an increasing role in inter-island travel. Their journey times are half those of ferries. This is great, particularly if your time is limited, but there are disadvantages. Both "cats" and hydrofoils are considerably more expensive and provide practically no view; it is like travelling in a high-speed water-borne bus. And neither are immune to the weather, for they are less able to bear high waves than ferries. Hydrofoils especially have also been known to stay in port through a scheduled departure simply because there were not enough passengers to justify the trip. There is no way to escape the uncertainties. ❏

LEFT: sailing into harbour. **RIGHT:** relaxing on a ferry.

MANAGING THE TOURISTS

Mass tourism has brought massive problems to Greece. Diverse remedies have been attempted, but there is still some way to go

Greece is essentially a small, jagged hump of rock and grey-green vegetation supporting an indigenous population of 10 million. Yet every summer, nearly as many foreign tourists descend on the country. By the early 1990s, more than eight million tourists visited the mainland and islands each year, pumping more than $3 billion into the economy annually.

Tourism had been either the second-largest or the largest foreign-exchange earner for Greece since the early 1970s. In recognition of this pivotal role, Greece's first Ministry of Tourism was founded to address long-neglected crises in the industry.

Growing pains

Greece's limited infrastructure and tourist facilities were both stretched to their limit. Popular islands teemed with hundreds of thousands of summer visitors. Streets that had been constructed for a donkey and two passers-by became rivers of slow-moving gawkers. Hotels were booked up far in advance, disappointing foolhardy travellers who arrived without a reservation.

Arid islands, supplied by tanker, had to ration water. Beaches were packed with sun-worshippers lying only inches apart. Nude sunbathers searching for the ultimate sybaritic experience appeared increasingly on family beaches. Native islanders, whose pleasures and priorities centred around the church and the community, were not amused.

Still less popular were thousands of young backpackers who arrived on the most crowded islands without pre-booked accommodation. They often had barely a drachma to their names, pushed up the local crime rate, and ended up sleeping on rooftops or beaches with nothing but the stars for cover.

Ferryboats to many islands were consistently overcrowded at high season. The craft themselves – often retired from more demanding

LEFT: tourists flock to the beaches in their thousands.
RIGHT: another charter flight arrives in Skiáthos.

North Sea or Baltic services, pending relegation to Southeast Asia, or the wrecker's yard – were nothing to write home about, either. Seats on island-hopping aeroplanes had to be booked two months in advance, and Athenians with island homes found they had to reserve their seats in spring for the entire summer.

Theoretical remedies

Even before tourism became the largest global industry, studies had predicted a future onslaught of young, low-income tourists, part of the estimated 2 billion travellers ranging around the globe in the new millennium, spoilt for choice in destinations.

The official Greek response, a consensus hammered out by the disparate elements of the Greek tourism industry convened by the first Tourism Minister Nikos Skoulas, was to emphasise quality clientele over quantity. Penniless backpackers were to be actively discouraged; upmarket, specialised tourism, involving high per-arrival spending, was to be promoted;

and the necessary infrastructure projects funded and built. It was further proposed to designate Greece as a "marine tourism country", to highlight the inland, monumental heritage, and to develop a higher level of professional services.

One immediate step taken was to forbid admission of charter-flight passengers without an accompanying room reservation, in a move to quash "hooliganism" among young tourists. This measure principally affected the British, roughly one in four arrivals. Athens also put a theoretical halt to licensing accommodation categories – mostly C-class hotels, and B-class rooms – on islands where there was an over-

PLANS FOR GROWTH

As part of the Skoulas tourism initiative, a dozen new full-service marinas were planned, and existing ones improved, with the help of the European Union's Integrated Mediterranean Programmes. Schools of tourism management were established, and a massive, coordinated overseas publicity campaign was undertaken, replete with some forgettable or ambiguous slogans ("Wherever you go, Greece awaits you"). New small-craft airports were opened on the smaller islands, bringing the Greek total to 36, and the domestic monopoly of Olympic Airways and its subsidiary, Olympic Aviation, was declared over.

supply, while simultaneously granting more permits for the construction of A- and luxury-class hotels, with generous incentives for supplementary facilities such as golf courses, tennis courts and convention halls.

But with the connivance of seat-only operators, the accommodation requirement was easily circumvented. The required vouchers soon became dummies, or were valid only for the first night, and in any case could not be enforced for EU nationals after 1993. Local bribes frequently neutralised national or urban controls on hotel building permits.

Reality bites

Ministry planners failed to recognise that, amid the early-1990s recessions, disposable income was unlikely to be available abroad to patronise all those grandiose projects. Poor accommodation distribution still plagues Greece. By early 1998 there were nearly 1 million licensed beds in hotels and *dhomátia*, with several provinces (such as Sámos and Iráklion) suffering from vast excess capacity, rarely full even in August, while other spots remain undersupplied.

Restored spas on Lésvos, a new marina on Híos (the one on Sámos has languished unfinished since 1991), the long-awaited restoration of Maniot towers as accommodation which promptly went bankrupt, all seemed like shuffling deckchairs on the *Titanic,* so inadequate were many aspects of Greece's chaotic infrastructure.

The nadir came in 1993, as the independent tourism ministry was temporarily reabsorbed into the economics ministry, and members of AITO, a group of independent British tour operators such as Laskarina and Sunvil, aired their grievances in *The Sunday Times*. The last straw was the sudden disappearance in mid-season of a critical ferry link, owing to a Byzantine wrangle between rival shipping companies and subsidising bureaucrats. With no subsequent improvement in boat or hydrofoil reliability, nor any Greek ministerial support for the AITO position, the islands concerned (Astypálea and Kastellórizo) were simply dropped from Laskarina's brochure.

The result: opt for a quality holiday on an offbeat, unspoiled island without an international airport – just what the ministry had encouraged – and there was no guarantee that you'd ever get there.

Hopes and prospects

Currently, a two-week, cheap-and-cheerful studio package, including flight, goes for about £350; a higher-quality package costs £400–450. For £100–200 more (or even the same price), British sunseekers can sample the exotic delights of Cuba, the Gambia, Goa or Florida. Individuals who love Greece, who have a connection with a particular place, and who speak a bit of the language, will continue to return regularly, but the country hasn't been trendy since the 1970s.

> **NUMBERS UP**
>
> Greece has seen a modest increase in tourist numbers in recent years – due to more "shoulder-season" bookings in spring and autumn.

The tourism industry's main task involves luring back significant numbers to what Greece does better or uniquely: clean seas, a high degree of personal safety, characterful inland villages, low-impact sports (venues for scuba diving, for instance, steadily increase). The other is to work on the weak points: unreliable transport; aging, brutalist-modern hotels and *dhomátia*; and indifferent cuisine.

The overcrowded-ferry abuses of 1996, when captains were fined for loading boats to double safe capacity, should never recur since the introduction of mandatory computerised booking and ticketing for all domestic sailings. Any lingering exceptions were winkled out by the September 2000 wreck of the *Express Samira*, which glaringly exposed the various shortcomings of Aegean shipping. Many rust-buckets have been junked since, and the bigger companies like NEL are ordering purpose-built, state-of-the-art boats rather than relying on cast-offs from northern Europe.

Since 1997 the National Tourist Organisation has produced annually an impartial printed ferry schedule, intended for overseas distribution *(see page 75)*. Several private competitors to Olympic Airways have emerged since the deregulation of the Greek skies, and if (as is perennially threatened) Olympic goes under and is inadequately "re-organised", these more efficient carriers may find themselves with a suddenly enlarged flight network.

Extensive restoration projects on the islands and mainland appeal to connoisseurs, but much more could be done with Greece's ample supply of medieval ruins. The level of cuisine in many resorts remains abysmal; locals retort that higher standards would be pearls before swine, and rail against the "supermarket tourists" who, having paid cut-rate fare and lodging, rub salt in the wound by self-catering, even without a kitchen. Cooking in hotel rooms is manifestly obnoxious, but offenders would probably splash out on taverna fare if it was more often worth paying for.

Some Greek tourism authorities still live in hope of a magic bullet which would simultaneously banish all cheapskates and lager-

louts, and bring malleable big-spenders rolling in. A wiser strategy, as Americans remain largely absent following the events of 11 September, and more Germans stay home because of economic uncertainties, would be to diversify the visitor portfolio. Already appreciative and relatively well-behaved central Europeans drive down to the north mainland, or fly in on packages; the Russian *nouveaux riches* have been arriving too. Weekend breaks and shopping visits by Turks to the border islands could be more actively encouraged.

With the big plans becalmed, the only certainty is that improvement will come in multifaceted increments. ❏

LEFT: queues at the charter terminal at Iráklion airport. **RIGHT:** tourism meets archaeology at Knossós.

SEA, SUN, SAND AND SEX

The arrival of single, female package tourists presented a challenge to local lads,

who on some islands saw seduction as a competitive sport

When the airport was built on Skiáthos in the mid-1970s, it put the island within three or four hours of direct flight from northern Europe. The number of visitors multiplied many times over, and the lifestyle of the islanders adapted rapidly.

Before the airport, Skiáthos was typical of

the small, relatively inaccessible Aegean islands. The unmarried men on the island might have assumed that unattached women were either old widows, who shrouded themselves in black and hobbled about on sticks, or their sisters. The others that existed were, without exception, under lock and key.

In the 1960s, most young Greek women were extremely restricted in their movements, and were kept closely tied to the family. There was therefore little prospect for romance, sex, or even an evening out with a girl for the would-be young man-about-town. The men saw the arrival of, in their eyes at least, sexually liberated women tourists as an opportunity not to be missed.

As with any country where sexuality has been repressed by strict segregation, and the young male population has an over-developed sense of *machismo*, Greece can be a troublesome place for single women to travel around – but this has not been helped by some of the tourists who have gone before them.

The northern Europeans disgorged from charter flights seemed to arrange matters differently from the women the local men were used to seeing (or not, as the case may be). Some of them travelled as couples but there were also a number of single women, some of whom, moreover, welcomed male company, be they fellow travellers, local fishermen or waiters in one of the many bars or restaurants.

A lexicon of early package tours was the four "Ss", the belief or hope that a beach in a hot country will produce the desired result: Sea plus Sun plus, bizarrely if you think about it, Sand equals Sex. With probably the best beaches in Greece, Skiáthos was inevitably going to be the setting for many such erotic expectations. The tourist industry boomed and gave the island a reputation as "the straight Mýkonos".

Some women, now respectably middle-aged, are commendably candid about their reasons for visiting Skiáthos back in the 1970s and 80s. Displaying an astounding lack of cultural sensitivity, they came looking for sex. This has, to a certain extent understandably, led some local men to expect the same of all foreign women – with predictable hassles.

Of course the tourists who came purely to sleep with a fisherman, waiter or, it must have seemed to some, any Greek man they could get their hands on, were always a minority and most women spent their time beating off advances rather than welcoming them. However, the idea of readily available sex became so dear to the hearts of some Greek men, they decided to invent a mythical "game" to complement the myth of available northern European women.

LEFT: a hopeful Greek boy entertains a visitor.
RIGHT: soaking up the sun on Rhodes.

Traditional word, new meaning

Kamáki literally means a fishing trident, or harpoon, but the word also refers to picking up or "hunting" foreign female tourists, and to the "hunter" himself (the sexual metaphor is obvious). It is a practice that has grown alongside the Greek tourist industry over the past 30 years, and whether it descends to physical harrassment or not, it is one which can become intensely irritating to any lone female traveller in Greece.

The rather sad exponents of *kamáki* like to imagine that sexual harrassment is acceptable as long as they can invent a set of rules to go with it – hence the claim that *kamáki* is a sophisticated game of seduction. This laughable claim is at once dispelled by its most common manifestation in the street, a kind of unappealing "cheeping" noise of the kind made to a budgerigar.

However, if you take the men's claims at face value, there are some "rules" that are common to all *kamáki*. Central to the whole pursuit is the idea that you can assign points, say from 1 to 10, to a woman – possibly based on nationality – which you earn if you have sex with her. It's not hard to imagine how a place on the scale might be decided and there is little point in going any further into it here. The aim, rather obviously, is to accrue as many points over a season (from June to September) and the one who has the most wins. One notable feature of this sad enterprise is its NIMBYism. The game's exponents will not risk the social approbrium that would come from targeting local women.

Whatever the repressed social situation of its origins, *kamáki* is not only blatantly insulting to foreign tourists, but also ignores the fact that contemporary Greek society now affords young Greek women much more sexual freedom, particularly in the major cities, up to and including cohabiting before marriage.

The best way to deal with these young and deluded males is to ignore them (or treat them with disdain), and to try and not let them spoil your holiday. Also, far more importantly, remember that the *kamáki* (who often are from outside the area) are unpopular among the vast majority of the local population, who will treat single women with respect as honoured guests, and feel that the *kamákis'* actions bring dishonour to the community. ❑

GREAT EXPECTATIONS

Stories abound of women whose holiday romances in Greece didn't turn out as they expected. One young woman, for example, arrived on Skiáthos late in the summer with the intention of remaining over the winter, but changed her plans after she was the target of predatory *kamáki* tactics.

She said later: "I arrived here carefree, honest and innocently trusting. It broke my heart when I had to acknowledge that you cannot trust 90 percent of what a Greek boy says to you, and that, however genuinely sensitive and warm he sounds, there are always ulterior motives. It's sad, it's true, but then this is a Greek island."

The reason for her disillusionment was that she had received – and seriously considered – a marriage proposal from a young fisherman who had had a number of partners that year.

But he had made it known, although not directly to her, that the marriage he was proposing would last only until the following spring, when he would have to break his promise in order to prey on more women that summer.

If that were not enough to demoralise the girl, she also discovered that at the end of the previous summer, and on exactly the same principles, he had married and subsequently divorced someone else.

WRITING THE GREAT NOVEL

Many authors – and would-be authors – decide that a Greek island is the perfect place in which to write a book. Some even achieve it

L awrence Durrell's somewhat sexist advice to Henry Miller in 1938 was "bring a woman", promising that in other respects his Greek island, lacking the more tiresome distractions of 20th-century society, was the perfect place to finish a novel. "We could sail and bathe in the morning, have a fine sunny lunch

with wine, then a long afternoon siesta, bathe before tea and then four hours' work in a slow rich evening." At the time, Miller was keen to finish a book and might have wondered about Durrell's idea of a hard day at the office.

Miller did finish the book (it was *Tropic of Capricorn*) and, although the extent to which it materialised on Corfu is unknown, the achievement ought to stand as a benchmark for the permanent presence that has since imposed itself on nearly every Greek island – writers wrestling with great works.

Most of them would have thrown a beach towel in with a typewriter or laptop and decamped to their island expressly to write a

book; others might have arrived for other reasons but been inspired by the amount of writing going on around them.

On one island, a book on local history had been in production for more than 20 years. It was by a clever Englishwoman who led a semi-reclusive existence in a primitive cottage high on a mountain. She would descend to the village once a week on a moped to do her shopping; otherwise nobody saw much of her. It was said that she'd come to the island to forget an unhappy love affair at Oxford.

The expatriate colony once published a little book about the island, and in it was an article by her which demonstrated convincingly the rigour of a trained historian. The article is probably as much as anyone will ever know about a project which had occupied most of her adult life. That year, she destroyed the manuscript. Asked why, she shrugged and said nothing.

Conspiracy of distraction

During the tourist season, a conspiracy of distraction forever drives a wedge between writer and great work. Durrell's invitation to Miller sets out some of them: the weather is magnificent and the sea so congenial that there is always a plausible excuse to dive in and remain there for some time.

Durrell's "fine sunny lunch with wine" is another of the yawning traps set for the island writer, especially the "with wine". By any criterion, expatriates who settle on islands are slightly odd. That makes them excellent company; it also means that, on the whole, they drink a bit.

Credit is extended everywhere to resident writers. The trusting and hospitable Greeks revere Homer and are willing to regard anyone who can type with two fingers as a potential heir. The less flattering explanation is that in winter there is no way off most islands except by boat, and creditors are likely to be lining the quay. Either way, their generosity can be a lifesaver because even writers who are in a position to have their banks at home send them money are often caught short.

Somewhere on the island there will be a wholesaler or a grocer who sells *oúzo* and brandy from the barrel – bring your own bottle. Short-term visitors are unlikely to have the time to find out who or where they are; expatriates, on the other hand, can find them blindfolded. Wine sold in huge bottles is commensurately cheap, and etiquette requires that, once opened, the bottle must be finished at one sitting.

One writer on the island discovered that, by reversing Durrell's timetable and applying himself in the mornings, he could turn out a slim volume of poetry per decade. Over lunch at his special table in a taverna below his house, he would discuss with another writer their respective great works. He was working on his third volume and was fairly confident that it would be ready by the turn of the millennium.

Bottle count

These were definitely lunches "with wine", and he would mysteriously arrange the bottles in a straight line on what seemed to be a constant compass bearing. (Greek waiters don't clear empty bottles; it is their way of keeping track of the ever-increasing numbers.)

A visit to the poet's house revealed that the view from the terrace bore down directly on the taverna and, in particular, on to "his" table. Concerned that too grand a lunch on the Durrell model might jeopardise work on volume three, the poet's wife had acquired a powerful pair of binoculars and turned the terrace into an observation post. From here she monitored the growing line of bottles that had been emptied by her husband and passing acquaintances, and if the situation appeared to be getting out of hand, she would descend imperially either to speak on the virtues of moderation or, *in extremis*, to march him off by the ear. The studied arrangement of the bottles, then, was a smokescreen. "He thinks that I can only see one," his wife revealed. "In that belief he is mistaken."

Whatever cloud may have been hanging over the third volume of poems, the first two were accomplished facts. Moreover, they were on sale in the local bookshop, a vindication for any writer whose credentials are called into question. Very few island writers are in a position to dispel doubt so triumphantly. Very few, indeed,

are on sale anywhere or, deep in their hearts, expect to be. It is enough merely to be writing a book, regardless of the outcome.

In the winter months, when all but one or two of the bars and tavernas are closed and the sea is too cold for swimming, there is nothing for the expatriate colony to do. It would be inconceivable, for example, to squander the need to call at the post office and at the bank by doing both on a single outing, even if post office and bank happened to be close neighbours.

Corfu cannot have had many visitors when Miller dropped in on Durrell in 1938, but Durrell's own literary output from his island base

proves that it can be done, if only by observing the sanctity of those four hours, either in the slow rich evening or, for a certain kind of poet, in the morning.

Less dedicated writers are more inclined to use the great novel to assuage Puritan misgivings about months of bone-idleness. It soothes the conscience and enhances the fun: after all, 150,000 completed words are a better memento of an island visit than a suntan or stamps registered in one's passport. All too often, of course, the great novel is never actually published – or indeed finished. But the possibility of its being completed provides the perfect excuse to return to the island for one more try. ❑

LEFT AND RIGHT: a look back in time; an antediluvian typewriter and several bottles of wine.

ISLAND WILDLIFE

The diverse island landscapes support a varied collection of flora and fauna.
Birds in particular, both resident and migrant, bring delight to ornithologists

Arrive at a Greek island in the heat of summer and you may feel you've inadvertently stumbled upon a little-known outpost of the Sahara. Arid brown countryside sheds clouds of dust each time the hair-dryer winds blow, dead tumbleweeds roll, and the only surviving plant life is in carefully nurtured village window-boxes.

Visit in spring, however and the picture is entirely different. Green leaves and coloured flowers cover the plains, hillsides and even areas of waste ground become gardens.

The first seedlings and new leaves sprout shortly after the first rains of autumn. Growth gathers pace through the cool but sunny winters then, a few weeks into the new year, the flowers start to open in the far southeast. Rhodes, Kárpathos and eastern Crete are followed in succession by western Crete, then the Peloponnese and the eastern Aegean. Spring arrives in the Ionian islands and Thássos as summer appears in Rhodes.

As the plants lead, so other wildlife follows. Insects increase, and the insect-eaters flourish; food-chains gear up for a spring and early summer of proliferation.

Plants a-plenty

Before mankind first settled in the region, the Greek islands had a mixture of some woodland, some tall, dense, impenetrably shrubby *maquis* vegetation, and much *garigue*. The latter consists of low shrubby bushes, which are often spiny and resist both the grazing of animals and the bare legs of walkers. Mixed together with the shrubs are fragrant herbs, colourful annuals and, enjoying protection from those spines, fragile orchids.

It is a myth that man and his flocks destroyed a verdant Greek Eden of continuous woodland: some larger islands had their own quota of

---

PRECEDING PAGES: goats on the Cretan mountains; donkeys in midwinter. **LEFT:** dolphins sometimes perform for ferry passengers. **RIGHT:** a European bee-eater conforming to its job description.

plant-munching animals – such as deer – long before any human arrivals. It was this that led to the flora's evolution of discouraging defences such as spines, bristles and foul tastes, which armed it well for the comparatively recent introduction of the domesticated sheep and goat. *(See also pages 92–3.)*

Reclusive mammals

Wild mammals occur on the islands, but most of them are secretive. Crete has its ibex-like wild goat or *agrími* (also called the *krí-krí*), a rare inhabitant of the White Mountains. With fears of its demise from over-hunting, some animals were transferred to the island of Dhía, near Iráklion, where they flourished and overpopulated – eating the rare native plants.

Elsewhere, the largest mammals are the badger, and the jackal of the eastern Aegean, but the one you are more likely to see is the stone-marten. This resembles a dark brown ferret, long, slim, agile and fast-moving. They are sighted both during the day and in headlights as they cross roads at night. They are frequent victims of the taxidermist's art, and many tavernas have a stuffed marten on the wall.

Most other mammals are small: rats (only common on Corfu), mice and shrews, and a variety of bats that can move from island to mainland and vice-versa.

The National Marine Park north of Alónissos is an important haven for the Mediterranean monk seal – the most endangered of all the world's seals. About 50 of a total world population of only 500 live here.

PYGMY PONY

On Skýros there is a very small wild horse, a unique breed very similar to the horses carved on the frieze of the Parthenon.

salty coastal pool, but visit Lésvos, Sámos and Límnos to see them nesting in quantity.

Much smaller, but most colourful, are the crested pink, white and black hoopoe, the bright blue and brown roller, and the multicoloured bee-eater. For many ornithologists, the most excitement comes from seeing the raptors – hawks, falcons, eagles and vultures, although the most frequent species is the common buzzard.

The larger species inhabit mountain areas, where gorges and cliffs provide secure nesting

Between islands, look out for common dolphins speeding alongside ferries.

Twitchers' territory

While the mammal-watcher may find him or herself under-employed, the bird-watcher should not be. The spring migration brings a variety of species north from Africa. Their final destination may be much further north, but the Greek islands may be their first landfall after the Mediterranean crossing. Some of the larger birds are most spectacular. Both black and white storks migrate through Greece, and nest on the way. Individual flamingos may turn up anywhere there is a

and the requisite isolation. Golden eagles may be the most romantic, but vultures are undoubtedly the most spectacular. Griffon vultures, sometimes in flocks of up to 20, patrol the skies, soaring effortlessly on broad wings the size of a door and a half. The scarcer lammergeier has narrow wings, the ultimate flying machine in its search for bones – or tortoises – to drop onto rocks and break open.

Reptiles and insects

The most abundant reptiles are lizards, some 21 species, of which the Balkan green lizard is perhaps the most conspicuous. Bolder and more stockily built is the iguana-like agama, sometimes called the Rhodes dragon, though it's also found in Corfu and several Aegean islands. This greyish rough-skinned lizard, when disturbed, often stays around for a few minutes to check out the danger.

Tortoises occur on many islands, though surprisingly not on the largest, Crete. Once gathered in tens of thousands for the pet-trade, they now lead safer lives wandering noisily through the underbrush. Their freshwater aquatic relatives, the terrapins, favour streams with bare muddy banks for sunbathing, but are wary and disappear quickly.

Marine loggerhead turtles are decreasing in

Aegean islands – they usually have a zigzag pattern down the spine, and move rather lazily.

Mosquitoes may seem the commonest insects at night, but Corfu is noted for its springtime fireflies, little flashing beacons that drift over damp fields and hedges after dark. Look for paler lights in the hedgerows and you may see glow-worms. During the day, butterflies are obvious, often in great quantity and variety. Some of the large hawk-moths may be seen during the day – the hummingbird hawk-moth, like its namesake, relies on superfast wingbeats to hover at flowers as it feeds.

Noisier are the huge, glossy blue-black

numbers as their nesting beaches are lost to tourism. They used to breed until recently on Crete, Kós and Rhodes – now they are restricted to a few semi-protected beaches on Kefalloniá and Zákynthos.

Snakes often cause alarm, but most are harmless, and all prefer to be left alone. Locals tend to overreact and attack any snake they see, though this is actually the best way to increase the chance of being bitten. Poisonous vipers do occur in some of the Ionian, Cycladic and east

FAR LEFT: the Mediterranean monk seal is a protected species. LEFT: a European roller. ABOVE: a griffon vulture soars. RIGHT: the once-endangered tortoise.

carpenter bees which spend much of their time looking for suitable nesting sites, usually a hollow cane. Noisiest of all is the cicada, an overgrown aphid, which perches – usually on a pine tree – and keeps up a deafening racket. Despite their size and volume, they are surprisingly hard to see. African locusts are really giant grasshoppers, though they never pillage in devastating swarms this side of the Mediterranean.

Praying mantids keep their barbed forearms in a position of supplication until an unwary insect moves nearby – then the mantid becomes a hungry atheist. Even the male of the species is devoured as he romances the female, his protein helping to nourish the next generation. ❏

THE ISLANDS IN BLOOM

The Greek islands are at their most abundant in spring and early summer, when every hillside and valley is decorated with glorious colour

Greece in spring is a botanist's dream and a gardener's despair. Some 6,000 species of wild plant grow in Greece and the islands, and in the spring (March to May) visitors may enjoy a magnificent cornucopia of flowers and fragrances.

Hillsides resemble giant rock gardens, while brilliant patches of untended waste ground outdo northern Europe's carefully tended herbaceous borders with ease. Winter rains, followed by a bright, hot, frost-free spring, produce a season's flowers compressed into a few, spectacular weeks before the summer's heat and drought become too much. By late May or June the flowers are over, the seeds for next year's show are ripening, and greens are fading to brown to match the tourists on the beaches.

SUMMER SURVIVAL

Except in the cooler, higher mountains, most plants go into semi-dormancy to survive the arid summer. The first rains of autumn, which could be in late September, but may be late November, tempt a few autumn bulbs into flower but also initiate the germination of seeds – plants that will grow and build up strength during the winter in preparation for the following spring when their flowers will again colour in the waiting canvas of the hills and valleys.

The richness and diversity of the flora are due in part to the islands' location between three continents – Europe, Asia and Africa – partly to the Ice-Age survival in temperate Greece of pre-glacial species, and partly to the wonderful variety of habitats. Limestone, the foundation of much of Greece, is a favoured home for plants, providing the stability, minerals, water supply and protection they need.

▷ **THE HILLS ARE ALIVE**
Sunshine, colour and quantity mark the spring flowering of the islands, as here in the mountains of Crete in mid-April.

△ **A GOOD REED**
Not bamboo – but it has similar uses. The giant calamus reed *(Arundo donax)* can be made into pan-pipes.

▽ **CUP OF MANY COLOURS**
Ranunculus asiaticus is an unlikely buttercup, with poppy-sized flowers in shades of white, pink, orange, red – and occasionally yellow.

▽ **SCARLET MEMORIAL**
The startling reds of *Anemone coronaria* mark the arrival of spring, and in myth represent the spilt blood of the dying Adonis.

▽ **HANDY BUSH**
The long flowering period of the native oleander makes it popular in gardens and as an ornamental roadside crash-barrier.

BEETLES, BEES AND BUTTERFLIES

The profusion of flowers and plants provides food for an equal profusion of insects. Butterflies are conspicuous from spring to autumn, including the swallowtail *(above)* whose equally colourful caterpillars feed on the leaves of common fennel. Its larger, paler and more angular relative, the scarce swallowtail, despite its name, is even more abundant.

Look for clouded yellows and paler cleopatras, reddish-brown painted ladies and southern commas, white admirals, and a myriad of smaller blue butterflies.

Butterflies, bees and day-flying hawkmoths tend to go for flowers with nectar, while beetles and flies go for the pollen. Some bugs even use the heat accumulated in the solar cup of many flowers in order to warm up their sex lives.

The leaves of plants feed armies of insect herbivores, which themselves are eaten by more aggressive insects. Some of the omniverous Greek grasshoppers and crickets are as happy munching through a caterpillar, or even another grasshopper, as the grass it was sitting on.

◁ **FIRE FENNEL**
According to legend, fire was brought to earth by Prometheus hidden in the smouldering stem of a giant fennel *(Ferula communis)*.

▽ **NATURAL FOOD**
Wild artichokes are painfully spiny to prepare for the pot, but their flavour is much prized by Greek country folk over the spineless cultivated variety, and their market price increases accordingly.

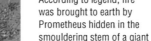

ISLANDS OUT OF SEASON

The onset of winter and the disappearance of the tourists brings a sudden and dramatic change to the smaller Greek islands

It is only when the charter flights have finally returned to base that the real character of a small island staggers out of its unseasonal hibernation. The larger islands are capable of absorbing a deluge of visitors without having to adopt a totally different identity. A visitor arriving in Crete in October would not discover, as could happen on a smaller island, that the police station had just closed and would not re-open until needed again late in the spring.

It is difficult to exaggerate the disfiguring impact when an island with a population measured in hundreds is swamped by 10 times as many people, all at the same time.

Quick change

Understandably dazed by the whole thing, the islanders have to find their feet again when everyone goes away. Superficially, the change into winter uniform is swift. Migrant waiters and kitchen staff pile on to departing ferries to look for winter jobs on the mainland. Awnings over pavement cafés are rolled up and stowed; the chairs and tables stacked and dragged away. Most of the shops are closed and padlocked.

A good sign that the islanders are feeling themselves again after the grinding hours they have put in during the season is the resumption of the evening promenade, an almost formal ritual in which small groups file from one end of the locally prescribed route to the other, and back again. Overtaking is apparently not allowed. Among them are the elderly and handicapped who are seldom seen in public during the season.

Winter visitors who join the throng are bound to attract curious glances from the traffic going in the opposite direction. The process of acceptance as an honorary member of the community is a ritual in itself. First, perhaps, a half-cocked eyebrow; later, a nod; then ultimately, triumphantly, a stop for a chat.

The promenade is a chance to observe all

LEFT: even the Cyclades see snow in winter.
RIGHT: stormy weather over Tínos.

kinds of island machinery in motion. Orthodox priests, symbols of a former propriety that doesn't stand a chance against the summer heathens, reassert their magisterial presence among the faithful. Office-holders and petitioners in the schismatic world of island politics fall into step beside the mayor for a mobile conference.

If the municipal elections are in sight, the plotting that goes on during the promenade will explode into campaigns which sound like the rumble of impending civil war. The party manifestos may commend or deplore, as the case may be, the state of the village drains, but the winner's powers of patronage are such that the outcome is regarded, not unrealistically, as a matter of economic life or death.

Visitors can skip politics, however, and still feel that they are part of local life. There are any number of religious festivals involving processions through the streets, the mayor and priests conspicuously linked in secular-clerical solidarity at the head of an enthusiastic brass band.

The locals have to buy food and other supplies, so there is never any difficulty getting hold of provisions. But the smaller islands are seldom self-sufficient, and if they have to rely on ferries – which are not nearly so frequent during the winter, and are likely to be cancelled in bad weather – there may be temporary shortages of most fresh produce.

Power failures which last more than a day cause a commotion because the bakeries can't function. The lesser kind go unnoticed (although not by writers with laptops needing recharging).

The fishermen sail at dusk and return at dawn but, for the rest of the male population, the

longer nights are the cue to bring out playing cards. Officially, no money changes hands, but passers-by can't fail to notice scraps of paper and meticulous accounting. In reality, there is a massive redistribution of the summer takings, although by the following spring most of the money is supposedly back where it started.

Winter visitors

Landlords don't expect to earn rent in winter, so when a visitor comes along out of season the negotiations are flexible. Prime accommodation on the sea may be worth a slight premium while the water is still at a tolerable temperature, although after September and before May there is hardly a beach that couldn't be annexed and occupied as private property.

If outdoor conditions are an important criterion, the southern islands are generally warmer. All over the Aegean, however, the winter wind will sometimes cut through to the bone, and houses that were not built specifically for the summer trade are more likely to have some form of heating. Tenants would be expected to pay for the fuel they use.

It is worth asking about vacant farmhouses; these have the added advantage that neighbours are always popping around with eggs, a bottle and an extra glass. This agreeable way of life can be had for a reasonable rent; not excluding lavish consumption of drink.

An insider's view

The English novelist Simon Raven spent the winter of 1960 on Hydra looking into "what goes on when winter comes, when the last epicene giggle has hovered and died in the October air". He decided he was among a bunch of atavistic pirates who, happily preoccupied by making money during the summer, reverted in winter to the old distrust of strangers who used to come only to spy on their illicit booty.

Hydra has since become accustomed to having a few foreigners stay on and, assuming the islanders never saw what Raven wrote about them, he would probably feel more comfortable among them now. The one impression formed then which he would not wish to change now is that only in winter could his eye make out what the island was really like. ❑

LEFT: an ancient provider of winter warmth on Ikaría.
RIGHT: January storm clouds over Hydra harbour.

PLACES

A detailed guide to all the island groups, with their principal sites clearly cross-referenced by number to the maps

The poet Odysseus Elytis once said: "Greece rests on the sea." It's an observation that few countries could claim with such authority. Some 25,000 sq km (10,000 sq miles) of the Aegean and the Ionian seas are covered by islands, the exact number of which has, in characteristic Greek fashion, been the topic of discussion and dispute. There may be 3,000 islands and islets, of which 167 are inhabited; there may be only 1,000, of which less than 60 are inhabited.

The frame of reference that defines a populated place is open to interpretation. Does a tiny outcrop, bare save for one shepherd and six goats, constitute an uninhabited island? Can an island totally deserted except for pilgrimages made annually to a small chapel at its summit claim to be inhabited?

The reality is perhaps immaterial; both visitors and inhabitants are more interested in sea and sky than in facts and figures. What is indisputable, however, is the sheer variety of landscape and experience to be found lurking behind the familiar images.

This is what we attempt to show here; islands with an ancient past and a modern outlook, the complex choice and the pure simple pleasures. In order to accommodate everything that is implied in the phrase "a Greek island" we have devoted space to tiny islands such as Ághios Efstrátios and Télendhos, as well as the well-known giants like Crete and Rhodes and the holiday favourites such as Corfu and Mýkonos. We do not ignore the familiar, popular islands, of course, but we explore them with typical Insight thoroughness, to search out the true heart of the place behind the tourist clichés.

So welcome aboard the ferry – and try not to be fazed by variations in spelling you will encounter. We have tried to be consistent in the way we spell place names, but when it comes to transliterating their language into Roman characters, the Greeks themselves are notoriously variable. Where there is more than one version of a place's name, we have indicated options. But be prepared to see different versions again on notices or road signs. For more on the Greek language, see the *Travel Tips* section at the back of this book. ❏

PRECEDING PAGES: Pythagório harbour, Sámos; fishing boats and the church – two important features of island life; lunchtime on Hydra. **LEFT:** passengers disembark from an Aegean ferry.

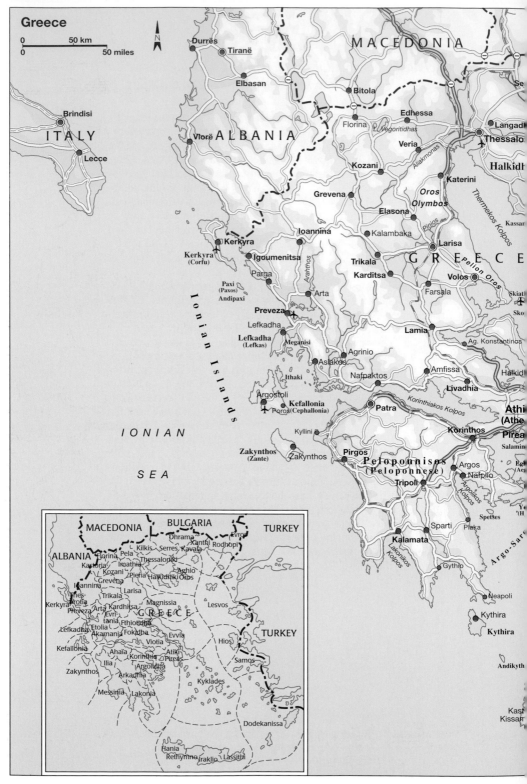

Greece

0   50 km
0   50 miles

N

MACEDONIA

Durrës
Tiranë
Elbasan
Bitola

Brindisi
ITALY
Lecce

Vlorë ALBANIA

Florina
L. Vegoritidhas
Edhessa
Langadi
Se

Veria
Thessalo
Aliakmonas

Kozani
Katerini
Halkidi

Grevena
Oros
Olymbos

Elasona
Kassar

Kalambaka
Pinios
Larisa
Thermekos Kolpos

Kerkyra
Kerkyra
(Corfu)
Igoumenitsa

Ioannina
Arakhthos

Trikala
GREECE
Pelion Oros

Parga
Karditsa
Volos

Paxi
(Paxos)
Andipaxi
Arta
Farsala
Skiat
Sko

Preveza
Lefkadha
Lamia
Ag. Konstantinos

Lefkadha
(Lefkas)
Meganisi

Agrinio
Aslakos
Amfissa
Halki

Ithaki
Nafpaktos
Livadhia

Argostoli
Kefallonia
(Cephallonia)
Poros

Patra
Korinthiakos Kolpos
Athi
(Athe

Ionian Islands

Kyllini
Korinthos
Pirea

IONIAN
Salamin

Zakynthos
(Zante)
Zakynthos
Pirgos
Peloponnisos
(Peloponnese)

Argos
Eg
(Aeg

SEA

Tripoli
Nafplio
Argolikos Kolpos

Spetses
Ye
'(H

Sparti
Plaka

Kalamata
Lakonikos Kolpos

Argo-Sare

Gythio

Neapoli

Kythira
Kythira

Andikyth

Kast
Kissam

MACEDONIA   BULGARIA   TURKEY

Dhrama
Xanthi Rodhopi
Evro

ALBANIA
Florina
Pela
Kilkis
Serres
Kavala

Kastoria
Imathia
Thessaloniki

Kozani
Pieria
Halkidhiki
Aghio
Oros

Grevena

Ioannina
Larisa

Thes-
protia
Trikala

Kerkyra
Arta
Kardhitsa
Magnissia
Lesvos

Preveza
Evri-
tania
Fthiotidha
GREECE

Lefkadha
Etolia
Akarnania
Fokidha
Evvia
TURKEY

Kefallonia
Viotia
Hios

Ahaïa
Korinthia
Atiki-
Pireas

Ilia
Argolidha
Samos

Zakynthos
Arkadhia

Messinia
Lakonia
Kyklades

Dodekanissa

Hania
Rethymno
Iraklio
Lassithi

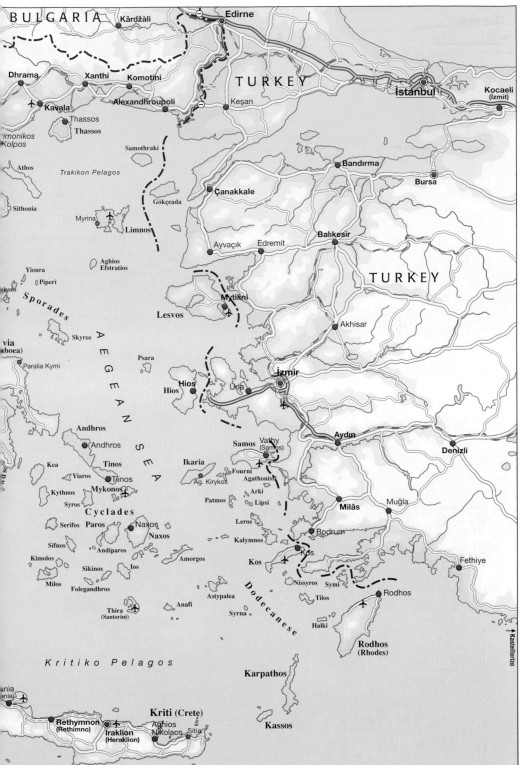

ATHENS STOPOVER

*Large and hectic, often spectacular, always exhilarating,
Athens can be simply exhausting. But if you have a
day or two to look around, there's plenty to see*

Map
on page
110

S ince Athens was suddenly elevated, unprepared, to the status of capital of the new Greek state after the War of Independence, it has grown haphazardly, and very fast. It never had a chance to mellow into venerable old age. Old and new sit side by side, and you can still sense the small pre-war city pushing through the huge sprawl of today's modern capital.

Occasionally, you come across what must have been a country villa, ensconced between tall office buildings, its owner still fighting against the tide, its windows hermetically closed against pollution and the roar of the traffic. However, the central squares have rid themselves of the temporary barricades and huge cranes marking the construction of the city's metro, and the clean, efficient trains are now running through the centre. More infrastructure projects, associated with the successful 2004 Olympics, have eased the pressure on the city.

Branching off from the frenzied central arteries are the minor veins of the city, relatively free from congestion. Most apartment blocks have balconies and verandahs, and there you can see the Athenians in summer emerging from their afternoon siesta in underpants and nighties, reading the paper, watching the neighbours, watering their plants, eating their evening meal. The hot weather makes life in the open air a necessity; this in turn means gregariousness, though nowadays the pale-blue flicker of television draws more and more people indoors.

LEFT: looking past the Acropolis out to sea (viewed from Lykavitós hill).
BELOW: shopping around Syntagma.

Ancient Athens

If your time in Athens is limited, it makes sense to start with the sights that are universally recognised as symbols of Ancient Greece, the monuments dating from Ancient Athens' "golden years", the 5th century BC. Seen from the right angle driving up the **Ierá Odhós** (the Sacred Way), the **Acropolis ❶** (summer: 8am–7pm; winter: 8.30am–3pm) still has a presence that makes the grimy concrete fade into insignificance. Climb up in the early morning, when crowds are thinnest, and a strip of blue sea edged with grey hills marks the horizon.

The **Propylaia**, the battered official entrance to the Acropolis built by Mnesikles around 430 BC, was cleverly designed with imposing outside columns to impress people coming up the hill. Parts of its coffered stone ceiling, once painted and gilded, are still visible as you walk through. And roped off on what was once the citadel's southern bastion is the small, square temple of **Athena Nike**, finished in 421 BC, is at present half-built following a restoration.

The Acropolis can look a little like a stonemason's workshop, much as it must have done in the 440s BC when the **Parthenon** was under construction as the centrepiece of Pericles' giant public works programme.

Supporting the porch of the Erechtheion, the Caryatids' faces still bear the pigments of ancient 'make-up'.

Some of his contemporaries thought it extravagant: Pericles was accused of dressing his city up like a harlot. In fact, the Parthenon celebrates Athena as a virgin goddess and the city's protector. Her statue, 12 metres (39 ft) tall and made of ivory and gold plate to Phidias's design, used to gleam in its dim interior. In late antiquity it was taken to Constantinople, where it disappeared.

Conservators have lifted down hundreds of blocks of marble masonry from the Parthenon, to replace the rusting iron clamps inserted in the 1920s with non-corrosive titanium (rust made the clamps expand, cracking the stone). The restorers also succeeded in identifying and collecting about 1,600 chunks of Parthenon marble scattered over the hilltop, many blown off in the 1687 explosion caused by a Venetian mortar igniting Ottoman munitions stored inside the temple. When they are replaced, as now on the north-facing Opisthonaos, about 15 percent more of the building will be on view. New blocks cut from near the ancient quarries on Mount Pendéli, which supplied the 5th-century BC constructors, will fill the gaps.

The **Erechtheion**, an elegant architecturally complex repository of ancient cults going back to the Bronze Age, is already restored. Completed in 395 BC, a generation later than the Parthenon, it once contained the supposed tomb of King Kekrops, a mythical founder of the ancient Athenian royal family, and also housed an early wooden statue of Athena.

The Caryatids now supporting the porch are modern copies. The four surviving originals are in the **Acropolis Museum** (summer: daily 8am–7pm; winter: Tues–Sun 8.30am–3pm, Mon 11am–5pm) to prevent further damage from the *néfos*, the ochre blanket of atmospheric pollution that can hang over Athens. The controversial new glass and marble museum building on D. Areopagitou, just below the Acropolis, is due to open in 2008. There were originally six

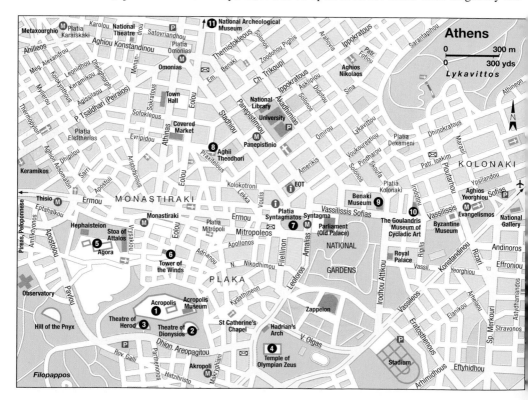

Caryatids: one was taken by the Ottomans and lost, another is in the British Museum in London, thanks to Lord Elgin. Their four sisters stare out from a nitrogen-filled case. The coquettish *koraï* reveal a pre-classical ideal: if you look closely, you can make out the traces of make-up and earrings, and the patterns of their crinkled, close-fitting dresses.

On the south side of the Acropolis lies the **Theatre of Dionysios ❷** (summer: daily 8am–7pm; winter: 8.30am–3pm). The marble seating tiers that survive date from around 320 BC and later, but scholars are generally agreed that plays by Aeschylus, Sophocles, Euripides and Aristophanes were first staged here at 5th-century BC religious festivals. A state subsidy for theatre-goers meant that every Athenian citizen could take time off to attend. Herod Atticus, a wealthy Greek landowner who served in the Roman senate, built another theatre on the south slope of the Acropolis in the 2nd century AD, as a memorial to his wife. The steeply-raked **Theatre of Herod Atticus ❸** is now used during the Athens Festival for performances of classical drama, opera and ballet.

Also in the 2nd century, the Roman Emperor Hadrian, a fervent admirer of classical Greece, erected an ornate **arch** marking the spot where the classical city ended and the provincial Roman university town began. Little of this Roman city can be seen beneath the green of the **Záppion Park**, and the archaeological area behind the towering columns of the **Temple of Olympian Zeus ❹** (summer: daily 8am–7pm; winter: 8am–3pm), but recent excavations in the corner of the Záppeio indicate that many Roman buildings stood in this area, at least as far as the stadium built by Herod Atticus. Work on the Temple of Olympian Zeus had been abandoned in around 520 BC when funds ran out, but Hadrian finished the construction and dedicated the temple to himself.

Map on page 110

In Ottoman times, the Erechtheion was used by the city's Turkish military commander as a billet for his harem.

BELOW: the Erechtheion by night.

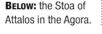

The Tomb of the Unknown Warrior, by Syntagma Square, is guarded by Evzónes, soldiers in traditional mountain costume. .

As the Acropolis was mainly used for religious purposes, so the ancient Greek **Agora ❺** (summer: daily 8am–7pm; winter: 8am–3pm) was employed for all public activities – commercial, political, civic, educational, theatrical, athletic. Today it looks like a cluttered field of ruins. If archaeologists had their way, the whole of Pláka might have been levelled. The reconstructed **Stoa of Attalos**, a 2nd-century BC shopping mall, is a cool place to linger among scents of ancient herbs replanted by the American excavators. The **Hephaisteion**, the Doric temple opposite, will help you appreciate that the Parthenon is truly a masterpiece. Across from the Agora, one corner of the **Painted Stoa** has been exposed in Adrianoú Street. This building gave its name to Stoicism, the stiff-upper-lip brand of philosophy that Zeno the Cypriot taught here in the 3rd century BC.

A 1st-century BC Syrian was responsible for the picturesque **Tower of the Winds ❻** (daily 8.30am–3pm), a well-preserved marble octagon overlooking the scanty remains of the Roman Agora. It is decorated with eight relief figures, each depicting a different breeze, and once contained a water-clock.

City streets

The heart of the modern city lies within a triangle defined by **Platía Omónias** (**Omónia Square**) in the north, **Platía Syntagmátos** (**Syntagma Square**) ❼ to the southeast and **Monastiráki** in the south. Except for three small cross-streets, no cars are permitted in this area, which has taken on a new lease of life. **Ermou**, once a traffic-clogged mess, is now a long pedestrian walkway with reinvigorated shops, enlivened by pavement buskers and push-carts. Many buildings have been refurbished, while the new lighting makes this an attractive area to wander in the evening in search of the perfect taverna.

BELOW: the Stoa of Attalos in the Agora.

The entire area is a huge sprawl of shops, more upmarket towards Syntagma Square. **Monastiráki** has a market selling a weird assortment of objects, where kitsch-collectors will find much to interest them. The old **covered market**, a 19th-century gem roughly half-way between Monastiráki and Omónia squares, is the city's main meat and fish market, crowded with shoppers milling between open stands displaying fish, seafood and any variety of poultry and meat you can imagine, all being loudly praised by vendors.

Pláka, the old quarter clustering at the foot of the Acropolis, has been refurbished and restored to its former condition (or rather to a fairly good reproduction of it), the garish nightclubs and discos have been closed down, motorvehicles prohibited (for the most part), houses repainted and streets tidied up. It has become a delightful, sheltered place to meander in. It is full of small beauties, too: look out for the Byzantione churches, the Old University, the fragmented ancient arches and walls.

Byzantine Athens is scantily represented: a dozen or so churches, many dating from the 11th century, can be tracked down in Pláka, and others huddle below street level in the shadow of the city's tall, modern buildings. They are still in constant use: passers-by slip in to light a yellow beeswax candle, cross themselves and kiss an icon in near-darkness before returning to the noise outside. One of the handsomest is **Ághii Theodhóri ❽**, just off Klafthmónos Square. It was built in the 11th century, on the site of an earlier church, in characteristic cruciform shape with a tiled dome and a terracotta frieze of animals and plants. The **Church of Sotíra Lykodhímou** on Filellínon Street dates from the same time, but was bought by the Tsar of Russia in 1845 and redecorated inside. It now serves the city's small Russian Orthodox community; the singing is renowned.

Map on page 110

The main tourist information office (EOT) is at Tsoha 24, tel : 210 870 7000. It provides free maps of Athens, brochures on the islands, ferry timetables and accommodation listings.

BELOW: the former palace on Syntagma Square now houses the Parliament.

Map on page 110

Socialising over a frappé (iced coffee) – and the obligatory mobile.

BELOW: stunning displays at the Byzantine and Christian Museum.

Athens' museums

The **Benáki Museum** ❾ (Mon, Wed, Fri and Sat 9am–5pm, Thur 9am–midnight, Sun 9am–3pm), at the northeast corner of the National Garden, houses a wonderfully eclectic collection of treasures from all periods of Greek history – including jewellery, costumes, the recreated interiors of two rooms from a Kozáni mansion, and two icons attributed to El Greco in the days when he was a young Cretan painter called Domenico Theotocópoulos. The beautifully laid-out galleries make this the most attractive museum in the city, which also has an excellent top-floor café and restaurant.

Near the Benáki is another museum with a world-renowned private collection on display. The **Museum of Cycladic and Ancient Greek Art** ❿ (Mon and Wed–Fri 10am–4pm, Sat 10am–3pm; *see also page 168*) features the beautiful prehistoric white marble figurines, dismissed as barbaric by turn-of-the-century art critics but include Picasso and Modigliani among their admirers. They come from graves in the Cycladic islands but scholars are still uncertain of their purpose. Also part of the museum is the Helen Strathou house, a beautiful Kolonáki neoclassical mansion. The nearby **Byzantine and Christian Museum** (Tues–Sun 8.30am–3pm), a mock-Florentine mansion built by an eccentric 19th-century duchess, contains a brilliant array of icons and church relics .

A real treat is the **Museum of Popular Musical Instruments** (Tues, Thur–Sun 10am–2pm, Wed noon–6pm) found at Diogenes 1–3, in Pláka. The collection was donated by the eminent Greek ethnomusicologist Fivos Anoyanakis and is housed in a neoclassical mansion. The many and varied musical instruments are well displayed and have listening posts nearby; an excellent introduction to the varied musical traditions of the country.

The **National Archaeological Museum** ⓫ (summer: Tues–Sun 8am–7pm, Mon 10.30am–5pm; winter: Tues–Sun 8.30–3pm) has reopened after a lengthy refurbishment, and holds the city's most important collection. Among the gems on display are the stunning gold work of the Mycenaean collection, the Akrotíri frescoes *(see pages 187–8)* and major bronze sculptures, including the wonderful Poseidon found off the coast of Évvia.

Athens by night

The night is long in this city. Athenians fiercely resist sleep, or make up for lost night-time sleep with a long afternoon siesta (*never* telephone an Athenian between 2pm and 6pm). Cafés and bars stay open until the small hours; they provide music (usually loud) and serve food (usually expensive).

Three o'clock in the morning, and the traffic still won't give up. Groups linger on street corners, goodnights take forever. The main streets are never entirely deserted. Perhaps this is one of the reasons why Athens is a safe city to walk in at night, except for the occasional bag-snatcher, for real violence is rare. The "unquiet generation" finally goes to bed; verandahs and balconies go dark, cats prowl, climbing jasmine smells stronger – and all the conflicting elements in the patchwork city seem momentarily resolved in the brief summer night. ❏

Coping with Piraeus

The port of Athens, Piraeus, is a city in its own right. Although it is an industrial city, with few concessions to the large numbers of tourists who pass through every year, it is easy to idle away a few hours while waiting to catch a ferry, even if there are few echoes of *Never on Sunday* these days. (The underworld moved to Athens during the puritanical colonels' dictatorship. Since then, successive mayors have been elected on a "smarten up Piraeus" ticket.)

For Piraeus ferries, get there one hour before sailing time so that you have half an hour to find the right quay before the boarding deadline: ships really do leave on time. It used to be the case that you didn't need to buy your tickets in advance, but computerised ticketing has put paid to that. For safety's sake, book as soon as you can.

The easiest way to get to Piraeus from Central Athens is on the metro (line 1; allow around 45 minutes for the journey). Alternatively, a bus leaves from Sýntagma, but this can be very slow. An express bus runs direct to Piraeus from Athens airport, and stops outside the Port Authority (OLP) passenger building on Aktí Miaoúli street.

Finding your boat can be confusing, but the ticket agent will be able to tell you which quay your ferry departs from. As a general guide: boats to the Cyclades depart from the quays opposite the metro station; boats to the Cycladic islands also go from the other side of Platía Karaiskáki (south of the metro); boats to Crete leave from Aktí Kondhíli on the northern side of the port; large catamarans, and Flying Dolphins to the Argo Saronic islands, depart from the quays close by Platía Karaiskáki (note that Flying Dolphin services for the Argo-Saronics no longer leave from Zéa Marina); and the Dodecanese are served by boats leaving from Aktí Miaoúli.

The radical cosmopolitan atmosphere for which Piraeus was famous 2,500 years ago still flourishes – the port and its industrial suburbs are left-wing strongholds – but few remains survive. A stretch of elegant 4th-century BC wall runs beside the coast road beyond Zéa Marina, and an amphitheatre backs on to the archaeological museum (Tues–Sun 8.30am–3pm) on Philhellínon Street, which is well worth visiting.

Its prize exhibits are two bronze statues found by workmen digging a drain in Piraeus: a magnificent *kouros* (6th-century BC figure) of a young man (known as the Piraeus Apollo), and a 4th-century helmeted Athena, looking oddly soulful for a warrior goddess. Both may have come from a shipment of loot overlooked by Greece's Roman conquerors in the 1st century BC.

The Hellenic Maritime Museum (Aktí Themistokléous; Tues–Sat 9am–2pm) is close by on Zéa Marina. Zéa Marina is crowded with medium-sized yachts – a floating campsite in summer – and you may also see huge, old-fashioned two and three-masters looking like small pirate ships, as well as sleek motor-yachts moored. Further round the headland are cafés and fish restaurants overlooking the Saronic Gulf. ❑

RIGHT: Piraeus is constantly busy with cruise liners, ferries and cargo ships.

THE IONIAN ISLANDS

*Corfu, Paxí, Lefkádha, Itháki, Kefalloniá,
Zákynthos, Kýthira*

The islands of the west coast are known in Greek as the *Eptánisa*
– the seven isles. However, the seventh island, Kýthira, lies off
the southern tip of the Peloponnese and, although it is linked by
history, culture and architecture, it remains quite isolated from the
other six islands.

During the 8th and 7th centuries BC, wanderers from Corinth
settled on the most northerly of the Ionian islands, bringing with
them a distinct culture. Two centuries later the secession of Corfu
from Corinth brought about the beginning of the Peloponnesian War.
Over the years the Ionians have had many warrior landlords, but it is
the long period of Venetian rule that has left the most indelible mark
on the islands.

Artists, craftsmen and poets were often sent to Venice for their
education, bringing back to the islands a cosmopolitan and international perspective. Even today, thanks to good air and sea links with
Italy, the islands have a distinctly Italian flavour   and that doesn't
only apply to the many pizzerias that jostle for space with tavernas
on many a harbour promenade.

It is the heavy rainfall which makes the Ionians among the greenest of Greek island chains. Olive groves and vineyards are reminders
that agriculture, rather than the dubious riches of tourism, still claim
a part in the economy. But it is this same unsettled weather that has
ruined many a traveller's holiday: from mid-September until mid-
May, rains can wash out any beach outing suddenly and without
warning. Fortunately, escape is never far away. The Ionians' links
with the mainland are very good, and several coaches daily at the
height of the season make the journey from Athens to Corfu (allow
at least 10 hours), via a connecting ferry service. It's also possible to
reach Kefalloniá or Zákynthos by bus and ferry from Athens.

Today the Ionians are threatened not by invaders (other than tour
companies) but by earthquakes. A series of quakes has at various
times beset the islands, the most recent and serious being in 1953.
Casualties were great and the beautiful Venetian-built capitals of
Kefalloniá and Zákynthos were flattened.

Reconstruction began almost immediately. The residents of
Argostóli in Kefalloniá put up makeshift buildings which still remain,
in order to resume busy, industrious lives. Zakynthians, however,
elected to recreate their Venetian city on a grand scale, using original plans and grids. These contrasting attitudes to tragedy tell an
island tale.   ❑

PRECEDING PAGES: Ássos on Kefalloniá; spring flowers bloom in an Ionian olive
grove. **LEFT:** an excursion to the Melissáni Cave, Kefalloniá.

CORFU

Few places have been as exploited for tourism as Corfu. Yet away from the package-tour resorts there is much to savour in this beautiful green island

Map on page 124

Strategically poised where the Ionian Sea becomes the Adriatic, almost within hailing distance of the mainland, Corfu (Kérkyra) has always been coveted, with a turbulent history and a long catalogue of invaders and rulers. The Venetians in particular left a rich legacy of olive groves, which for years provided a reliable living. The biggest current issue, which has united environmental activists and local municipalities against the agricultural ministry, is whether indiscriminate aerial pesticide spraying of the olives should continue.

There's evidence of habitation dating back 50,000 years, though Corfu enters history as 'Corcyra' in the mid-8th century BC, when it was colonised by ancient Corinth. By the 5th century BC, Corcyra had become a major, independent naval power, siding with Athens against Sparta (and Corinth) in the Peloponnesian Wars. After 229 BC, the island fell under Roman dominion, a relatively uneventful period.

Nearly eight centuries of Byzantine tenure from 395AD brought a measure of stability and prosperity, but latter years saw incursions and variable periods of domination by various groups of "barbarians", the Norman-Angevin Kingdom of the Two Sicilies, the Despotate of Epirus, and the Venetians. Weary of misrule and pirate raids, the Corfiots asked to be put definitively under the protection of Venice, who obliged in 1386 – and stayed for 411 years, successfully defying four Ottoman sieges. Napoleon dissolved what remained of the Venetian empire in 1797, and the French held the island until 1814 (except for the brief reign of the Ottoman/Russian-controlled "Septinsular Republic"). The British took over in 1814, staying for 50 years until all the Ionian islands were ceded to Greece as a sweetener for George I's ascent of the Greek throne.

During World War I, Corfu was the final destination of a retreating, defeated Serbian army; memorials and cemeteries from that era remain. In the next world war, the city suffered extensive damage in September 1943 under a German bombardment to displace the Italian occupiers, who had surrendered to the Allies; during their brief but brutal stay, the Nazis rounded up and deported Corfu's significant Jewish community, resident here since Venetian times.

LEFT: an elegant passage in Corfu town. **BELOW:** a memorial to a Venetian dignitary.

A multicultural capital

Corfu Town, known locally as **Kérkyra ❶**, occupies a slight peninsula on the east coast. The name is a corruption of *koryfo*, or "peak", there being two such on a Byzantine-fortified outcrop much altered as the **Paleó Froúrio** (daily 9am–7pm; entrance fee) by the Venetians during the 15th and 16th centuries, when they cut a canal to make the citadel an island. The more complete **Néo Froúrio** to the west (daily 9am–7pm; entrance fee) is strictly Venetian, and offers superb views over the tiled roofs of the town cradled between the two forts.

With its tottering, multi-storeyed Venetian-style apartments, and maze-like lanes ending in quiet plazas, the old town constitutes a flâneur's paradise; it was supposedly cleaned up prior to hosting the 1994 EU meeting, but you wouldn't know it. Vacant bomb-sites still yawn near the Néo Froúrio, and many main thoroughfares are blighted by touristic tat, but the backstreets are surprisingly unspoilt, festooned with washing-lines and echoing to pigeon coos. The elegant counterpoint to this is the easterly Listón, built by the French as a replica of the Rue de Rivoli in Paris. The name refers to local aristocrats listed in the Venetian Libro d'Oro, with sufficient social standing to frequent the arcades.

The Listón faces the Spianádha, a large and – today – grassy open space cleared by the Venetians to deprive attackers of cover. At pricey Listón cafés you can order *tsintsibira* (ginger beer), an enduring British legacy; others include cricket, played idiosyncratically on the Spianádha, and the enormous Victorian cemetery at the southwest edge of town, still used by the 7000-strong expat community.

The Spianádha is also the focus for Orthodox Easter celebrations, by far the

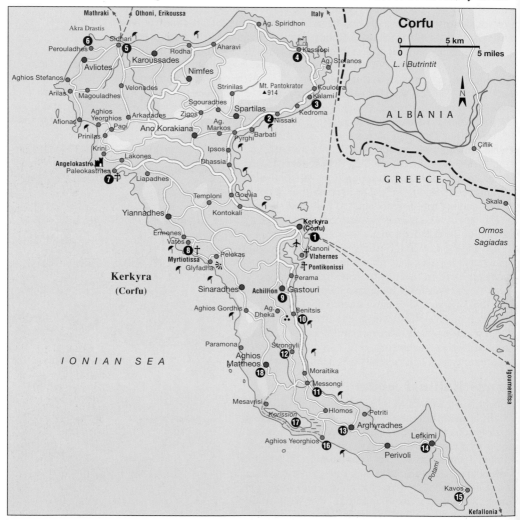

Map on page 124

best in Greece. On Good Friday eve, each parish parades its *Epitafios* (Christ's Bier) to the accompaniment of uniformed brass bands, playing dirges. On Saturday morning the relics of local patron saint Spyrídhon go walkabout, and then the tunes get jollier as townspeople shower pots and crockery from their balconies to banish misfortune. The Saturday midnight Resurrection mass finishes with fireworks launched from the Paleó Froúrio.

Both music and Saint Spyrídhon are integral parts of Corfiot life. Until destroyed by Nazi incendiary bombs, Corfu had the world's largest opera house after Milan's La Scala, and premières of major works took place here; there are still regular opera performances and thriving conservatories. Spyrídhon, after whom seemingly half the male population is named 'Spyros', was actually an early Cypriot bishop whose remains ended up here after the fall of Constantinople. Credited with saving Corfu from several disasters, his casket is processed four times yearly from his 16th-century shrine a block back from the Listón.

The White House at Kalámi, where Lawrence Durrell wrote Prospero's Cell *is now accommodation (top floor) and a taverna (ground floor).*

The town's two unmissable indoor sights are the **Asiatic Museum** (Tues–Sun 8.30am–3pm, entrance fee), a collection housed (together with changing exhibits) in the British-built Palace of SS George & Michael, plus the **Archaeological Museum** (Tues–Sun 8.30am–3pm; entrance fee), south of the Spianádha, with superb late Archaic art. Pride of place goes to the massive Gorgon pediment from a temple of Artemis at Paleopolis, but for some the smaller but more detailed pediment of a Dionysiac symposium, complete with the god, acolyte and lion, equals it. Both came from excavations in Mon Repos estate; just south of this at **Kanóni** are the photogenic islets of Vlahérna, with a little monastery and causeway to it, and Pondikoníssi, said to be a local ship petrified by Poseidon in revenge for the ancient Phaeacians helping Odysseus.

BELOW: the Paleó Froúrio.

Map on page 124

The north of the island

Northwest of town are busy resorts such as **Kondókali**, Komméno, Dhassiá and Ípsos, used by both Greek and foreign visitors. **Barbáti** is probably the first beach you would stop for. The coast between **Nissáki ❷** and **Ághios Stéfanos Sinión ❸** fancies itself a mini-Riviera with villas – there are almost no hotels – and secluded pebble coves lapped by turquoise water. Mass tourism takes over again at **Kassiópi**, important in antiquity but now with only a crumbled castle. Up the slopes of 906-metre (2,972-ft) **Mt Pandokrátor ❹** to Paleá Períthia, is a well-preserved Venetian-era village. Back on the coast, the little-frequented beaches between Kassiópi and **Aharávi** are a more pleasant alternative to over-developed **Ródha** and **Sidhári ❺**. From Sidhári ply the most reliable boats to the three small inhabited Dhiapóndia islets, **Mathráki**, **Othoní** and **Eríkoussa**.

West-coast beaches beyond Sidhári are superior, beginning at the quieter resort of **Perouládhes ❻**, continuing through **Ághios Stéfanos Avliotón**, Arílas and **Ághios Yeórghios Págon**. Beyond **Kríni** village looms the shattered but still impressive Byzantine-Angevin **Angelókastro**, guarding the approach to the beautiful double bay of **Paleokastrítsa ❼**, now swamped; best to admire it from above, at the namesake monastery or cafés in **Lákones** village. Beyond here, beaches resume at **Érmones**, but either **Myrtiótissa ❽**, small but beloved of naturists, or big, amenitied **Glyfádha**, are better, while **Ághios Górdhis** is a backpackers' paradise. Inland, Pélekashas famous coastal panoramas and sunsets.

The south of the island

Inland and south of Kérkyra, near Gastoúri, stands the pretentious **Achilleion Palace ❾**, built in 1890 for Empress Elisabeth of Austria, then acquired by Kaiser Wilhelm II. It once housed a casino, has hosted European Union meetings, and is now a museum of kitsch (daily 9am–4pm; entrance fee). **Benítses ❿** has seen its heyday come and go, though the village itself is passably attractive; **Moraïtika** and **Messongí ⓫** are by contrast unsightly, but local beaches are better.

Inland roads visit seemingly another island, winding around **Ághii Dhéka** hill. Due west of Messongí stands the **Gardhíki Pýrgos, ⓬** a crumbling octagonal castle of the Angevins in a curious lowland setting. The castle road continues to the fine Halikoúna beach at the northwest end of the **Korissíon lagoon ⓭**, a protected nature reserve and magnet for bird-watchers. From the nearby hill village of **Ághios Matthéos ⓮**, you've access to another long sandy beach, Paramónas.

Back on the main trunk road, Arghyrádhes gives access to the north-coast villages of Boúkaris and Petrití; protected from exploitation by a lack of beaches. In the opposite direction lies **Ághios Yeórghios Arghyrádhon ⓯**, developed during the early 1990s for what's delicately called "low-quality tourism", with only splendid Íssos beach to its credit. The Corfiots have deliberately quarantined the Club 18–30 set at **Kávos ⓰**. The underrated second largest town on Corfu, Lefkími **⓱**, goes about its business just inland, seemingly oblivious to its neighbour; the Lefkimians visit the beach at Boúka, the mouth of the river picturesquely bisecting Lefkími. ❏

ABOVE: the Achilleion Palace is stuffed with over-the-top statuary.
BELOW: Theotókos Monastery near Paleokastrítsa.

Working the Land

The silver olive trees that grace the Ionian landscape play more than just a picturesque part in island life. For thousands of years the olive and its oil have formed a staple part of not only the Greek diet, but the Ionian economy as well. But for most island farmers agricultural produce is for domestic use only. And the traditional, non-mechanised farming methods employed to produce it are forced on them by the islands' hilly terrain.

A typical farming community is a disorganised scatter of 20 to 100 houses closely packed together, with small yards containing chickens and the occasional pig (being fattened for Christmas). Most remote villages now have road communications and several fixed phones (plus a dozen mobile subscribers), but running water can often be a problem, especially at the height of summer.

A village on any Greek island that is farmed in the traditional way can usually be identified by the irregular fields which form its territory – an unusual visual aspect resulting from the system of splitting up the land to form inheritances and marriage dowries.

A remote village has probably three types of farmers. First, there's the large-scale goatherder with 100 to 500 animals, who purchases food such as maize, millet or animal-feed cake. He concentrates on producing kids or lambs for the peak periods of Easter and the New Year. The second is the small-scale farmer, who simply wants to keep his household supplied with bread, pulses (lentils, broad beans and chickpeas – the staple diet of winter) and vegetables. Finally, there's the single, elderly woman who owns a few goats and a few acres, and works them on her own.

Once the bitter winds of winter arrive, most small-scale farmers collect branches from wild bushes like the strawberry tree and bring them down from the hills by donkey for feed. In some remote villages the proportion of elderly people is quite high, and it is not unusual to see 80-year-olds scaling mulberry trees.

In spring, they take their animals to graze in fields away from the village. As the season progresses the ubiquitous vegetable gardens begin producing tomatoes, potatoes, beans and aubergines. These crops supplement the diet well into the summer but involve the investment of much time, labour and effort.

In June the work in the fields is back-breaking, for the grain harvest is reaped by hand with a sickle or scythe. The crop is laid out in the fields to dry, then carried back to be threshed. This is now usually done by machine, but on one or two remote, rugged islands, it is still done by walking a team of mules or donkeys over the crop strewn on the threshing cirques or *alónia* to smash the husks with their hoofs. Then it is winnowed and sieved.

These traditional farming methods are quickly disappearing. The exodus of the youth from the villages to the towns or the mainland to find work, plus competition with other European Union farmers, have meant that methods must change. The number of fields over-grown with scrub and crumbled terraces bear witness to this fact. However, this difficult but picturesque way of life does still exist; to witness it, you just need a sharp eye and a willingness to climb a few hills. ❑

RIGHT: gathering *horta* – wild greens

SOUTHERN IONIAN ISLANDS

Everything here, from architecture to food, has been influenced by the Italians, who continue to arrive in large numbers each August. Yet every Ionian island has its own character

Map on page 130

Paxí (**Páxos**), the smallest of the seven main islands of the Ionian archipelago, is 90 minutes by boat from Kérkyra (Corfu). Hilly and green, it has rugged west-coast cliffs, several sea-caves, and various pebble beaches. Páxi figures little in ancient history and mythology, when it was uninhabited, though Tim Severin in *The Ulysses Voyage* identifies the Homeric spring and dell of Circe as the modern one beside the late Byzantine **church of Ypapandí**, in the far north. Paxí acquired extensive olive groves and served as a hunting reserve for the Corfiot Venetian aristocracy, but was only systematically populated as of the 15th century. The gnarled olive trunks, their shimmering leaves likes coins tossed in the breeze, are emblems of the island, and provided the main livelihood before tourism – Paxí oil ranks among the best in Greece, having won many international medals. Dwellings, from humble cottages to baronial mansions, are tucked into hollows out of sight, and out of reach of the *maïstros*, the prevailing northwest wind; only during modern times have coastal view-villas appeared.

All boats dock at the small capital, **Gáïos ❶**, arrayed fan-like around its main square and sheltered by the two islets of **Ághios Nikólaos** and **Panaghía**, with respectively a Venetian castle and small monastery. Gáïos preserves narrow streets and a few grand 19th-century buildings with Venetian-style balconies and shutters, plus most island shops, though tavernas are undistinguished.

Paxí's single main road meanders northwest, through the olive groves and tiny hamlets consisting of a few houses, and perhaps a *kafenío* at lane-junctions. Locally sold walking guides point you along a maze of old walled paths, dirt tracks and paved lanes, which provide the best way to see the island. Reached by a side road, **Longós** on the northwest coast is the most exclusive resort, flanked by the popular beaches of **Levréhio** and **Monodhéndhri**, the latter with road access. The "motorway" ends at **Lákka ❷**, beloved of yachts and the majority of landbound tourists, with a better choice of food and lodging; small beaches like **Orkós** lie within walking distance.

The northeast coast of **Andípaxi** (Andípaxos) shelters two excellent beaches, well known to day-trippers but idyllic off-season. Only a dozen people live seasonally here, when three tavernas operate; Andípaxi's vineyards produce a heavy red wine favoured for local festivals, and a lighter tawny white.

Lefkádha (Léfkas)

Like Évvia, Lefkádha is barely an island, joined to the mainland by a floating drawbridge over a canal first dredged in ancient times. Greeks seasonally crowd the place, glad to find an island exempt from the prices and weather-whims of a ferry crossing. Yet

LEFT: inside the church of Ághios Dionýsios in Zákynthos town. **BELOW:** the ferry to Kefalloniá.

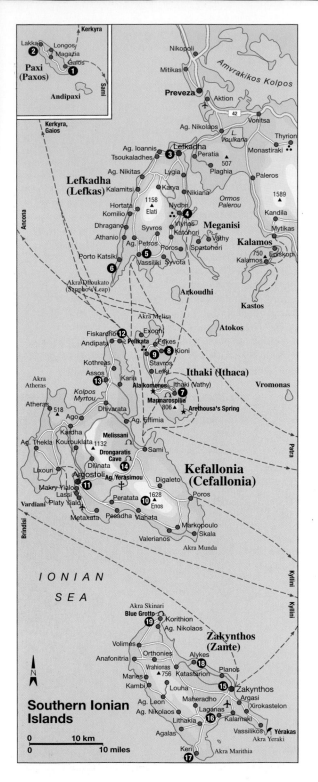

Kerkyra

Paxi
(Paxos)

Lakka
Longos
Magazia
Gaios

Andipaxi

Sami

Kerkyra,
Gaios

Nikopoli

Mitikas

Amvrakikos Kolpos

Preveza

Aktion

42

Ag. Nikolaos

L. Voulkana

Vonitsa

Thyrion

Ag. Ioannis
Tsoukaladhes

Lefkadha

Peratia

Monastiraki

507

Ag. Nikitas

Lygia

Plaghia

Paleros

Lefkadha
(Lefkas)

Kalamitsi

Karya

Nikiana

Ormos
Palerou

1589

Hortata
Komilio

1158

Elati

Nydhri

Kandila

Mytikas

Dhragano

Syvros

Mlynos

Meganisi

Athanio

Ag. Petros

Katohori

Poros

Vathy

Spartohori

Kalamos

Porto Katsiki

Vassiliki

Syvota

750

Episkopi

Kalamos

Akra Dhoukato
(Sappho's Leap)

Arkoudhi

Kastos

Akra Melisa

Atokos

Fiskardho

Exoghi

Erikes

Andipata

Pelikata

Kioni

Kothreas

Stavros

Lefki

Ithaki (Ithaca)

Akra
Atheras

Assos

Karia

Alalkomenes

Ithaki (Vathy)

Vromonas

Kolpos
Myrtou

Marmarospilia

806

Arethousa's Spring

Atheras

518

Dhivarata

Ago

Ag. Effimia

Kardha

Melissani

Ag. Thekla

Koutouklata

1132

Sami

Drongaratis
Cave

Dilinata

Argostoli

Ag. Yerasimou

Digaleto

Kefallonia
(Cefallonia)

Lixouri

Makry Yialos

Poros

Lassi

Peratata

1628

Vardiani

Platy Yialo

Enos

Metaxata

Pesadha

Vlahata

Markopoulo

Valerianos

Skala

Akra Munda

IONIAN

SEA

Akra Skinari

Blue Grotto

Korithion

Ag. Nikolaos

Volimes

Zakynthos
(Zante)

Orthonies

Alykes

Anafonitria

Vrahionas

Pianos

Maries

756

Katastarion

Kambi

Louha

Zakynthos

Ag. Leon

Maheradho

Argasi

Ag. Nikolaos

Laganas

Xirokastelon

Lithakia

Kalamaki

Agalas

Vassilikos

Yerakas

Akra Yeraki

Keri

Akra Marithia

N

Southern Ionian
Islands

0   10 km

0   10 miles

Lefkádha feels like the Ionian, with standard Venetian influences on speech and cuisine, the imposing fort of Santa Maura by the bridge, plus spear-like cypress and bright yellow broom in May carpeting the steep hillsides. Kefaloniá may be higher, but Lefkádha has a more rugged landscape, which has preserved rural lifestyles in the hill villages; the older women still wear traditional dress, while local crafts and foodstuffs are avidly promoted.

Lefkádha Town ❸ faces the canal and the lagoon enclosed by the Yíra sandspit; local topography provides safe mooring for numerous yachts on the southeast quay. Of all Ionian capitals, it's the most pedestrian-friendly; much of downtown is off-limits to cars. Municipal axis is Ioánnou Melá, which beyond lively Platía Ayíou Spiridhónos becomes Wilhelm Dörpfeld, in honour of the early 20th-century German archaeologist who attempted to prove that Lefkádha was in fact Homeric Ithaca. He is again duly revered in the excellent archaeological museum (Tues–Sun 8.30am–3pm). Also notable are several ornate Italianate churches dating from the late 17th or early 18th century, where arched windows and Baroque relief work sit oddly beside post-quake belfries modelled on oil derricks.

Lefkádha is the homeland of twentieth-century Greek poet Angelos Sikelianos, plus Lefcadio Hearn, the nineteenth-century writer born to American missionary parents here, who immortalized supernatural Japan in short stories. There are regular cultural links between the island and Japan, and streets commemorate both men.

Heading down Lefkádha's east coast, the little port-resorts of **Lygiá** and **Nikiána**, with pebble coves and fish tavernas, are the first places to prompt a stop. They're calmer than **Nydhrí ❹**, 20 km (12 mile) south of Lefkádha opposite a mini-archipelago of four islets. The view out to them is the reason Nydhrí has been earmarked for package-tourist development, since local beaches are frankly mediocre.

Until the 1970s it was a tiny fishing village, where Aristotle Onassis used to pop over for dinner from Skorpiós, his private island; there's a statue of the man on the quay now named for him, but no trace of exclusivity lingers. The one conventionally inhabited satellite island, **Meganíssi**, accessible by daily ferry, is an increasingly ill-kept secret; yachters already appreciate its quiet bays and attractive villages. The best escape for landlubbers lies 3 km (2 miles) inland, where the **Roniés waterfalls** prove suprisingly impressive, and indicative of abundant water at the heart of Lefkádha.

Beyond Nydhrí, Dörpfeld excavated extensively at Stenó and is buried on the far side of sumpy **Vlyhó** bay. The island ring road curls past Mikrós Yialós pebble bay and Sývota yacht harbour before descending to **Vassilikí ❺**, 40 km (25 miles) from town, one of Europe's premier windsurfing resorts. Boat tours are offered around Cape Lefkátas – where Sappho legendarily leaped to her death – to spectacular west-coast beaches, also accessible by roads of varying steepness. Southernmost **Pórto Kátsiki ❻** stars on every third postcard of Lefkádha; **Egremní** and **Yialós** are less frequented, while panoramic **Atháni** village has the closest tourist facilities. Further on, **Dhrymónas** is the most architecturally preserved settlement on the island, while **Kalamítsi** has an eponymous beach and "shares" **Káthisma**, Lefkádha's longest, with **Ághios Nikítas** (Aï Nikítas). The only port actually on the west coast has become a relatively upmarket resort, though worth avoiding in peak season. Beyond Ághios Nikítas' own little beach, **Pefkoúlia** stretches north to the headland dividing it from **Ághios Ioánnis**, the nicest section of Yíra beach, with its abandoned windmills. Overhead is the 17th-century monastery of **Faneroméni**, recently rebuilt in nondescript style.

Map on page 130

The church of Ághios Menás in Lefkádha town has a unique clock tower made of steel girders.

BELOW: fishermen in Lefkádha harbour.

Journeys inland thread through the half-dozen **Sfakiótes** hamlets occupying a fertile upland, where churches with Venetian belfries may be seen. The usual destination is **Karyá**, even higher and cooler, with a thriving crafts tradition and a vast central *platía* shaded by several giant plane trees.

Itháki (Ithaca)

Evidence that Itháki actually was the ancient home of Odysseus, wandering hero of Homer's *Odyssey*, is far from conclusive, but this hasn't stopped a Homeric "heritage industry" from revving up locally, with numerous streets and businesses named for characters in the epic, and the island's modest archaeological sites assiduously signposted as putative locales for various episodes.

Most ferries dock at the cheerful capital, **Vathý** ❼, occupying the head of a long bay. Though badly damaged by the 1953 quake, many buildings survived, while others (unlike on Kefalloniá) were rebuilt with good taste, incorporating traditional architectural elements. There are more tavernas and *kafenía*, especially along the quay, than in any other port town of this size. Several pebble beaches, if not Itháki's best, can be found close by; this is an island ideally sized for scooter exploration and walking.

Also near Vathý are several sites associated with Odysseus: the **bay of Phocrys** (now Fórkynos), the **Cave of the Nymphs**, the **spring of Arethoúsa**, and ancient **Alalkomenae** (Alalkoméni). Having landed at Phocrys, Odysseus climbed up the hill to the cave and hid the 13 tripods given him by King Alkinous of the Phaeacians (ancient Corfiots). Later, Odysseus met his loyal swineherd Eumaeus and son Telemachos at the spring; the track-and-path walk from Vathý to Arethoúsa takes 90 minutes, somewhat challenging but with good

In 1939 Itháki had a population of around 15,000; now it is under 3,000, thanks to mass emigration – particularly to Australia, the USA and South Africa – following the 1953 earthquake.

BELOW: Itháki's capital, Vathý.

views. Alalkomenae occupies a hillside 5 km (3 miles) west of Vathý, above the road between Fórkynos and the secondary port (and good pebble beach) of **Píso Aetós**; archaeologist Heinrich Schliemann excavated here, but most finds (now in the town museum) fail to match the Homeric era.

Itháki is almost pinched in two by an isthmus barely wide enough for the main corniche road. The northern half is more lushly vegetated and has better beaches; below **Léfki** village the secluded pebble bays of **Ághios Ioánnis** and **Koutoúpi** grace the west coast. **Stavrós**, 16 km (10 miles) from Vathý ❽, is Itháki's second town, with another small museum devoted to finds from local sites with a better claim to being Odysseus' possible home. These are a citadel on **Pelikáta** hill and, more intriguing, an excavation marked as "**School of Homer**" off the road to Exoghí. Walls and foundations, a few Mycenaean graves, steps carved into the rock and a vaulted cave-well lie exposed. In size and position, the place feels just right to be the base of a minor chieftain like Odysseus. **Exoghí**, highest village on the island, is seasonally occupied but offers superb views northeast. From Platrithiás village a paved drive goes to **Afáles** bay with its excellent sand-and-pebble patches, while another road loops through Ághia Saránda and Lahós, partly spared by the quake, en route to **Fríkes**. There are ferries here (to Kefalloniá and Lefkádha) and many yachts, though most visitors continue, past attractive pebble coves, to **Kióni** ❾, Itháki's most upmarket resort, where again various houses survived the quake. At either port, rooms are rare items in high season.

From Kióni you can walk up the cleared and profusely waymarked old path to Anoghí, a three-hour round trip; it's the best hike on the island, with only the last 20 minutes spoilt by the heliport and its access road. In half-deserted

Map on page 130

Stavrós is one of several places in Itháki claiming to be the site of Odysseus's castle, and marks its claim with this bust of the Homeric hero.

BELOW: red-tiled rooftops cluster round Kióni harbour.

Argostóli's museum tells the recent history of the island and its earthquakes in photographs.

Anoghí, there's a medieval church of **Kímisis tis Theotókou** (Dormition of the Virgin) with heavily retouched Byzantine frescoes and a Venetian belfry. Some 4 km (2 miles) south, the **monastery of Katharón** is by contrast a post-quake barracks structure, flanked by modern antennae, but the views over southern Itháki are unsurpassed.

Kefalloniá (Kefallinía, Cephalonia)

Kefalloniá is the largest and second most mountainous Ionian island, its population famous for a studied (often creative) eccentricity. It's recovering from being typecast as "Captain Corelli's Island", since political opinions expressed in Louis de Bernière's locally set blockbuster novel are not popular here.

The capital town of **Argostóli** , levelled by the 1953 earthquake, was rebuilt in utilitarian style and has a workaday feel, epitomized by meat and produce markets perched right on the commercial quay. From north to south, its names honour two islanders: Ioánnis Metaxás, 1930s dictator and defier of the Italians, and Andónis Trítsis (1937–1992), innovative architect, maverick politician and ultimately mayor of Athens. The heart of town is **Platía Vallianoú**, ringed by hotels and *kafenía*, though some trendy cafés have sprouted on pedestrianized **Lithóstroto**, beside its smart shops. Specific sights are limited to three museums, of which the **Korghialenios Historical and Folkloric Museum** (Mon–Sat, 9am–2pm; entrance fee) is the most interesting, with pictures of Argostóli before and after the quake.

West of town, at the mouth of Argostóli gulf, are the closest decent beaches: **Makrýs Yialós** and **Platýs Yialós**, crowded by patrons from **Lássi** package resort, under the airport flight path and not the island's best. Near the Doric rotunda of **Áyios Theodhóros lighthouse**, the "sea mills" at **Katavóthres** used to grind grain and generate electricity; salt water pouring down sinkholes here emerges three weeks later near Sámi, but the 1953 disaster reduced the flow to a trickle.

To the east looms **Mount Énos** (Ainos) ⓫, at 1,628 metres (5,340 ft) the highest peak in the islands and still partly covered with native firs (*Abies cephallonica*); two small reserves protect the remaining trees, much reduced by fires and loggers. The inclined south coastal plain at the base of the mountain, **Livathó**, is punctuated by a conical hill bearing the Venetian capital of **Ághios Yeórghios**, inhabited from Byzantine times until the 17th century. The impressive summit castle is has wonderful views. Aristocratic associations linger at certain Livathó villages: pre-quake stone walls enclose vast estates; Lord Byron lived at nearby Metaxáta in 1823; and Keramiés still harbours dilapidated pre-quake mansions and a huge olive mill. The largest beach in the area, with resort amenities, is **Lourdháta** (Lourdhá).

On the west shore of Argostóli gulf, reached by frequent ferries used by drivers and pedestrians alike to miss the tedious journey around, **Lixoúri** has long been eclipsed by rival Argostóli, but it's a pleasantly sleepy town with views to Zákynthos. People stay here for easy access to excellent red-sand beaches, such as **Mégas Lákkos** and **Xí**, southwest on the peninsula; en route you'll see how the fertile, grain-and-grape-planted terrain was heaved and buckled by the force of the quake.

Beyond Xí, **Kounópetra** ("rocking stone") no longer does so since 1953. North-west of Lixoúri, is the long fine-pebble beach of **Petáni**; exposed but spectacular.

The north side of Kefalloniá was less damaged by the quake, and surviving medieval houses in various states of repair, especially at **Vassilikiádhes** and **Mesovoúnia**, are poignant reminders of a lost architectural heritage. But the port resort of **Fiskárdho** emerged almost unscathed, and ruthlessly exploits the fact despite a lack of beaches. The atmosphere is very pukka, almost precious, and yachts congregate in force, dodging the occasional ferry to Lefkádha or Itháki. 'Fiskárdho' is a corruption of the name of Norman leader Robert Guiscard, who made Kefalloniá his headquarters but died here in 1085. On the west coast, the perfect horseshoe harbour of **Ássos** ⓭ sees only fishing boats and is the bet-ter for it; there's good swimming from the isthmus joining this partly preserved village to a pine-covered bluff, with its fine late sixteenth-century Venetian fort. A bit further south, **Mýrtos** is among the most famous – and overrated – beaches in the Ionians: coarse-pebbled and downright dangerous if a surf is up.

The water's calmer and the pebbles smaller at **Ayía Effimía**, a fishing village on the east coast; between here and the functional ferry port of **Sámi** lies the **Melissáni cave** ⓮, containing an underground lake with its roof partly open to the sky. Nearby another cave, **Dhrongaráti**, offers multicoloured stalactites and stalagmites, and occasionally hosts concerts.

Beyond Sámi, a good road threads attractively through vegetated scenery to underrated **Póros**, another ferry/yacht port with a backdrop of green cliffs. From here you loop around the coast to the busy resort of **Skála**, with its superb sand-and-gravel beach fringed by pines, and then around Cape Moúnda to all-sand **Kamínia** beach, Kefalloniá's principal turtle-nesting venue.

Kefalloniá is noted for its honey (thyme-scented), quince jelly and a local spe-ciality called riganáta *– feta cheese mixed with bread, oil and oregano.*

BELOW: the church is reflected by contemporary island life.

Map on page 130

"The reason they build their houses so lowe [in Zákynthos] is, because of the manifold Earthquakes which doe as much share this Iland as any other place in the World."

– THOMAS CORYAT, 1612

Zákynthos (Zánde)

"Zante, Fior di Levante", so said the Venetians, and its central plain – the most fertile in the Ionians – and eastern hills support luxuriant vegetation. The southeastern coasts shelter excellent beaches: some almost undeveloped, others home to notoriously unsavoury tourism. Zákynthos also has some of the most dangerous roads in the islands, so take extra care when driving.

The once-elegant harbour town of **Zákynthos** ⓯ had its public buildings and squares rebuilt approximately as before in reinforced concrete. Ferries dock by Platía Solomoú, named for native Dhionýsios Solomós, a 19th-century poet who wrote the words to the Greek national anthem. At the rear of his *platía*, the **Zákynthos Museum of Post-Byzantine Art** (Tues–Sun 8am-2.30pm, entrance fee) features icons rescued from quake-blasted churches, as well as numerous 17th- to 19th-century religious paintings of the Ionian School, founded by Cretan artists fleeing the Ottoman conquest, who met local artists strongly influenced by the Italian Renaissance. In medieval times people lived above the present town in **Bóhali** district, inside the huge *kástro*, mostly Venetian but with Byzantine foundations. Here, several tavernas provide superb views.

Regrettably, most of Zákynthos' 700,000 annual visitors don't stray far from adjacent **Laganás/Kalamáki** ⓰ beach resorts. Its explosive growth since the late 1970s is endangering the survival of loggerhead turtles *(see next page)*, which have nested here for millennia. Luckily, the tourist tat is easily skirted and Zákynthos shows its best side in remoter corners. The **Vassilikós peninsula**, beyond forgettable Argássi, has the island's best, most scenic beaches, culminating in **Ághios Nikólaos** and **Yérakas**, nearest the east cape.

Start a tour of the unspoilt western hill villages from **Kerí** at the far south cape, with its lighthouse; next stop would be **Kiloméno** ⓱, which largely survived 1953. Tourists are coached to **Kambí** to watch the sunset, but **Éxo Hóra** and **Mariés** are more characterful, with pre-quake churches and wells, vital in this arid region. Still further north, **Anafonítria** village offers an eponymous 14th-century monastery with a daunting gate-keep; plaques recall the local legend that St Dhionýsios forgave and sheltered his brother's murderer here. Nearby, the 16th-century monastery of **Ághios Yeórghios ton Krimnón** has a round lookout tower in its well-tended courtyard; just beyond is the overlook for **Shipwreck (Navághio) Beach**, the most photographed in the Ionians, where a rusty freighter lies half-buried in sand. Boat trips visit from **Pórto Vrómi**, below Mariés.

From Shipwreck, head east through grain fields, and the three **Volímes** villages noted for their honey and cheese, to reach the east coast near **Makrýs Yialós** pebble beach and the bleak port of **Ághios Nikólaos**, with both daily ferries to Kefalloniá and excursion boats to the **Blue Caves** ⓳, interconnecting grottos with spectacular light effects at the right hour.

Back towards town, you wind through **Alykés** (the calmest beach resort), past secluded bays favoured by Greeks, before hitting mass tourism again at **Planós**. An antidote to this, in the hills between Planós and Tragáki, is Dhimitris Avouris' exemplary stone-built **Skalia Cultural Centre/Théatro Avoúri**. ❏

BELOW: Shipwreck Beach, Zákynthos .

Turtles v. tourists

T he loggerhead turtle crawls out of the sea onto the moonlit beach of her birthplace, the island of Zákynthos. She has crossed the length of the Mediterranean to return, at last, to this spot. Summoning all her strength, the 90 kg (200 lb) reptile carefully selects a place in the sand where she digs a nest with her rear flippers. Into it she lays 100 soft eggs the size of a ping-pong ball, covers them with soft sand and returns exhausted to the sea to rest in the shallows. However, her labour may have been in vain. For on Zákynthos, thoughtless tourism is threatening these ancient creatures with extinction.

The survival of the loggerhead *(Caretta caretta)* is endangered before she even reaches the beach. It has been estimated that nearly half the nesting females may be maimed or killed by pedalos or the propellers of speedboats taking out waterskiers and para-gliders. Carelessly discarded litter from tourists creates another hazard, as turtles suffocate trying to swallow plastic bags which they mistake for jellyfish, a favourite food.

For the female turtle, the hazards increase when she slips ashore. Disorientated by the glittering lights of hotels and the strange noises coming from the tourists and tavernas, she may scurry back to the seas, uncertain where to deposit her eggs. Those that try to continue their labours may suffer the indignity of ignorant spectators brandishing torches and flashing camera lights, frightening the turtles back into the sea where the eggs may be released never to hatch.

The eggs that are successfully laid are often crushed by thoughtless motorcyclists, horse-riders and motorists who drive across the sand, packing it down so that it is impossible for the hatchlings to emerge. Beach umbrellas are unwittingly driven into nests, piercing the eggs. Tamarisk trees, planted in haste to shade sunbathers, pose another problem as hatchlings become tangled up in the roots. Even sandcastles may create holes which become shallow graves for the young turtles.

Hatching takes place from early August to late September – the time of year when most of the tourists arrive. The 6-cm (2½-in) hatchlings may emerge from their hazardous 50-day incubation and, instead of heading instinctively to the light on the horizon line at sea, frequently wander confused up the beach to the lights of the hotels and bars. This error brings death from exhaustion or dehydration.

Zákynthos did have the greatest concentration of nesting turtles in the Mediterranean. The Laganás bay coastline was once a favourite spot but, confused by the combination of boats, buildings and noise that tourism has brought, the turtles have abandoned the busy sands. The majority now nest in the more secluded beaches of Sekánia, Yérakas and Dáfni, where there is barely room for the activities of the bewildered reptiles. Only 800 turtles now breed on Zákynthos, barely half the number to be found here in the early 1980s.

The local Sea Turtle Protection Society, locked in frequent conflict with unscrupulous developers, and despairing of raising visitor consciousness, has succeeded in creating the National Marine Park of Zákynthos, encompassing the whole gulf between capes Yérakas to Kerí. Three levels of control restrict boating and land access; all affected beaches now have dawn-to-dusk curfews.❏

KÝTHIRA

Geographically nearer to Crete than to the Ionian group, this is one of Greece's quietest islands. Most visitors are Greeks from Athens – or Greek Australians returning home

I
n legend Kýthira, suspended off Cape Maléa in the Lakonian Gulf, was one of the birthplaces of Aphrodite (the other, stronger contender is in south-western Cyprus). Essentially a bleak, thyme-covered plateau slashed by well-watered and vegetated ravines, the island forms part of a sunken land bridge between the Peloponnese and Crete, from where many Venetian refugees arrived in the 17th century.

And an in-between sort of place it is, in many respects: it has two names (Tserigo was its Venetian alias); a history of Venetian and British rule like the bona-fide Ionian islands, but today governed from Piraeus along with the Argo-Saronics; an architecture that's a hybrid of Cycladic and Venetian; a pronounced Australian flavour, courtesy of remittances and personal visits from 60,000 emigrants Down-Under – and ubiquitous eucalypts.

Kýthira (also spelt Kýthera and Kíthira) frankly does not put itself out for outsiders. Accommodation is expensive and oversubscribed, good tavernas are thin on the ground. Habitually rough seas, which can play havoc with daily ferries from Neápolis on Cape Maléa, prompted the construction of an all-weather harbour at Dhiakófti in 1997, though local politics kept this from being fully operational until 1999. Despite all that, Kýthira seems increasingly popular as a haunt of trendy Greeks, thanks to regular hydrofoils and flights from Athens – plus the **Hóra ❶** (also known as **Kýthira**), one of the finest island capitals of the Aegean.

The imposing, flat-roofed mansions of the lower town date from the 17th to 19th centuries. The Venetian **kástro** overhead is of earlier vintage. Still intact is an elaborate domed cistern system, while up top a few rusty cannon guarding a Venetian church seem superfluous, given the incredibly steep drop to the sea at **Kapsáli**. This is the yacht harbour, and where most tourists stay, though its beach is mediocre.

The best beaches

Much better beaches lie east of Hóra at **Halkós**, south of **Kálamos** village, and at **Fyrí Ámmos**, east of Kálamos, with sea-caves to explore. North of Fyrí Ámmos, and easier to get to, more excellent beaches dot the east coast: **Kombonádha**, **Kaladhí** with a rock monolith in the surf at one end, and two – **Asprógas** and **Paleópoli** – to either side of Kastrí Point with its Minoan settlement, which was explored by Heinrich Schliemann in 1887.

The beachy strip ends at the fishing anchorage of **Avlémonas ❷**, where seemingly half the island's population turns up for weekend lunches at the main fish taverna. The diminutive octagonal Venetian fort at the harbour mouth is scarcely more than a gun emplacement. There's a better, 16th-century castle,

BELOW: a native of Kýthira.

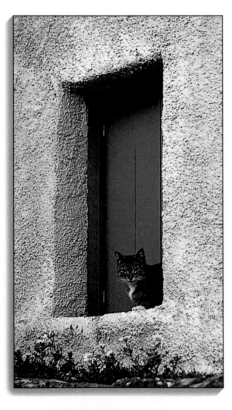

complete with a Lion of St Mark, at **Káto Hóra**, just outside the attractive village of **Mylopótamos ❸**, with a waterfall and abandoned mill in a wooded canyon. Like similar ones in the Cyclades, the Káto Hóra fortress was not a military stronghold but a civilian refuge from pirates, with derelict houses inside the gate.

Some 2.5 km (1½ miles) west of Káto Hóra, perched above the surf-lashed west coast, the black-limestone cavern of **Aghía Sofía ❹** (Jun–Sept; Mon–Fri 3–8pm, Sat–Sun 11am–5pm) is the best of several namesake caves on Kýthira. A 13th-century hermit adorned the entrance with frescoes of Holy Wisdom personified, and three attendant virtues, though the inner cave was never inhabited, being too remote and dry. (Locals insist that Aphrodite slept there, but today the only endemic life is a minute white spider.) About one-sixth of the cave, and marvellous stalactites and stalagmites, are open for visits.

Capital of Kýthira after 1248, the ghost village of **Paleohóra ❺** in the northeast of the island failed the pirate-proof test in 1537, when the notorious Barbarossa spotted and sacked it. The ruins, including six frescoed (and locked) churches, cover the summit of a high bluff plunging to the confluence of two gorges which unite as Kakí Langádha, reaching the sea at a small lake.

Potamós ❻, 2 km (1¼ miles) north of the Paleohóra turning, is Kýthira's second village, most notable for its Sunday-morning farmer's market.

Aghía Pelaghía, the now distinctly secondary ferry port with a scruffy beach, has come down in the world since **Dhiakófti** commenced working. More rewarding is **Karavás ❼**, the northernmost and prettiest of the ravine oasis-villages that Kýthira abounds in. This valley meets the sea at **Platiá Ámmos** beach; pebbly **Foúrni** cove lies adjacent. ❑

So many Kythirans (possibly 60,000) have emigrated to Australia that the post office in Hóra contains a Sydney telephone directory.

BELOW: Kapsáli harbour seen from Hóra high above.

ISLANDS OF THE SARONIC GULF

Salamína, Aegina, Póros, Hydra and Spétses

The five islands of the Saronic Gulf might best be described as "commuter" islands. As they are within a short ferry ride (or even shorter hydrofoil trip) from Piraeus, the temptation is to treat the islands as an extension of the mainland or, more specifically, suburbs of Athens.

Entrepreneurs have been quick to exploit the proximity. The one-day cruise from Piraeus calling at Aegina, Hydra and Póros is an extremely popular atraction for tourists visiting Athens (rivalled only by Delphi as the most enjoyable day spent out of town). When the cruise ships mingle with the ferries, the hydrofoils and the regular scheduled caiques, there is often a virtual traffic jam on the waters, and foreigners easily outnumber Greeks at most Saronic ports.

In spite of all this, these are Greek islands, not Athens suburbs – distinctive in character, rich in history and, behind the crowds and chi-chi boutiques, remarkably attractive. Salamis (Salamína) is renowned for the epoch-making battle in 480 BC which decided the outcome of the Persian Wars. Aegina (Éghina) is the site of the Temple of Aféa, one of the most important antiquities located on any Greek island.

Póros has been immortalised by US author Henry Miller in *The Colossus of Maroussi*, and Spétses by John Fowles in *The Magus*. Not to be outdone, since the 1960s Hydra (Ýdhra) has attracted artists, film-makers, well-heeled Athenians, trendy French and Italians, movie stars and other international celebrities. ❏

PRECEDING PAGES: donkeys patiently awaiting tourists at Hydra harbour; sausages for sale. **LEFT:** octopus drying on the washing line.

ARGO-SARONIC ISLANDS

Map on page 148

These five islands are all within easy reach of the mainland, and popular with Greek day trippers. Nevertheless, they are distinctive, rich in history and remarkably attractive

Salamína

This low, flat island (also called Salamis) is popular with Athenians but offers little of interest to visitors. It is the largest of the Saronic Gulf islands, but so close to Athens that most Greeks regard it as part of the mainland. The most fun to be had might well be on the ferry from Piraeus; the tiny caique laden with commuters reading tabloid newspapers threads its way between larger boats destined for more far-flung locations.

Salamína is best known for the 480 BC ancient naval battle in which the outnumbered Athenian ships routed Xerxes' Persian fleet, the Greek ships being the "wooden walls" that the oracle of Delphi had predicted would save Athens. Today the island is decidedly not posh. Its appeal is that it is not much developed and can be reached so quickly, just a few minutes' ride across from **Pérama** to the port of **Paloúkia**, a town with a strong naval presence and a couple of waterside tavernas.

Most of the inhabitants live in the island's capital, **Salamína (or Kouloúri) ❶**, which has both an archaeological and a folk museum. Boats also leave regularly from Pireaus harbour for Selínia, Paralía Kakís Víglas, Peráni and Peristéria on the east coast. The island's pride, the late 17th-century **Faneroméni Monastery**, is on the northwest coast, 6 km (3½ miles) from Salamína town. **Eándio ❷**, a pleasant village on the west coast, has a good hotel. From here you can go down to the southeast coast of **Peráni** and the small but very pretty little harbour of **Peristéria**.

Aegina

Aegina (or Aigina or Éghina) is close enough to be within easy reach of the mainland and far enough to retain its island identity. About an hour and a half by ferry from Piraeus, or 45 minutes by the hydrofoil, Aegina has had little trouble attracting visitors. Long a favourite Athenian retreat, it remains more popular among weekend smog evaders than among foreign tourists or Greeks from elsewhere.

Aegina's main produce is pistachio nuts, which you can buy at shops and stands along the harbour street. Shaped on the map like an upside-down triangle, Aegina's south is marked by the magnificent cone of **Mount Óros**, the highest peak in the Argo-Saronic islands, visible on a smog-free day from the Acropolis in Athens. The centre and eastern side of the island is mountainous; a gently-sloping fertile plain runs down to the western corner where Aegina town overlays in part the ancient capital of the island.

For a brief time (from 1826 until 1828) Aegina served as the first capital of the modern state of Greece. **Aegina town (Éghina) ❸** has several 19th-

LEFT: the massive church of Ághios Nektários, Aegina.
BELOW: traditional pottery made in the traditional way.

century buildings constructed when the country's first president, Ioánnis Kapodístrias (1776–1831), lived and worked here. The **Archaeological Museum** (Tues–Sun 8.30am–3pm), about 10 minutes' walk from the town's ferry quay, is the oldest in Greece and displays a number of interesting artefacts. The modern harbour, crowded with yachts and caiques, is next to the ancient harbour, now the shallow town beach north of the main quay.

Further north from the port stands the **Kolóna** ("column"), all that remains of the Temple of Apollo built in 520–500 BC. It was superseded by a late Roman fortress, fragments of which survive on the seaward side. Although from the sea the position of the temple looks unimpressive, the view from the hill in late summer is very pleasant. There is a small museum on the site (currently closed for renovation), and the reconstructed mosaic floor of an ancient synagogue.

The island's most famous ancient site is the **Temple of Aféa** (Aphaia) ❹ (summer: daily 8.15am–7pm; winter: 8.15am–5pm), in the northeast, above the often packed summer resort town of **Aghía Marína**. The temple stands at the top of a hill in a pine grove commanding a splendid view of the Aegean. Built in 490 BC, in the years after the victory at Salamis, it has been called "the most perfectly developed of the late Archaic temples in European Hellas". It is the only surviving Greek temple with a second row of small superimposed columns in the interior of the sanctuary. It is also quiet and beautiful, one of the most impressive ancient Greek temples you will see.

On the way to the Temple of Aféa you will pass by the **Monastery of Ághios Nektários**, the most recent Orthodox saint. Across the ravine from the large monastery is the abandoned medieval city known as **Paleohóra** (Old Town), where the islanders came to live after the island was sacked by pirates in the late

BELOW: a fisherman in Aegina harbour.

Map
on page
148

9th century. They were too open to attack down in the port, and lived up here until early in the 19th century. Most of the 38 churches left standing are in utter disrepair, but you can see the remains of many frescoes.

The west coast of the island is quite gentle, with a good sand beach at **Marathóna**, but better reasons to head in this direction are to enjoy a meal in one of the many fish tavernas along the harbour at **Pérdhika** ❺, or to go on by small hired boat to swim in pristine water at the beautiful beach on the little uninhabited island of **Moní**.

Angístri is the small island facing Aegina town. It was originally settled by Albanians, but more recently has been colonised by Germans, who have bought most of the houses in the village of **Metóhi**, above the port of **Skála**. The larger boats stop at Skála and the smaller boats from Aegina stop at the more attractive **Mýlos**. The island is not much developed but there are several hotels and tourism is increasing. The most attractive beach is on the southwestern coast by the small islet of **Dhoroúsa**.

Póros

Póros is separated from the Peloponnese by a small passage of water which gives the island its name – the word *póros* in Greek means "passage" or "ford". As you sail down the passage from the northern entrance, the channel opens ahead and **Póros town** ❻ comes into view. It is almost landlocked and one of the most protected anchorages in the Aegean. Your first glimpse of the town will be of the white houses and bright orange rooftops, with a clock tower on top of the hill. The effect is disarming. On the mainland opposite, the village of **Galatás** makes a wonderful sight, with its white steps and dark

Lemonódassos, opposite Póros on the mainland, is a huge lemon grove with 30,000 trees – and a taverna selling delicious fresh lemonade.

BELOW: the unique two-storey Temple of Aféa.

alleys, and extensive lemon groves. Sailing through Póros is so impressive that ferry captains often call out to passengers to hasten deck-side so as not to miss the extraordinary illusion that they are actually sailing through the streets of the town.

The town is built around several hills, one crowned with the blue and white clock tower. The climb to the tower is revealing – melons, grapes and flowers overhang domestic verandas. Staircases which begin with promise are apt to end in a villa-owner's market garden. Along the harbour pride of place is given to a busy meat market.

Many hotels have now been built on Póros, and prominent Athenians have owned holiday homes here for decades. The island has never been fashionable like Hydra or Spétses, but during summer it gets every bit as crowded as Aegina. In 1846, the Greek naval station was established on the peninsula, just before the narrow stream separating the small section of Póros town from the main part of the island. The site is now used for training naval cadets. This area contains several fine family mansions with well-tended gardens, and can be a refreshing place to stroll on a hot summer afternoon.

The main sight near the sea on Póros is the **Monastery of Zoödóhos Pighí** (Virgin of the Life-Giving Spring) ❼ on a wooded hillside (20 minutes from town by bus). Only a few monks still live there today. Noteworthy is a wooden, gold-painted iconostasis dating from the 19th century.

In front of the monastery, a road encircling the heights to the east climbs through the pine woods to the ruins of the **Sanctuary of Poseidon**, in a saddle between the highest hills of the island. From here came much of the stone used in building the Monastery of the Panaghía on Hydra. The temple was excavated at the turn of the century and little remains, but its setting is rewarding.

BELOW: eating out on Aegina's waterfront.

Hydra

The island of Hydra (or Ydhra, once Ydrea, "the well watered") now appears as a long, barren rock. But the harbour and lovely white and grey stone buildings built up around the town are incomparable, attracting the artistic and the fashionable since the 1950s, and many, many more ever since. It is one of the few places in the country that has reined in the uncontrolled growth of cement construction, and retained its original beauty, greatly helped by the banning of motorised transport from the island. Hydra town is a very popular destination and becomes packed during the summer and, especially, at weekends.

The heart of the island is its harbour-town, also called **Hydra (Ydhra)** ❸. All around the picturesque bay, white stone houses climb the slope accented by massive grey *arhontiká*, the houses built by the shipping families who made fortunes in the 18th and 19th centuries. Along the quay are the colourful shops of the marketplace, with the clock tower of the **Monastery of the Panaghía** in the centre. Much of the stone used in building this 18th-century monastery was taken from the ancient Sanctuary of Poseidon on the island of Póros.

The harbour, girded by a little thread of a breakwater, forms a soft and perfect crescent, its two ends flanked by 19th-century cannons. The town has many good tavernas and restaurants, as well as highly popular bars and discos. Some of the well-preserved and imposing *arhontiká* are open to visitors. The Athens School of Fine Arts has established a branch in the huge mansion built by Admiral Tombazis, which hosts artists of international acclaim. A Merchant Navy Training School occupies the Tsamádos House, and across the way are the Hydriot Archives.

The higher reaches of the town and the hills beyond remain surprisingly untouched, charming and full of Greek colour. Narrow alleys and steep stair-

Map on page 148

Tourism to Hydra was given a boost by the 1957 film Boy on a Dolphin, *starring Sophia Loren, which was set on the island.*

BELOW: a 19th-century bridge at Vlyhós, Hydra.

Map on page 148

Greece's national heroine of the War of Independence was a Spetsiot woman called Laskarína Bouboulína, who took command of her husband's ships after he was killed by pirates. Her house is behind the Dápia.

BELOW: reflections of Spétses.

cases lead from one quarter to the next. The uniformity of white walls is broken again and again by a century-old doorway, a bright blue window frame, a flight of striking scarlet steps, or a dark green garden fence.

An hour's walk upwards and inland leads to the **Convent of Aghía Efpraxía** and the **Monastery of Profítis Ilías**, while the **Zoúrvas Monastery** is to be found in the extreme east. Island beaches, however, are less impressive. **Mandhráki ❾**, northeast of town, has the only sand beach, but the southwest is more interesting. A wide path goes along the coast to **Kamíni** and **Vlychós**, with its early 19th-century arched stone bridge. There are some good tavernas in both Kamíni and Vlychós, and water taxis available to get you back to town.

Spétses

Spétses (or Spétsai) is the southernmost of the Argo-Saronic Gulf islands. In antiquity it was known as Pityoússa, "pine tree" island, and it is still by far the most wooded of the islands in the group. It also has more sandy beaches. Tourist development here is much more extensive than on Hydra but less than on either Póros or Aegina, and in recent years responsible planning, including banning cars outside of Spétses town, has helped keep the island's charm.

Although **Spétses town ❿** has its share of bars and fast-food places, the **Paleó Limáni** (Old Harbour) still radiates a gentle grace, its own particular magic that is apparent to even the short-term visitor. The 18th-century Italian-style mansions *(arhontiká)* one sees in this part of the town are now the property of wealthy Athenian families who return to the island every summer.

Like Hydra, Spétses was one of the main centres of activity during the Greek War of Independence, using its fleet of more than 50 ships for the Greek cause.

The island is distinguished for being the first in the archipelago to revolt against Ottoman rule in 1821, and the fortified harbour, still bristling with cannons, now surrounds the town's main square, the **Dápia** (a name sometimes applied to the whole town).

Although Spétses's fleet declined after the War of Independence, with the emergence of Piraeus as the main seaport, the traditions of shipbuilding continue unabated. The small museum (Tues–Sun, 8.30am–3pm) in the imposing *arhontikó* of Hadzighiánnis Mexís, a major shipowner in the late 18th century, contains coins, costumes, ship models, weapons and other memorabilia from the island's past.

Outside the town to the northwest is **Anarghýrios and Korghialénios College**, a Greek impression of an English public school. John Fowles taught here and memorialised both the institution and the island in his 1966 novel *The Magus*. The school no longer operates and the buildings are used only occasionally as a conference centre or for special programmes. This section of town is less posh than the Old Harbour and has some fine small tavernas.

The town beach by the Church of Ághios Mámas and the small beach in the Old Harbour are unattractive in contrast to the beautiful beaches of **Aghía Marína**, **Ághii Anarghyrí**, **Ághía Paraskeví** and **Zogeriá**, going around the wooded southern coast of the island from the east to the west ❏

Pipe Dreams

A note you're likely to see behind your bathroom door warns: "Throw your paper in the bin provided." Seasoned Hellenophiles know all about Greek plumbing and observe the no-paper rule, thus avoiding clogging and flooding. They also know that it's a good idea to carry tissues or *hartopetsétes* (napkins) nabbed from taverna tables, just in case. The cramped cubicles at the back of popular basic eateries seldom bear close inspection, with their overflowing bins, floors awash and no loo roll. In extremis the brand-name cry of "Softex" might bring emergency supplies.

Squat-over loos are becoming less common, though you still come across them in public conveniences. You might even come across a hole in the floor over the sea for instant and natural flushing. Some toilets can be grim, especially on ferries; even on the new and otherwise immaculate catamarans.

But in the main, toilet facilities in most tavernas and restaurants are adequate, with soap, towels and the ever-present bottle of *hloríni* (bleach). But perhaps the biggest mystery of all is why many bathroom fittings are straight out of a 1970s *Homes and Gardens*.

Visit the remotest of islands, the poorest of village rooms and you can be sure that *tó loutró* (the bathroom) will be sumptuously equipped and decorated. Colours outmoded in most countries (avocado, rose pink or even hard-to-clean maroon) are all the rage. Patterned tiles, the more garish the better, are a must, as are the bidet, shower with backless chair but no curtain, fancy taps and mirror-fronted bathroom cabinet.

The fact that there's rarely a shower tray, just a hole in the uneven floor down which you have to urge the water with the loo brush, and the door won't shut because it has been warped by the water, is neither here nor there. Sometimes even running water seems optional. But the matching suite is essential.

"Can we drink the water?" is a normal tourist question. "Where can we *find* the water?" is a specifically Greek inquiry. Lack of fresh water is a giant problem for many islands so you may have to drink bottled, and wait patiently for the waterboat to arrive. When the boat comes in there's usually a mad scramble as families with hosepipes fill their wells, jugs and containers. You too may have to make daily trips to the pump or village tap. Most countries take water for granted, but in arid Greece in high summer it is a precious commodity and conservation is the key to many communities' survival.

Some islands have Heath Robinson water systems that rely on pumps and bewildering pipework. Pondering over pressure, bores, cisterns, pumps and ball-cocks, you might be tempted to ask why you can't put paper down the pan. The answer lies in the bore of the pipes that were used all over Greece to take away the waste water. These are so narrow that the paper wending its way down is almost guaranteed to bung things up. Another reason is that, in many places, sewage is sent straight out to sea.

The pipes are being changed (very slowly), and better sewage treatment plants are being built, but for the time being you will still have to put the paper in the bin. ❑

RIGHT: a traditional village tap.

THE CYCLADES ISLANDS

Ándhros, Kéa, Tínos, Kýthnos, Sýros, Mýkonos, Sérifos,
Sífnos, Andíparos, Páros, Náxos, Mílos, Folégandhros,
Síkinos, Íos, Amorgós, Santoríni, Anáfi

The Cyclades fix in the mind memories and dreams of sun-drenched seascapes. The white cube houses, justly famous, have inspired many modern architects, Le Corbusier among them. The beaches are dazzling, the food fresh, fellow-travellers companionable, and the ferry connections so organised that short holidays can take in more than one "paradise".

For many people the Cyclades are Greece; other island chains are mere distractions from this blue Aegean essence. Of the 56 Cycladic islands, 24 are inhabited. The scenic highpoint is probably Santoríni. Southernmost of the Cyclades, dramatic Santoríni was created by a volcanic explosion about 3,500 years ago, and there is nothing like it. The spiritual centre remains Apollo's ancient Delos: "Cyclades" means a cycle around Delos.

There are two basic ferry routes. The first, eastern and central, takes in elegant Ándhros and religious Tínos, includes Mýkonos, Páros and Náxos – the backpackers' (and everyone else's) beat – calls briefly at undeveloped islets like Donoússa and Iráklia, and concludes in spectacular Santoríni. The second, western, arches by Kýthnos, Sérifos, Sífnos and Mílos; these are somewhat less popular, with different cultural attributes. Off both ferry routes, Kéa attracts Athenian weekenders.

The Cyclades were inhabited as early as 6000 BC. In the third millennium a fascinating culture flourished, with beautiful arts and crafts and lively commerce, as anyone who visits the Goulandris Museum of Cycladic Art in Athens will appreciate. This modern museum (on Neofytou Douka Street) is the world's first devoted to Cycladic art, which is most famous for its glittering marble female figurines.

And high culture continued to the Roman decline, with buildings, statues and poetry. Although this vast backdrop of culture and history might not be evident amidst the hedonistic jet-setters of Mýkonos or youthful merry-makers of little Íos, it is never very far away. One sunset over the Vale of Klíma, the marble-strewn valley in Mílos where the Louvre's Aphrodite (Venus de Milo to the Latinate) was discovered, is all that's needed.

As Greece's Nobel laureate poet, Odysseus Elytis, wrote: "Íos, Síkinos, Sérifos, Mílos – each word a swallow to bring you spring in the midst of summer." ❑

PRECEDING PAGES: the elaborate dovecotes of Tínos; "Little Venice", Mýkonos.
LEFT: view from a church on the rim of Santoríni's crater.

THE CYCLADES

Map on pages 162–3

From the hectic night-life of Mýkonos and Íos to the rugged beauty of Mílos and Sérifos, and the unspoilt seclusion of tiny Kímolos and Anáfi, there is something for all tastes among these islands

Ándhros

The red Ándhros soil makes everything glow sienna at sunset, especially on its bare northern heights. Ándhros was settled centuries ago by Orthodox Albanians; their stone huts of the north contrast with the whitewash and red tile of the other villages. Golden eagles and long-haired goats may be spotted here too. Farmland is divided by painstakingly built stone walls, unusual for the pattern of triangular slates incorporated into them. From **Kalyvári**, the northernmost hamlet, roads appear as no more than chalk marks, and a diaphanous blue haze unfolds in the late afternoon to blur the distinction between sky and sea.

The port town, **Gávrio**, is only that. **Batsí** ❶, 6 km (4 miles) south, is a pleasant Cycladic "fishing" town: whitewash, cafés, beaches, package tours, and development at the outskirts. On the east coast, **Ándhros town (Hóra)** ❷ remains remarkably unspoiled. It is because so many rich Athenians have weekend houses here – less than three boat hours from Athens – that tourism has not been assiduously pursued. The Goulandris shipping family has created the excellent **Modern Art Museum**, a few steps north of the main square (Jul–Sept; Wed–Mon 8am–2pm and 6–8pm; Oct–Jun: 8am–2pm). Works by modern Greek artists as well as European Modernists are featured. The sculpture garden, tiny and exquisite, is imbued with a modernist sense of play. The prize exhibit in the **Archaeological Museum** (Tues–Sun 8.30am–2.30pm), indeed one of the prize exhibits in all Greece, is the Hermes of Ándhros, a 2nd-century copy of Praxiteles' statue.

LEFT: looking down on Mýkonos.
BELOW: wind surfing on the Aegean.

Between Batsí and Ándhros town runs a long, deep valley, with terraces all the way up its sides toward the island's highest mountain range, which rises to 994 metres (3,261 ft). Sycamores, mulberries and walnut trees flourish amid acres of pine. Feeding all this verdure, a series of springs whirls down from the mountaintops, most notably at **Ménites**, where **Panaghía Koúmoulos** is sited. The spring is considered sacred; possibly there was a big temple to Dionysos here.

The **Monastery of Zoödhóhos Pighí** (Life-giving Spring) also claims to be on a sacred spot. Situated in the hills northeast of Batsí, the monastery is looked after by a diminishing group of nuns guarding a library of precious sacred manuscripts. Adjacent is a fountain on the eponymous spring.

Three km (2 miles) to the west, about an hour's walk from Gávrio, the remarkable Hellenistic tower of **Ághios Pétros** remains a mystery: what is it doing here? Turn off the main road at the "Camping Ándhros" signs south of the port, then follow the Ághios Pétros road. South of the Paleópolis/Hóra road is the most spectacular of Ándhros's 13 Byzantine monasteries, **Panáhrandou** ❸ (Wholly Immaculate) – over 1,000

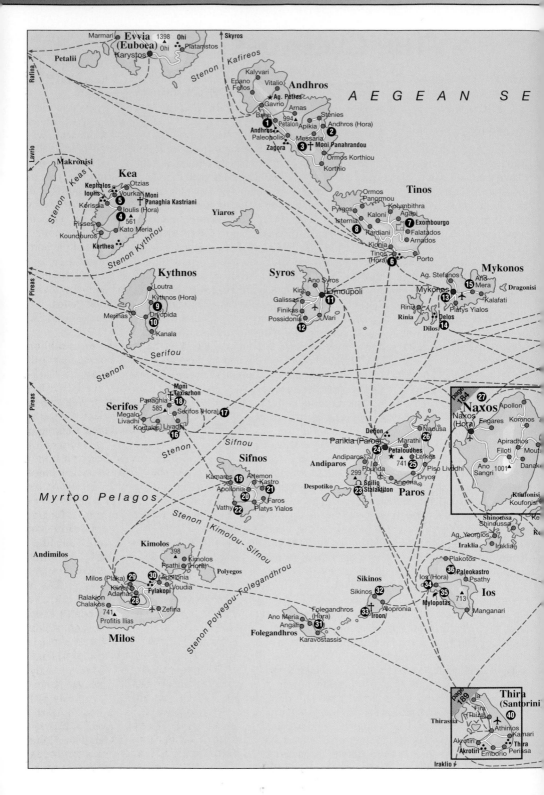

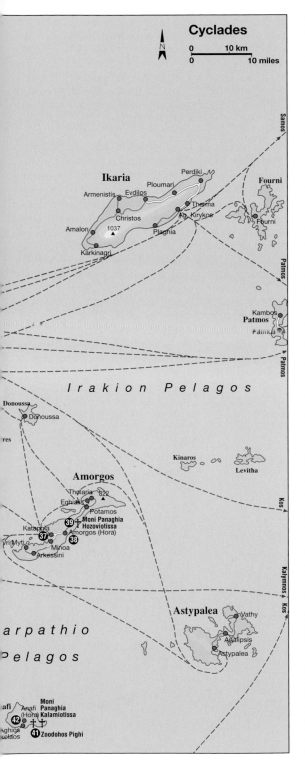

Cyclades

0   10 km
0   10 miles

Samos

Ikaria
Perdiki
Ploumari   Fourni
Armenistis Evdilos
Therma
Christos   Ag. Kirykos
Amalon   1037   Fourni
Plaghia
Karkinagri   Patmos

Kambos
Patmos
Patmos

Irakion Pelagos

Donoussa
Donoussa
res

Kinaros   Levitha

Kos

Amorgos
Tholaria 822
Eghiali
Potamos
Moni Panaghia
Katapola 39 Hozoviotissa
37 Amorgos (Hora)
Myti 38
Minoa
Arkessini

Kalymnos Kos

Astypalea Vathy

arpathio   Agrilipsis
Pelagos   Astypalea

afi Anafi Moni
(Hora) Panaghia
42   Kalamiotissa
ghios
olaos 41 Zoodohos Pighi

---

years old, it was founded in 961. The round trip on foot lasts about 3 hours (2 hours by donkey) from **Messariá**, a green valley town with the Byzantine Taxiárhis (Archangel) church.

Paleópolis, the ancient capital, doesn't give much hint of its past; but the Hermes statue in the archaeological museum was discovered here. From the road, 1,000 steps descend to a fine beach. A bit further south, the **Zagora** promontory is the site of a walled city-state that flourished in the 8th century BC, Homer's time. It is fenced and excavation work has stopped.

Ándhros has many beaches; the easiest to get to are **Nimbório** south of the port, the string of beaches between Gávrio and Batsí, and **Yiália** (near Steniés, north of Ándhros town) – plus a number of lovely remote coves such as **Ághios Péllos**.

Kéa

In the last century there were a million oaks on well-watered Kéa, and many still give shade. Olive trees, however, are lacking; since ancient times, the island has been noted for its almonds. Kéa's main town, **Ioulís (Hóra)** ❹, rides a rounded ridge overlooking the island's northern reach; it was a spot chosen precisely for its inaccessibility from foreign marauders. Kéa (popularly Tziá, in ancient times Kéos) is now popular with Athenians. As well as services to and from Pireaus, regular Kéa-bound boats leave from Lávrio, some 50 km (30 miles) from Athens, and land at **Korissía**, locally called **Livádhi**.

Hóra's **Archaeological Museum** (Tues–Sun 8.30am–3pm) doesn't contain much, but it's free. The **Lion of Kéa**, a 15-minute walk northeast of Hóra, is carved from granite; it is probably early Archaic. In legend it represents a lion brought in to eat evil Nereids. The maneless beast is almost 6 metres (20 ft) long.

The jagged west coast has many sandy spits, some inaccessible. **Písses** and **Koúndouros** are just two of the resorts that have sprung up to accommodate Athenian escapees. Close to Korissía is the bayside village of **Vourkári** ❺, with **Aghía Iríni** church, a Minoan excavation and an ancient road. A short distance to the north,

Cape Kéfala is the site of the oldest Neolithic settlement in the Cyclades.

Almost all Keans live in Hóra. The rest of Kéa is made up of resorts, of which the busiest, **Otziás**, in the north, has the pick of beaches. Each 15 August, pilgrims make their way to **Panaghía Kastrianí Monastery** to the northeast. The remains of four old Ionian cities – Koressia, Ioulis, Kartheia and Poiessa – testify to Kéa's one-time political importance. The first two are near their modern namesakes. Poiessa is near **Písses** and Kartheia near **Póles**, south of Káto Meriá.

Tínos

Tínos receives many thousands of visitors – but they are mostly Greek pilgrims here for the church, the **Panaghía Evangelístria** (Our Lady Annunciate). In 1823, the nun Pelaghía dreamt of an icon of the Virgin Mary; it was duly unearthed and the church was built to house it. The icon's healing powers have made **Tínos town (Hóra)** ❻ the Lourdes of Greece. Women fall to their knees upon arrival, and crawl painfully to the church (the marble steps are carpeted). Healing miracles are said to occur. On her feast days – 25 March (Annunciation) and 15 August (Assumption) – thousands of Greeks pour off the boats, including many gypsies in glittery clothes, for the procession of the little icon. The church complex is full of marble, precious votives (especially silver boats), and contains several museums. Religion is the point here, not antiquity.

The site of the temple of Poseidon and Amphitrite at **Kiónia** beach, one of the few ancient sites, is neglected, though the town's Archaeological Museum is worth a look (Tues–Sun 8.30am–3pm). Among the exhibits are: a 2nd- to 1st-century BC marble sundial from Kiónia that shows the time, the equinoxes and solstices; and a large number of artefacts from excavations at Exómbourgo.

BELOW: a modern café on Sýros.

Amidst the religious paraphernalia are also locally-produced jewellery and marble sculptures. Tínos is renowned for the latter – especially the fanlights – and there is still a marble-sculpture school in the village of **Pýrgos**. This is the place to see Tiniot artists at work. Tínos's other hallmark is Greece's most elaborate dovecotes. There are hundreds of them inland, a tradition started by the Venetians. Their pattern of triangular windows is echoed over doorways and in fences and window-shapes. It is a pliant symbol, which seems to represent anything from the shape of a sail to, certainly in Tínos's case, the Trinity.

For a sombre reminder of the Ottoman conquest, visit the peak of **Exómbourgo ❼**, 643 metres (2,110 ft) high, with its ruined fortress. Tínos was the last island to fall to the Turks, in 1723. A bus ride to Exómbourgo and beyond will also reveal some weird, mushroom-shaped, wind-sculpted rocks, especially above **Vólax** village, famed for its basket weaving, and a proliferation of chapels, many newly constructed.

Kolymbíthra in the north is Tínos's best beach. **Ághios Sóstis**, near **Pórto** on the south coast, is also a long decent stretch of beach, lightly commercialised.

The marble carvers of Tínos are famous throughout Greece for their intricate craftsmanship. Watch them at work in the village of Pýrgos.

Of the several monasteries to see, **Katapolianí**, near **Istérnia ❽**, is exceptional. Abandoned by monks, it is inhabited by a shy farm family who will heave the old door away from the chapel's entrance for the infrequent visitor. The bay of **Isterníon** is a fabulous hike from Istérnia. Take the marble steps to a dirt path which, after 10 minutes of dust and goat blockades, leads to a marble-cobbled path down to the sea. An asphalt road and caiques go there too. Beautiful **Kardianí**, the village southeast of Istérnia, is the island's most spectacularly set – though arcaded **Arnádos** gives it competition.

BELOW: doorways and dovecotes in Tínos.

Kýthnos

After iron mining operations ceased, Kýthnos lost its prime source of income. Foreign tourism has not supplemented it, but Athenian tourism has helped. Kythniots today are mainly dairy and livestock farmers. Elderly residents and visitors frequent the thermal baths at **Loutrá** (the island's medieval name was Thermia), on the northeast coast; therefore Kýthnos is very quiet. It is also quite barren. Bowers of blossoms cultivated in family gardens provide the only colour against the dun-coloured, flat landscape.

Mérihas on the west coast has most of the accommodation on Kýthnos. In summer, a "taxi-boat" runs from Mérihas to **Episkopí**, **Apókrisi** and **Kolóna** beaches. Landlocked **Kýthnos (Hóra) ❾** 6 km (4 miles) northeast of Mérihas, is exquisite. Whereas most Cycladic towns crawl spider-like over the area, Hóra follows a rectangular plan. Wood-beamed arches span across narrow streets to join two sides of one house. In the passages underneath, the rock pavements are playfully decorated in whitewash with fish, stylised ships, or flowers. There is a small main square, filled with sweet-smelling oleander. The fields at the back of the town rise gently away from the ravine to the south, dotted with farmhouses and tile-roofed chapels.

A walk to Loutrá (5 km/3 miles from Hóra) goes through the rural central plain. Cows sedately cross the road, udders swinging, and long-haired sheep

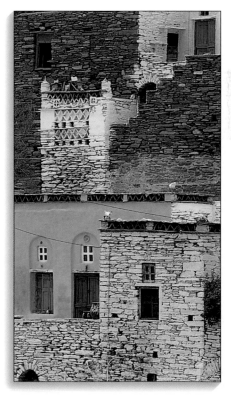

Much of Kýthnos's electricity is supplied by a "wind park" just east of Hóra and a "solar park" on the road to Loutrá.

cluster under the rare tree. The hot springs at Loutrá have coloured the soil reddish. Above Loutrá, at **Maroúla**, excavations have revealed the earliest known settlement in the Cyclades – from before 4500 BC. **Bryókastro** (Ancient Kythnos), a two-hour walk from Hóra, is a seaside ruin where the foundations of the old town are visible. A nearby islet fortress, glowering in the direction of Hydra and the Peloponnese, has also been excavated.

A stream bed splits **Dryopída** ❿ (the medieval capital) into two; the chambered Katafíki cave here is linked in legend with the Nereids. The town itself presents an appealing red-roofed spectacle, especially when seen from above.

Sýros

When Sýros ceased to be Greece's premier port in the late 1800s, it lost a lot of status. The island remains the capital of the Cyclades, but when Piraeus sapped its steam as a trade centre, Sýros was cut off and left, as one Greek guide says, "a grand but old-fashioned lady who lives on her memories of the good old days and on her half-forgotten glories." This is a shame, for with its excellent inter-island ferry links and low-key but useful facilities, Sýros can be a pleasant and rewarding place to stay.

Shipyards dominate the capital, **Ermoúpoli** ⓫. Sýros calls itself the "Manchester of Greece", which doesn't help its resort image, but shows how proud Syrians are of their industrial importance. Although little at first seems appealing about Ermoúpoli, the scent of roasting octopus and the lights of the quayside tavernas give it a festive air at night. And one of Greece's greatest *rembétika* musicians, Markos Vamvakaris, was a Syrian. A member of the famous Piraeus Quartet, his music remains popular in tavernas across the island.

BELOW: altar boys and girls of Sýros lead an Easter procession to mark the last Sunday of Lent.

Map on pages 162–3

Behind the harbour itself a few grace-notes appear: the area called **Ta Vapória** (The Ships), uphill from the shopping streets, is where you'll find many 19th-century neo-classical mansions (a few doubling as cheap hotels).

The marble-paved, plane tree-shaded main square, Platía Miaoúlis, is lined with imposing buildings in somewhat shabby condition. The Apollon Theatre, adjacent to the Town Hall, is modelled after La Scala in Milan; its recent renovation is still a point of pride. The tradition of the Saturday night stroll – young men on the prowl, women in new clothes, excited children – keeps the square lively. As you poke around the back streets, Ermoúpoli reveals itself as the most elegant neo-classical town in Greece.

The port is dominated by two hills, each capped by a church. On the lower, **Vrontádo**, stands the Greek Orthodox **Church of the Resurrection** (Anástasis). On the higher is **Áno Sýros**, the medieval Catholic quarter – Ermoúpoli is one of Greece's most Catholic towns – dominated by **Aghíos Yeórghios** church and Capuchin monastery (adjacent is a British World War I cemetery). Also here is the Vamvakaris Museum (Tues–Sun 10.30am–1pm, 7–10pm), dedicated to the life and music of the famous bouzouki composer and performer.

Fínikas, a beachside town in the southwest, is named after the Phoenicians, probably Sýros's first inhabitants. The island's south is softer and greener than the thinly populated north and has good beaches, namely **Possidonía ⑫** and **Vári** as well as Fínikas. At **Possidonía** (also known as Dellagrázia) there is a series of churches. Pythagoras's teacher, Pherekydes, the inventor of the sundial, was from here, and several caves bear his name. Up the west coast, **Galissás** and **Kíni** are emerging beach resorts. During the rule of the colonels, political prisoners were interned on **Yiáros**, the empty island to the north.

The name Sýros may be derived from Osiris, the Egyptian god of corn and the dead. Ermoúpoli was named by its founders, refugees from Híos, in honour of Hermes, the god of commerce.

BELOW: a stormy day on Sýros.

The Cycladic Bronze Age

Bronze age Cycladic peoples left behind beautiful artefacts that provide evidence of an organised and flourising culture, most famously in their stylised marble sculptures. The settlements and cemeteries excavated on a number of islands are generally considered to be the first complex, organised, settled communities in Europe.

The Early Cycladic Bronze Age is thought to have begun close to 3200 BC, and to have lasted until around 2000 BC. The later Bronze Age in the Cyclades falls into two general periods, referred to by scholars as Middle and Late Cycladic respectively. These increasingly display the influence of the Minoan culture of Crete and the move towards urban settlement. In general, the term Cycladic Culture refers to the Early Cycladic, and it is during this period that the individuality of the culture of the Cycladic islands is most evident.

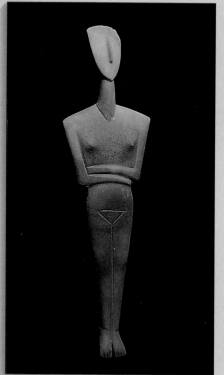

The settlements of the Early Cycladic were small, of around 50 people, comprising densely packed stone-built housing, usually only of one storey. Accompanying the settlements, outside the residential area, are cemetaries of small cist graves (rectangular graves lined with stone) and chamber tombs, clustered in family groups; the dead were inhumed in a contracted (foetal) position along with everyday objects. Much of the evidence we have of how Early Cycladic society functioned comes from these cemetaries.

The often stark differences in grave goods between tombs provides evidence of a stratified society. While some graves contain a very rich variety of artefacts, including gold and silver jewellery, others have very little, often only a single marble figure. How these differences between rich and poor were manifest in practice is a matter of conjecture, but many artefacts display a high degree of skill in their manufacture, indicating a class of skilled craft workers, and, as well as hunting, fishing, animal husbandry and agriculture, much trade was carried out from the Cycladic islands, pointing to the existence of a merchant class. The latter were, presumably, among the wealthier members of society. The Cycladic peoples were skilled sailors and had contact with the Greek mainland, Crete, Turkey, and even as far as the Danube Basin.

Of all the items left by these peoples, the marble figurines are both the most famous and, perhaps, most intriguing. Their importance is such that they are used as a 'diagnostic' tool by scholars to delineate the Cycladic Culture. The predominately female figures are generally around 20cm (8in) in length (though a very few near life-sized sculptures have been discovered) and are made of white marble. Almost two-dimensional in their execution, they have flattened oval heads and folded arms; many features would have been painted on to marble (on the face, only the nose is rendered in stone). It is conjectured from the position of the feet that they were intended to lie horizontally, but there is no conclusive evidence for this, just as there is no evidence for their function. Explanations from scholars range from their being apotropaic, to divinities, to ancestors. ❏

LEFT: a Cycladic figurine.

Mýkonos

If it weren't for Mýkonos's twisting dazzles of architecture, its plentiful beaches and chapels, and its reputation for shopping and sexy nightlife, this small blue and white island would be a dreary place. It is rocky and treeless, and there are no ancient sites. Yet people are irresistibly drawn here by the thousand. Why?

Mýkonos has made itself glamorous. Otherwise unprosperous, it has turned its ruggedness into a tourist-pleasing package that works – incidentally making it more expensive than the other islands.

Mýkonos town ⓭ has its legends, however, which include the bars, transvestite shows, fur and jewellery shops, and swish restaurants. The haggling for the fishermen's catch, for which they have to contend with Pétros the pelican, adds a touch of local colour. Later in the day, it's back to the tourists again. Luxury liners shimmer on the horizon while passengers are shipped ashore for shopping sprees, then horn-blasted reluctantly back, laden with sheepskins and gold bracelets.

The Alefkándra district, known as Little Venice because of its balconies jutting out over the sea, is the artists' quarter of Mýkonos.

It is possible to eschew all this and still enjoy Mýkonos. The **Folklore Museum** (Apr–Oct: Mon–Sat 5.30–8.30pm, Sun 6.30–8.30pm) and the **Archaeological Museum** (Tues–Sun, 8.30am–3pm), at different ends of Mýkonos's quay, are full of interesting objects, including grave stelae and a Hellenistic copy of a 5th-century cult statue of Herakles. And the town is the prettiest and most solicitously preserved in the Cyclades, with its wooden balconies loaded with flowers, red-domed chapels and billows of whitewash. The odd-shaped **Paraportianí** (Our Lady of the Postern Gate) is probably Greece's most photographed church. **Little Venice**, a row of buildings populated by artists and hanging over the sea at the north, is the least frenetic part of town.

BELOW: the windmills above Mýkonos town.

The mascot of the island is a pelican called Pétros. His predecessor had settled on the island after being blown off course by a storm. After a number of adventures, including an alleged kidnapping by a fisherman from Tínos, the original Pétros was killed when he was hit by a car in 1985. His replacement, who now inhabits the quayside scattering his pink feathers, was donated to the island by a German businessman.

Caiques start from Mýkonos town for **Dílos** ⓮, the sacred island that is the centre of the Cyclades *(see page 170)*. Or strike inland to **Áno Merá** ⓯ 7 km (4 miles) east, the only real village on the island, which is largely unspoilt by tourism. Its main attraction is **Tourlianí Monastery**, with red domes and an ornate marble tower. It houses some fine 16th-century icons and embroideries. On the road leading to Panórmos Bay and Fteliá beach lies the 12th-century Paleokástro convent (indefinitely closed because of a collapsed roof.) The reservoir lake in the island's centre attracts thousands of migrating birds.

Mýkonos is famous, indeed notorious, for its all-night bars and all-day beaches. For bars, you must inquire; the scene changes all the time. For beaches, **Paradise** is straight nude, **Super Paradise** gay nude, and both are beautiful; **Kalafáti**, reached via Áno Merá, is quiet; **Platýs Yialós** and **Psárrou** are popular with families. With the exception of **Pánormos Bay**, the north coast is exposed and windy.

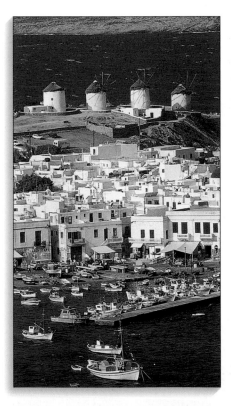

Map on pages 162–3

Ancient Delos

T he tiny island of Dílos (Delos in ancient times) is nirvana for archaeologists. Extensive Greco-Roman ruins occupying much of Dílos' 4 sq km (1½ sq miles) make the site the equal of Delphi and Olympia.

The voyage southwest from Mýkonos may be only 45 minutes but, as the caique heaves and shudders in the choppy sea, it can seem 10 times that long. Take a sweater or wear several layers as the sea breeze can be very stiff. Having accomplished these preliminaries it's then best to forget the physical and concentrate your mind on the metaphysical.

It was on ancient Delos that Leto, pregnant by Zeus, gave birth to Apollo. Delos, at that time a floating rock, was rewarded when four diamond pillars stretched up and anchored it in the heart of the Cyclades.

On arriving at Dílos, you should orient yourself to avoid getting lost among the ruins. Most of these occupy the two arms of a right angle. Ahead of you (the southern arm) are the theatre and mainly domestic buildings.

To the left is the sanctuary to which pilgrims from all over the Mediterranean came with votive offerings and sacrificial animals.

For nearly 1,000 years, this sanctuary was the political and religious centre of the Aegean and host to the Delian Festival every four years. This, until the 4th century BC, was Greece's greatest festival. The Romans turned it into a grand trade fair and made Delos a free port. It also became Greece's slave market where as many as 10,000 slaves were said to be sold on one day.

By the start of the Christian era, the power and glory that was Delos was waning and soon afterwards the island fell into disuse. During the next two millennia the stones were silent; then, with the arrival of French archaeologists in the 1870s, they began to speak.

Follow the pilgrim route to a ruined monumental gateway leading into the Sanctuary of Apollo. Within are three temples dedicated to Apollo – there is also a temple of Artemis – and parts of a colossal marble statue of Apollo which was destroyed when a massive bronze palm tree fell on it. Close by is the Sanctuary of Dionysos with several phalli standing on pedestals and Dionysiac friezes. Upstanding is a marble phallic bird symbolising the body's immortality.

Continue to the stunning Lion Terrace where five anorexic, archaic lions squat, apparently ready to pounce. Below this is the Sacred Lake and the palm tree which marks the spot of Apollo's birth.

Most visitors delight in that part of Dílos which was occupied by artisans rather than gods. Their houses, close to the port, are a regular warren of narrow lanes lined by drains from 2,000 years ago, with niches for oil lamps which illuminated the streets. The main road leads to the theatre which seated 5,500. It is unimpressive, but there are superb views from the uppermost of its 43 rows. Close to the theatre are grander houses surrounded by columns and with exquisite mosaics on their floors.

A word of warning: it is a good idea to stamp your feet loudly when exploring little-trafficked areas, to warn the snake population of your approach. They tend to nip at passing ankles when startled. ❏

LEFT: one of the guardians of the Lion Terrace.

Sérifos

A long tail of land slashes out to enclose **Livádhi** , the harbour of Sérifos. With a half a dozen each of tavernas, hotels, disco-bars and shops, Livádhi is a pleasant place to stay, with good beaches on either side. **Sérifos town (Hóra)** ⑰ clings closely to the mountain above, and has a precipitous beauty emphasised by the starker, taller mountains. Buses ascend to Hóra regularly, but the long flights of old stone steps (a half-hour climb) make for a more authentic approach.

Hóra has two parts: Káto (Lower) and Áno (Upper). The upper is the more interesting; its ridge leads in the west to the old ruined **kástro**. The view of the gleaming bay and other islands is spectacular. The beach that looks so inviting to the southwest, called **Psilí Ámmos**, really is.

The road is paved as far as the fortified Byzantine **Taxiárhon Monastery** to the island's extreme north. The scenic walk there from Áno Hóra's main square follows a wide fieldstone path. Numerous small bays with tiny, empty beaches lie below. Habitation is sparse, and there are just a few small farms along the way. After a good hour's walk, the village of **Kallítsos** appears at the far side of a steep valley. Marigolds and palm trees grow between the older houses; some abandoned stone huts straddle the palisade of rock overlooking the sea. Though there are no tavernas, a fresh-water fountain along the main cement path will refresh you.

The paved road cuts westward from here, leading to the Taxiárhon in about half an hour. The monastery sits directly on the roadside, opposite a small chapel and cemetery. The resident monk, Makários, one of Sérifos's two parish priests, will show you the ornate icon-screen and such rare treasures as lamps from Egypt and Russia and an ivory inlaid bishop's throne. Makários also fishes and raises livestock.

The rustic villages of **Galáni**, **Pýrgos** and **Panaghía** focus the magnificent valley beyond the Taxiárhon. You can cross this valley by one of two footpaths around the hill that bisects it, or stick to the road. The original, 10th-century **Panaghía** (Virgin) church is infamous for its 16 August feast-day (Xílo Panaghía), when lads and maidens used to rush in pairs to be the first to dance around the church's olive tree: the first couple to complete the dance would be allowed to marry during the year. Jealousy and feuding resulted, and when the island's youth started beating off unwanted competition with switches, a priest put a stop to the fighting. Now the priest is always the first to circle the tree.

Sérifos abounds in beaches, most of them accessible only on foot, and so unspoiled. **Megálo Livádhi** in the southwest is the island's second port (buses cross to it in the summer only). Once a mining centre, it is now rather forlorn.

Sífnos

Resplendent with olive trees, bougainvillea and wind-bent juniper, Sífnos may well be the greenest of the Cyclades, as often touted. The island's villages are flawlessly pretty and the valleys surrounding them are filled with dovecotes and monasteries. Indeed,

Makários, the monk who looks after the Taxiárhon monastery on Sérifos, has lived there alone since 1958.

BELOW: a miller inside a working windmill.

Sífnos is famous throughout Greece for its ceramics, particularly simple everyday pottery made to traditional designs from grey and red clay.

BELOW: Hrysopighí monastery, Sífnos.

even the island's harbour, **Kamáres** , has a pleasant aspect. Its mouth is narrow, formed by opposing mountain ridges that look like two dusty-flanked dinosaurs backing towards each other unawares.

Sífnos's central range of mountains softens as it meanders south; towards the empty north, it spreads into sand-coloured pyramids. The main road strikes through a steep, deep valley from Kamáres 5½ km (3½ miles) to **Apollonía** ⓴, the capital. Countless terraces cascade from the mountain tops; the pale soil makes it look as though a golden nectar were poured down over them, cooling in ridges along the way.

Sífnos was and is a potter's isle. In Kamáres, Fáros, Platýs Yialós and especially isolated Hersónisos, potters still set out long racks of earthenware to dry in the sun. Weaving and jewellery-making are the other crafts, the jewellery-making dating from times when Sífnos was rich in gold and silver. There are fine examples of local weaving in Apollonía's **folklore museum** (Tues–Sun 9.30am–2pm, 6–10pm; a notice on the door tells you where to find the curator).

Connected to Apollonía, **Artemón** (the towns are named for the divine twins Apollo and Artemis) is Sífnos's richest town, with mansions and old churches. The chief church, the **Kóhi** (Nook), in whose courtyard cultural events are held in summer, is built over a temple to Artemis. Down the block a plaque marks the house of mournful poet John Gryparis (1871–1942).

The oldest community is **Kástro** ㉑, the former capital perched 100 metres (328 ft) above the sea and 3 km (2 miles) east of Apollonía. Kástro's layout of concentric streets sets it apart from other settlements. Catalans and Venetians once ruled the town; the walls they built are still in evidence, as are some remains of an ancient acropolis. Most of the buildings are from the 14th century.

The big Venetian building in the centre of town is the **Archaeological Museum** (Tues–Sun 8.30am–3pm).

Sífnos's south shore settlements make tranquil beach-side bases. **Fáros**, on a clover-shaped bay, abounds in tiny churches. Sífnos's prettiest spot may be **Hrysopighí** (Golden Wellspring) **Monastery**, built in 1653 on an islet reached by a footbridge. It is no longer in monastic use and basic rooms can be rented in summer.

The adjoining beach of **Apókofto** (Cut-off) is lovely and sheltered, with a popular taverna. **Platýs Yialós** is crowded in summer and deserted in winter. A beach settlement with rooms, here backpackers feel most at home. Public notices primly advise that camping on the beach (there is a campsite) and nude bathing are prohibited, and that "cleanliness is the key to civilisation". Many glorious walks into the island's interior begin around this area.

A paint-blazed footpath leads from **Kataváti** just south of Apollonía to remote **Vathý ㉒**, a potter's coastal hamlet provided with a road only in 1993. Caiques make the trip from Kamáres in the summer, and there are tavernas and private rooms on the beach. Its sandy-floored bay is edged by a number of small coves, yet it is a man-made feature that makes Vathý so visually stunning: **Taxiárhis** (Archangel) **Monastery**, poised as though ready to set sail.

Andíparos

Once, 5,000 years ago, this small, pretty island was joined to Páros. A narrow channel now separates the two, plied by frequent car ferries and excursion boats bringing visitors to its famous cave, **Spílio Stalaktitón** (the Cave of the Stalactites) ㉓. At the entrance to the cavern stands the Church of Ioánnis Spiliótis

Map on pages 162–3

Hrysopighí Monastery has an icon with allegedly miraculous powers: it once destroyed the stone bridge to the islet, saving the monastery from pirate attack; then later saved Sífnos from plague (1675) and locusts (1928).

BELOW: the main attraction on Andíparos.

UNDERGROUND TOURISM

The Cave of the Stalactites (summer: daily 10.45am–3.45pm), the principal attraction on Andíparos, was discovered in the reign of Alexander the Great, around 330 BC, and has been attracting visitors ever since. Despite the predations of souvenir hunters, who have broken and removed stalactites for centuries, it is still a fantastic spooky chamber, full of weird shapes and shadows.

Almost as impressive as the stalactites and stalagmites are the inscriptions left by past visitors, including King Otto of Greece and Lord Byron. The oldest piece of graffiti has sadly been lost – a note from several individuals stating that they were hiding in the cave from Alexander the Great who suspected them of plotting his assassination. Another inscription (in Latin) records the Christmas mass celebrated in the cave by the French Marquis de Nointel in 1673.

In summer buses and boats run to the cave from Andíparos town, or else it is a two-hour walk. Then you descend more than 70 metres (230 ft) from the cave entrance to the vaulted chamber, surrounded by stalagmites and stalactites. There are concrete steps now, and electric lighting, but the effect is still breathtaking. The entire cave is actually twice as deep, but the rest has been closed because it is too dangerous.

(St John of the Cave). Buses run from **Andíparos town** to the cave, but most day-trippers bypass the pretty village, so it is relatively easy to find rooms here outside the month of August (the newer houses belong to Athenians).

Andíparos measures only 11 km by 5 km (7 miles by 3 miles), so there are no impossible distances. The beachside campsite on **Diapóri** bay faces a calm, shallow channel between two islets; at their end rise two sea rocks, the Red Tower and the Black Tower, visible from Parikía. The little ferry passes two islets; on one, Saliagos, British excavators in 1964 revealed a neolithic (dating from before 4000 BC) settlement, including a fat female figurine now in the Parikía museum. The other belongs to the Goulandris family, who established Athens's eponymous museum.

Good beaches and bars have lured to Andíparos some of Páros's former business. **Ághios Yeórghios**, on the south coast, has two tavernas and faces the goat island of **Despotikó**. South of the cave the **Faneroméni chapel** stands alone on a southeastern cape.

Páros

Parikía 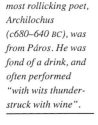 (also called Páros) is the attractive capital of this heavily trafficked island. In August, make sure you book ahead or get off the ferry quickly as the cheaper rooms go fast; though in the evening they are empty as most people are taking in the famous nightlife. Parikía is as pretty as Mýkonos, but not so labyrinthine. The beautiful 6th-century **Ekatontapylianí church** (Our Lady of a Hundred Doors) retains its Byzantine form, and includes a side chapel adapted from a 4th-century BC building. By the church is a **Byzantine Museum** (Tues–Sun 9am–1pm, 5.30–9.30pm). The **Archaeological Museum** (Tues–Sun

The ancient world's most rollicking poet, Archilochus (c680–640 BC), was from Páros. He was fond of a drink, and often performed "with wits thunderstruck with wine".

BELOW: Náousa, Páros, is now a fashionable village.

8.30am–3pm) has exhibits from across the island. The ancient **cemetery** is next to the post office. The Venetian **kástro** in the centre of town is built wholly of classical marbles. Páros has some of the world's finest marble; you can still visit the ancient tunnel-quarries in **Maráthi** and pick up a chip.

The island is loaded with beaches, many within easy walking distance of Náousa (*see below*). **Hrysí Aktí** (Golden Beach), on the east coast just north of **Dhryós** (which also has a good beach), is a perennial favourite. **Léfkes** , the Turkish capital, is the largest inland village. The settlement is very attractive and set in a beautiful location. There are several 17th-century churches, the two most prominent edged with an opaline-blue wash. Léfkes (Poplars) makes a good base for walking excursions, as the area is full of monasteries.

In beautiful **Náousa** ❷, on the north coast, the little harbour's colourful boats seem to nudge right up against the fishermen's houses. Though the village has become fashionable, with upmarket boutiques and restaurants, the harbour still retains its traditional charm. Caiques leave from here for several fine beaches; the world windsurfing championship is often held on Santa Maria beach.

One of the best walks from Léfkes is over the Byzantine cobbled road leading to **Píso Livádhi**, where a fold of rich Aegean blue separates Páros from the high, dark crags of **Náxos** ❷ (*see page 184*). Píso Livádhi itself has been spoilt by over-development for package tourists.

In the west is the much-visited **Valley of the Butterflies**, or **Petaloúdhes**, a big well-watered garden with huge trees. The black and yellow butterflies – actually Jersey tiger moths – are colourful and countless in summer (Jun–Sept: daily 9am–8pm). A wide road goes there, but no bus. The bus does, however, go to **Poúnda**, from where the small ferry sails to Andíparos.

Map on pages 162–3

The summer visitors to Petaloúdhes, southwest of Parikiá, are not butterflies but Jersey tiger moths.

BELOW: the baptism font at Ekatonpylianí church in Parikía.

Mílos

Mílos is a geologist's paradise. The colours and shapes of rocks, caves, cliffs, coastline and hot springs make it eerily beautiful. Snaking streams of lava formed much of the island's coastline. The lava dripped into caves and thickened as it hit the sea, thrusting up weird rock formations that take on animal shapes when caught in the purple shadows of the setting sun. The island has always been extensively mined, once for obsidian, now for bentonite, perlite, barite and china clay. The gaping quarries disfigure the landscape.

Modern Miliots are possessed of a quiet sophistication and worldliness. They have graciously adapted to the thin stream of tourism the island receives, concentrated in **Adamás** ㉘, the port, and Apollónia, a fishing village in the northeast. On the map, Mílos resembles a bat in flight; almost all the island's total population of 4,500 is in the eastern wings; the western wing is wildly beautiful. One way to kill time while waiting for a boat in Adamás would be to take a hot springs bath, if they were open, but the tiny entrance door in the concrete wall near where the boats dock is locked. Inside the **Aghía Triádha** church in Adamás, Cretan-style icons dominate. Links have always been strong between Mílos and the "great island": Cretan refugees founded Adamás in 1853 (though ancient tombs have been found on the site of the town), and was settled by Minoans who came to Mílos to trade obsidian.

The island's capital, **Pláka** (also called **Mílos**) ㉙ has both an **Archaeological Museum** (Tues–Sun 8.30am–3pm), which contains a cast of the famous Venus de Milo, and a **Folklore Museum** (Tues–Sat 10am–2pm and 6–9pm). The latter, set in an old house, is packed with diverse exhibits from rock specimens and goat horns to samples of native weaving. A hike to the **Panaghía**

Greek Street in London is named after the Miliot ghetto in Soho, populated by refugees from Mílos in the 17th century.

BELOW: the west coast of Mílos, with Andímilos islet in the distance.

Map on pages 162–3

Thalássitra (Mariner Virgin), the chapel above Pláka (follow signs for Anna's Art Dresses), and the old **kástro** walls gives a splendid view of the bay-bound Mílos and, on clear days, as far as Páros. The escutcheon on the church is of the Crispi family, who wrested Mílos from the Sanudi in 1363.

Southwest of Pláka lies the verdant **Vale of Klíma**, on whose seaside slope the ancient Miliots built their city. Excavations undertaken by the British School in Athens in the late 1800s uncovered a Dionysian altar here, and remains of an ancient gymnasium. There is even a Roman mosaic. Follow the catacombs sign, and then the track to the **theatre**. It is very well preserved, probably because of its Roman renovation.

Near the theatre, a marble plaque marks the spot where a farmer unearthed the Aphrodite of Mílos (Venus de Milo) in 1820. In a feat of robbery approaching that of the appropriation of the Parthenon marbles (though the French were the villains rather than the British this time) she was whisked off to Paris, never to return. The statue was probably carved in the 1st century BC – of Parian marble since Mílos lacks good stone. Mílos was long famous for producing superb statuary, wrought by succeeding generations of a family called Grophon. Other examples of Miliot sculpting include a (copied) bust of Asclepius in the British Museum and a Hermes in the Berlin Museum. More can be found in the Archaeological Museum in Athens.

Below the theatre lies one of the island's prettiest villages, **Klíma**, with brightly painted boathouses lining the shore. Further down the road from Pláka to Adamás are the **Christian catacombs**. Carved into the hillside, they are the earliest evidence of Christian worship in the country. The 291 tombs – which probably held as many as 8,000 bodies – have all been robbed, yet the site remains moving. Though cheerily lit by tiny electric lanterns, the frescoes and religious graffiti are hard to discern, and only the initial 50 metres (164 ft) are open to the public.

Ten km (6 miles) northeast from Adamás lies the rubble of the ancient city of **Fylakopí**, whose script and art resemble that of the Minoans. It flourished for a thousand years after 2600 BC. The famous flying fish fresco is now in Athens, but many objects are in the Pláka museum. All around Fylakopí are strewn flakes of obsidian, which was used for sharp tools before bronze became common; visitors came to Mílos for it from 7000 BC.

Mílos's polychrome geology is especially impressive here. Next to the site glitters the **Papafránkas cave**, where precipitous stone steps take you down for an atmospheric swim in a pool connected to the sea by an inlet running under a rock bridge. The multi-coloured rocks offshore, **Glaronísia**, can be reached by cruise boat from Apollónia.

Apollónia ㉚, a restful base in the northeast, is a popular resort with a tree-fringed beach. It is a good starting point for several short walks that give the full measure of Mílos's strange beauty. A short distance west along the coast (follow the town beach), four volcanic boulders do a ring dance atop a crest of sandstone; the feeling of movement is undeniable, though the rocks were petrified here centuries ago.

The Venus de Milo was entrusted to the French Consul in Istanbul (she probably lost her arms in transit), to keep her safe from the Turks. He promptly shipped her off to France, where Louis XVIII put her on display in the Louvre. She has been there ever since.

BELOW: Kímolos, seen from the coast of Mílos.

Most of the Cyclades islands that grew their own grain have windmills but, unlike this one in Síkinos, the majority have fallen into disuse.

BELOW: the steep terraced slopes of Folégandhros.

Kímolos

This tiny island – 35 sq km (14 sq miles), with a population of 800 – is an alluring presence for anyone who has been staying in Apollónia on Mílos. The distance between the two is just under a nautical mile. Kímolos's chalky cliffs, mined for Fuller's earth and tufa building blocks, turn a velvety rose at sunset and then seem to disappear in the evening haze. The boat takes only 20 minutes to cross the narrow channel from Apollónia to **Psáthi**, Kímolos's landing. Some ferries to Mílos also stop here. **Hóra**, the one town, is a 20-minute walk up from the quay. The 14th-century Venetian **kástro** above Hóra, sadly in an advanced state of decay, looks down on a row of windmills, of which one still grinds. The most interesting church is **Ághios Ioánnes Hrysóstomos**, built in the 14th century and well restored.

Kímolos, once a pirates' hideout, today provides a refuge from the more crowded islands. Although blessedly undeveloped, it has several beaches at Alykí, Klíma, Prássa, Bonátsi and Ellinikó, all within easy walking distance. Offshore from Ellinikó is Ághios Andréas, now an islet. Excavations there have revealed a significant and fascinating Mycenaean settlement. Prássa has a reasonable shingle beach and some rooms to rent.

Folégandhros

The vaulting steepness of Folégandhros's coast has deterred outside invasion over the centuries and so lent the islanders security. Despite its tiny size – 32 sq km (12 sq miles) populated by barely 500 people – its role in recent history has not been insignificant: many Greeks were exiled here during the country's 1967–74 military rule. Its ancient and early Christian ties with Crete were

Map
on pages
162–3

strong, and many paintings of the Cretan School can be found in its churches today. In myth, a son of King Minos founded the island.

Folégandhros abounds with bays, wild herbs and grapes. **Karavostássis**, the port, **Angáli**, at the waist of the island on the west shore, and **Ághios Nikólaos** above it, are the little-developed beaches. The recent spate of construction solved a summer "no rooms" problem; the campsite at **Livádhi** in the south provides a useful backup. From Livádhi it is possible to walk to one of the island's best beaches at **Katergó**.

There are buses to the capital, **Folégandhros** or **Hóra** ❸, a magnificently sited medieval town with an inner **kástro** high above the sea. **Hrysospiliá**, the "golden cave" near Hóra, gapes over the sea. It is rich with stalagmites and stalactites. Excavations show this was a place of refuge in the Middle Ages. It's only accessible to good climbers, who can get there by caique from Hóra.

The island's second village, **Áno Meriá**, comprises stone houses and farms; the surrounding hills are dotted with chapels. Historically, Folegandrian supplications were for rain – and still are, for on no other Cycladic island are wells and cisterns so closely guarded.

Síkinos

Rocky Síkinos, despite the usual variety of harbourside lodgings, couldn't be less like its larger neighbour, Íos. Although connected to Piraeus and other Cyclades twice or three times a week by ferry, and by caique to Íos and Folégandhros in summer, Síkinos so far seems to have shrugged off tourism. It also escapes mention in the history books for long periods of time, but there are antiquities and churches to be seen.

BELOW: Síkinos through a ruined kástro doorway.

The three beaches, **Aloprónia** (also the port), **Ághios Nikólaos** and **Ághios Yeórghios** to the north, face Íos. From Aloprónia harbour there's a regular bus or an hour's hike to **Síkinos town** , which consists of the simple village (**Hóra**) and the medieval **kástro**, with its wonderful village square arranged for defence. The abandoned convent of **Zoödóhos Pighí** sits above the town.

Perhaps even barer than Íos, Síkinos is a sparse island with few obvious diversions. One site of note, the **Iroön** ⓧ, near the village of **Episkopí**, stands on what was once thought to have been a temple to Apollo; this is now reckoned to be an elaborate Roman tomb, incorporated into a church during medieval times. Síkinos's old Greek name, Oenoe, testifies to the fact that the island once produced a celebrated wine *(oinos)*, but not any longer.

Íos

A tiny island with few historic attractions, Íos has drawn the young and footloose since the 1960s. The current influx, who flock here to live cheaply, drink and dry out in the blistering sun, are a faint echo of their hippie forbears, who camped here year-round; people no longer sleep on the beach at **Mylopótas** ⓧ.

The centre of Íos's nightlife shifts constantly about the tiny capital town, **Hóra** (also called **Íos**) ⓧ. Boutique shopping is minimal. But one thing people are sure to spend money on while here is drinking. Nightclubs stud the hill above Íos harbour, with another large cluster of bars in the Hóra. At around 11pm, beach stragglers break the quiet ready for night-time revels (a bus runs regularly between beach and harbour via Hóra). Once ensconced inside a bar, they could be anywhere in the western world. The island authorities are, however, keen to change the image of Íos and move to more upmarket tourism.

BELOW: a midnight Easter service.

Map on pages 162–3

The permanent effects of the tourist invasion have been twofold: Íos is no longer poor, and traditional life has virtually disappeared. Hóra is the only town; there are no small villages to keep up the old traditions. As one elderly resident recounts, weddings were once week-long feasts for all. Now, unless they are held in winter, they last an evening, as everyone is too busy tending tourist-related enterprises. However, with all the action and nightlife concentrated in Hóra, away from the town and its immediate area, it is still possible to find quiet corners and fairly unpopulated beaches.

Íos is not devoid of natural beauty or charm; even the bleary-eyed can see it. The harbour is one of the Aegean's prettiest. The hilltop Hóra, capped by a windmill, blazes with the blue domes of two Byzantine churches. Its layout and the palm trees that flank it look almost Levantine. Buses are frequent, and there is a long marble stairway from the port. The flat plain north of the harbour is filling up with new houses and at least one villa complex has been constructed on the main road.

Íos has many good swimming beaches, including the nude beaches north of the harbour. There are summer caiques to **Manganári Bay** in the south and **Psáthy** in the east. A half day's walk northeast ends at **Aghía Theodóti**, with beach and seasonal camping. A traditional *panaghíri* (saint's festival) is held at Theodóti church on 8 September, the only festival in which the entire island still participates.

Beyond the church are the remains of **Paleokástro** ㊱, an elevated fortress containing the marble ruins of what was the medieval capital. At a lonely spot toward the northern tip, behind the cove at **Plakótos**, is a series of prehistoric graves, one of which the islanders fiercely believe is Homer's.

BELOW: *tsouréki* traditional Easter sweet bread.

There are more than 40 churches and chapels in little Amorgós town, including Ághios Fanoúrios, the smallest church in Greece, which can accommodate a congregation of two.

Amorgós

The spine of mountains – the tallest is Krikelas in the northeast, at 822 metres (2,696 ft) – precludes expansive views unless you're on top of them. The southwesterly harbour town of **Katápola** ❸ occupies a small coastal plain. Trees overhang the quayside and thick orchards fringe the town. Unfortunately, new development is encroaching on the older Cycladic structures as Amorgós gets more summer tourist traffic each year.

Three important ancient cities once thrived here (many of the finds are now in Athens). At **Minóa** (just above Katápola) are very scant ruins of a gymnasium, stadium and temple to Apollo. **Arkessíni**, in the far southwest, comprises a burial site and a well-preserved Hellenistic fortress. **Aigialis** (Eghiális), above Amorgós's second northeastern harbour, was also an ancient colony; now only the ruined fortress is visible. As Semonides of Amorgos wrote around 650 BC, "The generation of men is like that of leaves."

The elevated **Hóra** (or **Amorgós town**) ❸, accessible by a regular bus service, is a cluster of whitewashed houses and numerous churches around a 13th-century Venetian castle, and a regulation row of windmills.

The island's two most famous churches are outside Hóra. **Ághios Yeórghios Valsamítis**, 4 km (2 miles) southwest, is on a sacred spring once believed to cure lepers and now watering someone's market garden; this church's pagan oracle was finally closed only after World War II. Half an hour east of Hóra, clinging to the side of a 180-metre (590-ft) cliff, the spectacular 11th-century Byzantine **monastery of the Panaghía Hozoviótissa** ❸ – one of the most beautiful in Greece – is home to a revered icon of the Virgin from Palestine (daily 8am–1pm). For the miraculous story of the chisel and vision of the church's building, take a copy of the church pamphlet.

BELOW: Panaghía Hozoviótissa monastery on the cliffs of Amorgós.

Below the monastery, **Aghía Ánna** beach beckons. To the southwest lie empty, secluded coves for bathing and sunning; a line of windmills edges the ridge above. The coastal ledges are covered with wild thyme and oregano, which release their pungent bouquet when crushed underfoot. A Hellenistic watchtower looking towards Anáfi marks the island's southernmost point, below Arkessíni.

The north of the island is characterised by high-perched villages, except for **Eghiális**, a small anchorage with accommodation and good beaches nearby. Some ferry boats, plus caiques from elsewhere on Amorgós, put in here. Beyond it is **Tholária**, surrounded by Roman tombs. Sheer rock faces notwithstanding, Amorgós is full of tiny, hidden beaches. Locally produced maps name them all and provide valuable information.

Anáfi

In legend, Apollo conjured up Anáfi to shelter Jason and the Argonauts when the seas grew rough and they risked losing the Golden Fleece. Apollo's shrine was built here in thanksgiving. Divine intervention has never again been reliable. Earthquakes originating on its volatile neighbour **Santoríni** ❹ (*see page 187*) usually shivered through Anáfi, causing tidal waves and a rain of volcanic detritus. Anáfi's appearance has

Map
on pages
162–3

probably not altered much since then: it still looks like a rough boulder heaved up out of the sea and kept in place only by the goodness of a tenacious god.

However, a different god is involved now: **Zoödóhos Pighí** (Lifegiving Wellspring) **Monastery ❹** was erected over the old shrine in the island's southeast corner. Extensive courses of marble masonry in its walls are believed to be remnants of the old temple. Above the monastery soars the smaller monastery of **Panaghía Kalamiótissa**, high on a pinnacle that is Anáfi's most distinctive feature.

Fewer than 300 people live on the island today, surviving mainly by fishing and subsistence farming. Summer tourism, mostly German, has boosted the economy only slightly, and the island makes few concessions to those who come. However, recent years have seen an increase in visitors, attracted by Anáfi's peace and quiet, and superb south-facing beaches. It is served by a twice-weekly caique from Santoríni and several ferries from Piraeus.

The south-facing harbour, **Ághios Nikólaos**, has rooms available in summer. A short bus ride or half-hour walk up, the main town, **Hóra** (or **Anáfi**) **❷**, offers a wider choice and finer setting, and life in the quiet streets has so far been unaltered by tourism. A ruined Venetian **kástro** reigns overhead. Feast days on Anáfi – 10 days after Easter and 8 September – are occasions for all-out dancing, eating and drinking.

Hikes eastward lead first to the beach at **Klisídi** (with seasonal taverna) and then to half a dozen more, all superb, before reaching the two monasteries. The interior is virtually empty, except for the rubble of another Venetian castle above central Roúkounas beach. Goat paths amble aimlessly; follow them, for Anáfi remains a hawk-haunted place for solitude. ❑

BELOW: a sunny back street.

THE BACK ISLANDS

The so-called "Back Islands" near Náxos were once thickly populated. Now **Donoússa**, **Iráklia**, **Shinoússa** and **Koufonísi** have populations of 100 to 200 each, while **Kéros** is completely uninhabited. For Iráklia, Shinoússa and Koufoníssi there are ferries twice or thee times a week, and smaller boats from Náxos. Donoússa has ferry connections four times a week, and is served by caiques from Náxos, Páros and Santoríni in summer. No boats go to Kéros. A stay on any of the Back Islands means, at least out of season, accommodation with local families and a very low-key existence. Water is scarce on all of them.

Hilly Donoússa is covered with vineyards; views from the harbour take in the barren Makáres islands and the grand profile of Náxos. Iráklia has two settlements: the harbour, Ághios Yeórghios, and Hóra, just over an hour's hike above. Shinoússa's hilltop Hóra has a medieval fortress at its back; Messariá is a tiny beach settlement on the north coast. Koufoníssi (its neighbour, Káto Koufoníssi, belongs mainly to goats) has an actual hotel, and an east coast beach with a seasonal taverna. Kéros was a third-millenium BC burial site. Much of the Cycladic material in great museums comes from here, and if you put in to Kéros, the police will want to know why.

NÁXOS

Mountainous Náxos is the largest of the Cyclades. It offers lush green valleys, even in the height of summer, and sweeping sandy beaches

Naxian marble has always been prized. It was used for the famous lions of Delos (see page 170).

BELOW: the Portára gateway at the unfinished temple of Delian Apollo.

Náxos is the largest, most heroic, most magnificent of the Cyclades. High mountains, long beaches, inaccessible villages, ruins, medieval monasteries, and fascinating history make any visit here too short. Hemmed in by the Cyclades' highest mountains, the interior recalls the more forbidding parts of the Peloponnese. **Mount Zas** – or Zeus, who was born in a huge bat-filled cave here – is 1,001 metres (3,284 ft), but not difficult to climb. **Hóra** (**Náxos town**) ❶ is a labyrinthine chaos of Venetian homes and castle walls, post-Byzantine churches, Cycladic to medieval ruins, and garden restaurants.

Hóra is divided into sections whose place names reflect the port's long Venetian occupation. The **Catholic Cathedral** at the east of the town demarcates the Fontana section. The residential Borgo quarter behind the main *platía* is splendidly Cycladic. Higher up, within the walled **kástro**, live descendants, still Catholic, of the Venetian overlords; look for their coats of arms over doorways. The former French School, built into the ramparts, now houses the **Archaeological Museum** (Tues–Sun 8.30am–3pm). Just north of Hóra is the Grotta area, with the remains of a Cycladic settlement (c2500 BC).

On an islet (connected by a causeway) to the north of Hóra's ferry dock, a colossal free-standing marble door frame marks the entrance to the **Temple of**

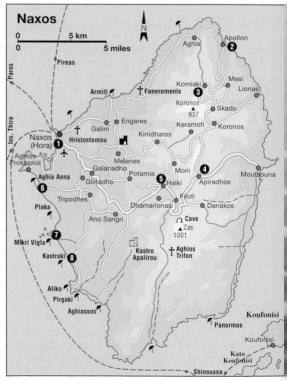

Naxos

Delian Apollo of 530 BC. It was never completed, despite the efforts of Lygdamis, Náxos's energetic tyrant. If it had ever been finished, it would have been Archaic Greece's largest temple.

On the northern shore of Náxos is the resort town of **Apóllonas ❷**, three hours from Hóra by the daily bus. A huge 6th-century BC *kouros* (statue of Greek god), probably bearded Dionysos, lies on the hillside above it, abandoned when the marble cracked. (Another cracked *kouros* reposes in a splendid garden 10km/6 miles east of Náxos in Melanés, near the road to Kourohóri.)

The rest of the island is a sumptuous wilderness, ripe for exploration by anyone with the time and stamina (or hired means of transport) to do it justice. The rural villages of Náxos are numerous and unpredictable, with reception to foreigners varying enormously from one to another. Olive and fruit trees grow densely around them, concealing Byzantine churches and crumbling Venetian manors. Four villages on the road back from Apóllon to Hóra are particularly worthy of attention: Komiakí, Apíradhos, Filóti and Halkí.

Komiakí ❸, the highest village on the island, is extremely attractive, has wonderful views over the surrounding terraced vineyards, and is where the local *Kitrón* liqueur originally came from. **Apíranthos ❹** was first settled by Cretan refugees in the 17th and 18th centuries; the dialect is noticeable. The town, whose streets are marble, even looks Cretan. Its little **Archaeological Museum** (open daily: if closed, ask someone where to find the guard) contains some rough-carved reliefs that are unique and uninterpretable. In the school a teacher has set up a museum of local minerals.

Filóti, on the slopes of Mount Zas, is Naxos's second largest town. The festival, which starts on 14 August, sees the village celebrate with three days of eating, drinking and dancing. Near Filóti a bad road leads (14km/9 miles) southeast to the Heímarros Tower, strongly built in the 3rd century BC.

The Trageá valley, from Filóti to Halkí, is all olive trees, amid which are several Byzantine churches. This region is excellent walking country and numerous routes are possible here. **Halkí ❺**, the Trageá's main town, has several fine churches, the best being **Panaghía Protóthronis** (First-Enthroned Virgin), founded in 1052. The 13th-century Annunciation fresco over the sanctuary is a masterpiece. Next to the church is the 17th-century Grazia tower. Many such towers, which the Venetian lords built to guard their holdings, can be seen throughout Náxos.

Goats and migrating birds are southeastern Naxos's chief inhabitants. On the way to Halkí a good road branches off to **Moní**, whose restaurants are justly popular for their mountain views. On the way to Moní the road passes the **Drosianí**, or Church of the Dewy Virgin, which has rare early medieval frescoes.

It is only since the early 1990s that Náxos has become known for its beaches. Some of the best in all the Cyclades are on the west coast of the island, facing Páros. **Ághios Yeórghios** south of the port is the most popular. **Aghía Anna ❻** (partly nude) has a good number of rooms to rent; **Plaka ❼** beyond it is less crowded, with 5 km (3 miles) of sand; and **Kastráki ❽**, furthest south, offers blissful solitude. ❑

The gigantic kouros *at Apóllonas, left unfinished in around 600 BC, weighs 30 tonnes and is 10.5 metres (34 ft) long.*

BELOW: relaxing at midday.

SANTORÍNI

Santoríni's whitewashed villages cling to volcanic cliffs above beaches of black sand. It is an island shaped by geological turmoil, and one of the most dramatic in all Greece

Entering the bay of Santoríni on a boat is one of Greece's great experiences. Broken pieces of a volcano's rim – Santoríni and its attendant islets – form a multicoloured circle around a deep lagoon that, before the eruption, was the island's high centre. When the volcano blew (c1500 BC), Minoan ships sank, earthquakes followed, and sunsets were affected globally for years. The island's long crescent, formed of petrified lava, seems at sunset to reflect fire still from the dormant volcano.

Thíra (or Thera) is its ancient and official name. Greeks however prefer its medieval name, Santoríni, after Saint Irene of Salonica, who died here in 304. **Firá** (or **Thíra**) ❶, the capital, sits high on the rim, its white houses (many barrel-vaulted against earthquakes) blooming like asphodels. The town is largely pedestrianised, its winding cobbled streets terraced into the volcanic cliffs. Firá has an **Archaeological Museum** (Tues–Sun 8.30am–3pm; free Sun) and a cultural festival every September. The **Mégaron Gýzi Museum** (daily 10.30am–1.30pm and 5–8pm) is housed in a beautiful 17th-century mansion that was spared in the 1956 earthquake. The collection includes engravings, documents, paintings and prints featuring Santorinian landscapes, pre-quake photographs and island maps from the 16th to the 19th century.

LEFT: the churches of Ía. **BELOW:** white houses, purple sea.

Despite August's touristy atmosphere, for most of the year Firá is quiet. Although it is packed with jewellers, boutiques and cave-like discos, it has the power to charm. A sunset drink at a cliffside café – contemplating the rust-and-purple striated cliffs, blue bay, twinkling lights and sensual white lines of its architecture – remains unforgettable. Some boats put in at **Skála Firá**, 580 steps below Firá (*skála* means staircase in Greek), but most dock at **Athiniás**, 10 km (6 miles) further south.

Ancient Thíra

To the east of Firá, the land smoothes out into fertile fields. A few bare hills push up again in the southeast. On one of them sits **Ancient Thíra** ❷ (Tues–Sun 8.30am–3pm). Founded by Dorians in the 9th century BC, it was occupied by 5,000 Romans until an earthquake knocked it down for good. The foundations of the ancient buildings are still clear.

In the south, **Akrotíri** ❸ (Tues–Sat, 8.30am–3pm), a Minoan town preserved in volcanic ash like Pompeii, continues to be excavated under a roof built to protect the remains. The town clearly had comfortable two-storey houses, good plumbing and attractive little squares, and a walk through it brings the past to life. No bones have been found, which implies that the inhabitants, though they had to leave in a hurry, knew of the coming eruption. But if you want to see

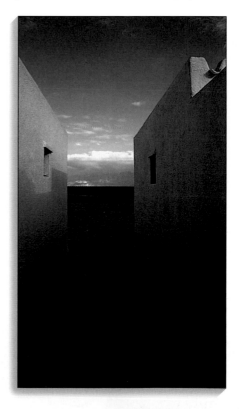

You don't need to walk up the 580 steps from Skála Firá to Firá, or charter a donkey: there is also a cable-car.

BELOW: houses teeter over the top of Ammoudía bay.

the beautiful frescoes, pots and furniture that have been found there you must, to the islanders' chagrin, go to Athens' Archaeological Museum (*see page 114*). Near Akrotíri and Kókkini Ámmos beach, the Glaros taverna serves sweet, lava-nurtured Santoríni wines in dented tin jugs.

Santoríni's population swells from 9,000 to 70,000 in summer, and most of the visitors congregate in the capital. Though Firá is most developed, many other places offer plentiful accommodation. **Ía (Oía)** , on the island's north-ernmost peninsula, is perhaps Greece's most photographed village. Ía has been beautifully restored since, in 1956, a severe earthquake sent a layer of lava sliding down over the houses. Afterwards, people dug their way back inside their homes. Life is marginally quieter here than in Firá, with fewer bars and tavernas, and earlier closing hours.

A steep walk down twisting stone steps from the western end of town ends at **Ammoudiá** beach, overhung by houses. Beautiful cave houses converted into expensive hotels are a speciality of Ía. The gentle hike along the caldera's edge from Ía to **Imerovígli** (north of Firá) allows you to experience the cruel reds and purples of the petrified lava and the island's tempestuous geology. The volcano is only dormant, not extinct; it still emits gas and steam at 80°C (175°F) and earthquakes are always a disturbing possibility.

Every year there are more places available to stay and eat in **Kamári** ❺ and **Périssa** ❻, busy resorts on the east coast. Périssa has the main campsite. Both have roasting hot black pebble beaches (at Périssa, the strand is 8 km/5 miles long). They make a good starting point from which to climb to Ancient Thíra (if you don't take a taxi or bike) and then Mount Profítis Ilías, the next hill inland. The museum in **Profítis Ilías Monastery** exhibits tools and even complete work-

Map below

shops of the various crafts practised here by monks since its founding. But remember, the remaining monk in charge is not obliged to keep regular hours for tourists. The hours that Profítis Ilías is open to the public tend to be erratic: try to ascertain whether the monastery is open before setting out on your climb.

It is also possible to walk to the monastery from **Pýrgos** ❼, an island village on the central plain. Yellow wheat sheaves, grapevines twisted into wreaths Santoríni-style, tiny thick-skinned tomatoes (grown without water for concentrated flavour), and riots of wild spring flowers – all growing out of angry-looking pumice soil – make up the island's gentler side. Small caves used as toolsheds, barns and sometimes even as homes, occasionally yawn up from wide stretches of grassy fields.

The last stretch of road before tiny **Monólithos**, near the airport (a 45-minute walk from Firá), is lined with hollowed-out sandstone formations that emit eerie piping noises when the wind rushes through them. There's quite a good beach here too. One of the island's best tavernas, Psistaria O Kritikos, is further south near **Kamári**, a tourist resort with a good, if very crowded, beach. Buses run frequently, or you can take a taxi or tour for wine tastings at one of Santoríni's wineries. (Bus transportation on the island is unexpectedly good, with regular services augmented by excursion buses to places like Akrotíri.)

The blazing whiteness and sensual lines of Cycladic architecture are doubly disarming in Santoríni, against the smoky purple banks of the old lava, and from every port-side passage there is a sombre, fantastic view to be seen of the ocean-bound volcano with "Burnt Islands" at its centre. Lights twinkle across the strait on the islet of **Thirassía**, sparse in vegetation and inhabitants, seemingly many miles away from the tourist bustle of Santoríni. ❑

Volcanic Santoríni is believed by many to be the origin of the lost kingdom of Atlantis, which was swallowed up by the sea.

BELOW:
Firá at night.

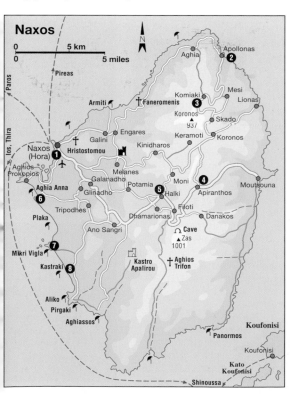

MIXING PIETY WITH PLEASURE

Greek religious festivals – and there are many – celebrate saints' days and other events in the religious calendar with devotion and high spirits

Greek island life is punctuated throughout the year by saints' days and religious festivals or *panighýri*. As there are around 300 saints in the Orthodox calendar, there is an excuse for a party most days of the year.

Easter is the most important festival (often preceded by a pre-Lenten carnival). It's a great time to visit, with traditional services marking the Resurrection everywhere from humble chapels to mighty monasteries. Colourful, noisy and potentially dangerous – in Kálymnos they throw dynamite to ensure Christ has truly risen – it's like Firework Night and Christmas rolled into one.

During Holy Week, or *Megáli Evdhomádha*, churches are festooned in black. On Maundy Thursday monks on Pátmos re-enact the washing of Christ's feet at the Last Supper. On Good Friday the *Epitáfios*, or bier of Christ, is decorated by women and paraded through the streets at dusk *(above)* as they sing hymns.

On Easter Saturday the churches are decked in white. On the stroke of midnight everything is plunged in darkness as the priest lights the first candle from the holy flame to represent the light of the world, and intones: *"Hristós anésti"* (Christ has risen). This is the signal for all the congregation to light their candles. Fireworks explode, rockets soar, dynamite sometimes shatters windows, and everyone plays conkers with their red-dyed eggs. Families then break the Lenten fast with Easter soup made from lamb's offal, with lemon, rice and spring onions.

On Easter Sunday there's great rejoicing as a lamb or kid is barbecued outdoors over charcoal with the usual music and dancing. There are often parties on Easter Monday, and in some islands an effigy of Judas is filled with fireworks and burned.

▽ **AFTER MIDNIGHT**
In the early hours of Easter Sunday, crowds head home in candle-lit processions. Families mark the sign of the cross over their door with their candle to bring good luck.

▷ **SCARLET SHELLS**
Hard-boiled eggs, dyed red to symbolise the blood of Christ, are cracked in a game like conkers on Easter Day.

◁ **EASTER TWISTS**
A sweet, twisted bread called *tsouréki* is made for Easter in various shapes, often with a red egg in the centre.

◁ MONDAY MAYHEM

"Clean Monday" is the end of the pre-Lenten carnival, with exuberant celebrations on some islands, including kite-flying and flour fights.

▽ STEPS TO SALVATION

Devout women crawl in penance to the church of the Panaghía Evangelístria on Tínos, at the feast of the Assumption in August.

◁ MOUNTAINTOP MASS

Saints' days are celebrated by *panighýri* (festivals) at hundreds of small chapels throughout the islands. Here, Cycladic islanders honour Aghía Marína, the protector of crops, on 17 July.

△ ALL DRESSED UP

In Ólymbos, the remote mountain village on Kárpathos, the eldest daughter or *kanakará* wears her traditional costume and dowry of gold coins for major festivals.

◁ EASTER PARADE

Priest and villagers join in traditional chants in an Easter procession on Páros.

CELEBRATING ALL YEAR ROUND

Greeks mix piety and pleasure with gusto for all their festivals, from the most important to the smallest fair. The biggest religious festival after Easter, the Assumption of the Virgin *(Panaghías)* on 15 August, draws Greeks home from all over the world.

Following the long liturgy on the night of the 14th, the icon of the Madonna is paraded and kissed. Then there's a communal feast – and the party can go on for days. The celebrations are spectacular in Kárpathos, with dazzling costumes, special dances and traditional songs.

Every month there are festivals on the islands for everything from sponges to snakes, and national holidays like *Óhi* or "No Day" (28 October), with patriotic parades to mark the Greeks' emphatic reply to Mussolini's surrender ultimatum.

Celebrations begin the night before feast days and everyone in the community takes part, from babies to grannies. Patron saints are honoured with services followed by barbecues, music and dance. The picture above shows the feast of Ághios Dimítris on Síkinos in October, which is conveniently when the first wine is ready to drink.

THE SPORADES AND ÉVVIA

Skiáthos, Skópelos, Alónissos, Skýros and Évvia

The Sporades – in English, "sporadic" or "scattered" – are a group of four islands in the northwest Aegean. Évvia, lying stretched along the Greek mainland to the south of the Sporades, is Greece's second largest island, after Crete.

Mainlanders have long recognised Skiáthos's beaches as the best in the Aegean and made an annual pilgrimage. They are now outnumbered by foreigners, and the fact that there are shops that sell nothing but expensive fur coats and will accept any conceivable credit card is a forecast of what to expect.

In spite of a rich history, Alónissos is the least developed island in terms of tourism, while Skópelos, more recently and self-consciously the senior partner among the trio, is a compromise. Skýros, the largest and in many ways the most interesting of the Sporades, is detached from the others. It is like a scaled-down version of Crete, with an independent spirit and a deeply entrenched local culture impervious to the events that constantly swirl around it. Évvia has not been spoilt by tourism. Its diverse landscape and rich history make it almost a microcosm of the whole country.

While hopping between Skiáthos, Skópelos and Alónissos is very easy, and Évvia has many connections to the nearby mainland, Skýros involves a longer trip; but they all are connected now by hydrofoil. Skiáthos alone among them has an international airport with several (charter) flights daily in summer, mainly from Britain, Germany and Scandinavia, and domestic connections. Skýros has an airport but, apart from a feeder service from Athens, it is reserved for the Greek Air Force. Ferries and hydrofoils run to all the islands from Vólos and Ághios Konstandínos on the mainland.

The islands are what's left of a mountain range which snapped away from the mainland in a geological convulsion and "sank". They lie within a narrow band where prevailing winds and other factors produce reliable rainfall and lush vegetation, notably pine forests. The rains do not intrude in summer. Instead, the *meltémi*, a northerly wind, helps to hold temperatures down a little.

The traditional trade route between the Mediterranean and the Black Sea via the Bosphorus passes the Sporades. Since antiquity, bad weather has brought unexpected and often unwanted callers, including distressed invasion fleets (for example, Xerxes) and pirates. Yet major archaeological sites are surprisingly few.

World War I produced a postscript to the strategic location: it was on a convoy heading for Gallipoli that the poet Rupert Brooke died. Skýros rose into view, and it was here that they buried him. ❑

PRECEDING PAGES: three Orthodox priests; in attendance at a traditional Greek baptism, Síkinos. **LEFT:** the Karababa Turkish castle near Halkídha, Évvia.

THE SPORADES

Once exclusive resorts for the rich and famous, the Sporades now attract Greek and foreign holidaymakers alike, whether for the nightlife of Skiáthos or the quieter charm of Alónissos

Map on page 200

Skiáthos

The scythe of **Koukounariés** is used as evidence on thousands of picture postcards that the Aegean can produce the kind of beach normally associated with the Caribbean. Propriety would prevent as many postcards from featuring **Krassí ❶** (colloquially "Banana Beach") because it caters for nudists. The fact that no one cares whether bathers at Banana Beach strip off or not is typical of the easy-going, relaxed nature of the people of Skiáthos as a whole.

The island has beaches for all occasions, not least because some among the supposed 60 will always be sheltered wherever the wind is coming from. Koukounariés and Banana Beach are near neighbours at the end of the twisting, busy 18-km (11-mile) coast road from the town; there are dozens of beaches along it and several more beyond, many with a taverna or at least a kiosk selling drinks and sandwiches. A path leading down from the road usually promises a beach at the end; with luck it won't be as crowded as Koukounariés.

Round-the-island boat trips pass the rocky and otherwise inaccessible northern shoreline where the only human construction is the **Kástro ❷**, the abandoned 16th-century capital once connected to the rest of the island by a single drawbridge. For 300 years the islanders huddled on this wind-buffeted crag, hoping the pirates would pass them by. During the last war Allied soldiers hid out there, waiting for evacuation by a friendly submarine. Nowadays it is an obligatory stop for the excursion caiques, after they have dipped into three technicolour grottoes and dropped anchor at **Lalaria**, a cove famous for its smooth, round stones, and before they proceed to a beach taverna for lunch.

A moped or hired car is necessary to follow the unpaved roads looping through the mountains. They provide stunning views as well as the chance to pop into monasteries which, with the Kástro, are more or less the only buildings of historic interest. Of these, the grandest and closest to town is **Evangelistría**, with the **Panaghía Kehrías** and **Kounístra** also worth a visit should the beaches pall.

The bluff above the quiet beach at the end of the very busy airport runway has produced fragments suggesting a prehistoric settlement, but neither it nor the rest of the island has ever been properly excavated. Fires started by the Nazis destroyed most of the pretty pre-war town.

But **Skiáthos ❸**, the port village, makes up in liveliness what it may lack in architectural merit. In fact, its nightlife is probably the most important consideration, after the beaches, for the type of visitor which Skiáthos attracts in large numbers in August. The preferences of the fast-living set change constantly,

LEFT: Skiáthos has beaches to rival the Caribbean.
BELOW: an ancient citizen of Skýros.

but it is not difficult to spot which places are in vogue at any particular time, whether one's preference is for beer and blues, wine and Vivaldi or tequila and 1950s rock and roll. The lights are brightest but also the tackiest along **Papadhiamántis**, the road that bisects the two hills on which the town stands, and along the *paralía* or waterfront. The atmosphere is a bit classier and quieter around **Polytéhniou** and the cobbled alleys above the port.

Expect restaurants, with international flavours as well as Greek, rather than tavernas and be prepared to pay accordingly, especially along the seafront. Plate-smashing and other forms of sociable anarchy are at a safe distance out of town; to the fury of taxi drivers and the regular bus operators, the tavernas concerned lay on special transport from the main dock.

Skópelos

Skópelos's traditional stone farmhouses (kalívia) all have distinctive outdoor ovens where the island's famous plums were dried to become prunes.

An enduring image of Skópelos, for anyone who has been there in August, is the way in which the famous local plum is picked, examined, wiped and, before being popped into the mouth, given a final polish with the thumb. And who, on sailing or driving along the coast between Glóssa and Skópelos town and knowing a particular local tale, would not be on the look-out for the spot which best fitted the dénouement?

It seems that a rampaging dragon had proved itself to be invulnerable to conventional weapons. The local priest, one Reginos, was implored to direct a sermon at the beast, the islanders having heard enough of them to think that it might do the trick. Finding itself as bored as they had been, the dragon reared away and fled until it could go no further. The pious Reginos followed doggedly and, on cornering his quarry on a clifftop, prepared to deliver another one. Despairing at the

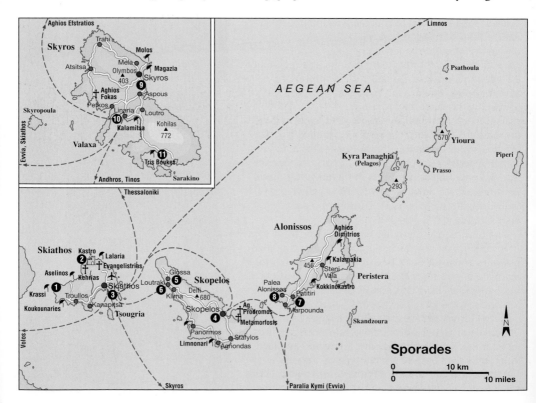

Map on page 200

prospect, the dragon dived off, and the impact on landing created one of the indentations which are characteristic of the deeply rugged coastline.

Visitors waiting in Vólos rather than Ághios Konstandínos for passage to Skópelos (the alternative is to fly to Skiáthos and catch a Flying Dolphin hydrofoil or ferry from there) might enjoy visiting the archaeological museum; on display are the contents of a grave discovered on the island fairly recently (Tues–Sun, 8.30am–3pm). The gold crown and ornate weapons almost certainly belonged to Stafylos, a Minoan who colonised Skópelos and then went on to be crowned its king.

The island's distinguished past is not so much demonstrated by prominent historical sites as by the exceptionally fine houses in **Skópelos town ❹**, a handsome amphitheatre around a harbour lined with bars and tavernas under mulberry trees. Skópelos escaped earthquakes and Nazi vindictiveness and is therefore the most "authentic" and traditional of the three northern Sporades (Skýros being in a class of its own). Slate roofs, wooden balconies, hand-painted shop signs and flagstone streets give it a serenity and dignity rarely found in Skiáthos in season. On the other hand, beaches are not the island's forte. It has far fewer than Skiáthos and Alónissos – mostly on the south and west coasts – though nudists are welcomed at **Velánio**, just beyond the family beach at **Stáfylos** (where the king's tomb was found). As compensation, Skópelos offers forested hills for spectacular walks to 40 monasteries and 360 churches, 123 of which are tucked among the houses above the port, which in turn is crowned by a Venetian castle planted on ancient foundations.

Glóssa ❺, the island's other town, is something of an oddity in that the people who live there have a pronounced dialect which, together with houses whose features are not like other island architecture, suggests that at some time they immigrated from Thessaly. They seem to have made themselves welcome: other islanders refer approvingly to their "exaggerated hospitality".

The main road on the island runs south from the port of **Loutráki ❻**, where Glóssa used to stand before it moved up the mountain for safety's sake, along the west coast, then loops back to Skópelos town. It is an attractive run which includes a number of hamlets, beaches and **Panórmos**, where there are a few remains of a city which probably existed in 500 BC. The wise money is on the dragon having made its desperate departing leap somewhere around Panórmou Bay. Now yachts park in one of its fjordlike inlets and tavernas ring its shores. Further south along the coast road, **Agnóndas** is a tiny harbour with beachside tavernas that are popular with locals.

Alónissos

This island is full of ghosts whispering what might have been. On the hill above **Patitíri ❼**, the last port on the Vólos/Ághios Konstandínos ferry and hydrofoil routes, is the **Hóra**, also called **Paleá Alónissos ❽**, the former capital destroyed by an earthquake in 1965. This compounded the blow the islanders had already suffered when all their grapevines withered and died from phylloxera only 15 years earlier.

Alónissos seems to have been ever thus: the previous capital, Ikos, literally disappeared when the

BELOW: Skiáthos harbour.

ground on which it stood toppled into the sea. The submerged remains of the capital, off **Kokkinókastro** beach, are an important part of the Sporades Marine Park, and may be explored with a snorkel but not with scuba tanks (this is a general rule in protected parts of the Aegean to prevent pilfering and damage). The Sporades Marine Park was established in 1992 around Alónissos and neighbouring islands. The main aim of the park is to provide sanctuary, and conserve declining fish stocks, for the severely endangered Mediterranean monk seal, of which there are less than 500 worldwide.

Of the famous wines which were once shipped all over ancient Greece in urns stamped "Ikion", there is no longer any trace. Yet in 1970, paleolithic evidence was found which could mean that Alónissos was singled out for habitation before any other island in the Aegean, perhaps as early as 100,000 BC, and it was considered a prize over which Philip of Macedon and the Athenians fought bitterly.

The way the island has adjusted to its unrealised potential and bad luck is something for which many visitors should be grateful. Its people are laid-back and charming, its atmosphere cheerful and unpretentious. It is also the least developed of the Sporades, a much quieter island surrounded by an interesting collection of islets. Some of them are off-limits to tourists and fishermen alike, protected areas within the Marine Park reserved for the endangered monk seal and other rare fauna. **Yioura**, for example, is home to a unique breed of wild goat and also has a cave that is full of stalactites and stalagmites – some islanders like to believe it was once occupied by a protective cyclops. The cave and the islet of **Pipéri** may not be visited, but caiques leave Patitíri on calm days for excursions to the closer islets of **Peristéra** and **Kyrá Panaghía**, where sheep roam and there are a couple of monasteries to glimpse.

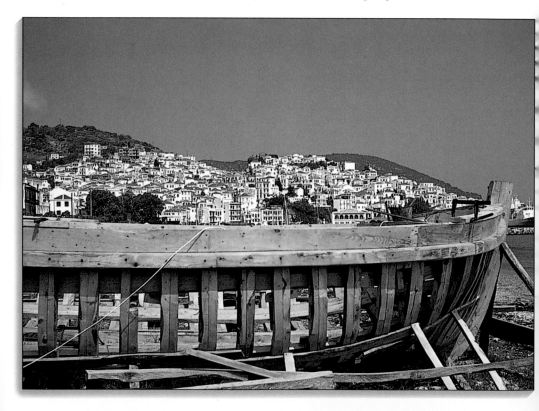

The fishing round Alónissos is excellent too, and many swordfish are taken in the waters around the island. In the absence of proper roads, apart from the one to **Stení Vála**, caiques are the most practical form of transport. There is a fleet of them waiting every morning at Patitíri to take bathers to the beach of their choice. The terrain is rugged and walking therefore quite demanding, but motorbiking is much safer here than on the winding roads of Skiáthos and Skópelos.

The path from Patitíri up to Paleá Alónissos is steep, but the old town is served by a bus and is well worth a visit. Thanks largely to the efforts of foreigners who spied a bargain and bought up the old ruins, it is fast coming back to life. Boutiques are springing up in once-abandoned courtyards, and there are several bars and tavernas commanding stunning views, as well as providing restorative drinks and delicious food.

Skýros

The main character in Skýros's Carnival goat dance, staged just before Lent, is a *yéros* (old man) who wears a mask made out of goat skin; by shaking his hips he rings the many sheep bells hanging from his waist. The second figure is the *koréla*, a young man dressed and behaving as a woman. Foreign visitors enjoying the spectacle ought to know that the third figure (the *frángos*), a buffoon who has a large bell strapped to his back and blows into a seashell, represents, well, a foreigner. Islanders might politely point out, however, that he is specifically a western European of the 17th century.

Visitors should not take the mockery to heart. Skýros does not have to put up with so many of them that their presence becomes intrusive, and in many ways the island goes on in its own sweet way as it has always done. The Greek Air

Map on page 200

Skýros has some unique miniature horses, which have been bred exclusively on the island since ancient times. They may be the same breed as the horses depicted on the Parthenon frieze.

BELOW: the Faltaïts Museum above Skýros town.

Map on page 200

The Faltaïts Museum (summer: daily 10am–1pm and 6–9pm; winter: 10am–1pm and 5.30–8pm), in a mansion north of town, is a private collection presenting the life of the island through local art and crafts, books, costumes and photographs.

BELOW: sunset over the Aegean. **RIGHT:** carnival characters.

Force, for instance, has taken over what was once a lovely beach at the northern edge of the island, but nobody will be aware of their presence except on the rare occasion when a pilot buzzes the **Magaziá** beach on the northeast coast, below Skýros town. The Skyrians are more interested in the quietly growing strength of their summer season, and their own way of life. Older islanders will still wear traditional clothes as a matter of course.

Behind their characteristic pebbled entrances the cubist houses contain amazing collections of craft work and other prized objects, many of them originally pirate booty. Carved wooden furniture passed down though the generations is often rather too small to be practical, so the islanders hang a lot of it on the walls. The Skyrians also produce wonderful pottery, which you can find in a couple of shops along the main street up in town and from two producers down in the Magaziá area near the Hotel Hydroussa in Skýros town.

Skýros town ❾ is on the northern half of the island on the east coast, high above the long sand beach at the Magaziá. Life in the town is played out all along the meandering main street, which runs from the telephone exchange (OTE) past the raised, largely ignored square to the northern edge of town, where a statue of a naked man representing Immortal Poetry (in memory of Rupert Brooke, who is buried on the island, *see below*) commands the view. A side street wanders up to the **kástro**, the old Byzantine/Venetian castle on the heights from which, in legend, Theseus was thrown to his death.

The beach below town runs from the Magaziá all the way down to **Mólos**, and there are some more stretches of beach, although not as attractive, farther along the northeast coast near **Polýhri**. On the west side of the island there are pleasant sandy coves at **Linariá ❿**, just past the port, and **Péfkos**. The central section of this part of the island is wooded, as is the northern coast from just past the airport down to the little bay of **Atsítsa** which has, as required, a little taverna by the water.

Skýros was probably originally two islands, the halves joining near where there is now a road linking Linariá, the main port, with the little village of **Aspoús** on the way to Skýros town. The southern sector of the island is mountainous and largely barren, and visitors are unlikely to venture below **Kolimbádha** unless they are heading for **Pénnes** beach or **Trís Boúkes ⓫**.

Trís Boúkes, the site of **Rupert Brooke's grave**, is about a 30-minute drive from Kolimbádha, and Pénnes another 15 minutes more over a reasonable, wide dirt road. The beaches at **Paghiá** and **Skloúka** just north of Kolimbádha are lined with a growing number of summer homes but have none of the appeal of the beaches in the north of the island. The real appeal of the southern part of Skýros is from the sea, for cliffs along most of the coast, from Pénnes all the way around to Achílli Bay near Aspoús, fall straight down into the sea. These cliffs are inhabited by a few wild goats and seemingly innumerable Eleanora's Falcons, which can be seen darting around the heights all the way over to Skýros town. Excursions by boat can be arranged at Linariá, where the ferries dock. ❑

ÉVVIA

*Greece's second largest island is largely unspoilt by tourism,
and little known by outsiders. Although it is barely separated
from the mainland, Évvia has a rich, independent history*

O n the map, Évvia (Euboea) looks like a large jigsaw puzzle piece just
slightly out of position. The island's main town, Halkídha, is close enough
to the mainland for an elderly drawbridge and a new suspension bridge to
make easy connection. Aristotle is supposed to have been so frustrated in trying to understand the tides here in the narrow channel, which are highly irregular and sometimes quite fast, that he killed himself by jumping into the waters.

In antiquity the two most prominent cities were Chalcis (modern Halkídha)
and nearby Eretria, both of which became powerful trading cities, establishing
colonies in Syria, the Aegean islands, Italy and Sicily. After the Persian wars
Évvia came under Athenian control, from which it revolted in 411 BC. Thereafter
it was under either Athenian or Theban rule until the Macedonians arrived in 338
BC, then the Romans in 194 BC. This evolved into Byzantine control, which
lasted until the Venetians captured the island in 1210. The Venetians ruled the
island for over 250 years, until it was taken by the Ottoman Turks in 1470.
Évvia became part of Greece in 1830, after the Greek War of Independence.

Halkídha (**Halkís, Chalkís**) ❶ is now an industrial town, but the **kástro**,
with its **Emir Jade** mosque (now a museum), and the **Church of Aghía
Paraskeví** are worth visiting, as is the **Archaeological Museum** in the new
town (Tues–Sun 8.30am–3pm). There is also a syna-
gogue, built in the middle of the 19th century and still
used by the last few members of the Jewish Roman-
iote community. **Erétria** ❷ to the south is a crowded
summer resort where the ferries land from Skála
Oropoú on the mainland. This is a town to pass
through (as is Halkídha), but the small **Archaeological Museum** is very good (Tues–Sun 8.30am–3pm).

The road south along the gentle coast is dotted with
villages and summer homes until just before **Alivéri**
where it turns inland. From **Lépoura** to the north, the
main road goes through the hamlet of **Háni
Avlonaríou**, with the large and unusual 14th-century
Church of Ághios Dimitríos, before continuing
through often beautiful hilly farmland to drop down to
the east coast village of **Paralía** (or Stómio), where a
small river reaches the sea. The wide new road then
runs along the shore, through **Platána**, to the harbour
at **Paralía Kymi** and the boat to Skýros.

In general, the southern part of the island is drier
and less green. The turning for the south is at
Lépoura. On the main road between **Almyropóta-
mos** and **Polypótamos** along the narrowest part of
the island, there are views from the road down to the
sea on both the east and the west. Near the village of
Stýra ❸ are the ruins of three buildings of huge
stone, known locally as Dragon Houses (*dhraóspita*).
These remains are of great age but unknown date.

BELOW: the new
bridge to Halkídha.

Map below

Neá Stýra, 4 km (2½ miles) away on the coast, is a resort town with direct ferry connections (40 minutes) to the small port of Aghía Marína on the west coast of Attica. **Marmári**, another resort/port village farther down the coast, has frequent ferry boat connections with Rafína (1 hour 15 minutes). The main town in the south is the prosperous town of **Kárystos ❹** with a long beach, also connecting with Rafína on the mainland.

North of Halkídha, the small village of **Stení ❺** on the slopes of **Mount Dhírfys** (1,743 metres/5,718 ft), is a favourite goal for Athenians seeking clean air and grill restaurants. **Prokópi ❻**, on the main road, was built beside the Keréa River on land purchased by Englishman Edward Noel in the 1830s. The old family home of the Noel-Bakers, his descendants, is now available for holiday lets, and pottery, painting and yoga courses are run on the estate. The town was settled after 1923 by refugees from Asia Minor who brought with them the relics of an 18th-century saint, St John the Russian, canonised in 1962. The saint's relics are in the unattractive cement church in the central square.

Límni ❼ on the west coast is a pretty and convenient 19th-century town, though the nearby beaches are unimpressive. A long stretch of truly outstanding beach is farther north, after the ancient but still functioning baths at **Loutrá Edhipsoú ❽**, from **Gregolímano** and **Aghios Yeórghios** all the way around the triangular point of the peninsula. The east coast is mountainous, dropping sharply to the sea, but there are a few beaches, such as **Angáli**, **Paralía Kotsikiás**, **Psaropoúli** and **Ellinká**, of which the last is the smallest and prettiest.

The famous bronze statue of Poseidon poised to throw a trident, now in the Archaeological Museum in Athens *(see page 114)*, was found in 1928 in the sea off **Cape Artemesion** (Ákti Artemíssio) on the northern coast. ❏

Prokópi is famed for its honey, which you can buy in the village in a variety of flavours, including thyme, orange-flower and pine.

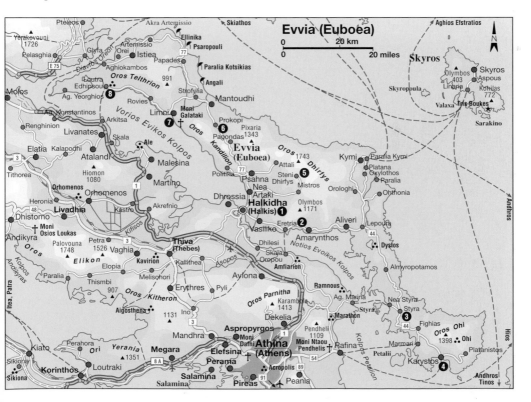

Evvia (Euboea)

THE NORTHEAST AEGEAN

Thássos, Samothráki, Límnos, Ághios Efstrátios,
Lésvos, Psará, Híos, Ikaría, Sámos

The islands of the northeast Aegean have little in common other than a history of medieval Genoese rule. The northerly group, comprising Thássos, Samothráki and Límnos, has few or no connections with the south Aegean; indeed Thássos belongs to the Macedonian province of Kavála, and Samothráki to Thracian Évros. This close to the mainland, and with a short summer season, the Greeks' own affection for these convenient islands takes precedence over foreign package tourism. Except for marble-cored Thássos, these isles – as well as Lésvos – are of volcanic origin, their gentle slopes thinly covered by lava-tolerant oak trees.

Lésvos, Híos and Sámos to the southeast once played leading roles in antiquity, colonising across the Mediterranean and promoting the arts and sciences, though little tangible evidence of ancient glory remains. All three islands served as bridges between Asia Minor and the rest of the Hellenic world and were, in fact, once joined to the coast of Asia Minor until Ice-Age cataclysms isolated them. Turkey is still omnipresent on the horizon, just 2 km (1 mile) away across the Mykale straits at Sámos. Politically, however, the two countries are often light years apart, something reflected in absurdly inflated fares for the short boat trip across.

Híos, Sámos and Ikaría are rugged limestone and schist (with a bit of granite too on Ikaría), forested with pine, olive and cypress. Delicate spring and autumn wildflowers, especially on Sámos, heighten their appeal, and numerous small mammals and birds thrive, having migrated over from Anatolia before the rising sea marooned them. Beaches, fairly evenly distributed across the group, vary from long shores of fist-sized pebbles to sheltered, sandy crescents.

As ever, transport to, between and on the bigger islands varies with the population and level of tourism. Samothráki has a skeletal bus service and overpriced ferries from Alexandhroúpoli; Thássos by contrast has frequent buses and regular car ferries from Kavála and Keramotí. Límnos and Lésvos have regular flights and sailings from Piraeus and Thessaloníki, plus each other; Híos is linked daily with Athens and Lésvos, less regularly with Sámos or Ikaría, and – unlike northern neighbours – not at all by charter to northern Europe. Ikaría is similarly remote, though like adjacent Sámos it is connected to certain Cyclades. Sámos itself could rank as an honorary Dodecanese island: it has ferry and hydrofoil links with all isles from Pátmos to Kós, and receives far more international charters than runner-up Lésvos. ❏

PRECEDING PAGES: the Roman aquaduct on Lésvos; a grim reminder of the 1822 massacre on Híos. **LEFT:** votive candles burn in Mytilíni's fortress chapel, Lésvos.

THÁSSOS, SAMOTHRÁKI AND LÍMNOS

Map
on page
216

*Greece's most northerly islands do not see much package
tourism, but they offer more than enough by way of ancient
ruins, empty beaches and picturesque villages*

Thássos

Just seven nautical miles (12 km) from mainland Macedonia, Thássos – always
a favourite retreat of northern Greeks – has recently welcomed a cosmopolitan
assortment of foreigners. Yet the island seems relatively unspoiled, with package
tourism well quarantined. Mountainous, almost circular, Thássos is essentially a
giant lump of marble, mixed with granite and schist, crumbling into white beach
sand at the island's margins. Lower elevations, covered in vast olive plantations, remain attractive, but "the Diamond of the North" *(Dhiamándis tou Vorrá)*
had its lustre severely dulled by forest fires in 1981, 1985, 1989 and 1993,
which were deliberately set by developers wanting cheap building land. Thássos is now three-quarters denuded of its original pine forest, which survives
only in the northeast. Elsewhere, only the inland villages and a thin fringe of surrounding vegetation were saved. The bus service around the coastal ring road is
adequate, though most visitors rent motorbikes or cars (Thássos is small enough
for a long day tour). The east and south coasts have the better beaches; the west
coast has access to most inland villages.

LEFT: Hóra
(Samothráki) at
sunset. **BELOW:**
off-season sewing.

Thássos' past glory is most evident at the harbour
capital of **Liménas** (or **Limín**, also known simply as
Thássos) ❶, where substantial remnants of the ancient
town have been excavated; choice bits of the ruined
acropolis overhead are illuminated at night. The
biggest area, behind the picturesque fishing harbour
which traces the confines of the old commercial port,
is the **agora**. The nearby archaeological museum is
closed indefinitely for a major overhaul to accommodate a backlog of finds.

Beginning at the **Temple of Dionysos**, a path permits a rewarding walking tour of the ancient walls
and acropolis. First stop is the Hellenistic **theatre**
(open but dug up for re-excavation). Continue to the
medieval fortress, built by a succession of occupiers
from the masonry of a temple of Apollo. Tracing the
course of massive 5th-century BC walls brings you to
the foundations of a **temple of Athena**, beyond which
a rock outcrop bears a **shrine of Pan**, visible in badly
eroded relief. From here a vertiginous "secret" stairway plunges to the **Gate of Parmenon**, the only
ancient entry still intact, at the southern edge of town.

The first village clockwise from Liménas, slate-
roofed **Panaghía** ❷, is a large, busy place where life
revolves around the *platía*, with its plane trees and
four-spouted fountain. **Potamiá**, further down the valley, is far less architecturally distinguished: visitors
come mainly for the sake of the **Polygnotos Vaghis**

Museum (summer: Tues–Sat 9.30am–12.30pm, 6–9pm; Sun 10am–1pm; winter: mornings only), featuring the work of the eponymous locally-born sculptor. Beyond, the road plunges to the coast at Potamiá Bay.

Locally made honey, candied walnuts and tsípouro, the firewater of northern Greece, are favourite souvenirs of Thássos.

Skála Potamiás, at its south end, is all lodging and tavernas, with more of that to the north at **Hryssí Ammoudhiá**. In between stretches a fine, blond-sand beach. There are even better strands at **Kínyra**, 24 km (15 miles) from Liménas, but most one-day tourists schedule a lunch stop at one of the several tavernas of **Alykí ❸** hamlet, architecturally preserved thanks to adjacent ruins: an ancient temple and two atmospheric Byzantine basilicas. The local topography of a low spit, sandy to the west, nearly pinching off a headland, is strikingly photogenic. So too is the **Convent of Arhangélou Miháïl** 5 km (3 miles) to the west, high above a barren coast – but mainly from a distance; it has been renovated rather hideously since 1974.

At **Limenária ❹**, now the island's second town, mansions of departed German mining executives survive. More intriguingly, perhaps, it's the starting-

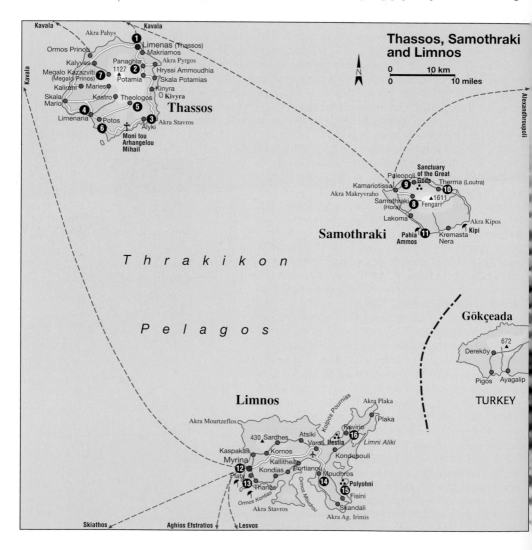

Map on page 216

point for a safari up to hilltop **Kástro**, the most naturally pirate-proof of the inland villages. Beyond Limenária, there's little to compel a stop other than side roads up to the villages from their *skáles*, relatively recent – and scraggy – shore settlements built once the seas had been cleared of marauders.

Theológos ❺, actually reached from the over-developed resort of **Potós ❻**, was the island's Ottoman capital, a linear place where most houses have walled gardens. **Mariés** sits piled up at the top of a wooded valley, just glimpsing the sea. By contrast **Sotíros** enjoys phenomenal sunsets, best enjoyed from its central taverna under enormous plane trees. Of all the inland settlements, **Megálo Kazazvíti** (officially **Megálo Prínos**) ❼ has the grandest *platía* and the best-preserved traditional houses, snapped up and restored by outsiders. Ground-floor windows still retain iron bars, reminders of pirate days.

Samothráki

Samothráki (or Samothrace) raises forbidding granite heights above stony shores and storm-lashed waters, both offering poor natural anchorage. Homer described Poseidon perched atop 1,611-metre (5,285-ft) **Mount Fengári**, the Aegean's highest summit, watching the action of the Trojan War to the east. Fengári and its foothills occupy much of the island, with little level terrain except in the far west. Its southwest flank features scattered villages lost amid olive groves varied by the occasional poplar. North-facing slopes are damper, with chestnuts and oaks, plus plane trees along the numerous watercourses. Springs are abundant, and waterfalls even plunge directly to the sea at **Kremastá Nerá** in the south. Only the west of the island has a rudimentary bus service, though most roads are paved now.

Tourism is barely developed, and the remaining islanders prefer it that way. In its absence the population has dipped below 3,000, as farming can only support so many. Boats and occasional hydrofoils dock at **Kamariótissa**, the functional port where rental vehicles are in short supply.

Hóra or **Samothráki ❽**, the official capital 5 km (3 miles) east of Kamariótissa, is more rewarding, nestling almost invisibly in a circular hollow. A cobbled commercial street serpentines past sturdy, basalt-built houses, many now unused. From outdoor seating at the two tavernas on Hóra's large *platía*, you glimpse the sea beyond a crumbled Byzantine-Genoese fort at the edge of town.

Samothráki's other great sight lies just outside the ancient capital **Paleópoli ❾**, 6 km (3½ miles) from Kamariótissa along the north-coast road. From the late Bronze Age until the coming of Christianity, the **Sanctuary of the Great Gods** was the major religious centre of the Aegean. Local deities of the original Thracian settlers were easily syncretised with the Olympian gods of later Aeolian colonists, in particular the Kabiri, or divine twins Castor and Pollux, patrons of seafarers (who needed all the help they could get in the habitually rough seas hereabouts).

The sanctuary ruins (Tues–Sun 8.30am–sunset) visible today are mostly late Hellenistic, and still eerily impressive, though overgrown. Obvious monuments include a partly re-erected temple of the second initiation; the peculiar round *Arsinoeion*, used for

Unlike the elitist Eleusinian Mysteries, the Samothracian cult of the Kabiri was open to all comers, including women and slaves. But, as at Eleusis, the details of the rites are unknown, for adherents took a vow of silence.

BELOW: the hamlet of Kástro, Thássos.

sacrifices; a round theatre area, for performances during the summer festival; and the fountain niche where the celebrated Winged Victory of Samothrace, now in the Louvre, was discovered.

Some 6 km (3½ miles) further east, hot springs, cool cascades and a dense canopy of plane trees make the spa hamlet of **Thermá** (**Loutrá**) ❿, the most popular base on the island, patronised by an uneasy mix of the elderly infirm and young bohemian types from several nations. Hot baths come in three temperatures and styles – including outdoor pools under a wooden shelter – while cold-plunge fanatics make for **Gría Váthra** canyon to the east. Thermá is also the base camp for the climb of Mount Fengári, a six-hour round-trip.

The villages south of Hóra see few visitors, though they lie astride the route to **Pahiá Ámmos** ⓫, the island's only sandy beach. From **Lákoma** village, it's about 8 km (5 miles) by improved track to the beach, where a single seasonal taverna operates. Beyond Pahiá Ámmos, you can walk to smaller **Vátos** nudist beach, but you'll need a boat – or to drive clockwise completely around Samothráki – to reach the gravel beach of **Kípi** in the far southeast.

Límnos

Dominating the approaches to the Dardanelles, Límnos has been occupied since Neolithic times, and always prospered as a trading station and military outpost, rather than a major political power. The Greek military still controls much of the island's extent, including half of the huge airport, belying an otherwise peaceful atmosphere. The volcanic soil dwindles to excellent beaches, or produces excellent wine and a variety of other farm products. The surrounding seas yield plenty of fish, thanks to periodic migrations through the Dardanelles.

Most things of interest are found in the port-capital, **Mýrina** ⓬, or a short distance to either side – luckily, since the bus service is appalling. Volcanic stone has been put to good use in the older houses and street cobbles of Mýrina, while elaborate Ottoman mansions face the northerly town beach of **Romeïkós Yialós**, with its popular cafés. The southerly beach of **Tourkikós Yialós** abuts the fishing port and contains half a dozen seafood tavernas.

Mýrina's admirable **Archaeological Museum** (daily 8am–7pm) holds finds from the island's major dig sites. Public evidence of the town's Ottoman period is limited to an inscribed fountain and a dilapidated, circular dervish hall behind a supermarket, both near the harbour end of the long market street. Festooned over the headland above town, the ruined local **kástro** is worth climbing up to for sunset views.

The road north from Mýrina passes the exclusive **Aktí Mýrina** resort en route to good beaches at **Avlónas** and **Ághios Ioánnis**. In the opposite direction lie even better ones at **Platý** ⓭ and **Thános**, with tiered namesake villages on the hillsides just above. Continuing southeast from Thános brings you to **Evgátis**, acknowledged as the island's best beach.

Sadder relics of more recent history flank the drab port town of **Moúdhros** ⓮ – two Allied cemeteries maintained by the Commonwealth War Graves Commission. During World War I, Moúdhros was the

The 4th-century BC statue of Victory (Athena Nike) was discovered in 1863 by a French diplomat, Charles Champoiseau, who immediately sent it to Paris. The Greek government has long demanded its return, but so far has had to settle for a plaster copy.

BELOW: a figure near Thermá, Samothráki, points to the coastal campsite.

Map
on page
216

principal base for the disastrous Gallipoli campaign. Of roughly 36,000 casualties, 887 are interred outside Moúdhros town on the way to **Roussopoúli**, while 348 more lie behind the village church at **Portianoú**, across the bay.

The major archaeological sites on Límnos are all a long trip away, in the far east of the island. **Polyóhni** ⓯, southwest of Roussopoúli, was a fortified town even older than Troy, but was destroyed by an earthquake in 2100 BC and never rebuilt. **Ifestía** on the north coast was the ancient capital and the largest city on the island until the Byzantine period. The foundations of a temple of Hephaistos and a Roman theatre are visible. Across the bay at **Kavírio** ⓰ was a sanctuary to the Kabiri, the Great Gods. Not much remains to be seen except the stumps and bases of columns.

A tiny wedge of land south of Límnos, **Ághios Efstrátios (Aï Strátis)** is without doubt the most desolate spot in the Northeast Aegean – all the more so since a 1967 earthquake devastated the single village. Owing to junta-era corruption, reparable dwellings were bulldozed and the surviving inhabitants (nearly half were killed) provided with ugly, prefabricated replacement housing on a grid plan. This, plus two dozen surviving old buildings on the left, is what you see if you disembark from the regular ferries stopping here on the Rafína-Límnos-Kavála route, or (in summer) the small ferry based in Límnos – together these constitute Aï Strátis's lifeline, as all supplies must be imported.

Fish are the only thing in local abundance. There's little arable land aside from the valley partly clogged by the prefabs. This inevitably sad settlement can muster perhaps 200 permanent residents. There are a couple of taverna-cafés and three pensions for tourists, most of them Greek. None of the beaches, within 90 minutes' walk to north or south, is likely to contain another soul. ❑

In the Polyóhni ruins, archaeologists discovered a hoard of gold jewellery from the 3rd millennium BC. It is now on display in Athens.

BELOW: an old boat-builder's yard on Límnos.

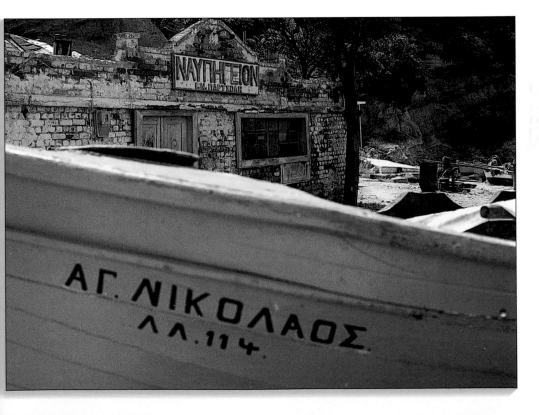

LÉSVOS, HÍOS, IKARÍA AND SÁMOS

These were some of Ancient Greece's wealthiest islands, and there are many impressive relics of their former prosperity, as well as reminders of their dramatic, more recent history

Map on page 222

Lésvos

Greece's third largest island, measuring 70 by 40 km (43 by 25 miles) at its extremities, Lésvos is the antithesis of the *nisáki* or quaint little islet. Between far-flung villages lie 11 million olive trees producing 45,000 tonnes of oil every year. Shipbuilding, carpentry, ouzo-distilling and pottery remain important, but none rivals the olive, especially since it complements the second industry of tourism. Nets to catch this "black gold" are laid out in autumn, as soon as the tourists leave.

With its thick southern forests and idyllic orchards, Lésvos was a preferred Roman holiday spot. The Byzantines considered it a humane exile for deposed nobility, while the Genoese Gattilusi clan kept a thriving court here for a century. To the Ottomans it was "the Garden of the Aegean", their most productive, strictly governed and heavily colonised Aegean island.

Following 18th-century reforms within the empire, a Christian land-owning aristocracy developed, served by a large population of labouring peasants. This quasi-feudal system made Lésvos fertile ground for post-1912 Leftist movements, and its habit of returning Communist MPs since the junta fell has earned it the epithet "Red Island" among fellow Greeks. The years after 1912 also saw a vital local intelligentsia emerge, but since World War II Lésvos's socio-economic fabric has shrunk considerably with emigration to Athens, Australia and America. However, the founding here in 1987 of the University of the Aegean brought hope for a cultural revival.

LEFT: a mosaic from Néa Moní, Híos.
BELOW: a beach in the Gulf of Yéra, southeast Lésvos.

Mytilíni ❶, the capital (its name a popular alias for the entire island), has a revved-up, slightly gritty atmosphere, as befits a port town of 30,000. It's interesting to stroll around, though few outsiders stay. Behind the waterfront, assorted church domes and spires enliven the skyline, while Odhós Ermoú one street inland contains an entire bazaar, from the fish market to a clutch of excellent but pricey antique shops. On the headland to the northeast sits the medieval **kástro** (Tues–Sun 8am–2.30pm), with ruins from various eras. Behind the ferry dock is the two-wing **Archaeological Museum** (summer: daily 8am–7pm; winter: Tues–Sun 8.30am–3pm) featuring Hellenistic mosaics depicting scenes from Menander's comedies and interesting grave *stelae*.

More noteworthy are two museums at Variá, 4 km (2½ miles) south of town. The **Theophilos Museum** (Tues–Sun 9am–2pm, 5–8pm, free Sun) contains more than 60 paintings by locally-born Theophilos Hazimihaïl, Greece's most celebrated naïve painter.

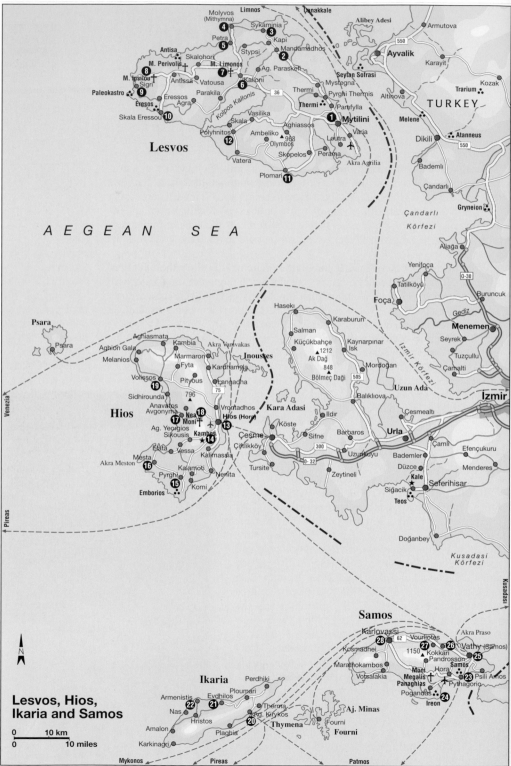

The adjacent **Thériade Museum-Library** (Tues–Sun 9am–2pm, 5–8pm) was founded by another native son who, while an avant-garde art publisher in Paris, assembled this collection, with work by Chagall, Picasso, Léger and others.

The road running northwest from Mytilíni follows the coast facing Turkey. **Mandamádhos ❷**, 37 km (23 miles) from Mytilíni, offers a surviving pottery industry and, on the outskirts, the enormous **Monastery of the Taxiárhis**, with its much-revered black icon. At **Kápi** the road divides; the northerly fork is wider, better paved and more scenic as it curls across the flanks of Mount Lepétymnos, passing by the handsome village of **Sykaminiá ❸**, the birthplace of novelist Stratis Myrivilis.

You descend to sea level at **Mólyvos** (sometimes known by its ancient name, **Míthymna**) **❹**, the linchpin of Lésvos tourism and understandably so: the ranks of sturdy tiled houses climbing to the medieval castle are an appealing sight, as is the stone-paved fishing harbour. But its days as a colony for bohemian artists and alternative activities are over, with package tourism dominant since the late 1980s. **Pétra ❺**, 5 km (3 miles) south, accommodates the overflow on its long beach; inland at the village centre looms a rock plug crowned with the **Panaghía Glykofiloússa** church. At its foot the 18th-century **Vareltzídena Mansion** (summer: Tues–Sun 8.30am–7pm, closes earlier in winter) is worth a look, as is the frescoed church of **Ághios Nikólaos**.

From Pétra, head 17 km (11 miles) south to **Kallóní ❻** and the turning for **Límonos Monastery ❼**, home to small ecclesiastical and folklore museums, before continuing west towards the more rugged half of the island, with its lunar volcanic terrain. Stream valleys foster little oases, such as the one around **Perivolís Monastery** (daily 8am–7pm), 30 km (19 miles) from Limónos,

Map on page 222

The Theophilos Museum in Mytilíni contains the largest collection of works by Greece's most famous naïve painter.

BELOW: the harbour of Mytilíni.

Lésvos claims to produce the finest olive oil in all Greece. The olives are harvested in November and December, and pressed within 24 hours of being picked.

decorated with wonderful frescoes. After 10 km (6 miles), on top of an extinct volcano, the **Monastery of Ipsiloú** ❽ contemplates the abomination of desolation – complete with scattered trunks of the "Petrified Forest", prehistoric sequoias mineralised by volcanic ash.

Sígri ❾, 90 km (56 miles) from Mytilíni, is a sleepy place flanked by good beaches, and very much the end of the line, though it has recently become an alternative ferry port. Most people prefer **Skála Eressoú** ❿, 14 km (9 miles) south of Ipsiloú, for a beach experience. In particular, numerous lesbians come to honour Sappho, who was born here.

Southern Lésvos, between the two gulfs, is home to olive groves rolling up to 968-metre (3,176-ft) Mount Ólymbos. **Plomári** ⓫ on the coast is Lésvos' second town, famous for its ouzo industry. Most tourists stay at pebble-beach **Ághios Isídhoros** 3 km (2 miles) east, though **Melínda** 6 km (4 miles) west is more scenic. **Vaterá**, with its 7-km (4½-mile) sand beach reckoned the best on the island, lies still further west, reached by a different road. En route, you can stop for a soak at the restored medieval spa outside **Polyhnítos** ⓬, 45 km (28 miles) from Mytilíni. Inland from Plomári, the remarkable hill village of **Aghiássos** nestles in a wooded valley under Ólymbos. Its heart is the major pilgrimage church of **Panaghía Vrefokratoússa**, which comes alive for the 15 August festival, Lésvos' biggest. Local musicians are considered among the island's best; they're evident at the pre-Lenten carnival as well, celebrated here with gusto.

Híos

BELOW: a distinctive church in Pyrghí.

Although Híos (often spelt Chíos) had been important and prosperous since antiquity, the Middle Ages made the Híos of today. After the Genoese seized control here in 1346, the Giustiniani clan established a cartel, the *maona*, which controlled the highly profitable trade in gum mastic. During their rule, which also saw the introduction of silk and citrus production, Híos became one of the wealthiest and most cultured islands in the Mediterranean.

In 1566 the Ottomans expelled the Genoese, but granted the islanders numerous privileges, so that Híos continued to flourish until March 1822, when poorly armed agitators from Sámos convinced the reluctant Hiots to participate in the independence uprising. Sultan Mahmut II, enraged at this ingratitude, exacted a terrible revenge. A two-month rampage commanded by Admiral Kara Ali killed 30,000 islanders, enslaved 45,000 more, and saw all settlements except the mastic-producing villages razed. Híos had only partly recovered when a strong earthquake in March 1881 destroyed much of what remained and killed 4,000.

Today Híos and its satellite islet Inoússes are home to some of Greece's wealthiest shipping families. The catastrophic 19th century ensured that **Híos town** or **Hóra** ⓭ (pop. 25,000) seems off-puttingly modern at first glance. But scratch the ferro-concrete surface and you'll find traces of the Genoese and Ottoman years. The most obvious medieval feature is the **kástro**. Moated on the landward side, it lacks a seaward rampart, destroyed after the 1881 earthquake.

Just inside the impressive **Porta Maggiora** stands the **Giustiniani Museum** (Tues–Sun 9am–3pm), a worthwhile collection of religious art rescued from rural churches. Off a small nearby square is the Muslim cemetery, with the tomb of Kara Ali – the massacring admiral, blown up along with his flagship by one of Admiral Kanaris's fire-boats in June 1822. Still further inside lies the old Muslim and Jewish quarter, with its derelict mosque and overhanging houses. Christians were required to settle outside the walls.

The lively bazaar extends south of central **Platía Vounakíou**, with Aplotariás as its backbone – fascinating alleys between this street and Venizélou culminate in a wonderful *belle époque* meat-and-produce gazebo. Also on Platía Vounakíou, the **Mecidiye Mosque** serves as a Byzantine Museum (Mon–Fri 9am–2pm), merely a warehouse for lapidary fragments; the **Archaeological Museum** (Tues–Sun 8.30am–2pm), well lit and laid-out, is more interesting.

Heading south out of Hóra you pass through **Kámbos** ⓮, a broad plain of high-walled citrus groves dotted with the imposing sandstone mansions of the medieval aristocracy, standing along narrow, unmarked lanes. Many were destroyed by the earthquake, while a few have been restored as accommodation or restaurants. Irrigation water was originally drawn up by *manganós* or water-wheel; a few survive in the centre of ornately paved courtyards.

The onward road heads southwest towards mastic-producing southern Híos, with the 20 villages collectively known as the *mastihohoriá*, built as pirate-proof strongholds by the Genoese during the 14th and 15th centuries. Each village is laid out on a dense, rectangular plan, with narrow passages over-arched by earthquake buttresses, and the backs of the outer houses doubling as the perimeter wall.

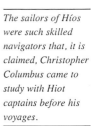
Map on page 222

The sailors of Híos were such skilled navigators that, it is claimed, Christopher Columbus came to study with Hiot captains before his voyages.

BELOW: stringing tomatoes to dry in Pyrghí, Híos.

Most of the houses in the mastic village of Pyrghí are incised with black and white geometric patterns, known as xistá.

BELOW:
scraping resin off a mastic tree.

Pyrghí ⑮, 21 km (13 miles) from Hóra, is one of the best-preserved *mastihohoriá*. A passageway off its central square leads to Byzantine **Ághii Apóstoli** church, decorated with later frescoes. In Pyrghí's back alleys, tomatoes are laboriously strung for drying in September by teams of local women. Some 11 km (7 miles) west, **Mestá ⑯** seems a more sombre, monochrome labyrinth, which retains defensive towers at its corners. Several three-storeyed houses have been restored as accommodation. Such quarters are typically claustrophobic, though, and guests will appreciate the nearby beach resorts of **Kómi** (sand) and **Emboriós** (volcanic pebbles).

With your own car, the beautiful, deserted west coast with its many coves is accessible via **Véssa**. Between **Kastélla** and **Elínda** bays, a good road snakes uphill to **Avgónyma ⑰**, a clustered village well restored by returned Greek-Americans. Just 4 km (2½ miles) north perches almost-deserted, crumbling **Anávatos**, well camouflaged against its cliff. Here in 1822, 400 Hiots leapt from it to their deaths rather than be captured.

Some 5 km (3 miles) east, **⑱** (summer: daily 8am–1pm, 4–8pm; winter: 8am–1pm, 4–6pm) forms one of the finest surviving examples of mid-Byzantine architecture, founded in 1049 by Emperor Constantine Monomachus IX on a spot where a miraculous icon of the Virgin had appeared. It suffered heavily in 1822 and 1881, first with the murder of its monks, plus the pillage of its treasures, and then with the collapse of its dome. Despite the damage, its mosaics of scenes from the life of Christ are outstanding. The outbuildings have lain in ruins since the events of the 19th century. By the gate, an ossuary displays the bones of the 1822 martyrs together with generations of monks. The paved road eventually takes you to castle-crowned **Volissós ⑲** in the northwest. To

UP A GUM TREE

The mastic bushes of southern Híos are the unique source of gum mastic, once the basis for many products: it was popular in Istanbul as chewing gum and was allegedly used to freshen the breath of the sultan's concubines; the Romans had their toothpicks made from mastic because they believed it kept their teeth white and prevented tooth decay; the "father of medicine", Hippocrates, praised its therapeutic value for coughs and colds; and lately some practitioners of alternative medicine have been making even more ambitious claims on its behalf.

The first stages of the mastic production process are basically unchanged since ancient times. The villagers set off from the *mastihohoriá* on late summer mornings, some on donkeys, some in pick-up trucks. They make incisions in the bark of the trees, which weep resin "tears". These are carefully scraped off and cleaned of leaves or twigs.

In the final stage, the raw gum is sent to a central processing plant where the "tears" are washed, baked and formed into "chiclets". Some 150 tons of mastic are produced annually, most of it exported to France, Bulgaria and Saudi Arabia for prices of up to $35 a kilo.

Map on page 222

either side of this half-empty village are the island's finest beaches – and visible scars from a series of 1980s fires which burnt two-thirds of Híos's forests.

Despite provincial appearances, the peaceful, green islet of **Inoússes** (Oinoússes), some 16 km (10 miles) north of Híos harbour by regular caique, is actually the wealthiest territory in Greece, home to the Livanos, Lemos and Pateras shipping families. Appropriately, a marine academy that trains many seamen for Greece's merchant fleet stands at the west end of the quay, with a small private maritime museum in the centre of the single town. Small but decent beaches lie to either side.

The tiny islet of **Psará**, 71 km (44 miles) to the west of Híos, derives its name from the adjective *psarós* (grey) – and a grey place it is, especially since 1824, when 14,000 Ottoman troops landed here to avenge continued harassment of their shipping by Psaran Admiral Kanaris, who commanded the third largest Greek fleet after those of Hydra and Spétses. Some 27,000 islanders died – many blowing themselves up in a ridge-top powder magazine rather than surrender – and only about 3,000 escaped. The Ottomans burned any remaining buildings and vegetation.

Today about 350 inhabitants remain on melancholy Psará, its bleakness relieved only by occasional fig trees and one cultivated field in the west. Besides the lone port village, there's just a deserted monastery in the far north, frequented once yearly at its 5 August festival. Six beaches lie northeast of the port, each better than the one before, though all of them catch tide-wrack on this exposed coast. Just a few tourists trickle over from Híos, either on the thrice-weekly Miniotis Line ferry from Híos town, or on a summer-only caique from Volissós of similar frequency; ferries call rarely from Sígri on Lésvos, Límnos and Kavala.

The Massacre of Chios, *an 1824 painting by Delacroix depicting the slaughter of 1822, caused controversy in Europe and won much sympathy for the Greek cause.*

BELOW: the Turkish cemetery on Híos.

Ikaría

This narrow, wing-shaped island is named after the mythical Ikaros (Icarus), who supposedly fell into the sea nearby when his wax wings melted. One of the least developed large islands in the Aegean, Ikaría has little to offer anyone intent on ticking off four-star sights, but appeals to those disposed to an eccentric, slightly Ruritanian environment. During both the 1930s and 1970s dictatorships, the island served as a place of exile for hundreds of communists. The locals thought they were the most noble, humanitarian folk they'd ever met, and still vote Communist in droves – not quite what Athens intended.

Ághios Kírykos ⑳ is the capital and main southerly port. It is little more than a sleepy fishing village, its tourist facilities geared to the clientele at the neighbouring spa of **Thermá**. Taxis are far more reliable than the bus for the spectacular 41-km (25-mile) drive over the 1,000-metre (3,300-ft) Atherás ridge to **Évdhilos ㉑**, the north-facing second port, a small, relaxed resort.

Another 16 km (10 miles) takes you past **Kámbos**, with its sandy beach and ruined Byzantine palace, to the end of the asphalt at **Armenistís ㉒**. It is only here that foreigners congregate, for the sake of excellent beaches – Livádhi and Mesakhtí, just east – though the surf can be deadly.

Nás, 4 km (2½ miles) west, is named for the *náos* or temple of Artemis Tavropolio, on the banks of the river which drains to a popular pebble cove. **Yialiskári**, a fishing port 4 km (2½ miles) east, is distinguished by its photogenic jetty chapel. There are few bona fide inland villages, as the proud Ikarians hate to live on top of each other, and keep plenty of room for orchards between their houses. Above Armenistís are four hamlets lost in pine forest, collectively known as **Ráhes**. At **Hristós**, the largest, people cram the café-bars all night,

Apparently impervious to the irony, the Greek Air Force has adopted the doomed aviator Ikaros as its patron.

BELOW: sailing the Aegean in style.

sleep until noon, and carry belongings (or store potent wine) in hairy goatskin bags. The surrounding countryside completes the hobbit-like image, with vertical natural monoliths and troglodytic cottages for livestock made entirely of gigantic slate slabs. Dirt roads are abysmal, especially towards the south coast, where the few hamlets are more easily reached by boat.

Foúrni, one of a mini-archipelago of islets southeast of Ikaría, lives from its thriving fishing fleet and boatyards. Seafood dinners figure high in the ambitions of arriving tourists, who mostly stay in the main, surprisingly large port town. A road links this with Ághios Ioánnis Hryssóstomos in the south and idyllic Hryssomiliá in the far north, the only other habitations, but path walking (where possible) and boat-riding are more relaxing ways of getting around. The best of many beaches are at **Kámbi**, one ridge south of the port, or at **Psilí Ámmos** and **Kálamos** on the north.

Sámos

Almost subtropical Sámos, with vine terraces, cypress and olive groves, surviving forests of black and Calabrian pine, hillside villages, and beaches of every size and consistency, appeals to numerous package tourists. Half a dozen wild fires since 1986 – the worst in July 2000 – and heavy commercialisation have blighted the eastern half of the island, but impassable gorges, the Aegean's second highest mountain and beaches accessible only on foot hold sway in the far west.

Natural endowments take precedence over man-made ones, as evidence of ancient glory is sparse, and Sámos has an identity problem owing to a 15th-century depopulation and later recolonisation. First settled in the 13th century BC,

Map on page 222

In July 1912, a Dr Malahias declared Ikaría liberated from the Turks. For three months it was an independent republic with its own money and stamps.

BELOW: the remote chapel of Yialiskári, Ikaría.

One column is all that remains of Polykrates' great temple to Hera. He planned it to be the largest temple in Greece, but it was never completed.

BELOW: *kouros* in the Archaeological Museum, Vathý.

by the 7th century Sámos was a major maritime power thanks to its innovative *triremes* (warships), still shown on local wine labels. A "golden age" ensued under the rule (538–22) of Polykrates, a brilliant but unscrupulous tyrant who doubled as a pirate. Wealth, however accumulated, supported a luxurious capital of 60,000, and a court attended by the likes of philosopher-mathematician Pythagoras, the astronomer Aristarchus and the bard Aesop. Decline ensued with Polykrates' death at the hands of the Persians, and the rise of Athens.

Heavily commercialised **Pythagório ㉓** occupies the site of Polykrates' capital, three of whose monuments earned Herodotus' highest praise: "I have spoken at greater length of the Samians because of all the Greeks they have achieved the three greatest constructions." From the immense harbour mole constructed by ancient slaves (the first of the great constructions), you watch Mount Mykale in Turkey majestically change colour at dusk.

The 1,040-metre (3,412-ft) **Evpalínio Órygma** (Eupalinos' Tunnel), an aqueduct built by Polykrates through the hillside northwest of town, is the second construction, and one of the technological marvels of the ancient world. Surveying was so good that two work crews beginning from each end met with no vertical error and a horizontal one of less than one percent. You can visit much of it (Tues–Sun 8.30am–2.30pm) along the catwalk used to remove spoil from the water channel far below. The ruins of the third construction, the **Hera Temple (Iréon) ㉔**, lie 8 km (5 miles) west of Pythagório, past coastal Roman baths and the airport. Polykrates' grandiose commission was never actually completed – and Byzantine builders dismantled it for cut stone.

Vathý or **Sámos town ㉕**, built along a deep inlet on the north coast, is the capital and main port, founded in 1832. Tourism is less pervasive here, though many do call at the **Archaeological Museum** (Tues–Sun 8.30am–2.30pm), one of the best in the provinces, with a rich trove of finds from the sanctuary of Hera. Given pride of place is a 5-metre (16-ft) nearly intact *kouros* (male votive statue), the largest ever found. The small-objects collection in a separate wing confirms the Middle-Eastern slant of worship and clientele at the temple: orientalised ivories and locally cast griffin's heads.

Áno Vathý, the large village clinging to the hillside 2 km (1 mile) southeast, existed for two centuries before the harbour settlement. A stroll will take you through steep cobbled streets separating 300-year-old houses, their overhanging second storeys and plaster and lath construction more akin to northern Greece and Anatolia than the central Aegean.

The first stop of note on the north-coast road is **Kokkári ㉖** after 12 km (7½ miles), a former fishing village now devoted to tourism. The original centre is cradled between twin headlands, and windsurfers enjoy the long, westerly pebble beach. Overhead loom the now much denuded crags of **Mount Ámbelos** (1,150m/ 3,773ft), formerly a favourite of hikers. Paths go up directly from behind Kokkári, while cars climb a road just past Avlákia to **Vourliótes ㉗**, a thriving village with several tavernas on its photogenic square. The monastery of **Vrondianí**, 3 km (2 miles) east, co-hosts the island's liveliest festival (7–8 September).

The coastal highway continues west to **Karlóvassi** , 34 km (21 miles) from Vathy. It's a sprawling, somewhat dishevelled place, lumped into four districts, and with little tourist infrastructure. **Néo**, the biggest, has cavernous, derelict warehouses down by the water, vestiges of the leather-tanning trade which thrived here before 1960. **Meséo** is more villagey, as is **Áno** (or Paleó), lining a vegetated valley behind the sentinel church of Ághia Triádha. **Limín**, just below Áno, has most local tourist facilities, including a daily ferry service.

The shore west of here has some of Sámos' best beaches, including sand-and-pebble **Potámi**, visited by most of Karlóvassi at weekends. Beyond here, you must walk to a pair of remote, scenic beaches at **Seïtáni**. Karlóvassi lies roughly halfway around an anti-clockwise loop of the island. Head south, then east through an interior dotted with small villages of tiled, shuttered houses and stripy-domed churches. There are few special sights: you will mostly encounter elderly men drinking coffee, contractors mixing cement or itinerant greengrocers with pickups fitted with loud-hailers to hawk their wares

At the **Ághii Theodhóri** junction, choose southwest or east. The former takes you through **Marathókambos** and its port to **Votsalákia**, Sámos' fastest-growing beach resort. Better, more secluded, coves lie further west along the road curling around the base of **Mount Kérkis** (1,433 metres/4,700 ft), which forms the west end of the island. The refuge of several hundred *andártes* between 1943 and 1948, it's usually climbed from Evangelístria convent on the south or Kosmadhéï on the north – either way a full day's outing.

Returning to Pythagório, schedule stops in **Pýrgos** for a can of local honey, and at the **monastery of Megális Panaghías**, just below Mavratzéï, which has the best (if smudged) frescoes on Sámos, dating from after 1586. ❑

Pythagório (formerly Tigáni) was renamed as recently as 1955, to honour the great Samian Pythagoras – an irony, since the mathematician exiled himself in disgust at the greed of the tyrant Polykrates.

BELOW: fishing boats in Pythagório harbour.

THE DODECANESE

*Rhodes, Kárpathos, Kássos, Hálki, Kastellórizo, Alimiá,
Tílos, Sými, Níssyros, Kós, Psérimos, Astypálea, Kálymnos,
Télendhos, Léros, Lipsí, Pátmos, Arkí, Agathoníssi*

The term "Dodecanese" is relatively new to the Greek vocabulary. For the four centuries that these far-flung islands were ruled by the Ottomans, they were known, incongruously, as the southern Sporades. At the beginning of the 20th century, in response to the withdrawal by the Young Turks of historic privileges granted by various sultans, 12 islands (*dhódheka nisiá* in Greek) jointly protested. Their rebellion failed, but the name stuck – hence the Dodecanese (*Dhodhekánisos* in Greek).

In fact, there are and always have been more than 12 islands in this archipelago. Depending on how you count, the chain consists of 14, 18 or (including every desert islet) even 27 islands. The only point of agreement is that the number of principal inhabited islands is never lower than 12.

The 19 islands included in these chapters are divided into three sections. Rhodes appears separately, for it is the capital and main transport hub of the province. The collective term "Southern Dodecanese" has been coined to include the islands immediately around Rhodes, which are easiest reached from overseas by an initial charter flight into the mother island, followed by a feeder flight or ferry – even to distant Kastellórizo, the proverbial "inset" island, rarely included on maps of Greece.

"Northern Dodecanese" islands, on the other hand, use Kós as a touchdown point, though some, such as holy Pátmos, are also easily reached from Sámos in the northeast Aegean. Seasonal hydrofoils based on Rhodes, Kálymnos and Sámos fill in the gaps between aircraft and conventional boats.

The Dodecanese were Greece's final territorial acquisition in 1948. Before that they were ruled (briefly) by the British; before that, there was a two-year occupation by the Germans, who had succeeded the Italians on their capitulation in late 1943. They in turn had ruled since 1912 with delusions of recreating the Roman Empire, leaving rashes of Art Deco follies on each island to mark their passing. The Italians had taken over from the Ottomans, who had ousted the Knights of St John in 1523 and (except for Rhodes and Kós) administered these islands mostly with benign neglect. Thus, to walk the streets of Kós or Rhodes is to witness a cultural patchwork: a minaret on one corner, an Italian villa on another, facing each other across an expanse of excavated Hellenistic foundations, all overshadowed by the fortifications of the crusading Knights. ❏

PRECEDING PAGES: twilight at the entrance to Mandhráki harbour, Rhodes; tomatoes strung up to dry. **LEFT:** old man, old book.

RHODES

According to the ancient Greeks, Rhodes is "more beautiful than the sun". Even today's brash resorts cannot dim the appeal of its benign climate, entrancing countryside and unique history

The capital of the Dodecanese and fourth largest Greek island, Rhodes (Ródhos) has long been on the package-tour trail. It's a reduced-VAT port, thronged from May to October by Scandinavians in search of Valhalla via cheap booze. Stylish Italians swarm the streets in August, and the British beer-and-bouzoúki brigade also abound, propping up the hundreds of bars in town and the built-up outskirts. Rhodes spells fun for the young, free and single.

But far from the madding crowds in Neohóri (Rhodes New Town) and the serried ranks of umbrellas and sunbeds on the northern beaches, you can still find a more unspoiled island light years away from the tasteless T-shirts and tawdry knick-knacks of the resorts. Frequent bus services run down both coasts from beside the "New Market", but it's worth hiring a car, jeep or powerful motorbike if you really want to explore deserted beaches, remote monasteries and castles perched above citrus groves.

Patchwork history

The legacy of ancient Greeks, crusading knights, besieging Ottomans and colonial Italians forms a fascinating palimpsest in Rhodes town, from castle turrets to the ancient street-plan. There are temple pillars and Byzantine churches, mosques with minarets, plus the twin bronze deer guarding the waters of Mandhráki harbour where perhaps the Colossus once stood.

This wondrous statue depicting Apollo Helios, the work of local sculptors Kharis and Lakhis, stood over 30 metres (100 ft) tall. Impressive by any standards, legend made it even more so by describing it as standing astride the harbour entrance. But to do so it would have to have been more than 10 times its original size, an impossible engineering feat. Wherever it actually was, the monument stood until it collapsed in an earthquake in 226 BC. The bronze was sold for scrap in the 7th century AD.

Under the Byzantine empire, Rhodes was governed by the Genoese – until the Knights of St John, who had fled Jerusalem via Cyprus, captured the city in 1309, beginning a rule that lasted 213 years, under 19 Grand Masters. They substantially refortified the city, and raided Ottoman shipping. Finally, in 1522, Sultan Süleyman the Magnificent took the city after a six-month siege that pitted 200,000 warriors against 650 knights. The Grand Master and 180 surviving brethren surrendered and were allowed safe conduct to Malta. The Ottomans held the island for 390 years. Churches were converted to mosques, and Christians were banned from living within the city walls.

In 1912, Italy occupied Rhodes while at war with Turkey, and embarked on a massive archaeological

LEFT: medieval windmills on Mandhráki harbour.
BELOW: the Apollo temple at Monte Smith.

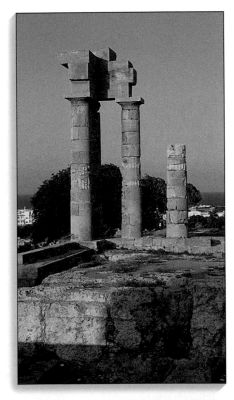

The bronze deer guarding the port recall the time when the island was plagued by snakes. The Delphic oracle suggested the introduction of stags, who did the trick by spearing the serpents with their antlers.

BELOW: selling boat excursions on Mandhráki quay.

construction programme. During World War II, when Italy capitulated in 1943, the Germans took over. Rhodes was liberated by the Allies in 1945, and the Greek flag hoisted in 1948 when the Dodecanese became united with Greece.

These days, the island is still under siege – by tourists. Present-day **Rhodes town (Ródhos) ❶** divides neatly into the New Town, Neohóri, settled by Greeks in Ottoman times, and the Old City. The contrast is marked: fast food, designer clothes and techno-beat versus cobbled streets and a village feel.

The New Town

Here, smart shops abound, peddling Lacoste, Trussardi and Benetton. Inexpensive umbrellas are big business and you can have any logo embossed. Watch the world go by and the yachts bobbing from one of the expensive, touristy pavement cafés at **Mandhráki** port. Marginally cheaper are cafés inside the **covered market (Néa Agorá) Ⓐ** among fishmongers, butchers and wonderfully heaped-up produce. Cheap *souvlákia* and fresh orange juice are available, and there's a good bakery.

Mandhráki's quay buzzes night and day with caricature artists, popcorn vendors, sponge-sellers and touts hawking daily boat trips. Excursion boats leave by 9am for the island of Sými, calling first at Panormítis Monastery, or down the east coast to Líndhos. Hydrofoils depart from the base of the jetty, while full-sized ferries leave from the commercial harbour, a 15-minute walk east.

Mandhráki, guarded by the round bastion-lighthouse of **Ághios Nikólaos (St Nicholas' Fort) Ⓑ**, is also an established port of call on the international yachting circuit, with local charters too. By the harbour entrance stands a cluster of Italian Art Deco: the Governor's House with its Gothic arches, the **church of the Annun-**

ciation (**Evangelismós**) **C** next door, and across the way the post office, town hall and municipal theatre in quick succession. Opposite the theatre, the **Mosque of Murad Reis D** stands beside one of the island's larger Muslim graveyards. On the other side of this is the **Villa Cleobolus**, where Lawrence Durrell lived from 1945 to 1947. A stroll along the waterfront brings you to the grandly named **Hydrobiological Institute** (summer: daily 9am–9pm; winter: 9am–4.30pm) at the island's north cape – actually an aquarium, with the live specimens in the basement.

Inland Neohóri thumps with nightlife, revellers spilling out of the bars onto the pavements in high season. A sign reading "A balanced diet is a drink in each hand" represents the prevailing philosophy. There are said to be more than 200 bars packed into an area measuring less than one square kilometre. Orfanídhou in particular is informally dubbed "Skandi Street" after the new Vikings.

In the municipal gardens beneath the Old City walls, there are *Son et Lumière* performances (**Íhos kai Fos E**) every evening, re-enacting the siege of Süleyman the Magnificent. Pay as you enter – but check with the box office that the performance for that session is in your language.

Some 2 km (1 mile) southwest of Mandhráki, **Monte Smith** – more correctly, Ághios Stéfanos hill – offers panoramic views over the town. This was the site of Rhodes' Hellenistic acropolis, with a stadium, a heavily restored *odeion* and evocatively re-erected columns of an Apollo temple dating from the 3rd century BC. In the far south of the new town, en route to Líndhos, **Rodhíni Park**, home of the ancient rhetoric school, turns up modern babble during August with a wine festival every evening (8pm–midnight; entrance fee includes unlimited wine). The grounds with their gardens, lakes and bridges were refurbished in 1996, and incorporate some rock-cut Hellenistic tombs.

Maps:
244
& below

Monte Smith, the hill to the west of town, is named after the British admiral Sir Sidney Smith who kept watch from here for the Napoleonic fleet in 1802.

BELOW: in the Archaeological Museum.

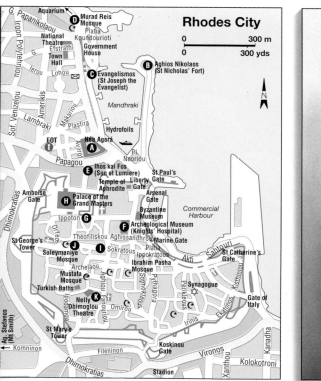

The most famous item in the Archaeological Museum is the marble Aphrodite dating from the 1st century BC, the inspiration for Gerald Durrell's Reflections on a Marine Venus.

BELOW: the courtyard of the Knights' Hospital.

The old city

The medieval walled town, with its ramparts, 11 surviving gates and narrow cobbled streets, is so well preserved a visitor half expects to bump into a Crusader. Recognized as a UNESCO heritage site, its monuments are now getting some long-needed maintenance. Many of the streets follow their right-angled ancient predecessors: in the maze-like Ottoman quarters, it's easier to get lost.

Step through the northernmost **Liberty Gate (Pylí Eleftherías)** into **Platía Sýmis** to view the foundations of an Aphrodite temple. The adjacent **Platía Arghyrokástrou** is flanked by the Inn of the Order of Auvergne and the **Decorative Arts Collection** (Tues–Sun 8.30am–3pm), with costumes, ceramics and carved woodwork gathered from old houses across the archipelago. Just opposite stands the **Byzantine Museum** (Tues–Sun 8.30am–3pm), situated in the former Knights' cathedral, now known as **Panaghía Kástrou**. Much of its collection of icons and frescoes rescued from rural chapels has moved to the Palace of the Grand Masters *(see below)*.

Next stop is the 15th-century **Knights Hospital** ❻, now the **Archaeological Museum** (Tues–Sun 8.30am–3pm). Among the badly labelled and displayed exhibits is the famous, sea-eroded Aphrodite Thalassia, Durrell's Marine Venus, the star of the Hellenistic statuary gallery.

From here the **Street of the Knights (Odhós Ippotón)** ❼ leads in medieval splendour straight uphill to the Palace of the Grand Masters. Italian-restored, and preserved from commercialisation, the thoroughfare houses the inns of the Knights as they were divided by linguistic affinity. The Inn of France, emblazoned with heraldry of several Grand Masters, is the most imposing.

The **Palace of the Grand Masters** ❽ itself (Mon 2.30–9pm, Tues–Fri

8.30am–9pm, Sat–Sun 8.30am–3pm) was almost completely destroyed when a munitions store in the nearby church of St John exploded in 1856, killing 800. During 1937–39 it was hastily rebuilt by the Italians as a holiday retreat for King Victor Emmanuel and Mussolini, neither of whom ever used it. Traipse up the grandiose staircase to ogle the ostentatious upper-floor decoration, including Hellenistic mosaics transferred here from Kós. The ground floor houses an excellent medieval exhibit which, with its displays on the Knights' tenure and sacred art transferred from Panaghía Kástrou, is certainly the best museum on Rhodes.

The main commercial thoroughfare is **Sokrátous ❶**, a "Golden Mile" packed with fur and leather shops, jewellers, lace and embroidery stalls, and every other kind of tourist paraphernalia imaginable. Sokrátous links **Platía Ippokrátous** and its ornate fountain with the pink **Süleymaniye Mosque ❷** at the top of the hill. It's currently shut and under scaffolding, as are most Ottoman monuments here. The old town still has a sizeable Turkish minority, though since 1948 they deliberately keep a low profile. One such monument that's still working, and esteemed by Orthodox and Muslim alike, is the *hamam* (Turkish baths, signed as **Dhimotiká Loutrá**; erratic hours) on Platía Ariónos.

The other local minority which dwelt here were the Jews, who were deported to Auschwitz by the Nazis in June 1944. Few returned, and their **synagogue** on Simíou is essentially maintained as a memorial. Behind the *hamam* on Andhroníkou, the Nélli Dhimóglou dance troupe offers a glimpse of traditional culture in the **Nélli Dhimóglou Theatre ❸** (Mon, Wed, Fri, 9.20pm). For other nightlife, growing numbers of pubs and bars are appearing in the Old City, albeit at a lower decibel level than in Neohóri.

Map on page 241

The magnificent walls of the Old City date from the 14th century and are up to 12 metres (40 ft) thick in places. The only way to get on to them is on an organised walk. Tours start at the Palace of the Grand Masters (Tues and Sat, 2.45pm).

BELOW: the Museum of Decorative Arts.

The west coast

Rhodes' west coast is the damper, windier, greener side of the island, with agriculture on a par with tourism. Scrappy shingle beaches have failed to slow hotel construction at **Ixiá** and **Triánda**, busy resorts that blend into each other and Neohóri. A road leads inland 5 km (3 miles) from Triánda to the site of **ancient Ialyssós ②** (Tues–Sun 8am–7pm), better known today as **Filérimos**, after the Byzantine monastery established here. Of the old city, only a Doric fountain and some Hellenistic temple foundations are evident. The restored Gothic **monastery**, with its vaulted chambers, original fish-mosaic floor and rampant bougainvillea is the main attraction.

Kremastí, back on the coast, is famous for its annual festival of the Virgin (15–23 August), but is otherwise eminently avoidable. The airport lies between here and **Paradhíssi** village, often resorted to for solace when homeward charters get delayed (a common occurrence). Just past Paradhíssi, another inland turning leads to a famous Rhodian beauty spot, the **Petaloúdhes** or "Butterfly

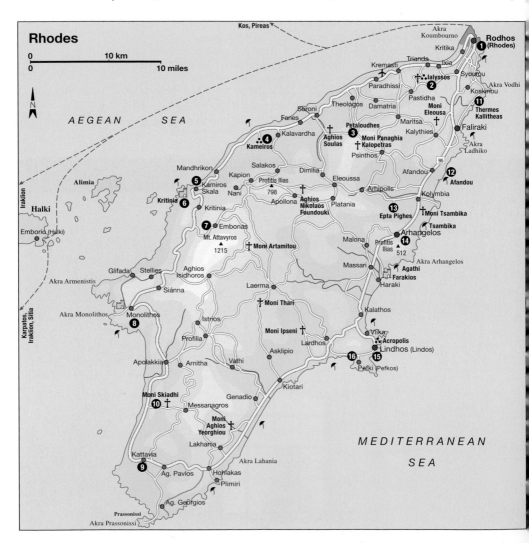

Valley" ❸. The access road crosses the canyon about halfway along its length. Head upstream or downstream, along paths and over bridges, past the *Liquidambar orientalis* (sweet-gum) trees on which Jersey tiger moths roost during summer. Black and yellow when at rest, they flash bright red wing-tops in flight. From the top of the valley, about 6 km (4 miles) inland from **Soroní** on the coast road, a dirt track leads to the **monastery of Ághios Soúlas** which has a major festival on 29–30 July featuring donkey races.

The other big tourist attraction of the west coast, 32 km (20 miles) from Mandhráki, is **Kamíros (ancient Kameiros)** ❹, excavated in 1929. Though no single monument stands out, it's a remarkably complete Doric townscape, without the usual later accretions. Unusually, there were no fortifications, nor an acropolis on the gently sloping hillside.

Back on the coast **Skála Kamírou** (also **Kámiros Skála**) ❺ is a small port with heavily touristed fish tavernas, and afternoon ferries for the tiny island of **Hálki** opposite. **Kritinía** ❻ castle just overhead, one of the Knights' rural garrisons, is today a dilapidated shell but merits a visit for the views out to sea.

The interior and far south

Inland, at the base of 1,215m (3,986ft) Mount Attávyros, **Émbonas** ❼ is the centre of the Rhodian wine industry. Products of the private Emery winery are considered the best. Numerous meat-orientated tavernas serve lunch and "Greek Night" suppers to coach tours. The road skirts the base of the mountain through conifer forest en route to the attractive village of **Siánna**, famous for its honey and *soúma* – a strong grape-distillate spirit that's deceptively smooth. Some 4 km (2½ miles) further, flat-roofed **Monólithos** ❽ village

Map on page 244

Filérimos monastery, an Italian restoration of the original, has many 14th-century wall-paintings and mosaics.

LEFT: bringing in the grapes at Émbonas. **BELOW:** the modern Trianda Hotel.

BELOW: ancient
Kameiros.

gives access to the eponymous castle perched on a narrow pinnacle, with a 200-metre (656-ft) sheer drop all around.

Inland Rhodes is the perfect antidote to the tourist extravagances of the coastal resorts, its rolling hills still partly wooded despite fires started by arsonists since the late 1980s. The late Byzantine church of **Ághios Nikólaos Foundouklí**, 3 km (2 miles) west of **Eleoússa**, has good frescoes. You can continue west to densely shady **Mount Profítis Ilías** (798m/2,618ft), and descend by cobble trail to the village of **Salakós**, where "Nymph" brand spring water is bottled.

Alternatively, from **Apóllona** on the mountain's south side, a rough track (jeeps only) leads directly to **Láerma**, and thence through pines to the Byzantine **monastery of Thári**, reinhabited in 1990 by monks who oversaw the cleaning of its vivid 13th-to-15th-century frescoes. The track continues southeast to **Asklipío** village, where slightly later frescoes in the church of Kímisis Theotókou are in better condition owing to the dry climate. Together these constitute the finest Byzantine art *in situ* on the island.

From Asklipío you emerge on the southeast coast at **Kiotári** and **Yennádhi**, stretches of open gravel beach; well developed with large hotels at Kiotári. Further south, **Plimýri** is sandy and more sheltered, while **Prassoníssi** (Leek Island) at Rhodes' south tip is tethered by a broad, sandy causeway favoured for training by windsurfers. The main island coast road loops back to Monólithos via the villages of **Kattavía** ❾ (which has a church with remarkable frescoes and ancient sculptures) and **Apolakkiá**, between which stretches wild, surf-pounded beach.

Most inland villages here are moribund, with house owners off in Rhodes town or overseas. They've sold up en masse to Germans at **Lahaniá** near Plimýri, though the wonderful square with its taverna and twin fountains under

a plane tree remains traditional. From here head northwest to the fine hilltop village of **Messanagrós**, with its 13th-century chapel hunched amid the larger foundations of a 5th-century basilica. If you're overtaken by darkness and can't face the drive back to town, the kindly keepers at **Skiádhi monastery ⑩** just to the west may invite you to use the guest quarters.

The east coast

The east coast, sandier and more sheltered than the west, with a warmer sea, was only developed for tourism after the 1970s, though much of it remains unspoiled. **Koskinoú** is famous for its ornate doorways and intricate pebble-mosaic courtyards. Immediately downhill, the spa of **Thérmes Kallithéas ⑪**, undergoing restoration, is a splendid orientalised Art Deco folly of the Italians, complete with domed pavilion and palm trees. Below the spa, a pair of sandy coves flanked by rocky headlands are popular with divers.

Wall-to-wall hotels characterise **Faliráki**, the popular package resort bursting with the young, carefree and single. There are dozens of bland eateries and dance bars behind the long sandy beach, where every kind of watersport, plus para-gliding, is on offer. Immediately south looms **Cape Ladhikó**, with its "Anthony Queen" (sic) cove where Quinn starred in *The Guns of Navarone*. Beyond the cape stretches the long pebble-sand beach of **Afándou ⑫**, scarcely developed except for the 18-hole golf course just inland. At a junction still further south, a seaward turning leads through the Italians' model-farm scheme of the 1920s at **Kolýmbia** to another resort ranged around a small volcanic cove.

Heading inland, you reach the leafy glades of **Eptá Pighés** (Seven Springs) **⑬**, one of the island's most popular beauty spots. The springs of the name feed a small

Map on page 244

Skiádhi monastery has a miraculous icon of the Panaghía (Blessed Virgin) which supposedly bled when it was stabbed by a heretic in the 15th century.

BELOW: a full moon over Líndhos.

reservoir dammed by the Italians to irrigate their Kolýmbia colony. Explore a claustrophobic aqueduct-tunnel leading to the pond, or eat at the popular taverna under the trees in the company of screaming peacocks and geese. The Greek answer to fertility drugs, **Tsambíka Monastery**, teeters high on the volcanic headland behind Kolýmbia, overlooking a sandy namesake beach to the south. The otherwise undistinguished church is a magnet for childless women, who come as barefoot pilgrims to revere an 11th-century icon at its 8 September festival.

If a childless woman conceives after praying at Tsambíka Monastery, the child is named Tsambíkos or Tsambíka, names unique to Rhodes.

BELOW: a popular beach at Péfki.

Arhángelos ⑭, 29 km (18 miles) from Rhodes town, is the island's largest village, famous for its *koureloúdhes* (rag rugs), pottery and leather crafts – all goods duly pitched at a large, mostly German, package-tour contingent, here despite the inland position. Good beaches are not far away, however, **Agáthi**, for example, reached via the little resort and fishing port of **Haráki**, overlooked by the crumbled Knights' castle of **Feraklós**.

Líndhos

There are regular buses to cover the 56 km (35 miles) from Rhodes town to **Líndhos (Lindos) ⑮**, but it's more relaxing to take a boat trip and enjoy the coastal scenery. Huddled beneath yet another Knights' castle, Líndhos, with its tiered, flat-roofed houses, appears initially to be the dream Greek village. Medieval captains' mansions – some open for viewing – have ornate gateways and vast pebble-mosaic courtyards. Near the main square, a Byzantine church preserves 18th-century frescoes. The hottest spot on Rhodes, its narrow lanes teem with day-trippers in high season. Donkeys, the Lindian taxi, haul tourists up the steep gradient to the ancient acropolis, with its scaffolded Temple of Lindian Athena. It's more accurately a Temple of Tourism, with women selling lace on the way up.

Líndhos in general is a shrine to sun, sea and sex. At night the village throbs to the beat of numerous bars, while by day the sand lining the northerly port below is sardine-can dense. The southern harbour, with a quieter beach, is known as St Paul's Bay, honouring the Apostle who landed here in AD 58. The tiny church dedicated to him celebrates a *panighíri* on 28 June.

Ancient Lindos dates back to the Bronze Age, thanks to the only protected harbour on the island aside from Mandhráki. With such barren surroundings, it always lived from the sea. In the 1960s, the light and shade playing on the nearby jagged mountains attracted Italian, German and British painters, hangers-on and hippie drop-outs. Past alumni include the late astrologer Patric Walker and various members of Pink Floyd, but Líndhos' days as a hippie-artist colony are long over, superseded by the era of mass tourism. Supermarkets cater to every foreign whim, and tavernas even do sweets – it's hard to believe you're in Greece.

Around the limestone headland, **Péfki (Péfkos) ⑯** is a good deal less frenetic than Líndhos, originally an annex of the latter but now a package resort in its own right; beaches are small and hidden. At **Lárdhos**, 4 km (2½ miles) west, the long, gravelly beach is obvious, and the village elders have embarked on ambitious development, undeterred by the cancellation of a second civilian airport to have been built nearby. ❑

Italian Architecture in the Dodecanese

The Italians occupied the Dodecanese from 1912 until 1943. Because of the Fascist associations, anything connected with the occupation is usually seen in a bad light, nonetheless, much of the work the Italian administration undertook was very interesting. The Italians reconstructed the historic centres in Rhodes and Kos and built many public buildings, doing much to reconstruct Kos after an earthquake in 1933. On Leros they built the naval air base and Porto Lago new town.

In Rhodes, all public services were placed in a new administration centre (Foro Italica) outside the old city, centred on Fascist Party Headquarters with a tower and all-important speaker's balcony. Beyond was the new city's tourist area, which included the La Ronda Sea Baths (now Flli) and the aquarium.

The Kallithea Baths are the best of the architecture of this period in terms of size, quality, and how well the buildings are set into the natural landscape. Art Deco style appeared in the Fascist Youth Building and in the Rhodes Stadium. The La Ronda Baths mixed abstract Ottoman influence with Art Deco; also evident in the aquarium and, in more simplified form, in the Customs House. Buildings in a "neo-Crusader" style, such as the Bank of Rome building, were also constructed.

The later phase of Italian rule (1936–41) stressed the perceived continuity between the Knights Hospitallers and Italian rule. This was done by "purifying" such buildings as the Hotel of the Roses, the Courthouse, the Fascist Party Headquarters, and the Italian Club, by removing what were considered foreign decorative elements and facing them with poros stone. At the same time many buildings constructed by the Knights were restored as symbols of Italian rule.

In this later phase, Italian architecture in the Dodecanese became more monumental and rigidly symmetrical. The Piazzo del' Impero was surrounded by these new buildings, including the Puccini Theatre, which is probably the most important building of Italian rationalism in the Dodecanese. ❏

THE SOUTHERN DODECANESE

The islands farthest from the mainland – they didn't even become part of Greece until 1948 – have developed a distinct character, culture and architecture

Kássos

Kássos is the southernmost Dodecanese island, and the poorest. Remote and barren, its plight was accentuated by a comprehensive Ottoman massacre in 1824. Before and since Kassiots took to the seas, distinguishing themselves as pilots, and helping to dig the Suez Canal. In six clustered villages on the north flank, many houses lie abandoned: summer sees a homecoming of expatriated Greek-Americans, especially for the major festivals, 17 July (Aghía Marína) and 15 August (Assumption of the Virgin).

The capital, **Frý ❶** (pronounced "Free"), is a bit shabby but does have a couple of tavernas and an attractively enclosed fishing port, the Boúka, with a narrow entrance, set against a mountain backdrop. **Emboriós** down the coast was the old commercial port, now silted up but still picturesque. The only conventional tourist attraction is **Seláï** stalactite cave beyond **Aghía Marína**, the most attractive inland village.

Except at peak season when a few mopeds appear, you face long, shadeless hikes to get anywhere. The only half-decent beach, for instance, is **Hélatrós**, nearly four hours' walk from Frý in the southwest, via **Ághios Yeórghios Hadhión**, one of two rural monasteries. The indolent should take up offers of boat excursions to better beaches on the offshore islets of **Makrá** and **Armathiá,** which has a spectacular beach.

Frý has a tiny airstrip with puddle-jumper planes to Rhodes, Kárpathos and Sitía (Crete). Fares are affordable, and a flight may be your only option in heavy seas, when inter-island ferries skip the poor anchorage west of the Boúka.

Kárpathos

Wild, rugged and sparsely populated, Kárpathos is the second largest Dodecanese island, marooned in crystalline sea roughly halfway between Rhodes and Crete. With vast expanses of white-sand beaches, usually underused, and craggy cloud-topped mountains soaring to almost 1,200 metres (3,937 ft), it makes up in natural beauty for what it lacks in attractive villages or infrastructure.

Direct seasonal flights serve Kárpathos from overseas; the alternative involves a domestic flight or ferry from Rhodes. The capital and southerly harbour of **Pigádhia ❷** (also known as **Kárpathos**) has undergone a tourism boom in the last few years; in any case the town only dates from the mid-19th century, and had little beauty to lose before eyesore concrete blocks went up. Many families have returned wealthy from America, and you're as likely to hear "Have a nice day" as *"Kaliméra"*.

PRECEDING PAGES: windmills on Kárpathos. **LEFT:** all dressed up for the festival of St John. **BELOW:** a traditional Ólymbos interior.

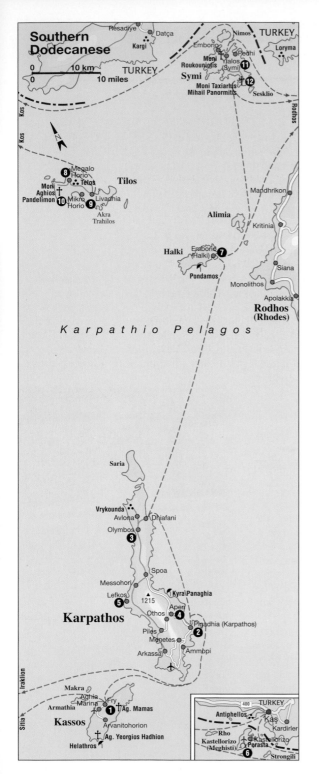

Just north of Pigádhia, massively sandy **Vróndi** beach, with windsurfers and kayaks for rent, sweeps past to the 5th-century basilica of **Aghía Fotiní**. Otherwise you can drive 7 km (4½ miles) south to **Ammopí**, the island's longest established resort, with its three coves, (two sand, one pebble).

Northern Kárpathos is easiest visited via the port of **Dhiafáni**, served both by local caiques from Pigádhia and all main-line ferries. A jetty built in 1996 has made the previous, precarious transfer ashore in small boats history. Dhiafáni is peaceful and congenial except in August, with coastal walks to the beaches in either direction, but most use it as a stepping-stone to reach **Ólymbos ❸**, the island's most distinctive village, which clings to the mountainside 600 metres (1,968 ft) up.

Remote Ólymbos feels like the capital of a separate island. Older houses consist of one divided room built around a central wooden pole, the "pillar of the house", to which are attached embroideries and usually a wedding portrait of the owners, complete with a *stéfano* or wedding wreath. On a raised wooden platform behind a carved rail is rolled-up bedding, plus chests of dowry linens and festival clothes.

The rest of the room is crammed with plates, lace, crochet and other souvenirs – a kitsch explosion of fairground colours – gathered by seafaring relatives from ports around the world. Even modern villas have their front room decked out in the same way, with the TV draped in garish mats, a shrine for family photos and icons.

Ólymbos long existed in a time warp, but tourism by amateur anthropologists has dragged the place into the modern era, and the locals are now well used to visitors. It's best to stay the night, when you'll hear the Dorian-influenced local dialect in the tavernas and see the women clomp off to the terraces below at dawn, in their high leather boots. Older women still wear traditional costumes (intricately embroidered jackets, scarves and pinafores) on a daily basis

Map on page 254

as well as for festivals, though lately a good deal of the embroidery is imported.

Bread and biscuits are baked in communal ovens. The flour was formerly ground by the village's half-dozen 18th-century windmills, two of which were restored as working museum-pieces in the mid-1980s.

Organised tours serve Ólymbos, complete with bus transfer up from Dhiafáni, but the north is wonderful for walking. Besides the hike between the two, there's the half-day trek via **Avlóna** hamlet to **Vrykoúnda**, where a cave-shrine of St John the Baptist is the focus for a major festival on 29 August.

Exploring further afield can be arduous: paved roads are rough, the many dirt ones appalling, and filling stations few. Mopeds should thus be avoided for long trips, as they'll run out of petrol – and when the *meltémi* wind buffets the west coast you can be blown off the road by gusts. There are buses and pricey taxis to less remote mountain villages like **Menetés**, with vine-covered streets; **Apéri ❹**, the elegant medieval capital, said to have the highest per capita income in Greece; **Óthos**, the highest on the island at 400 metres (1,312 ft), where an old Karpathian house serves as a craft museum; and **Voládha** just across a mist-swirled ridge, with a tiny Venetian citadel.

Many of Kárpathos' better beaches are most easily reached by excursion boat. Among these, on the east coast, are **Kyrá Panaghiá** (with the most facilities and a lovely pink-domed church), or lonelier, more unspoilt **Aháta** and **Ápella**. **Arkássa** on the western shore is a growing resort, popular with both Greeks and foreigners, between a Mycenaean-Classical acropolis at **Paleókastro** and the working fishing port of **Finíki**. **Lefkós ❺**, further north, presents an outstanding topography of headlands sheltering three horseshoe bays of white sand; there are plenty of places to stay and eat.

Ólymbos was virtually cut off from the rest of Kárpathos for centuries. The road from the south was only completed in 1979.

BELOW: clouds gather over Ólymbos.

On 1 May every year, wreaths made of wild flowers and garlic are hung outside homes to ward off evil. On some islands, the wreaths are burnt as part of the celebrations on St John's Day (24 June).

BELOW: the port of Kastellórizo.

Kastellórizo

Kastellórizo's alias, Meghísti, means "Biggest" – biggest, that is, of a local mini-archipelago, for this is actually one of the smallest inhabited Dodecanese islands. It's also the first point in Europe, coming from the east, as signs on the quay proudly announce to wandering yachts, and only a few nautical miles away from Turkey where locals go shopping. Before 1900, Kastellórizo was a thriving town of 14,000, supported by its schooner fleet. The sale of the fleet, World War I bombardment, and an earthquake in 1926 sent the island into terminal decline, despite its role during the 1930s as a sea-plane halt.

The final nail in the coffin came in July1944, when a fuel depot exploded, levelling more than half the port. The town had already been looted, and few chose to return after the war, when the population dropped to about 200. The US even tried to persuade Greece to cede Kastellórizo to Turkey in 1964 in exchange for limited hegemony in Cyprus. Recovery from this nadir is due to the return of expatriate "Kassies" from Perth and Sydney to build retirement homes, and the island's use as the location for the Oscar-winning film *Mediterraneo*, which spurred a wave of tourists.

This limestone island is fringed by sheer cliffs, with no beaches at all. What remains of the red-roofed port town, **Kastellórizo**, is overseen by a half-ruined, red-stone Crusader castle, responsible for the island's Italianate name. The keep houses a small museum (Tues–Sun 7am–2.30pm) of local finds, relocated here from the quayside mosque, while beyond in the cliff-face is Greece's only Lycian house-type tomb.

Also worth seeing is the remote monastery of **Ághios Yeórghios toú Vounoú** with groin vaulting, pebble flooring and the frescoed subterranean crypt-chapel

of Ághios Harálambos. Boat trips go to the satellite islet of **Rhó**, or to the cathedral-like Blue Grotto of **Perastá ❻** on the southwest coast which, according to locals, rivals its namesake in Capri. The cave is about 45 metres (147 ft) long and 28 metres (92 ft) high, and the rays of the morning sun create spectacular effects inside. The journey there is a 90-minute round-trip, plus time to swim in the deep, glowing waters.

Kastellórizo lies 70 nautical miles (114 km) from Rhodes, and ferries make the long trip only two or three times a week. The tiny airstrip receives three to seven weekly flights from Rhodes, though seats can fill days in advance. Tourist facilities have improved vastly since the 1990s, and are priced accordingly; the half-dozen tavernas are good value, except for two aimed at yachties.

Map on page 254

Hálki

Ninety minutes by boat from Kámiros Skála on Rhodes, Hálki (also spelt Chálki) is pretty, welcoming and "arrived", despite being barren and harsh, and lacking a fresh water supply. **Emborió (Hálki) ❼**, the harbour and only settlement, has numerous waterfront tavernas and abundant accommodation in its restored Neoclassical mansions, though most of these are block-booked from April to October by three British tour companies. **Ághios Nikólaos** has the highest bell-tower in the Dodecanese, nearly matched by a free-standing clock-tower nearby.

The island's only sandy beach – artificially supplemented – is at **Póndamos** bay, 400 metres (440 yards) west, just overhead, **Horió** village has been deserted since the 1950s but offers spectacular views from its crumbled Knights' fortress. Tarpon Springs Boulevard, built with money from Hálki sponge fishermen who

Hálki was a fertile island until seawater infiltrated its water-table. Now fresh water is imported by tanker.

BELOW: fishing still plays a major role in the Dodecanese economy.

emigrated to Florida, has been extended to the monastery of **Ághios Ioánnis** in the northwest of the island. Without a lift, it's a good two-hour walk from Horió. There are no other good roads, so pebble coves like **Aréta** and **Dhýo Yialí**, on the north shore, or Trahiá under the castle, are reached by boat excursion. Otherwise you can walk to less inspiring **Yialí** or **Kánia**.

Floating between Hálki and Rhodes, **Alimiá** (aka **Alimniá**) island has been mostly deserted since World War II, despite having a fresh-water spring and excellent anchorage. The inhabitants aided the Allies under the very noses of the Italian forces manning submarine pens here. When they were detected, the islanders were deported to Rhodes and Hálki as punishment, and the few returners left again in the 1960s. With yet another Knights' castle, a pretty church, pebbly beaches, clear waters and ruined houses strafed by bullet holes, the island is now a popular picnic spot for both locals and tourists, and seasonally home to Halkian sheep.

Tílos

Tranquil and unspoiled, Tílos has only seen tourism since the late 1980s. It has several thousand goats but only about 500 people (80 in the winter). Though the island is bare on its limestone heights, neighbouring Níssyros deposited rich lava soil in the lowlands, which with ample ground-water allows the Tíliots to farm. Indeed before the 1970s it was the granary of the Dodecanese, with undulating fields of wheat visible far out to sea.

The island's capital, **Megálo Horió** ❽, is an inland village, topped by a Venetian castle that incorporates a Classical gateway and stone from the ancient acropolis. It looks south over an orchard-planted plain to red-sand **Éristos** beach, the best on Tílos. The harbour and main resort of **Livádhia** ❾ has a

long shingle beach, behind which development is accelerating at an alarming rate. There are now half a dozen good tavernas, a score of hotels and even some low-key nightlife. You can walk or moped to most good beaches, so boat trips are only offered when numbers justify. The closest are Lethrá, Stavrós and Thólos, with the Knights' castle of Agriosykiá (one of seven here) en route. Just west of Livádhia is the ghost village of **Mikró Horió**, abandoned in the 1950s. There's another castle here, and a late-hours bar in a restored house.

The trans-island road passes another fort and a cave at **Harkádhi**, in which the fossilised bones of tiny mastodons (extinct elephants) were found in 1971. The bones are kept in a small museum in Megálo Horió.

At **Ághios Andónios** beach, the surf washes over the petrified remains of three sailors, trapped by an eruption of Níssyros. The road's end is the 15th-century **monastery of Aghíos Pandelímon** , tucked into a spring-fed oasis-ravine. Since 1999 a caretaker family has been in residence, and will open for visitors at reasonable hours. The church has a few frescoes and a fine marble floor. The big island knees-up is here, running for three days from 25 July and including the famous "Dance of the Cup". Almost as important is the 23 August festival at **Panaghía Polítissa monastery** near Livádhia, for which special boats are laid on from Rhodes the previous day.

For centuries Sými was the sponge-diving capital of the Aegean, until it was surpassed by Kálymnos (see page 270).

Sými

As you approach Sými on a day-trip boat from Rhodes, flotillas of boats flee the port of **Yialós**  for remote beaches around the island. The foreign "residents" and overnighters are escaping the daily quota of trippers. Yialós (also called Sými) is a stunning spectacle with its tiers of pastel-coloured houses. But it is

LEFT: island woman. **BELOW:** the ferry from Rhodes approaches Pédhi.

Map on page 254

The Symiots have been renowned for their boat-building since antiquity. In legend they built the Argo in which Jason sailed off to find the Golden Fleece.

BELOW: local transport in Horió.
RIGHT: Yialós, Sými.

a town with two faces. When the tour boats hoot their arrival, it becomes a mini-Rhodes, with mediocre waterside tavernas touting for business, and stalls selling imported spices and sponges, plus other knick-knacks. As soon as the trippers leave in mid-afternoon, peace is restored: there's room to walk on the quay and you'll get stronger drink.

Symiots are famous as boat-builders and you can still see boats taking shape at the Haráni yards. Until it was surpassed by Kálymnos after World War II, Sými was also the sponge-diving capital of the Aegean, a role assured by an Ottoman imperial grant of monopoly in the trade. The Treaty of the Dodecanese, in which Nazi Germany formally surrendered the islands to the Allies, was signed in Les Katerinettes restaurant on 8 May 1945.

Built in a protected gulch and thus stiflingly hot in summer, Yialós is beautiful at night when the bay reflects the lights from the houses above. Popular with the yachting fraternity, but still relatively unspoilt because of limited accommodation, the "Hydra of the Dodecanese" has plenty of bars and tavernas scattered about. It's not, however, an island for the unfit, the elderly or the very young, who would have to manage the 357 steps of the **Kalí Stráta**, the broad stair-street climbing to the upper town of **Horió**. Follow arrows to the worthwhile local **museum** (Tues–Sun 10am–2pm), which highlights Byzantine and medieval Sými. Overhead is the Knights' castle, built on the site of – and using material from – the ancient acropolis.

The only other significant habitation is the valley of **Pédhi** to the east, where flat land and a few wells allow vegetable cultivation. On the south side of the bay here, reached by a marked trail, is the naturally sandy beach of **Ághios Nikólaos**, the only one on Sými.

Beyond Haráni, the coastal track heads north, then west to the bay of Nimborió, where a Byzantine floor mosaic and catacombs can be found up behind an artificial strewn sand beach. The only other notable sacred art outside the museum is at the monastery of **Mihaïl Roukouniótis**, west of Horió, with a peculiar piggy-back church and vivid 18th-century frescoes in the upper one.

Other beaches are pebble; walk across the island, through the remaining juniper forest, to **Ághios Vassílios** in the southwest (no facilities), or take an all-day boat excursion to **Ághios Yeórghios Dhyssálona**, **Nanoú** or **Marathoúnda** (only Nanoú has a taverna) on the east coast.

The most important monastery is **Taxiárhis Mihaïl Panormítis** ⓬ in the far south. The Archangel Michael is the patron of local sailors, and his feast day (8 November) brings seafaring pilgrims to Panormítis from all over the Aegean. Even though the monastery was raided and stripped of its possessions during the last war, the central church is still atmospheric, with its myriad oil lamps set in the midst of a giant pebble-mosaic courtyard; a small museum displays votive offerings from seamen. Things are tranquil once the tour boats have gone – it's usually the first stop coming from Rhodes – and you can rent a cell for whatever you wish to pay, but the compound doors are locked at 9.30pm sharp. ❏

THE NORTHERN DODECANESE

Closer to Turkey than to Greece, these islands have a discernible eastern influence. As well as the Ottomans, the Italians and the Knights of St John have also left their mark

Map on page 264

Astypálea

Bleak, butterfly-shaped Astypálea, with just under 1,500 inhabitants, is geographically nearer to the Cyclades than the Dodecanese. It belongs administratively to the latter group, yet in architecture and culture bears more resemblance to the former. On a clear day both Amorgós and Anáfi appear distinctly on the horizon. In recent years Astypálea's notoriously bad ferry connections have improved, enough to ensure export of the abundant local fish, though still not enough to suit package-tour operators. In high summer the few hotels do fill up, while Athenians have renovated old houses in the capital as summer residences. A domestic airport operates, a single stretch of road has been paved, taverna food has improved, and houses are whitewashed more frequently, but further momentous change is unlikely.

Many visitors stay in the principal (and functional) port of **Péra Yialós** or **Skála**, which dates from the Italian era. A long stair-street connects Skála with the capital, also called **Astypálea ❶**, which incorporates the medieval **Hóra**, the finest such in the Dodecanese outside of Pátmos. A line of derelict windmills trails off to the northwest; at the pinnacle of things sits the tan-walled **kástro**, not for once a legacy of the Knights of St John, but a 13th-century effort of the Venetian Quirini clan. Until the 1950s several hundred islanders dwelt inside it, but now all is desolation, except for two fine churches: **Evangelístria**, supported by the groin vaulting of the northwest entrance, and **Ághios Yeórghios**.

LEFT: St John's monastery, Pátmos. **BELOW:** the black volcanic shore of Níssyros.

Just west of the Hóra ridge, **Livádhia ❷** is the island's second resort, between citrus orchards and a sandy but somewhat scruffy beach. Better beaches, like nudist **Tzanáki**, and taverna-equipped **Ághios Konstandínos**, lie further southeast, out on the western "wing". **Kaminákia** and **Vátses** beaches beyond are usually visited on boat excursions.

The "body" of the butterfly is a long isthmus, just 100 metres (110 yards) across at its narrowest point, by Stenó and Mamoúni beaches. **Maltezána** (officially **Análipsi**) to the east has become another resort, more through proximity to the airport than any intrinsic merit. The only habitations on the eastern "wing" are **Éxo Vathý**, and **Mésa Vathý**, the road's end and favoured by yachters. A single bus plies between Livádhia and Maltezána, via all points in between; otherwise it's one of three elusive taxis, or a rented moped.

Níssyros

In legend Greek Poseidon, pursuing the Titan Polyvotis, tore a rock from nearby Kós and crushed his adversary beneath it. The rock became Níssyros. The groaning of the Titan is still audible beneath the surface of the

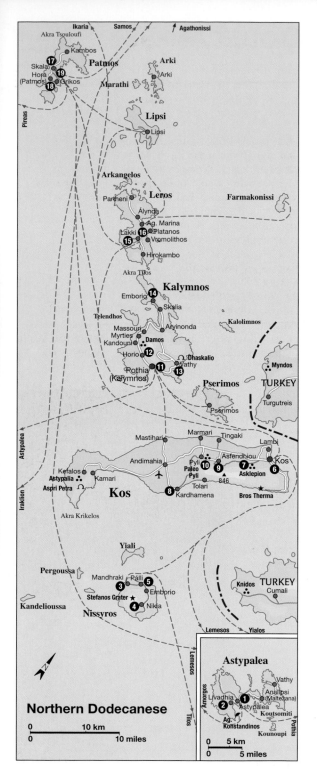

Northern Dodecanese

0   10 km
0   10 miles

Astypalea

0   5 km
0   5 miles

caldera in Níssyros's most impressive feature, the volcano which forms the heart of the island. Currently dormant, it was last active in 1933, and vulcanism still dominates Níssyros, from black pebbles on the shore to a sulphurous spa.

Once you're away from its harbour, **Mandhráki** proves an attractive capital. Wooden balconies hang cheerfully from tall, white houses ranged around a central communal orchard. Overhead, the Knights' castle shelters the monastery of Panaghía Spilianí, while to the south, the Doric citadel of **Paleókastro** is more impressive.

Mandhráki by night is lively, with many tavernas and *kafenía* found, unusually, inland. There are few hotels, as most folk come just for the day from Kós to tour the volcano. In some establishments, you can order *soumádha*, a non-alcoholic drink now imported made from almonds. The island's green interior – from which wild almonds have sadly disappeared – is best appreciated by walking some of the remaining trail system.

The main **Stéfanos** crater, 260 metres (853 ft) across, punctuates the nearly lifeless Lakkí plateau, 13 km (8 miles) southeast of Mandhráki. Occasional buses make the trip. With stout shoes, you can visit the caldera floor, braving a rotten-egg stench. Yellow crystals form around hissing steam vents while mud boils out of sight – the voice of Polyvotis.

The Greek power corporation made exploratory geothermal soundings here until 1993, but departed in the face of islander hostility – though not before ruining the best local walking trail.

Two scenic villages perch above Lakkí: **Emborió**, virtually abandoned and bought up for restoration by outsiders, and lively **Nikiá** , with a quirky round *platía* and a few *kafenía*. The Emboriots moved down to the fishing port of **Pálli** . The biggest sandy beach is 6 km (3½ miles) around the northeast coast, at **Pahiá Ámmos**. West of Páli, the old spa at **Loutrá** has been well restored with EU funds.

Kós

The second largest Dodecanese in population, Kós is third largest in size after Rhodes and Kárpathos. It follows the lead of Rhodes in most things: a sea-transport hub for a gaggle of surrounding islands; a shared history, give or take a few years; a similar Knights' castle guarding the harbour, plus a skyline of palms and minarets; and likewise an agricultural economy displaced by tourism.

However Kós is much smaller than Rhodes, and much flatter, with only one mountain, Dhíkeos, rising to 846 metres (2,775 ft) in the southeast. The margin of the island is fringed by excellent beaches, most easily accessible by motorbike or even push-bike. Despite the presence of cycle-paths – a Greek first – Kós is by no means unspoilt, and even early or late in the season you'll have plenty of company. Visits in mid-summer, especially without a reservation, are emphatically not recommended. Yet the obvious over-development has compensations: surprisingly good restaurants scattered across the island, ample water-sports opportunities, and a good infrastructure (including a cinema in summer and winter).

Although the Minoans colonised the site of present-day **Kós town ❻**, during the late Bronze Age and Classical eras, the main island city-state was Astypalaia, on the far southwestern cape of Kéfalos, an ally of Rhodes in the Dorian Hexapolis. Spartan sacking during the Peloponnesian War and a subsequent earthquake (Kós is very susceptible to them) forced a relocation to the northern site, a process completed by the mid-4th century BC. According to Strabo, the new town was a success: "She was not large but inhabited in the best way possible and to the people visiting her by sea pleasant to behold."

Yet another earthquake in 1933 devastated most of Kós Town, except for the Ottoman bazaar of Haluvaziá, but gave Italian archaeologists a perfect excuse

Map on page 264

Kós has been inhabited since Neolithic times. Between 1500 and 1100 BC it had a powerful naval fleet, which took part in the Trojan War.

BELOW: boats take excursions from Kós to Níssyros.

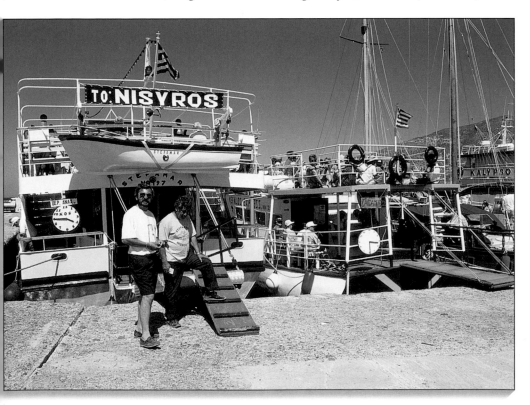

The 18th-century Defterdar mosque in Platía Eleftherías is still used by Kós Town's 50 or so Muslim families, but is not open to the public.

BELOW: the remains of the Asklépion.
RIGHT: in Kós's Archaeological Museum.

to excavate the ancient city comprehensively. Hence much of the town centre is an archaeological park, with the ruins of the Roman *agora*, the eastern excavation, lapping up to the 18th-century Loggia Mosque and the "Plane Tree of Hippocrates", under which the father of medicine is said to have taught. It is not really 2,500 years old, though it probably is one of the oldest trees in Europe, now dependent on a life support system of metal scaffolding.

The western digs offer covered mosaics and the Xystós, the colonnade of an indoor running track. Just south stand an *odeion*, sometimes used for summer performances, and the **Casa Romana** (Tues–Sun 8.30am–3pm), a restored Roman villa with more mosaics and murals. The Italian-founded **Archaeological Museum** (Tues–Sun 8am–2.30pm) on Platía Eleftherías has a predictable Latin bias in exhibits, though the star statue, purportedly of the great healer Hippocrates, is in fact Hellenistic.

Hippocrates himself (c460–370 BC) was born and practised on Kós, but probably died just before the establishment of the **Asklépion ❼**, the ancient medical school 4 km (2½ miles) southwest of town. The site (Tues–Sun 8.30am–3pm) impresses more for its position overlooking the straits towards Turkey than for any surviving structures. Their masonry was thoroughly pilfered by the Knights to build their massive **castle** (Tues–Sun 8am–2.30pm), which unlike the one at at Rhodes was strictly military. It's a double fort, the smaller inner one dating from the mid-15th century, the outer circuit completed in 1514.

Between the Asklepion and Kós Town, pause at **Platáni**, roughly halfway, to dine at one of three excellent Turkish-run tavernas. As on Rhodes, most local Muslims have chosen to emigrate to Turkey since the 1960s. There was a small Jewish community here too, wiped out like the Rhodian one in 1944, leaving

behind only the marvellous Art Deco **synagogue** by the town *agora*. The road east of town dead-ends at **Brós Thermá**, enjoyable hot springs which run directly into the sea. West of town, within easy cycling distance, are the package resorts of **Tingáki** and **Marmári** with their long white beaches, and the less frantic **Mastihári**, with a commuter boat to Kálymnos. All three of these take a back seat, tourism-wise, to **Kardhámena ❽** on the south coast, 25 km (15 miles) from Kós Town but just 7 km (4½ miles) from the airport. It's the island's cheap-and-cheerful resort, with little to recommend it aside from suggestively-named cocktails and a long, sandy and jam-packed beach. The only cultural diversion is the Knights' castle near **Andimáhia**, a two-hour walk inland for the energetic.

The map is on page 264

The Asklépion, Kós's ancient medical school and hospital, has two underground chambers with a statue of Aphrodite, believed to be where venereal diseases were treated.

In the far southwest, facing Níssyros, are more scenic and sheltered beaches, with names like "Sunny" and "Magic". At nearby **Ághios Stéfanos**, twin 6th-century basilicas are the best of several early Christian monuments. The Kéfalos headland beyond saw the earliest habitation of Kós: **Áspri Pétra** cave, home to Neolithic man, and Classical **Astypalaia**, the birthplace of Hippocrates, of which only the little theatre remains.

The appealing villages on the wooded northern slopes of Mount Dhíkeos, collectively known as the **Asfendhioú ❾**, have retained their traditional character, with whitewashed houses and attractive Byzantine churches. At Ziá, tavernas seem more numerous than permanent inhabitants, and are especially busy at sunset and after. Asómati's vernacular houses are slowly being bought up and restored by foreigners. The forest that surrounds the villages, the only one on the island, provides welcome relief from the heat in summer.

On the western flank of Mount Dhíkeos, the Byzantines had their island capital at **Paleó Pylí** (Old Pylí) **❿**, today a jumble of ruins – including three 14th-

BELOW: the massive castle built by the Knights at Kós.

Although the sponge-diving industry has declined in Kálymnos (see page 270) there are still workshops in Póthia where you can see sponges being cleaned and trimmed.

BELOW: the silver-domed cathedral of Ághios Hristós on Póthia waterfront.

century churches with frescoes – below a castle at the head of a spring-fed canyon. Modern Pylí, 3 km (2 miles) downhill, paradoxically offers something more ancient: the Harmyleio, a subterranean Hellenistic family tomb with 12 niches.

Psérimos

Tiny Psérimos (population c. 25), between Kós and Kálymnos, can be reached from either, though tourist excursions from Kós won't give you a full day here. This is apparently because the massive crowds of day-trippers, who come to flop on the long beach here, exceed the capacity of the few tavernas amid the 30 or so buildings, so lunch may now be taken somewhere on Kálymnos. If you do elect to stay the night, you'll find the islanders more receptive once the excursionists have departed. At sunset, local women wade into the sea, skirts held high, in rarely seen relaxation.

The sea is perfect for children, for several hundred feet away from the shore the water is still only shoulder-deep. If you tire of the main beach – which doubles as the main street – there are others, not as good in the east and north of the islet, or you could visit the monastery of Grafiótissa. After dark, the only sounds will be the wind rustling through calamus thickets, or the tinkle of goat bells.

Kálymnos

First impressions of Kálymnos, north of Kós, are of an arid, mountainous landmass with a decidedly masculine energy in the main port town of Póthia. This is due to the former dominant industry, sponge-diving, only lately supplanted by tourism and commercial fishing. But the former mainstay *(see page 270)* is amply evident in the home décor of huge sponges and shell-encrusted amphorae,

Map on page 264

souvenir shops overflowing with smaller sponges, and (in autumn) uproarious celebrations of returned divers in the port's bars and cafés – which single women may choose to avoid.

Póthia ⓫ itself, the second largest town in the Dodecanese with a population of about 16,000, is noisy, colourful and workaday Greek. Its brightly painted houses rise in tiers up the sides of the amphitheatric bay. To the northwest loom two castles: Hryssoherías, the Knights' stronghold, and the originally Byzantine fort of Péra Kástro, above the medieval capital of Horió ⓬, which is still the island's second town.

The east coast is harsh and uninhabited except for the green, citrus-planted valley extending inland from the fjord of Vathýs ⓭, which comes as a surprise amid all this greyness as you round a high curve in the road. Plátanos and Metóhi hamlets used to live from the sweet-smelling mandarin and orange orchards here, though many of these are now for sale. Yachts call at the little port of Rína, from where there are boat trips to the nearby cave of Dhaskalió, a place of ancient worship, and purportedly of refuge during the Italian era. The limestone strata are riddled with other, visitable stalactite caves. The best are Kéfala in the far southwest, and Skalía and Kolonóstilos in the far north.

Most visitors stay at the beach resorts on the gentler west coast, locally referred to as Brostá ("Forward"). Locals and Greek vacationers tend to gravitate towards beaches at Kandoúni and Linária, though less developed Platýs Yialós just north is reckoned the island's best. Foreign package tourists patronise Myrtiés and Massoúri, two adjacent, heavily developed resorts. At Myrtíes, also the port for the idyllic islet of Télendhos, a riot of vegetation – palms, hibiscus, grape arbours – adorns tavernas, rooms and *dhomátia*.

Póthia has an orphanage where, until recently, Orthodox priests would come to choose a bride before they were ordained. A woman without a dowry was reckoned to have little chance of finding a husband outside the Church.

BELOW: quiet times on Kálymnos.

Sponge Diving

K álymnos has been a sponge-fishing centre from ancient times, although a combination of fishing restrictions and marine blight have diminished the trade in recent years. Sponges come in various grades: coarser for industry, or finer for cosmetic and artistic use. Although cheap artificial sponges now dominate the market, many people will still pay extra for the more resilient natural sponge.

Sponges were traditionally "cured" in two stages. First the divers trod them underfoot on the caique deck to "milk" them of unwanted organic matter; then they strung them together and dropped them back into the sea for a few more days of cleaning.

Sponge-curing can be observed in Póthia factories (particularly at the Astor Sponge Workshop, open daily 10am–6pm in summer). Older operations have stone tubs of salt water, others bubbling vats of dilute acid which bleach the sponges – a concession to tourist tastes which actually weakens the

fibres. After this optional process, they're rinsed in salt water again and finally laid out to dry in the factory courtyard.

Over the years sponge-fishers developed various methods of gathering their quarry: spearing them in shallow water; dragging a heavy blade and net along the sea-bottom so that everything – stones and seaweed as well as the odd sponge – got pulled up together; and diving.

In the old days, divers used to sink themselves with heavy stones tied to their waists. Holding their breath, they scraped off the rock-fixed sponges spied from the surface. They could usually get two or three before they had to surface for air. Better divers could dive to 40 fathoms before the "machine" was introduced late in the 19th century.

The "machine" is the local term for the first diving apparatus, which consisted of a rubber suit with a bronze helmet connected to a long rubber hose and a hand-powered air-pump. The diver was let out on a long cable and given enough air-hose for his final depth, where he could stay much longer thanks to the constant air supply. Too long and too deep, as it turned out. Compressed air delivered to divers at the greater depths bubbled out of solution in their bloodstream as they rose, invariably too rapidly. The results of nitrogen embolism – known as the "bends" – included deafness, incontinence, paralysis and often death.

By the 1950s the physiological mechanism was understood and the carnage halted, but too late to help hundreds of Kalymnian crewmen. Although the "machine" now seems quaintly antiquated, it was innovative enough for its time to enrich the boat captains and sponge wholesalers.

Ironically, the increased efficiency in sponge-harvesting helped to wind up the industry. The Greek seabed was stripped bare, and Kalymnian boats had to sail increasingly further afield. Over-exploitation of Mediterranean sponge beds was the rule even before a virus devastated them during the late 1980s. Today, sponge divers are a rare breed, but two or three caiques still set out from Póthia in late April for six months of sponge diving. ❑

LEFT: the "machine" that revolutionised diving.

You could escape the crowds by heading north towards **Aryinónda** and **Emborió** , the end of the road 19 km (12 miles) from Póthia, but at a price: beaches are rough shingle rather than comfortable round gravel, and the bus service beyond Massoúri is sparse to non-existent. In any case, Kálymnos is just the right size to explore by moped or on foot, and boat excursions are also offered.

Télendhos

Seen from Myrtiés on Kálymnos at dusk, the bulky islet of Télendhos resembles a snail; others claim to see the silhouette of a petrified princess, jilted here by her lover. The caique from Myrtiés runs every 20 minutes in the summer, from dawn until late, and (optimistically) once or twice daily in the winter. Prepare to share the boat with boxes of tomatoes, piles of blankets, and other household goods. The fishermen who are the most frequent passengers are graced with wonderful manners: even if she is three times younger, a lady will not be allowed to stand while they remain seated.

The single waterside hamlet huddles under mammoth **Mount Ráhi** (458 metres/1,502 ft). Halfway up the north side of this, a long trek away, is the fortified monastery of Ághios Konstandínos. Less energetic souls content themselves with the ruined Byzantine monastery of **Ághios Vassílios**, at the north edge of the hamlet, or the Byzantine baths at **Ághios Harálambos**. Télendhos is more upmarket than nearby Psérimos, and less set in the day-trip mentality. Most tavernas are stylish and friendly, and accommodation designed with intent to lure custom over from the main island. Beaches are limited both in number and size. The best is scenic **Hohlakás**, 10 minutes west, with coin-sized pebbles.

Télendhos was joined to Kálymnos until AD 554, when an earthquake sundered the two. Buildings of a town that sank into the resulting channel are supposedly visible in exceptional circumstances.

Léros

Léros, with its half-dozen deeply indented bays, looks like a jigsaw puzzle piece gone astray. The deepest inlet, that of **Lakkí**  (now the main ferry port), sheltered an important Italian naval base from 1923 onwards, and from here was launched the submarine that torpedoed the Greek battleship *Elli* in Tínos harbour on 15 August 1940.

Today Lakkí town seems bizarre, an Art Deco experiment far too grand for the present token population. The institutional buildings, reminders of colonial subjugation, have only been restored in 2001, the landscaped squares and wide boulevards spookily empty. Ferries in all directions tend to arrive after dark, when the prevailing shabbiness is masked by glamorous illumination. The local atmosphere is not cheered by the presence of three hospitals for handicapped children and mentally ill adults, substandard conditions in them prompting an uproar when exposed in the late 1980s. More timid travellers thus give Léros a miss, which means that the island is mostly spared the excesses of industrial-strength tourism.

The rest of the island is more inviting, particularly the fishing port of **Pandéli**, with its waterfront tavernas, just downhill from the capital of **Plátanos**, draped over a saddle, with a well-preserved Knights' castle and its Panaghía toú Kástrou church. South of both, **Vromólithos** has the best easily accessible and

BELOW: fishing nets drying in the sun.

car-free beach on an island not known for good, sandy ones. In most places sharp rock reefs must be crossed. **Ághia Marína**, beyond Plátanos, is the hydrofoil harbour and, like Pandéli, offers good tavernas.

Álynda, 3 km (2 miles) north around the same bay, is the oldest established resort, with a long beach right next to the road – and a poignant Allied War Graves cemetery containing casualties from the Battle of Léros in November 1943, when the Germans ousted an insufficiently supplied British commando force.

In ancient times Léros was sacred to Artemis, and on a hill next to the airport runway are knee-high remains of the goddess's "temple" – now thought to be an ancient fort. Artemis' reputed virginity lives on in the place name **Parthéni** (*parthenos* is the Greek for virgin), the other side of the airport: an infamous concentration camp during the junta, now a scarcely more cheerful army base. Things perk up at the end of this, with one of the island's better beaches, **Blefoútis**, with a popular taverna.

Other bays tend not to be worth the effort spent getting there. **Goúrna**, in the west, is long, sandy and gently shelving, but also windy, backed by rubble and devoid of facilities. **Xirókambos** in the south refuses to face the facts of a poor beach as it struggles to be a resort; caiques from Myrtiés on Kálymnos call here in season.

Lipsí

The name Lipsí (sometimes spelt Leipsoí) is supposed to derive from Kalypso, the nymph who held Odysseus in thrall for years. The little island (population 700) has been transformed by tourism and a regular ferry service since the 1980s. The single harbour town (also called **Lipsí**) has been spruced up, accom-

The ancient worship of the goddess Artemis may be responsible for one custom peculiar to Léros: all property is inherited down the female family line.

BELOW: twilight over Télendhos.

modation has multiplied, bulldozer tracks and paved roads creep across the landscape, and mopeds are now available to explore them.

An extraordinarily long esplanade links the ferry quay with the village centre, marked by the three-domed cathedral of Ághios Ioánnis. Behind this is the main square with some cafés and the town hall, whose ecclesiastical museum has some amusing exhibits. As befits a dependency of Pátmos, the older houses have their windows outlined in bright colours which change by the year, just as in Skála. Beaches are scattered across the island. The best and sandiest are the town beach of **Liendoú**, **Platýs Yialós** in the northwest, with a seasonal taverna, and **Katsadhiá**, a double cove in the south, facing Léros, with two tavernas.

Lipsí appears green, but farming is dependent on well water; there is only one spring in the west of the island. Though tractors and pumps are audible by day, nights are given over to the sea's lapping, the crowing of errant roosters, or a snatch of music from one of three bars.

Three remoter islets north of Lipsí are far less developed and can be more easily reached from Pátmos. The permanent population of **Arkí** is just 45, and falling. There's no real village, beach, fresh water, or ferry dock. Electricity is solar, and two ferries each call once a week. Likewise two tavernas keep rooms for guests. **Maráthi**, across a channel, gets some day-trips from Pátmos for the sake of its sandy beach. It is inhabited only in summer, when there are a couple of places to stay. **Agathoníssi**, off towards Sámos, is more of a going concern with its three hamlets and population of about 160. Connections are better too, with hydrofoils dovetailing well with the small ferries. Most tourists stay at the little port of **Ághios Yeórghios**, with a convenient beach. More secluded beaches lie around the headland at Spiliás, or in the far east of the island at Thóli.

Map on page 264

BELOW: café society in Lipsí.

The monastery of St John was built as a fortress to protect its treasures from pirates (there are even slits for pouring boiling oil over attackers). The massive walls were restored after an earthquake in 1956.

BELOW: a courtyard in St John's Monastery, Pátmos.

Pátmos

Pátmos has been indelibly linked to the Bible's Book of Revelations (Apocalypse) ever since tradition placed its authorship here, in AD 95, by John the Evangelist. The volcanic landscape, with its strange rock formations and sweeping views, seems suitably apocalyptic. In 1088 the monk Khristodoulos Latrenos founded a monastery here in honour of St John the Theologian (as the Evangelist is known in Greek), which soon became a focus of scholarship and pilgrimage. A Byzantine imperial charter gave the monks tax exemption and the right to engage in sea-trade, concessions respected by the island's later Venetian and Ottoman rulers.

Although Pátmos is no longer ruled by the monks, their presence tempers the rowdier elements found in most holiday resorts. There is just one, remote nudist beach on the island, nightlife is genteel and those who elect to stay (as opposed to those who arrive by hydrofoil from Kós or Sámos) appreciate the unique, even spiritual, atmosphere that Pátmos exudes once the day-trippers have departed.

Skála ⓘ is the port and largest village, best appreciated late at night when crickets serenade and yacht-masts are illuminated against a dark sky. By day Skála loses charm, but all island commerce, whether shops, banks or travel agencies, is here. Buses leave regularly from the quay for the hilltop **Hóra** ⓘ, but a 40-minute cobbled path short-cutting the road is preferable.

Hóra's core, protected by a massive, pirate-proof fortress and visible from a great distance, is the **Monastery of St John the Theologian** (May–Aug: Sun and Tues–Wed 8am–1pm, 2–6pm, Mon and Thur–Sat 8am–1.30pm; Sept–Apr: hours vary). A photogenic maze of interlinked courtyards, stairways, chapels and passageways, it occupies the site of an ancient Artemis

Map on page 264

temple. The Treasury houses the most impressive monastic collection in Greece outside Mount Áthos. Priceless icons and jewellery are on display, though the prize exhibit is the edict of Emperor Alexios Komnenos granting the island to Khristodhoulos. The library (open only to ecclesiastical scholars) is diminished from its heyday but still contains 4,000 books and manuscripts.

Away from the tourist thoroughfares, Hóra is silent, its thick-walled mansions with their pebble courtyards and arcades the preserve of wealthy foreigners who snapped them up in the 1960s. Short-term rooms are thus hard to come by, but there are a few good tavernas and, from Platía Lótzia in the north, one of the finest views in the Aegean, taking in at least half a dozen islands on all but the haziest of days.

Just over halfway up the path from Skála to Hóra stands the small **Monastery of the Apocalypse** (same hours as main monastery), built around the grotto where John had his Revelation. A silver band on the wall marks the spot where John laid his head to sleep. In the ceiling is a great cleft in the rock through which the divine Voice spoke.

The rest of the island is inevitably something of an anticlimax, but the beaches of Pátmos are surprisingly good. Buses connect with the resort of **Gríkos** ⓓ, whose population in winter falls to a dozen people, and to the fertile village of **Kámbos**, whose beach is popular with Greek families. The biggest sandy beach is **Psilí Ámmos** in the far south, accessible by boat trip or a half-hour walk from the road's end and favoured by naturists. Beaches north of Skála include (in order) **Melóï**, with a good taverna and the island campsite; long **Agriolivádhi**; isolated **Livádhi Yeranoú**, with an islet to swim to; and finally **Lámbi**, with irresistible, multicoloured volcanic pebbles and an excellent taverna.   ❑

BELOW: a young monk at St John's Monastery.

CRETE

Greece's southernmost island – and the largest – is characterised by soaring mountains, a proudly independent people, and unique remains of the first great European civilisation

Map on pages 288–9

Crete (Kríti), claimed by many Greeks to be the most authentic of the islands, is by far the largest. It stretches 256 km (159 miles) east to west and is between 11 and 56 km (7 and 35 miles) wide. A massive mountainous backbone dominates, with peaks stretching skywards to over 2,400 metres 7,874 ft). In the north the mountains slope more gently, producing fertile plains, while in the south they plunge precipitously into the sea. Megalónissos (Great Island) is what Cretans call their home and "great" refers to far more than size.

Great can certainly be applied to the Minoan civilisation, the first in Europe and one with which Crete is inexorably entwined. Visitors by the thousand pour into the ruins of Knossós, Festós, Mália and Káto Zákros, before heading towards one of the scores of excellent beaches. With two major airports, Crete cannot be classified as undiscovered, but through its size and scale it manages to contain the crowds and to please visitors with widely divergent tastes. While a car is essential for discovering the best of the island, car hire is, unfortunately, comparatively expensive.

Most of Crete's 500,000 people live in the north. The mountains to the south, honeycombed with caves, nurture a proud and ruggedly independent people whose fierce mustachioed menfolk still sometimes dress in jodhpurs, black leather knee-boots and black crochet headscarves. Unlike islands more integrated with the mainland, Crete has its own songs, characterised by the *mantinádes*, and its own dances, such as the spectacular *pentozáli*. These are almost invariably accompanied by the *lýra*, a ubiquitous Cretan instrument.

For more than half the year snow lies on the highest peaks, which provide a dramatic backdrop to verdant spring meadows ablaze with flowers. This, as botanists and ornithologists know well, is *the* time to visit. The former arrive to view more than 130 plant species that are unique to the island, while the latter are thrilled by more than 250 types of birds heading north. These migrants briefly join such rare residents as Bonelli's eagle and Eleonora's falcon. And it is in spring that the island is redolent with sage, savory, thyme and oregano. Dittany however is the endemic Cretan herb – did you know that bathing in an infusion of dittany increases sexual desire?

Crete, much more than other Greek islands, is a place both for sightseeing and for being on the beach. Minoan ruins are the major magnets: as well as the archaeological sites, the Archaeological Museum in the capital, **Iráklion ❶**, houses a unique collection of artefacts from Europe's oldest civilisation. But there are also Greek, Roman and Venetian remains

PRECEDING PAGES:
Ághios Nikólaos by night; sunset on the mountains of Crete.
LEFT: the harbour at Haniá. **BELOW:** fresco at the Palace of Knossos.

for which many tourist authorities would give their eye teeth, and literally hundreds of Byzantine churches, many with rare and precious frescoes. These paintings often have a distinct Cretan style recognisable by elongated figures and attention to detail. (Many churches will be locked: enquire at the nearest café for the key.) Dozens of monasteries have fallen into disuse, but others still function and have rich treasures and histories.

Homer's "island of 100 towns" can also be called an island of 100 beaches. Some are simply a place where a boat can be beached, but many are superb stretches of sand. On some, nudity, though not officially sanctioned, is tolerated. The season is long, stretching from Easter until late autumn.

Minoan glory

Most of the Minoan ruins visited at such renowned sites as Knossós, Festós, Mália and Káto Zákros date from the neo-palatial era (1700–1380 BC). Great unfortified palaces, brilliantly decorated, were built and beautiful pottery and magnificent jewellery, used for both religious purposes and personal adornment, were produced.

The first palaces, which were built during the proto-palatial period (2000–1700 BC) and of which scant remains exist today, are generally thought to have been destroyed by an earthquake. Debate still rages as to what brought the neo-palatial era to an end. By the post-palatial period (1300–1100 BC) the Minoan leadership in the eastern Mediterranean was waning, and by the Early Iron Age (1100–650 BC) Crete was under the sway of mainland Greece. Surviving Minoans – Eteo-Cretans – retired to the mountains and continued to maintain their old traditions.

BELOW: large pots *(píthi)* are still made as in Minoan times.

Iráklion (Iráklio, Heráklion)

The capital of Crete since 1971, Iráklion has a population of 120,000 and is the fifth largest city in Greece. It vaunts the highest per capita income of any Greek city, but this does not show in the civic infrastructure. Look not for extensive elegance or great public works. Much of Iráklion resembles a building site because of the tendency of the inhabitants to spend money on starting buildings without sufficient capital for completion.

Most tourists head for the Minoan ruins of Knossós, but this should be combined with a visit to the outstanding **Archaeological Museum** (summer: Tues–Sun 8am–7pm, Mon 12.30–7pm; winter: Tues–Sun 8am–5pm, Mon 12.30–7pm) in order fully to comprehend the site and its contents. The tourist office is almost next door, and both are moments away from the cinema, cafés and restaurants of **Platía Eleftherías** (Freedom Square) **Ⓑ**, popular with both local people and visitors.

Iráklion's other major attractions, other than the Minoan, are from the Venetian era, testifying that this was Crete's most prosperous period in historical times. Head seawards to the old harbour and visit the Venetian **Arsenali Ⓒ** (covered boat-building yards) and the restored **Koúles fortress Ⓓ** (Tues–Sun 8.30am–3pm) whose three high-reliefs of the Lion of St Mark announce its provenance. Observe Mount Yioúhtas, ever present in the background, resembling a recumbent figure said to be that of Zeus. The fortress is illuminated after dark – a fine spectacle from the quayside cafés.

A few minutes to the west of the old harbour on S. Venizélou Street is the **Historical Museum Ⓔ** (Mon–Fri 9am–5pm, Sat 9am–2pm), with collections from early Christian times onwards.

The Archaeological Museum in Iráklion is best visited in the afternoon, when it is quieter. You can take a break in the garden café – but remember to retain your museum ticket for re-admission.

BELOW: the Venetian fort overlooking Iráklion harbour.

Iráklion's Morosíni Fountain, built by the Venetians in the 1620s, originally had a giant statue of Poseidon on top (matching the sea gods around the basin below the lions) but he went missing during the Turkish occupation.

Head towards the city centre and the upmarket cafés of **Platía Venizélou** (Venizélou Square, also known as Lion or Fountain Square) which takes its popular names from the stylish 17th-century **Morosíni Fountain ❻** and guardian marble lions. Overlooking the square is the Venetian **Loggia ❼** (city hall) flanked by the churches of **Ághios Márkos ❽** and, in its own little square, **Ághios Títos ❶**. All three of these buildings have been heavily restored. Since 1966, when it was returned from St Mark's Basilica in Venice, the skull of St Titus, St Paul's apostle to Crete and the island's first bishop, has been housed in Ághios Títos.

Walk south through the "market street", redolent with tantalising smells, jammed with people and resonant with decibels, but now very touristy (the true city markets now take place in Iráklion's suburban streets) and then west to the cathedral of **Ághios Minás ❶**. More interesting than the cathedral is the **Icon Museum** (Mon–Fri 10am–1pm), housed in the small church of **Aghía Ekateríni ❶**, which contains some exquisite icons, six of them the work of the 16th-century master, Mihaíl Damaskinós.

Challenging but rewarding is a circumambulation of the 15th-century city walls which, in their day, were the most formidable in the Mediterranean. The walls stretch for nearly 4 km (2½ miles) and in parts are 29 metres (95 ft) thick. En route, pause a moment at the tomb of the great Irákliot author and iconoclast Níkos Kazantzákis to enjoy the views and perhaps to consider the brief inscription on fear, hope and freedom.

The best beaches near Iráklion are at **Ammoudára**, just west of town, and at **Karterós**, **Toumbroúk** and **Amnissós** to the east. The latter, which was the port for **Knossós**, has the best sands but is under the flight path to the airport.

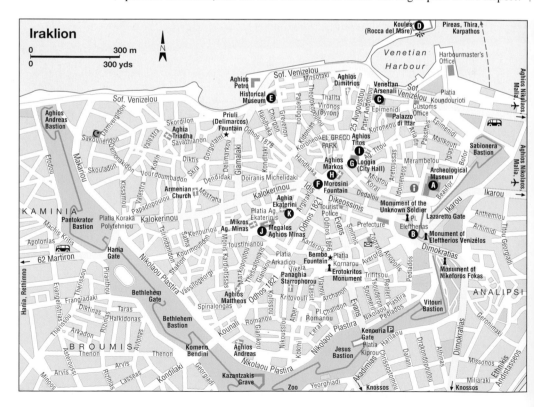

To Knossós and beyond

Several short excursions from Iráklion will delight any lover of Minoan sites, providing opportunities to view the attractive countryside and to savour village life. The most famous site, of course, is the palace of **Knossós** ❷, a mere 5 km (3 miles) southwest of the city centre, and easily reached on a No. 2 bus from Iráklion. *(For a full exploration of the remains at Knossós, see pages 302–3.)* In and around the village of **Arhánes** ❸,12 km (8 miles) south of Knossós, are three churches with interesting frescoes and icons, three Minoan sites, and an excellent new museum. **Turkoghitoniá** has a Minoan palace; **Fourní** possesses the most outstanding cemetery in the prehistoric Aegean; and the remains of a Minoan temple have been unearthed at **Anemóspilia**.

A steep climb from Arhánes (allow 1 hour) leads to the summit of **Mount Yioúhtas** (811 metres/2,660 ft), from where you can admire the panorama while griffon vultures soar overhead. At the top are a Minoan peak sanctuary, a 14th-century chapel and caves in which Zeus is said to be buried.

Týlissos ❹, 13 km (8 miles) southwest of Iráklion, possesses three well-preserved small palaces or large villas (daily 8.30am–3pm) and is one of the few present-day villages to retain its original prehellenic name. Twenty kilometres (13 miles) further west on the same road, the elongated village of **Anóghia**, where wool is spun and where many homes have looms, is a weaving and embroidery centre. Many Anoghians wear native dress with the picture-book men looking like rebels in search of a cause. This is no stage setting: Anóghia has a long tradition of resistance and revolt. The village was razed in 1821 and 1866, and in 1944 the entire male population of the village was killed by German troops.

Maps:
City 284
Area 288

Human remains found at Anemóspilia suggest that when the temple was destroyed by an earthquake (around 1700 BC) a priest was in the act of ritually sacrificing a youth.

BELOW: a market street in Iráklion.

Zorba's Legacy

Seldom has a fictional character so engulfed its creator as did Zorba the Greek swallow Níkos Kazantzákis (1883–1957), the best-known Greek writer of the modern era. Although Kazantzákis's output was large and varied, it is to the rugged, warm and happy-go-lucky Zorba that he owed his reputation.

At least, that was so until another of his books was also made into a film, *The Last Temptation of Christ*. When this book was first published, the Orthodox Church sought to prosecute him. When the film was screened in 1988, many church leaders the world over sought to have it banned. In - Athens, priests marched on the cinemas where the movie was playing and screens were slashed.

When Kazantzákis was born in 1883, Crete had not yet become a part of the Greek nation but was still embroiled in attempts to free itself from the Turkish yoke, a struggle which drove the Kazantzákis family to move

to the island of Náxos soon after Níkos was born. But it is here on the "Great Island" that he is buried: once a Cretan, always a Cretan – indeed, no self-respecting Cretan refers to his- or herself as a Greek.

Yet, because of his non-conformist views and writings, Kazantzákis was denied burial in a Christian cemetery with the full rites of the Orthodox church. He was buried in the Martinengo bastion of the Iráklion walls, from where there is an inspiring view over the Cretan mountains. His modest tomb carries this inscription: "I hope for nothing. I fear nothing. I am free." A statue in Eleftherías (Freedom) Square in Iráklion honours him more than does his grave tucked away on the town's battlements.

His admirers will make for the Kazantzákis Museum in the village of Mirtiá (24 km/ 15 miles) due south of Iráklion (when Kazantzákis was born here, it was called Varvári). Well arranged displays illustrate his personal, literary and political life both in Greece and abroad, with one room entirely devoted to Zorba. And in the Historical and Ethnographic museum in Iráklion, a complete room has been set aside to represent a study of Kazantzákis.

Those who favour fiction rather than fact have much to see in Crete. Ierápetra was the home of Madame Hortense, the French courtesan who featured in *Zorba*. Visitors may be shown where her still body was washed and where, even before the body was cold, the old harpies rushed in and stripped her apartment of all her possessions. A French courtesan who was the model for Kazantzákis's Madame Hortense did indeed live in Ierápetra during the early 20th century.

Much of *Zorba* was filmed in Pláka and, high above it, Kókkino Horió, which lie on the coast midway between Réthymnon and Haniá. Here habitués of the local tavernas may not recall the name of Kazantzákis but remember well that of Anthony Quinn. Then, in the northwest corner of the Akrotíri Peninsula, there is Stavrós with its pleasant beach, shallow waters and towering cliffs – known to the locals as "Zorba's Mountain" – where the film's climax was shot. ❑

LEFT: Spýros Hrisofákes of Ierápetra with a photograph of the original Madame Hortense.

Map on pages 288–9

From Anóghia the road climbs to the magnificent **Nída plateau**, from where it is a 20-minute uphill stroll to the **Idean Cave**; this was the nursery, if not the birthplace, of Zeus. Here the god was hidden and guarded by the Kourétes, who clashed their weapons to drown the sound of his cries, while the nymph Amalthée fed him goats' milk. Climbers might wish to push on to the summit of **Mount Ida (Psilorítis)** ❺, at 2,456 metres (8,058 ft) the highest point on Crete. A guide can be hired: allow up to 8 hours for the round trip.

East from Iráklion

Return to Iráklion and continue eastwards along the expressway for 24 km (15 miles), but then forget the "express". You have reached the Cretan Riviera, a stretch best avoided, with the resorts of **Hersónissos** ❻, **Stalídha** (Stális) and **Mália** ❼, notorious for their tourist tat. However, the beaches have good sand, even if most of it is occupied by tourists. Hersónissos has scanty Greek and Roman remains while close to the beach near Mália is a renowned Minoan site. Stalída has to settle for native palm trees.

The **Palace** at Mália (Tues–Sun 8.30am–3pm), traditionally associated with King Sarpedon, brother of Minos, is contemporary with that at Knossós. The ruins are not as extensive as those at Knossós or Festós but, even without a Knossós-style reconstruction, are more readily understood. The remarkable number of store rooms and workrooms, as well as the simpler style of architecture, suggests a country villa more than a palace. Recent excavations have unearthed the Hrysólakkos (Golden Pit) from the proto-palatial period (1900–1700 BC). This name is derived from the numerous gold artefacts found in this enormous necropolis.

Black crochet headscarves (along with baggy jodhpurs and high boots) are the traditional dress still worn in many parts of Crete.

BELOW: woven goods in Anóghia.

There are thousands of cloth-sailed wind pumps across the Lasíthi Plain, but only a few are still used to pump up water for irrigation.

From either Mália or Hersónissos, twisting mountain roads lead up to the **Lasíthi Plateau ❽**, around 840 metres (2,756 ft) above sea level and 57 km (36 miles) from Iráklion. This fertile and impeccably cultivated land supports a cornucopia of potatoes and grain crops, apples and pears. The visitor can well believe that Crete was the granary of Rome, and may recall Pliny's statement that whatever is produced in Crete is incomparably better than that produced in other parts. However, you will rarely see the unfurled sails of the 10,000 wind-pumps that irrigate the rich alluvial soil.

Proceed counter-clockwise around the plateau. **Psyhró** is the starting point for the descent to the giant **Díktian Cave**, supposedly the birthplace of Zeus. Before leaving the plain, try to visit **Tzermiádho** and its **Trapéza Cave**, which is the mythical home of Kronos and Rhea, the parents of Zeus. In Ághios Yeórghios is the Cretan Folklore Museum (Tues–Sun 9am–4pm) with household, craft and agricultural exhibits.

Eight km (5 miles) after leaving Mália, the main coastal road passes the chapel of **Ághios Yeórghios Selenáris**. Public transport often stops here to allow passengers to give thanks for a journey completed and to pray for a safe continuation. Such roadside shrines are not uncommon at the midpoint of dangerous roads.

Head safely on to **Ághios Nikólaos ❾**, 69 km (43 miles) from Iráklion, invariably abbreviated by tourists to "Ag Nik" and once the St-Tropez of Crete. This picture-postcard tourist paradise, overlooked by the eastern mountains, is magnificently situated on the Gulf of Mirabello. Here, and at neighbouring **Eloúnda ❿** (10 km/6 miles away), are some of the island's best and most expensive hotels. Unfortunately Ághios Nikólaos does lack a decent beach,

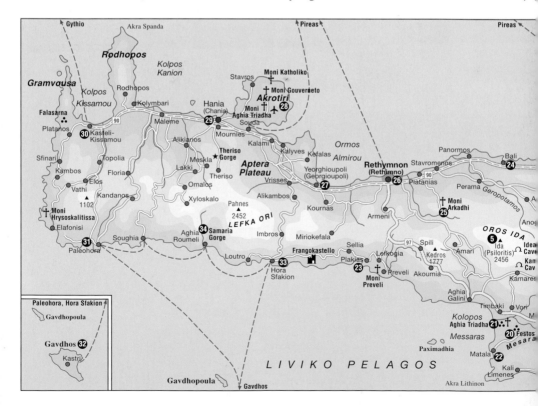

having built a football pitch over its best one, although there are some passable sands a couple of miles to the east. Restaurants and hotels, discos and cafés cluster Ághios Nikólaos's Mandhráki harbour and the small, so-called, bottomless lake. The latter is connected to the harbour by a canal. Although it is not what most visitors come here for, the town does have a pleasant archaeological museum (Tues–Sun 8.30am–3pm) and folk museum. Also worth seeing is the Byzantine church of Ághios Nikólaos.

The nearby island of **Spinalónga** with its ruined Venetian fortress is readily reached from Ághios Nikólaos by boat. (In 1589 the Venetians made the peninsula of Spinalónga an island by cutting a canal.) Aristotle Onassis considered building a casino here, but fortunately did not.

Clinging to the hillside 11 km (7 miles) from Ághios Nikólaos is **Kritsá ⑪** "the largest village in Crete", where lovely frescoes adorn the church of **Ághios Yeórghios**. Immediately below Kritsá is the church of **Panaghía Kerá** (Mon–Sat 9am–3pm, Sun 9am–2pm), which is Crete's greatest Byzantine treasure. The entire interior is a picture-book bible consisting of 12th- to 15th-century frescoes. Indicative of changing times, until a few years ago Panaghía Kerá was a functioning church: it is now a museum and charges admission.

A couple of miles beyond and above Kritsá are the ruins of **Lató**. The pleasure here lies not so much in the fairly extensive remains of a Greco-Roman city but the superb views. From the northern acropolis, look across plains covered with an infinity of olive and almond trees to the coast and to Ághios Nikólaos (once the port for Lató) and beyond, to the Gulf of Mirabello and the Sitía mountains. To sit here and absorb the view with the background music provided by the bells of unseen sheep is to feel completely at peace.

Lake Voulisméni at Ághios Nikólaos was said to be bottomless, and the home of spirits. Unromantic modern surveyors have found that it is about 70 metres (230 ft) deep and fed by an underground river.

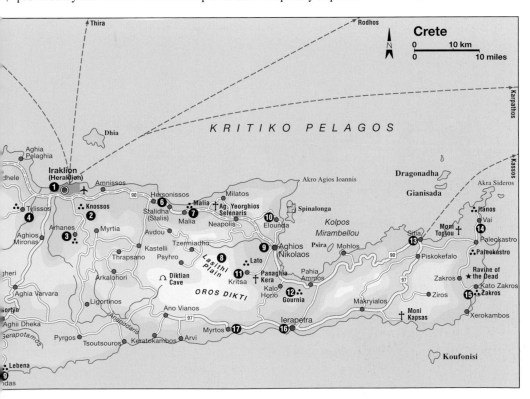

The 16th-century Venetian fortress on Spinalónga, near Ághios Nikólaos, was used as a leper colony until 1957 – the last in Europe.

BELOW: Sitía harbour.

Leave Ághios Nikólaos and head eastwards for Sitía. After 19km (12 miles), **Gourniá** ⓬ is reached (Tues–Sun 8.30am–3pm). Spread over a ridge, overlooking the sea, are remains, not of another palace, but of streets and houses of a Minoan town, the best preserved on the island. Especially in spring, when the site is covered with a riot of flowers and their perfume fills the air, even those bored with old stones will be delighted to be here.

A few miles further and a poorly surfaced side road drops to the unspoiled fishing village of **Móhlos**. The tiny island opposite, which can be readily reached by strong swimmers, bears the same name as the village and has scanty Minoan ruins. Some way beyond is the larger island of **Psíra** where a Minoan town and port are being excavated. (Both islands can, on occasions, be reached by boat from Ághios Nikólaos.)

Sitía ⓭, 70 km (43 miles) from Ághios Nikólaos, is a somewhat laid-back town which, to the delight of visitors and the chagrin of locals, has not yet hit the big time. Here are the almost obligatory Venetian fort, archaeological museum (Tues–Sun 9am–3pm), and a disappointing beach. There is also a folklore museum.

Toploú Monastery, its tall 16th-century Italianate bell-tower beckoning like the minaret of a mosque, stands in splendid isolation in the middle of nowhere beyond Sitía. The monastery derived its name from a renowned artillery piece (*top* is Turkish for cannon) which formerly protected it. The monks also had other methods of protecting themselves: observe the hole above the monastery gate through which they poured hot oil over their assailants.

After a further 9 km (6 miles) is **Váï** ⓮, renowned for its myriad palm trees and the large, sandy beach that suggests far-away tropics. Don't believe it. The

palm trees are native, not the species associated with desert islands, and the beach is usually crowded. For a more relaxed time, better make for the quiet, palm-free **Ítanos**, a couple of miles farther north.

Southwards from Vaï is **Paléokastro**, which hit the headlines because of outstanding finds at the largest Minoan town yet to be uncovered. Beaches about a mile away, especially at the southern end of the bay, are worth visiting. Further on is **Ano Zákros**, the starting point to **Káto Zákros** ⑮ (summer: 10am–5pm; winter: Tues–Sun 8.30am–3pm), the fourth great Minoan site. Hikers will prefer to make their way from Upper to Lower Zákros by walking through the spectacular **Ravine of the Dead**, where caves were used for Minoan burials.

The ruins at Káto Zákros, 43 km (27 miles) from Sitía, are from the neo-palatial era, but there are intrusions from the proto-palatial era. They are often waterlogged because Crete is tipping over longitudinally, with its eastern end sinking below and its western end rising above the water table. The main dig has its customary central courtyard and royal, religious and domestic buildings and workshops radiating outwards. Close by are the remains of a Minoan town and of a sheltered Minoan harbour, ideally situated for trade with the Levant and Egypt. As at many Minoan sites, the setting is everything.

Unusually, the dig at Káto Zákros is privately funded. In the 1960s Dr Nikólas Pláton, director of the Archaeological Service, was asked by the Pomerances, a New York business couple, if any Minoan sites had still to be excavated. Yes, he told them. So what, they asked, was the problem? Money, was the reply. With that, the Pomerances underwrote the dig with no strings attached.

Back at Gourniá, a flat road crosses the island's isthmus to **Ierápetra** ⑯ (35 km/22 miles from Ághios Nikólaos), the largest town on the south coast.

Map on pages 288–9

The plantation of palm trees at Vaï, which has existed since Classical times, may be unique in Europe. The trees are now fenced in to protect them.

LEFT: Vaï's palm-fringed beach.

Over the past decade Ierápetra has enjoyed a boom, not only because of tourism but also because of market gardening and the uncovering of archaeological sites. The town, scarcely atmospheric, has a promenade at the rear of a not-so-good beach, an archaeological museum and a small Venetian fort.

Fifteen km (9 miles) to the west lies the pretty village resort of **Mýrtos** , which takes advantage of mild weather to remain open through the winter. Eastwards 24 km (15 miles) from Ierápetra is the new and inchoate summer resort, and reasonable beach, of **Makryghiálos**. From here a side road leads to the 14th-century **Kapsás Monastery**, built snugly into the cliffs at the entrance to a gorge. Monks will show you, encased in a silver casket, the skull of Gerondoyánnis, a 19th-century faith healer who is a kind of cult figure. Káto Zákros is practically round the corner, but cannot be reached without returning to Makrýialos and then taking the twisting mountain roads to Sitía.

South from Iráklion

Head south from Iráklion, over a lower point in the island's spine, and you reach the very centre of the island, at **Aghía Varvára**. Straight on brings you to a breath-taking view of the Plain of Mesará. Rich soil and a benign climate make this a cornucopia where the wild flowers are said to be taller and larger than anywhere else in Crete.

At the edge of the plain, 40 km (25 miles) from Iráklion, is the almost sacred village of **Aghíi Dhéka** (Holy Ten), with its heavily restored medieval church into which are incorporated fragments from the nearby site of Górtyn. Aghíi Dhéka is renowned because in AD 250, during the persecution of the Christians, 10 men were executed who are not only among the most revered of Cretan

BELOW: Zarós in the Plain of Mesará.

saints, but also glorified as the first in a long line of Cretans willing to sacrifice themselves to oppose the tyrannical occupiers of their beloved island.

After another 1 km (½ mile), you reach **Górtyn (Górtys)** ⑱. This was the capital of the Romans who came to Crete in the 1st century BC to settle feuds but who stayed to conquer. Outstanding and upstanding are the Roman *odeion* and a triple-naved basilica (daily 8am–7pm). The latter is by far the best preserved early church in Crete and was built to house the tomb of St Titus, Crete's first bishop, who died in AD 105. However, the most renowned artefacts are some stone blocks incorporated into the *odeion*. About 2,500 years ago more than 17,000 characters were incised on these to produce the Code of Górtyn, which consists of rules governing the behaviour of the people.

Those in search of more classical ruins, of health and good swimming, might wish to head south to **Léndas** ⑲ (72 km/45 miles from Iráklion) over a mountainous road that provides magnificent vistas. Nearby ancient **Lebéna** was the port for Górtyn, and its therapeutic springs made it a renowned healing sanctuary with an **Asklipíon** (temple to Asklipiós, the god of healing). Traces of this sanctuary, with mosaic floors and large baths, can be seen. In an attempt to equal if not emulate the ancients, nude bathing is popular at Léndas's best beach, beyond the headland at the western end of the village.

Festós (Phaestos) ⑳, Crete's second great Minoan site, occupies a magnificent location 16 km (10 miles) west of Górtyn (summer: 8am–7pm; winter: 8am–5pm). Most of the remains are from the neo-palatial period, although part of the floor plan of the proto-palatial palace is discernable. State-rooms, religious quarters, workshops, store-rooms and functional plumbing can all be identified. An outstanding sight is the Grand Stairway.

Map on pages 288–9

The text of the Code of Górtyn is written in "ox-plough" fashion, reading left to right along one line, then right to left along the next.

BELOW: shepherds milking in the mountains.

The remains of two palaces can be seen at Festós: the first was built around 1900 BC and destroyed by an earthquake 200 years later; the other was seriously damaged around 1450 BC, possibly by a tidal wave.

BELOW: Mátala's sandstone caves.

Nearby, again on a glorious site with views of the Libyan Sea, are the attractive Minoan ruins of **Aghía Triádha** ㉑ (winter: 8.30am–3pm; summer: 8am–7pm) whose exact function – palace or villa – still causes speculation.

Next, on to **Mátala** ㉒, 70 km (43 miles) from Iráklion. The resort first gained renown when the sandstone caves in the cliffs around the small, excellent sandy beach became home to the world's hippies, and Joni Mitchell wrote a song about it. Today the small village can be busy, yet not frenetic. The scenic 30-minute walk south to Red Beach is highly recommended, though Kómmos beach to the north is much larger and has a recently excavated Minoan site.

The larger south coast resort of **Aghía Galíni** also lies on the Gulf of Mesará, though a little further west (70 km/43 miles from Iráklion by the most direct route). If Mátala proved too boisterous, Aghía Galíni will be far more so. The harbour, with a short wide quay and a tiny main street jammed with tavernas and bars, is enclosed within a crescent of steep hills covered with modest hotels. Nightlife goes on into the wee small hours. Not for the faint-hearted.

Into western Crete, and **Plakiás** ㉓ is reached, with its five large beaches and spectacular mountain backdrop, 112 km (70 miles) from Iráklion. An almost mandatory pilgrimage is the 13 km (8 miles) to the **Monastery of Préveli** (daily 8.30am–1.30pm, 3.30–8.30pm), passing en route the evocative ruins of the **Monastery of Ághios Ioánnis**. Préveli has a superb position, an interesting museum whose highlights include a piece of the True Cross, and a courtyard fountain with the inscription "Wash your sins, not just your face". At one time, the monastery's vast estates stretched from the Libyan to the Cretan seas. Below the monastery is a beach from where Allied troops in World War II escaped to waiting submarines after being sheltered by the monks.

Further along the coast to the west is the Venetian castle of **Frangokástello**, close-by an excellent sandy beach. In 1828, 385 freedom fighters from Sfákia were killed here; it is said that the mysterious *dhrossoulítes* (dew men), an atmospheric mirage that occurs in late May, are their ghosts.

Map on pages 288–9

West from Iráklion

Back in Iráklion, an oleander-lined expressway runs west towards Réthymnon. Some, however, might prefer more leisurely travel on the picturesque but winding old road. Alternatively, leave the new road 25 km (16 miles) from the capital to arrive in **Fódhele (Phódele)**, a small village rich in orange trees and locally made embroidery. A restored house here is said to be the birthplace in 1545 of Domínikos Theotokópoulos, better known as El Greco. Fódhele's fame may be fleeting, for the latest word is that El Greco was probably born in Iráklion. Back on the expressway, turn seawards after a further 18 km (11 miles) to reach the idyllic resort of **Balí ㉔**, which is clustered around three small bays at the foot of a hill.

At **Stavroménos** or **Plataniás**, just before Réthymnon, turn southeast for the beautifully situated **Arkádhi Monastery ㉕** (daily 8am–1.30pm, 2.30–8pm), 80 km (50 miles) from Iráklion, Crete's most sacred shrine. In 1886, the monastery, sheltering hundreds of women and children, was attacked by the Turks. Rather than surrender, the abbot ordered that gunpowder stored in the now roofless room in the northwest corner of the courtyard be ignited, thus killing both enemy (1,500 Ottoman soldiers died in the blast) and refugees. This act of defiance brought the plight of the Cretans to the public eye and gained for them the sympathy and assistance of much of Europe.

When Arkádhi Monastery exploded, one infant was blown into a tree and survived. She grew up to become a nun.

BELOW: Arkádhi Monastery.

A Cretan Myth

King Minos, mythical king of Knossós, was the son of Zeus and the Phoenician princess Europa. Zeus had seduced Europa while in the form of a bull and taken her off to Crete, where Minos and his brothers, Rhadamanthys and Sarpedon, were born. Minos spent nine years in the Dhíkti cave with his father learning the arts of kingship, after which he banished his brothers and became the sole ruler of Crete.

Wishing to consolidate his power, Minos asked Poseidon for a boon and the god provided a white bull to be sacrificed. However, Minos could not bring himself to kill the beautiful animal and sacrificed another in its place. This enraged Poseidon, who made Pasiphae, the wife of Minos, fall in love with a bull.

Daedalus, an ingenious member of the court, built a model of a cow for Pasiphae in which she could hide while the bull mounted her. The result of this was the half-man, half-bull Minotaur. Minos was furious when he found out about Pasiphae's son and ordered Daedalus to build a labyrinth under the court where the Minotaur was to live.

In the meantime the white bull had been taken to the Peloponnese by Herakles as one of his 12 tasks. There it did great damage and Minos's son, Androgeus, set out to hunt it. While out hunting, Androgeus was killled by a jealous Athenian rival. Minos immediately sent his fleet to Athens and after a long war, defeated the Athenians.

The Cretan king then demanded a tribute; the sacrifice six young men and six young women of Athens every year. They were to enter the labyrinth where they would be killed by the Minotaur.

One year Theseus, the son of the king of Athens, was selected for the sacrifice. While on Crete he met and fell in love with Ariadne, the daughter of Minos, who promised to help him. She passed Theseus a ball of thread to mark his way through the labyrinth to prevent him getting lost. He entered the maze and killed the Minotaur. On his escape he and Ariadne fled to Athens. ❑

Map on pages 288–9

Réthymnon (Réthimno) **㉖**, 77 km (48 miles) from Iráklion, which prides itself on being Crete's intellectual capital, still possesses an intact old town with a small, picturesque Venetian harbour. Its major attraction is a quayside choc-a-bloc with colourful but expensive fish restaurants guarded by an elegant lighthouse. West of the harbour is the immense ruined **Fortétsa** (Tues–Sun 8am–8pm), said to be the largest Venetian castle, and from where excellent views may be enjoyed. Réthymnon's other attractions – the **Rimóndi Fountain**, the **Archaeological Museum** (Tues–Sun 8.30am–3pm) and the **Neradzés Mosque** – all lie between the harbour and the fortress.

Venetian houses with unexpected architectural delights can be found in the narrow streets linking these sights, while Ottoman features in the shape of minarets and overhanging wooden oriels give Réthymnon a Turkish-style raffishness. Besotted shoppers, especially those in search of leather and textiles, will find their nirvana in narrow, crowded Arkadhíou Street. Sun-worshippers will make for Réthymnon's wide beach. There are decent sands, backed by a palm-shaded promenade which starts immediately east of the harbour and stretches for several miles past the new part of town.

Réthymnon and Haniá to the west are joined by an expressway and an old road. Leave the highway after 23 km (14 miles) and enter **Yeorghioúpoli (Georgioúpoli) ㉗** at the mouth of the River Armyrós. This delightful princely hideaway has a good long beach and a eucalyptus-shaded square.

Áptera, a flat plateau above Kalýves, provides not only excellent panoramas of the enormous **Gulf of Soúda** and the **Akrotíri peninsula ㉘**, but also insights into Crete's history. Visit the recently restored monastery of **Ághios Ioánnis Theológos**, the ruined Turkish fort, and the Greco-Roman remains (Mon–Fri 8am–7pm, Sat–Sun 8am–3pm). The name Áptera (Wingless Ones) is derived from the Sirens.

Haniá (Chaniá, Khaniá) ㉙, 59 km (37 miles) from Réthymnon, is Crete's second city and its capital until 1971. It is a larger version of Réthymnon and claims to be one of the oldest continuously inhabited cities in the world. Its jewel is the boat-free outer Venetian harbour. The quayside is wide and backed by characterful, colourful old buildings of the Venetian Quarter, whose reflections shimmer in the water. The ambience is of the Levant and this is the place for the *vólta,* the evening stroll.

The restored 17th-century **Mosque of Hassán Pasha,** the oldest mosque in Crete, stands at one end of the quay and is now the tourist office, while the restored **Firkás Sea Fortress**, which houses the naval museum (Tues–Sun 10am–4pm), occupies the other end. Here in December 1913 the king of Greece officially raised the national flag for the first time on Crete. The Old Town, where artisans, especially leather workers, still occupy workshops, can be entered from this point by way of Angélou and Theotokopoúlou Streets. Both have splendid examples of domestic Venetian architecture. On Theotokopoúlou is the 15th-century church of San Salvatore, which now houses the excellent collections of the **Byzantine and Post-Byzantine Museum** (summer: daily 8.30am–5pm; winter: Tues–Sun 8.30am–3pm).

"The appearance of the town [Haniá] was striking, as its irregular wooden buildings rose up the hill sides from the sea, interspersed with palm trees, mosques and minarets. There was no mistaking we were in Turkey."

– HENRY FANSHAW TOZER, 1890

BELOW: Réthymnon harbour.

The lighthouse at Hánia, designed like a minaret, dates from the period 1830–40, when Crete was handed over to Egypt in reward for helping the Turks crush the rebellious Greeks.

BELOW: Hánia harbour in the early morning light.

The **Archaeological Museum** (summer: Tues–Sun 8am–7pm, Mon 12.30–7pm; winter: 12.30–3pm) occupies the church of the Franciscan Friary, one of the best preserved and largest of a score of Venetian churches. The church of **Ághios Nikólaos**, after various architectural and religious conversions, displays both a minaret and a campanile. Another example of ecumenicalism is the small, drab Orthodox Cathedral, built by a grateful Turkish Muslim whose son's life had been saved by the intervention of the Virgin Mary.

In the New Town, visit the lofty glass-roofed cruciform **market**, opened by Venizélos in 1913. A wonderful place to pick up bits for a picnic, the market overflows with vegetables, fruit, fish, meat, herbs and spices, cheese and wine.

Those with a sense of history will visit **Mourniés** and **Thériso**, villages south of Haniá. The house in which Venizélos was born, now a museum, is in Mourniés. From here, a delightful journey through the Thériso Gorge brings the visitor to the village of that name. Much revered by the Cretans is the house of Venizélos's mother, which served as a revolutionary headquarters and is now a national shrine.

Akrotíri, a limestone peninsula stretching northeastwards from Haniá, is full of interest. First visit the hill of **Profítis Ilías**, where revolutionary Cretans gathered in 1897 to demand union with Greece. Here are the simple graves of Venizélos and his son Sofoklís.

Other graves, 1,527 of them, are found at the nearby immaculately maintained **Commonwealth Cemetery**, where British and Commonwealth troops killed during the 1941 Battle of Crete are buried. Equal honour is given to three times that number of Germans who are buried in the well-tended cemetery at **Máleme**, 16 km (10 miles) west of Haniá. And on the western outskirts of

Haniá stands a massive memorial topped by a diving eagle honouring Germans killed while attempting to oppress the Cretans: an unusual example of tolerance.

Farther out on the Akrotíri, 16 km (10 miles) from Haniá, is the important **Monastery of Aghía Triádha** (closed 2–5pm). A further 4 km (2½ miles) away and reached by a deteriorating road, is the **Gouvernéto Monastery**, a century older. Both have many treasures and shaded courtyards where visitors can chat with monks. From Gouvernéto a rough 40-minute downhill scramble leads to the abandoned, enchanting and possibly enchanted **Katholikó Monastery**, concealed in a ravine populated only by goats. Dating from about 1200, this is, if not the oldest, certainly one of the first monastic settlements on Crete.

St John the Hermit is thought to have lived and died in a cave near the Katholikó Monastery.

West from Haniá

The road west from Haniá hugs the coast, passing several busy small resorts that merge imperceptibly with each other, before arriving at the **Kolymbári** crossroads. Proceed westwards through low hills. Emerge through a cleft to memorable views of the plain of Kastéli and the Bay of Kíssamos, enclosed within the peninsulas of Rodhopós and Gramvoúsa. These are sometimes compared to a bull's horns, but more resemble rabbit's ears on the map. The road makes a tortuous descent to the plain and to pleasant but rather characterless **Kastéli-Kíssamos (Kastélli)** ❸, with its wide, broad beach, Roman ruins and a seldom open museum (42 km/26 miles from Haniá).

Turn left at **Plátanos** and a twisting road, reminiscent of a corniche, leads after 44 km (28 miles) from Kastéli, to **Váthi** and several splendidly frescoed Byzantine churches. From Váthi a poor, dusty road through a ravine leads, after 10 km (6 miles), to the **Hrysoskalítissa Convent** (7am–sunset). The name

BELOW: shadows in the afternoon.

**Map
on pages
288–9**

*The Samariá Gorge
is the home of the
rare and elusive
Cretan wild goat, the
agrími or krí-krí.*

BELOW: the
"Gates", Samariá
Gorge. **RIGHT:**
maintaining the
boat at Ayía Galíni.

means Golden Stairway and refers to one of the 90 steps descending from the
terrace being made of solid gold. Failure to recognise that step is considered proof
that you have sinned. From Hrysoskalítissa the road terminates at the broad sands
of **Elafonísi**, bordering a shallow lagoon; this is one of best spots on the whole
island for beach lovers, and can become very crowded in summer.

Around the corner to the southwest lies **Paleóhora** ❸ (76 km/47 miles from
Haniá), a self-contained resort that has a ruined castle and both sand and shingle
beaches, the latter for windy days. Occasional boats leave for **Gávdhos** ❸
island, Europe's southernmost point.

Hóra Sfakíon (Sfakiá) ❸, 75km (47 miles) by road from Haniá, is the home
of the Sfakians, who epitomise the independent Cretans. It's a small, cliff-
hanging, picturesque port with a brave past. Sadly, its sole *raison d'être* today
– but don't tell this to the Sfakians – is to transfer exhausted tourists returning
by ferry from their Samariá Gorge excursion.

Samariá Gorge

The most exciting and spectacular adventure which Crete offers the average
visitor is a walk through the **Gorge of Samariá** ❸ (1 May–31 Oct: daily
6am–3pm; entrance fee), at 18 km (11 miles) one of the longest in Europe. The
walk starts by descending a steep stairway at Xylóskalo, 1200 m (3,937 ft)
above the sea, at the southern end of the vast Omalós plain, itself a 45-km (28-
mile) tortuous drive from Haniá. Within a couple of kilometres' walking, the
path is 600 metres (1,968 ft) lower, then after a further 8 km (5 miles), the
abandoned village of Samariá and its church come into view. Stop and admire
the church's lovely 14th-century frescoes: an opportunity to regain your breath
without loss of face.

The going now gets tough and involves criss-
crossing the river-bed. Be warned: flash floods can
occur and wardens' warnings should be observed. The
gorge narrows and the walls soar straight upwards for
300 to 600 metres (1,000–2,000 ft). Soon after
passing the church of Aféndis Hristós, the **Pórtes**
(Gates) are reached and the gorge, scarcely penetrated
by sunlight here, is little more than 3.5 metres (11 ft)
wide. However, only a giant can, as sometimes
claimed, stretch out and touch each side of the gorge.

The park is under the strict aegis of the Haniá
Forest Service which specifically forbids singing,
among other activities. Even the most innocent of
botanists will be delighted by the gorge, and
ornithologists have been known to spot bearded
vultures overhead.

And so to **Aghía Rouméli** and the church of the
Panaghía. However, all is not over: this is old semi-
abandoned Aghía Rouméli and the goal is new Aghía
Rouméli on the coast. This means a further 3 km
(2 miles) of hot and anticlimactic walking before
celebrating with that longed-for swim or cold drink.
Refreshed, the only practical exit from the gorge,
other than retracing the same route, is by boat
eastwards to Hóra Sfakíon or westwards to Paleóhora.
There are no roads; allow four to six hours for the
walk along the gorge. ❏

CENTRE OF EUROPE'S FIRST CIVILISATION

Until a century ago, the Minoan civilisation was little more than a myth. Now its capital is one of the largest and best restored sites in all Greece

Knossós is a place of questions, many of them unanswered. Some visitors to the site find the concrete reconstructions and repainted frescoes (often from very small existing fragments) aid comprehension. But for many, used to other, more recent, ruins that are clearly defensive or overtly religious, the site is mysterious. Can we hope to look back at fragments of a culture from 3,500 years ago and understand its imperatives and subtleties?

In legend, Knossós was the labyrinth of King Minos, where he imprisoned the minotaur, the human-bovine child of his wife Pasiphae. In reality, the role of the Minoan palace was probably not in the modern sense of a palace, but perhaps as an administrative and economic centre, unified by spiritual leaders.

Among the 1,300 rooms of the main palace were both the sacred and the commercial: lustral baths for holy ceremonies; store rooms for agricultural produce; workshops for metallurgy and stone-cutting. Nearby are the Royal Villa and the Little Palace.

Try to visit early or late in the day (better still, visit out of season), to avoid the worst of the substantial crowds, and to avoid being swept along by the flow. Look for the subtle architectural delights – light wells to illuminate the larger rooms; hydraulic controls providing water for drinking, bathing and flushing away sewage; drains with parabolic curves at the bends to prevent overflow.

The site is open 8am–7pm daily in summer, and 8am–3pm in winter (admission fee).

△ **OVERVIEW**
The scale of the site is most apparent from the air – nearly 2 hectares (4 acres) of palaces ruled a population of perhaps 100,000.

▽ **EMPTY VESSELS**
Huge earthenware jars, *píthi*, were used to store grain, olive-oil, wine or water. Similar jars are still made in a few Cretan villages today.

△ **CHAIR OF STATE**
The throne room, possibly a court or council room, has a gypsum throne flanked by benches, and frescoes of griffins. These may have symbolised the heavenly, earthly and underworldly aspects of the rulers.

△ THE PLAY'S THE THING
The theatre was used for plays and processions. An engineered road, one of the oldest in Europe, leads from here to the Little Palace.

▽ ALL AT SEA
The fresco in the Queen's apartments (which included an *en suite* bathroom) features dolphins, fishes and sea urchins.

◁ BULL AND GATE
A (replica) fresco depicting the capture of a wild bull decorates the ramparts of the north entrance, leading to the road to Knossós' harbour at Amnissos.

▽ DILEMMA OF HORNS
The famous double horns now sitting on the south façade were once regarded as sacred symbols, though perhaps this is an overworking of the bull motif of the site.

◁ COLOUR CODING
The South Propylon (pillared gateway) has near life-size frescoes of processionary youths, including the famous slender-waisted cup-bearer. In Minoan art, male figures were coloured red, female white.

CONTROVERSIAL EXCAVATIONS

In 1878 a local merchant, Mínos Kalokairinós, uncovered a fragment of the remains at Knossós, but the Turkish owners of the land prevented further excavation and even the wealthy German Heinrich Schliemann couldn't afford their asking price when he attempted to buy the site.

However, once Crete gained autonomy from the Turks at the turn of the century, the way was open for the English archaeologist Arthur Evans (later knighted) to purchase the area and begin excavating. He soon realised that this was a major discovery. He worked at Knossós over a period of 35 years, though by 1903 most of the site had been uncovered.

Evans' methods of using concrete to reconstruct the long-gone timber columns, and to support excavated sections of wall have received much criticism. While these preserved some of the structure *in situ*, it also involved much interpretative conjecture on the part of Evans (pictured above with a 1600 BC steatite bull's head from the Little Palace).

Excavation continues to this day, under subtler management.

INSIGHT GUIDES
TRAVEL TIPS

CONTENTS

Getting Acquainted

The Place

Area 131,950 sq km (50,950 sq miles), including around 25,050 sq km (9,670 sq miles) of islands.
Capital Athens.
Population nearly 11 million. Greater Athens and Piraeus have a population of over 4 million. The most populated island is Crete, with just over ½ million inhabitants.
Language Modern Greek.
Religion Predominantly Greek Orthodox Christianity, with small minorities of Muslims, Catholics, Jews and Christian evangelical sects.
Currency Euro.
Weights and measures Metric.
Electricity 220V, round two-pin plugs.
International Dialling 30 (country code for Greece), followed by the entire 10-digit number, starting with 2 for landlines and 6 for mobiles.
Time Zones Two hours ahead of Greenwich Mean Time.

The People

Although about 40 percent of the population lives in Athens, the city is often called Greece's largest village. Traditionally, Greeks have rarely moved far from their village roots, although – with more and more young people moving to cities – chronic depopulation of the countryside has become a serious problem. Even the most jet-setting businessman is home-loving and much of the Greeks' social life is centred round the family. Children are adored (and given more licence than you might allow your own).

A nation of many passions, from football and basketball to politics, which can be very partisan, the Greeks love nothing better than discussing the meaning of life. If you strike up a conversation in a taverna, expect to while away an hour or two – especially during election time, when the whole country buzzes with political fervour and speculation.

Geography

Mainland Greece is made up of Attica, the Peloponnese, central Greece (more poetically known as Roúmeli), Thessaly, Epirus, Macedonia and Thrace. The highest mountain is Ólympos, straddling the border between Thessaly and Macedonia, at a height of 2,917 metres (9,570ft).

The coast is a series of so many coves and inlets that it runs to 15,000 km (9,320 miles), and the Mediterranean reaches its deepest point at the 4,850 metres (15,912ft) Oinoussa Pit off the south coast of the Peloponnese.

The hundreds of islands that spill out into the Mediterranean and Aegean are divided into groups: the Ionian archipelago to the west, the Sporades and Évvia in the central Aegean, the Cyclades and Dodecanese running out southeast from Athens, and the northeast Aegean islands just off the Turkish coast. The largest islands are Crete, Corfu, Kefalloniá, Rhodes, Lésvos and Sámos, all famous for their vegetation, though the flora throughout Greece is remarkable.

Government

Greece is a republic with a president, elected by parliament, who holds ceremonial executive power. The parliament has 300 elected members led by the prime minister.

King Constantine went into exile in December 1967 following the April seizure of power by the infamous colonels' junta, and the monarchy was abolished by a referendum held after the collapse of the dictatorship in 1974. Since then two parties, New Democracy (conservative) and PASOK (leftish) have taken turns at governing; PASOK was in power from 1993 to 2004, winning in both the 1996 and the 2000 elections under first Andreas Papandreou, then Kostas Simitis. The 2004 poll was won by New Democracy under Kostas Karamanlis, who was re-elected in 2007.

Economy

About 23 percent of the land is arable, and the country produces fruit, vegetables, olives, olive oil, wine, currants, grain, cotton and tobacco. Its natural resources include the minerals bauxite, lignite and magnesite, while building slate and marble are extensively quarried. Crude oil deposits are limited, with just a single field off Thássos currently exploited. About 15 percent of the labour force works in mining and manufacturing, producing textiles,

chemicals and food products. Shipping is still an important source of revenue, but tourism is the largest foreign currency earner.

In 1981 Greece became the 10th member of the European Union, with full integration at the end of 1993; it adopted the euro as currency in February 2002. The late 1980s and 1990s had already seen a huge rise in the cost of living throughout the country, and the euro seems to have only accentuated this – a shock for anyone who remembers it as a "cheap and cheerful" destination. Although it is no longer the place for bargain-basement holidays, Greece remains good value for foreign travellers, with restaurant meals and accommodation about the same as rural Spain or France.

Climate

If you visit Greece in the summer months bring lightweight, casual clothing. If you visit during the winter months, bring the same kind of clothes you would wear during spring in northern Europe or the northern part of the United States: that is, be ready for rainy, windy days and temperatures ranging between 3° and 16°C (40° and 60°F).

On the whole, islands are ill-equipped for visitors during the winter months. Heating can be basic or non-existent, boats infrequent, food tinned on the smaller islands and amenities scarce. The tourist season is officially "over" in late October, although it extends well into November on Rhodes and Crete, but ends mid-September inthe north. Should you find yourself on the pertinent islands during this period, you will be treated to a curious spectacle: an emerging ghost town. Cafés and shops close down daily, sometimes locking their doors directly after you have left, and remaining closed until the following April or even May.

In general, the north coast of each island is subject to more summertime gales and cooler temperatures than the protected south coast; be sure to check on a map exactly where a holiday resort is before making a final booking. Many travellers underestimate the differences in climate between individual island chains. The green, cool Ionian islands, for instance, are prone to rainy spells from mid-September through to the end of April. By contrast, the southern coasts of Crete and Rhodes can offer swimming for the hardy as late as mid-December. If planning to visit any island between mid-September through to the end of April, a good rule to follow is this: the further south the island is geographically, the better the sunshine rate will be.

Religion

The Greek Orthodox Church still exerts enormous influence on contemporary life, both in mainland Greece (including Athens) and the islands. Sunday is the official day of rest, and even in mid-season in some tourist areas, shops and activities are suspended. Excursion boats from island to island, for example, might well be running to schedule, but what no one bothers to point out is that nothing on the destination island will be open when you arrive. Always enquire beforehand when planning anything on Sundays.

The most important holiday in Greece is Easter, celebrated by the Greek Orthodox calendar and usually a week or two to either side of Catholic Easter. It is advisable to find out before booking a spring holiday exactly when Easter is, as services, shops and even flights experience disruptions during Easter period.

On 15 August, the Assumption of the Virgin Mary, many places hold a *panigýri* (celebration) to mark the reception into heaven of the *Panaghía*, as the Madonna is known in Greek. Greeks make pilgrimages from all over the country to Tinos in the Cyclades where the icon of the Panaghía Evangelístria is said to work miracles. The most colourful festival of the Virgin, however, takes place on 15 August in the hillside town of Ólymbos on the island of Kárpathos, where the women wear brilliant traditional dress and the *panigyriá* can last for days.

Nearly every day is a cause for celebration for someone in Greece. Instead of marking birthdays, Greeks have *yiortés*, name days, which celebrate Orthodox baptismal names. When the day commemorates a popular name-saint like John or Helen, a quarter of the nation has a party. You'll hear locals say: "*Yiortázo símera*" (I'm celebrating today). To which you may reply: "*Hrónia pollá*" ("Many years", in other words, many happy returns).

Seasonal Averages

- January–March
6–16°C (43–61°F)
- April–June
11–29°C (52–84°F)
- July–September
19–32°C (66–90°F)
- October–December
8–23°C (46–73°F)

Planning the Trip

Visas and Passports

Citizens of EU nations, as well as Switzerland and EEA countries, have unlimited visitation rights to Greece; your passport will not be stamped on entry or exit. With a valid passport, citizens of the USA, Canada, Australia and New Zealand can stay in the country for up to three months (cumulative) within any six-month period, with no visa necessary. To stay longer, you must obtain a permit from the nearest Aliens' Bureau; however this is lately proving nearly impossible (and very expensive) to obtain. Citizens of all non-EU/EEA countries should contact the nearest Greek embassy or consulate about visa and permitted length-of-stay requirements, which are liable to change again in future.

Customs

There are no official restrictions on the movement of goods within the European Union, provided the goods were purchased within the EU. It is no longer necessary for EU nationals to exit their home-country customs through a red or green channel.

Duty-paid goods

If you buy goods in Greece for which you pay tax, there are no restrictions on the amounts you can take home. EU law has set "guidance levels", however, on the following:
- **Tobacco** 800 cigarettes, or 400 cigarillos, or 200 cigars or 1kg of tobacco.
- **Spirits** 10 litres
- **Fortified wine/wine** 90 litres
- **Beer** 110 litres
  If you exceed these amounts you must be able to prove the goods are for personal use.

Duty-free goods

Since the abolition of duty-free concession within the European Union, all goods brought into Greece from EU countries must be duty-paid. In theory there are no limitations to the amount of duty-paid goods that

can be brought into the country. However, cigarettes and most spirits are much cheaper in Greece than in Britain and Ireland (government duty is much lower), so waiting until you reach your destination to buy these goods will save you money.

For travellers from non-EU countries, allowances for duty-free goods brought into Greece are:
- **Tobacco** 200 cigarettes, or 100 cigarillos, or 50 cigars, or 250g of tobacco.
- **Alcohol** 1 litre of spirits or liqueurs over 22 percent volume, or 2 litres of fortified, sparkling wine or other liqueurs.
- **Perfume** 60cc of perfume, plus 250cc of *eau de toilette*.

Non-EU residents can claim back Value Added Tax (currently between 6 and 18 percent) on any items costing over €120, provided they export the item within 90 days of purchase. Tax-free forms are available at tourist shops and department stores. Keep the receipt and form. Make your claim at the customs area of the airport when departing.

Currency restrictions

There are no limits on the amount of euros visitors can import or export. There are no restrictions on travellers' cheques, but cash sums of more than $10,000 or its equivalent should be declared on entry.

Importing cars

Visitors arriving with their own car are allowed to circulate for up to six months without formality; after that the bureaucratic fun begins, and people intending to establish residence will find that it's usually cheaper and easier to buy a Greek-registered car than try to import their overseas motor. Cars detected circulating after the initial six-month period without valid road tax are liable to seizure by customs/tax undercover agents.

Health

Greece has few serious diseases apart from those that you can contract in the rest of Europe or the United States. Citizens of the USA, Canada and United Kingdom do not need any vaccinations to enter the country.

Insurance

British and EU residents are entitled to free medical treatment in Greece as long as they carry a European Health Insurance Card (obtainable from post offices or on-line: www.ehic.org.uk). However, this guarantees only the most basic health care: you are only entitled to use one of the lowest-grade state hospitals, and will have to pay for your own medicine, so it is advisable to take out private medical insurance. You will have to pay for private treatment up front, so you must keep receipts for any bills or medicines you pay for to make a claim. If you plan to hire a motor scooter in Greece, you may have to pay an insurance supplement to cover you for accidents.

Money Matters

The Greek currency is the euro (*evró* in Greek), which comes in coins of 1, 2, 5, 10, 20 and 50 cents (*leptá*) , plus 1 and 2 euro, as well as notes of 5, 10, 20, 50, 100, 200 and 500 euro (the latter two denominations are rarely seen).

All banks and most hotels buy foreign currency at the official rate of exchange fixed by the Bank of Greece. Though it's safer to carry most of your currency in travellers' cheques, it is also worth carrying a limited sum in US dollars or sterling. When you can't find a place to cash cheques, there will usually be a shop or post office able to convert those currencies into euros. Exchange rates go up or down daily. To find the current rate, check displays in bank windows, or the newspapers; you can read the tables even in Greek.

Credit/debit cards

Many of the better-established hotels, restaurants and shops accept major credit cards, as does Olympic Airways and the larger ferry companies or travel agents. The average pension or taverna does not, however, so be sure to enquire if that is how you intend to pay. You will find that most brands of card are accepted by the numerous autoteller machines, upon entry of your PIN number. Surcharges on credit

cards, and many debit cards used in ATMs are very high, often amounting to over 4 percent of the transaction value. However, you will find that this is the most convenient and least expensive way of getting funds, and many of the machines operate around the clock.

What To Pack

Clothes

If you visit Greece during the summer months, you will want to bring lightweight, casual clothing. Add a pullover or jacket to this and you will be prepared for the occasional cool night breezes. Lightweight shoes and sandals are ideal in the summer, but you will also need a pair of comfortable walking shoes that have already been broken in. If you plan to do any rigorous hiking on the islands bring sturdy, over-the-ankle boots with a good tread; leather will be more comfortable in summer temperatures than high-tech synthetic materials.

In general, both Greeks and tourists dine in casual dress. You will only need formal dress if you plan to go to fancy establishments, casinos, formal affairs and so on. If you visit Greece during the winter months, which can be surprisingly cold, bring the same kind of clothes you would wear during spring in the northern part of the United States or central Europe.

Toiletries

Most international brands are widely available, except on the smallest islands. Tampons and sanitary towels are more likely to be sold in supermarkets than pharmacies.

Sun protection

A hat, sun cream and sunglasses are also highly recommended for protection from the intense midday

Dress Codes

The Greeks will not expect you as a tourist to dress as they do, but scuffed shoes, ripped jeans or visibly out-of-date clothing are considered offensive.

In certain places and regions, you will encounter explicit requirements or conventions concerning the way you dress. To enter a church, men must wear long trousers, and women sleeved dresses. Often dresses or wraps will be provided at the church entrance if you do not have them. Not complying with this code will be taken as insulting irreverence.

Some specific areas have their own dress codes. On Mýkonos, for example, male and female tourists alike will shock no one by wearing shorts or a swimsuit in most public places. But this same apparel will be severely alienating in a mountain village in Crete, or in any other area that is less accustomed to tourists. The best approach is to observe what other people are wearing and dress accordingly.

sun (sophisticated sun creams of up to SPF30 are widely available in pharmacies and cosmetics shops).

Adaptors

220v AC is the standard household electric current throughout Greece. Non-dual-voltage shavers and hair dryers from North America should be left at home in favour of versatile travel models – they can be bought on the spot in Greece. Greek plugs are the standard round, two-pin European continental type, different from those in North America and the UK; plug adaptors for American appliances are easy to find, three-to-two-pin adaptors for UK appliances much less so, so these are best purchased before departure.

Universal plug

Greek basins often aren't equipped with plugs, so if you want water in your sink a universal plug is essential.

Film

Film is widely available in a range of formats and speeds, at competitive prices, though if you require something esoteric, it's best to bring your own.

Torch

Pack one, as walking home from island tavernas can be tricky if there's no moon. If you forget, Maglites or the like are sold widely.

Drugs and Medicines

Greek pharmacies stock most over-the-counter drugs, and pharmacists are well trained. The Greeks themselves are some of the champion hypochondriacs and potion-poppers of Europe, and all manner of homeopathic or herbal remedies and premium-ingredient dietary supplements are available. Many formulas that would be obtainable only on prescription elsewhere, if at all, are freely obtainable in Greece. So you should have no problem obtaining most medicines (except on the smaller islands).

Essential drugs, made locally under licence, are price-controlled,

with uniform rates all over the country – eg a tube of 1% hydrocortisone cream costs less than €1.50 – but discretional sundries and anything imported can be expensive (eg, a packet of four water-resistant French-made bandages for €3.50). If you want to be absolutely sure, pack a supply of your favourite remedies to last out the trip, but check labels carefully – codeine (a key ingredient in some painkillers such as Panadol and Solpadeine) is banned in Greece.

Greek authorities take the unauthorised use of drugs very seriously indeed; this is not the country in which to carry cannabis.

Getting There

By Air

Greece has good air connections with all six continents and is serviced by numerous international airlines. Charter flights generally operate from mid-April to the end of October, even into November to Rhodes and Crete. There are ways of flying in at a much lower cost than the standard airline fares and it's a good idea to check the Internet and ask travel agents' advice before buying a ticket.

The airlines' own websites are often a good source of discount tickets, matching (or nearly so) the prices offered by general websites like Expedia or Travelocity, and being e-tickets are loss-proof.

The majority of schedule airline passengers travelling to Greece make Athens' Eleftherios Venizelos Airport (tel: 210 353 0000) their point of entry, though a number of services (from the rest of Europe only) arrive at Thessaloníki's Macedonia Airport.

However, a number of airlines now fly direct to some of the islands. For example, you can fly to Mýkonos, Rhodes, Crete and Corfu with EasyJet (www.easyJet.com) who acquired GB Airways in 2007; Thomson (www.thomsonfly.com) flies to Rhodes, Corfu, Crete and Zakynthos; and Ryanair (www.ryanair.com) to Crete.

Between Venizelos Airport, central Athens and Piraeus there are various connecting services. The light-rail suburban train line connects the airport to Dhoukíssis Plakendías, the new terminus of the metro network, from where you can take metro Line 3 to Sýndagma or Monastiráki. Some Line 3 metros surface at Plakendías and run to the airport. Tickets (metro and suburban) to Monastiráki from the airport cost €6 one way, €10 return. The suburban train also runs to Pireas.

The bus is cheaper (€2.90; tickets valid on all forms of public transport for 24 hours, but only one airport trip). The E94 express bus (every 10–20min; 7.30am–midnight) from outside Arrivals goes to Ethnikí Ámyna metro station; the E95 express runs to Sýndagma (every 20–30min; 24 hours a day), and the E96 to Pireás port (every 20–40min; 24 hours).

A taxi from Venizelos Airport to the centre of Athens will cost about €30, plus €3 airport surcharge, depending on time of day/night and your final destination, plus €0.30 for each piece of luggage over 10 kilos. Traffic congestion has improved since the opening of the Attikí Odhós (ring road) round northern Athens, but the journey time can still be over an hour.

By Sea

Most visitors entering Greece by sea do so from the west, from Italy. You can catch a boat to Greece from Venice, Ancona, Trieste and Bari, but the most regular service is from Brindisi.

Daily ferry lines (less frequent in the low-season) connect Brindisi with the three main western ports: Corfu, Igoumenítsa and Pátra. Corfu is a 9-hour trip; Igoumenítsa 11 hours; and Pátra 16 to 18 hours, depending on whether you take a direct boat or one that makes stops in Corfu and Igoumenítsa. The "Superfast" ferries between Ancona and Pátra offer an efficient 22-hour crossing.

Igoumenítsa is the ideal port of call for those setting off to see Corfu. Pátra is best if you want to head directly to Athens or the southern Ionian islands. Regular buses and trains connect Pátra and Athens (4 hours by bus, 5 hours by train). If you plan to take your car on the boat, you should definitely make reservations well in advance. Otherwise, arriving a few hours before the departure time should suffice, except during peak seasons when booking in advance is essential for seats or berths.

By Land

From Europe The most direct overland route from northwestern Europe to Greece is a long one: 3,000 km (1,900 miles) from London to Athens – a rather arduous and impractical travel option if you're just trying to get to Greece for a brief holiday.

There are one or two remaining, reputable **bus** lines that connect Athens and Thessaloníki with many European cities (the journey, though, is very long and uncomfortable, taking 3½ days from London for example, and little cheaper than the flight).

The various **trains** you can take from northwest Europe will take about as long as the bus, and cost considerably more, but fares include the Italy–Greece ferry crossing, and may get you to Greece feeling more intact. **From Asia via Turkey** If you are travelling strictly overland to Greece from Asia you will pass through Istanbul and cross into Greece at the Évros River. The road is good and the journey from Istanbul to Thessaloníki takes approximately 15 hours; several bus companies serve the route.

The train has the appeal of following the route of the old Orient Express, with better scenery than the road. But, unless you're a great rail fan, the travel time can be off-putting: 17 hours by the timetables, up to 19 hours in practice, including long halts at the border.

Another popular option is to take one of the small boats between western Turkish ports and select Greek islands just opposite. Fares are overpriced for the distance involved, but it is undeniably convenient. The most reliable links are from Çesme to Híos and Kusadasi to Sámos.

Specialist Operators

Your local overseas branch of the Greek National Tourist Organisation (see page 310) can usually provide a list of that country's tour operators and specialist agents offering holidays in Greece. Otherwise, here are a few suggestions for something unusual:

• **Archaeological tours**
The Traveller, 92 Great Russell Street, London WC1B 3PS;
Tel: 020 7436 9343
www.the-traveller.co.uk
• **Bicycle tours**
Classic Adventures, USA;
tel:1-800-777-8090;
www.classicadventures.com
• **Birdwatching**
Limosa Holidays, UK;
tel: 01263 578143;
www.limosaholidays.co.uk
• **Botanical tours**
Marengo Guided Walks, UK;
tel: 01485 532710;
www.marengowalks.com
• **Horse-riding**
Equitour, Hampshire, UK;

tel: 0800 043 7942;
www.equitour.co.uk
• **Sail-and-trek mixed tours**
Hellenic Adventures, Minneapolis, USA; tel: 1-800-851-6349;
www.hellenicadventures.com
• **Walking holidays**
ATG, 274 Banbury Road
Oxford OX2 7GH;
tel: 01865 315678;
www.atg-oxford.co.uk
Exodus, Grange Mills, Weir Road, London SW12 0NE;
tel: 0845 863 9600;
www.exodus.co.uk
Ramblers Holidays, Welwyn Garden City; tel: 01707 331133;
www.ramblersholidays.co.uk
Waymark Holidays, First Choice House, Crawley, UK; tel: 0870 950 9800; www.waymarkholidays.co.uk
• **Writing workshops/holistic holidays**
Skyros Centre, 9 Eastcliff Road, Shanklin, Isle of Wight PO37 6AA;
Tel: 01983 86 55 66;
www.skyros.co.uk

Practical Tips

Tourist Information

Tourist offices

If you would like tourist information about Greece during your trip, visit the nearest Greek National Tourist Organisation – GNTO, or EOT in Greek. They provide information on public transport, as well as leaflets and details about sites and museums. There are over a dozen regional GNTO offices across the country. The new head office in Athens is at Tsóha 24; tel: 210 870 7000, www.gnto.gr.

On many of the islands there are semi-official municipal tourist information centres open from June to September. These are usually prominently sited near the centre of the main town, and provide all the local information you might need. Some can even help with finding accommodation.

Tourist Police

The Greek Tourist Police are often a mine of information too. A branch of the local police and found in most large towns, they can be helpful in providing information about hotels as well as fielding a wide variety of travel questions.

Business Hours

All banks are open 8am–2.30pm Monday to Thursday, and close at 2pm on Friday. ATMs are now everywhere – even the smaller islands will have at least one – and this is how most people obtain cash nowadays.

The schedule for business and shop hours is more complicated. Business hours vary according to the type of business and the day of the week. The main thing to remember is that businesses generally open at 8.30 or 9am and close on Monday, Wednesday and Saturday at 2.30pm. On Tuesday, Thursday and Friday most businesses close at 2pm and reopen in the afternoon from 5pm to 8.30pm (winter), 5.30 or 6pm to 9pm (summer).

You'll soon learn that schedules are very flexible in Greece (both in business and personal affairs). To avoid disappointment, allow ample time when shopping and doing business. That way, you may also enter into the Greek spirit of negotiation, in which a good chat can be as important as the matter of business itself.

Telecommunications

The cheapest way to make telephone calls is to buy a telephone card from a kiosk and use a (usually noisy) phone booth. Cards come in three sizes: 100 units, 500 units and 1,000 units, with the largest ones representing the best value. Otherwise, you may still find a telephone kiosk at which you can pay a few euro-cents for a local call.

You can also make long-distance calls from the dwindling number of kiosks which have a cardphone, free-standing street-corner cardphones, or from the new-style coin-op counter phones which take assorted euro coins, often found in hotel lobbies and restaurants. Calls from hotel rooms typically have a minimum 200 percent surcharge on top of the standard rates – to be avoided for anything other than brief local calls.

Many post offices offer fax services; larger towns usually have at least two cybercafés – rates range from €4 to €7 per hour.

Greece has one of the highest per-capita mobile-phone usage rates in the world, and a mobile is an essential fashion accessory for any

Emergency Numbers

The following numbers work country-wide:
- **Police** 100
- **Ambulance** 161
- **Fire brigade, urban** 199
- **Forest fire reporting** 191
- **Tourist police 171** (Athens only; in other parts of Greece, ring 210 171)

Elsewhere, hotel staff will give you details of the nearest hospital or English-speaking doctor.

self-respecting Greek. Foreign mobile owners will find themselves well catered for, with thorough coverage and reciprocal agreements for most UK-based services. Calls within Greece are affordable, but the cost of overseas calls mounts up quickly. North American users will have to bring a tri-band apparatus to get any joy. If you're staying for any amount of time, you will find it better to either buy a pay-as-you-go phone from one of the four Greek providers (Vodaphone, Cosmote, Telestet, Q-Telecom) or, if feasible, buy just a SIM card for the apparatus you've brought along.

Postal Services

Most local post offices are open weekdays from 7.30am until 2pm. However, the main post offices in central Athens (on Eólou near Omónia Square and on Sýndagma Square at the corner of Mitropóleos Street) are open longer hours on weekdays, as well as short schedules on Saturday and Sunday.

Postal rates are subject to fairly frequent change; currently a postcard or light letter costs 65 euro-cents to any overseas destination. Stamps are available from the post office or from many kiosks (*períptera*), which may charge a 10–15 percent commission. But make sure you know how much it is to send a letter or postcard, as kiosk owners tend not to be up to date with latest international postal rates.

If you want to send a parcel from Greece, do not to wrap it until a post office clerk has inspected it, unless it's going to another EU country, in which case you can present it sealed. Major post offices stock various sizes of cardboard boxes for sale in which you can pack your material, as well as twine, but you had best bring your own tape and scissors.

Letters from abroad can be sent Post Restante to any post office. Take your passport or other convincing ID when you go to pick up mail.

Greek National Tourist Organisation Offices

United Kingdom
4 Conduit Street, London WIS 2DJ
Tel: (020) 7495 9300
Fax: (020) 7287 1369
Email: info@gnto.co.uk
www.visitgreece.gr
United States
Olympic Tower, 645 Fifth Avenue, 9th Floor, New York,NY 10022
Tel: (212) 421 5777
Fax: (212) 826 6940
E-mail: info@greektourism.com

Australia
37 Pitt Street, Sydney NSW 2000
Tel: (02) 9241 1663/5
Fax: (02) 9241 2499
Email: hto@tpg.com.au
Canada
1500 Don Mills Road, Suite 102, Toronto, ON M3B 3K4
Tel: (416) 968 2220
Fax: (416) 968 6533
E-mail: grnto.tor@on.aibn.com
www.greektourism.com

Medical Treatment

For minor ailments your best port of call is a pharmacy. Greek chemists usually speak good English and are well-trained and helpful, and pharmacies stock a good range of medicines (including contraceptives) as well as bandages and dressings for minor wounds.

Certain pharmacies are open outside of normal shop hours and at weekends, on a rotating basis. You can find out which are open either by looking at the bilingual (Greek/English) card posted in pharmacy windows or by consulting a local newspaper. In big cities, and major tourist resorts such as Crete or Rhodes, one or two pharmacies will be open 24 hours a day.

There are English-speaking GPs in all the bigger towns and resorts, whose rates are usually reasonable. Ask your hotel or the tourist office for details.

In Athens, the doctors' roster can be obtained by dialling 105; get the 24-hour pharmacy roster by dialling 107.

Treatment for broken bones and similar mishaps is given free of charge in the state-run Greek hospitals – go straight to the casualty/emergency ward. The EU form E111 is generally not even requested, your statement of EU nationality usually being sufficient. For more serious problems you should have private medical insurance. If you have a serious injury or illness, you are better off travelling home for treatment if you can.

Greek public hospitals lag behind northern Europe and the US in both their hygiene and standard of care; the Greeks bring food and bedding when visiting sick relatives, and must bribe nurses for anything beyond the bare minimum in care.

Security and Crime

Greece is still one of the safest countries in Europe. Despite the indulgence of the Greek popular press in luridly publicised antics of certain Albanians and Romanians, violent crime remains relatively rare. Sadly, however, petty theft does occur, and it is now the norm to lock cars and front doors in the countryside.

Because of tightened security considerations it is unwise to leave luggage unattended anywhere except perhaps in a hotel lobby, under the gaze of the desk staff. Belongings inadvertently left behind in a café will still usually be put aside for you to collect.

Animal Hazards

Nearly half the stray dogs in rural areas carry echinococcosis (treatable by surgery only) or kala-azar disease (leishmaniasis), a protozoan blood disease spread by sandfleas.

Mosquitos can be a nuisance in some areas of Greece, but topical repellents are readily available in pharmacies. For safeguarding rooms, accommodation proprietors often supply a plug-in electric pad, which vapourises smokeless, odourless rectangular tablets. If you see them by the bed, it's a good bet they'll be needed; refills can be found in any supermarket.

On the islands, poisonous baby pit vipers and scorpions are a problem in spring and summer. They will not strike you unless disturbed, but do not put your hands or feet in places (such as drystone walls) that you haven't checked first. If you swim in the sea, beware jellyfish whose sting is usually harmless but which can swell and hurt for days.

On beaches, it is worth wearing plastic or trekking sandals to avoid sea urchins (those little black pincushions on rocks that can embed their very sharp and tiny spines into unwary feet, which then break off). A local Greek remedy is to douse the wound with olive oil and then gently massage the foot until the spines pop out, but this rarely works unless you're willing to perform minor surgery with pen-knife and sewing needle – which should be done, as spine fragments tend to go septic.

Tipping

Menu prices at most cafés, restaurants and *tavérnes* include a service charge, but it is still customary to leave an extra 5–10 percent on the table for the waiters.

Just as important as any such gratuity, however, is your appreciation of the food you eat. Greek waiters and restaurant owners are proud when you tell them you like a particular dish.

Foreign Embassies in Athens

All embassies are open from Monday to Friday only, usually from 8am until 2pm, except for their own national holidays (as well as Greek ones).

• **Australia** Level 6, Thon Building, corner Kifisiás and Alexándras (Ambelókipi metro); tel: 210 870 4000.
• **Canada** Yennadhíou 4, Kolonáki, (Evangelismós metro); tel: 72 73 400.

Drinking Water

Carrying a large plastic bottle of mineral water is a common sight in Greece, but it is rather deplorable, as sunlight releases toxic chemicals from the plastic into the water, and the spent bottles contribute enormously to Greece's litter problem. Buy a sturdy, porcelain-lined canteen and fill it from the cool-water supply of bars and restaurants you've patronised; nobody will begrudge you this. Although unfiltered tap water is generally safe to drink, it may be brackish, and having a private water supply is much handier. On the mainland and larger islands, certain springs are particularly esteemed by the locals – queues of cars, and people with jerry-cans, tip you off. If you do want bottled water, it can be bought almost anywhere that sells food, even in beach cafés and tavernas.

Media

Print

Many kiosks throughout Athens and other major resorts receive British newspapers, plus the *International Herald Tribune*, either late the same afternoon or, more usually, the next *Athens News* in colour (online at www.athensnews.gr) is interesting and informative, with both international and local news, particularly good for the Balkans, and complete TV and cinema listings. *Odyssey* is a glossy, bi-monthly magazine created by and for the wealthy Greek diaspora, somewhat more interesting than the usual airline in-flight mag.

Radio and TV

ER 1 and ER 2 are the two Greek state-owned radio channels. ER 1 is divided into three different "programmes". The First (728 KHz) and Second (1385 KHz) both have abundant Greek popular music and news, some foreign pop and occasional jazz and blues. Third (665 KHz) plays a lot of western classical

• **Ireland** Vassiléos Konstandínou 7 (by National Gardens); tel: 72 32 771.
• **South Africa** Kifissiás 60, Maroússi; tel: 210 61 06 645.
• **UK** Ploutárhou 1, Kolonáki (Evangelismós metro); tel: 72 72 600.
• **USA** Vasilísis Sofías 91, Ambelókipi (Mégaro Mousikís metro); tel: 72 12 951.

music. ER 2 (98 KHz) is much like the first two programmes.

The BBC World Service offers news on the hour (plus other interesting programmes and features). The best short-wave (MHz) frequencies to pick up the BBC in Athens are as follows: 3–7.30am GMT: 9.41 (31 m), 6.05 (49 m), 15.07 (19 m) 7.30am–6pm: GMT–15.07 (19 m) 6.30pm–11.15pm GMT–9.41 (31 m), 6.05 (49 m). Additionally, a plethora of private stations broadcast locally from just about every island or provincial town, no matter how tiny.

There are two state-owned and operated television channels (ET1 in Athens, ET3 in Thessaloníki) and a half-dozen private television channels (Antenna, Net, Mega, Star, Alpha and Alter). Often they transmit foreign movies and programmes with Greek subtitles rather than being dubbed. Several cable and satellite channels are also broadcast, including Sky, CNN and Super Channel.

Etiquette

The Greeks are at heart a very traditional nation, protective of their families and traditions. So to avoid giving offence it is essential to follow their codes of conduct.

Locals rarely drink to excess, so drunken and/or lewd behaviour is treated with at best bewilderment, at worse severe distaste (or criminal prosecution, as many young louts on Rhodes have learned to their cost).

Nude bathing is legal at only a few beaches (such as on the island of Mýkonos), but it is deeply offensive to Greeks. Even topless sunbathing is sometimes not sanctioned, so watch

for signs forbidding it on beaches. The main rule of thumb is this: if it is a secluded beach and/or a beach that has become a commonly accepted locale for nude bathing, you probably won't offend anyone.

Despite assorted scandals and embarrassing espousal of retrograde issues in recent years, the Greek Orthodox Church still commands considerable respect in Greece, so keep any unfavourable comments about the clergy or even Greek civil servants to yourself.

Women Travellers

Lone female visitors may still be targeted for attention by predatory Greek males, especially around beach bars and after-hours discos, but in general machismo is no longer any more a problem than anywhere else in southern Europe. Inexorable changes in Greek culture mean that Greek women have much more sexual freedom than previously, especially in the cities. There is now little controversy in their spending time with their male counterparts, up to and including cohabiting before (or instead of) marriage.

In remote areas, many Greeks are still highly traditional and may find it hard to understand why you are travelling alone. You will not feel comfortable in their all-male drinking cafés.

Travelling with Kids

Children are adored in Greece, and many families are still highly superstitious about their welfare – don't be surprised to see kids with

Public Holidays

The Greeks like their festivals and celebrate them in style, so most business and shops close during the afternoon before and the morning after a religious holiday, as well as the day itself.

• **1 January** Protohroniá/New Year's Day
• **6 January** Aghía Theofánia/ Epiphany
• **Moveable** Katharí Dheftéra Clean Monday (First Day of Lent)
• **25 March** Evangelismós/ Annunciation
• **1 May** Labour Day
• **Moveable** Megáli Paraskeví/ Good Friday
• **Moveable** Orthodox Easter (Pásha), Easter Monday
• **Moveable** Aghíou Pnévmatos/ Pentecost Monday (50 days after Easter)
• **15 August** Assumption (Apokímisis) of the Holy Virgin
• **28 October** "Óhi" Day, National Holiday
• **25 December** Hristoúyenna/ Christmas Day
• **26 December** Sýnaxis tis Theotókou/Gathering of the Virgin's Entourage

amulets pinned to their clothes to ward off the evil eye. So expect your own kids to be the centre of attention. Children are given quite a bit of leeway in Greece and treated very indugently.

Children are allowed to stay up late and are routinely taken out to eat in tavernas. However, you may have to put your foot down when shop owners offer free sweets or strangers are over-indulgent towards your own children.

Photography

Although Greece is a photographer's paradise, taking photographs at will is not recommended. Cameras are not allowed in museums, and you may have to pay a fee to take photographs or use your camcorder at archaeological sites. Watch out for signs showing a bellows camera with a red "X" through it, and do not point your camera at anything in or near airports – most of which double as military bases – or any site which is remotely sensitive.

Prints can be processed just about anywhere in Greece, but slides are usually sent to Athens or Thessaloníki, so wait until you get home to have them processed.

"Greek Time"

Beware Greek schedules. Although shops and businesses generally operate the hours indicated on page 310, there is no guarantee that when you want to book a ferry or buy a gift, the office or shop will actually be open.

Siesta (mikró ýpno in Greek) is observed throughout Greece, and even in Athens the majority of people retire behind closed doors between the hours of 3pm and 6pm. Shops and businesses also close, and it is usually impossible to get much done that day until late-afternoon or early evening. To avoid frustration and disappointment, shop and book things between 10am and 1pm Monday to Friday.

Since 1994 Athens has experimented with "straight" hours

during the winter to bring the country more in line with the EU, but this seems to be discretionary rather than obligatory, with some stores observing the hours and others adhering to traditional schedules – which can be rather confusing. So far it has not caught on across the rest of the country.

The shops in Athens' Pláka district remain open until 10pm or longer to take advantage of browsers, and tourist shops throughout the country usually trade well into the evening in summer. But butchers and fishmongers are not allowed to open on summer evenings (although a few disregard the law), and pharmacies (except for those on rota duty) are never open on Saturday mornings.

Getting Around

By air

Flying is considerably more expensive than travelling by boat, bus or train (three times more than a ferry seat, just under double the price of a boat berth), though still reasonable when compared to the price of domestic flights in other countries. For example, the single one-hour ATR flight between Athens and Sámos costs about €90.

Greece's national airline, Olympic Airways, has had management and labour troubles for years, and there have been on-going attempts to privatise it. Strikes, mechanical faults and working to rule have in the past caused some flights to be cancelled or delayed, so leave plenty of leeway in your domestic flight arrangements if you have to be back in Athens for an international flight. You can reserve seats, pay fares and collect timetables at any Olympic office, and at numerous on-line travel sites, including Opodo, www.opodo.co.uk. Island flights are often fully booked over the summer, so book at least a week in advance. Olympic can be reached on tel: 210 966 6666 or low-cost number 801 114 4444 (from within Greece only), or on the web www.olympicairlines.com.

Currently the only alternative is Aegean Airlines, which flies from Athens and Thessaloníki to a number of the islands, including Corfu, Rhodes, Kos, Mýkonos and Sámos. Their nationwide low-cost number is 801 11 20000, or you can book online: www.aegeanair.com.

By bus

A vast network of bus routes spreads across Greece; the KTEL is a syndicate of bus companies whose buses are cheap, generally punctual and (eventually) will take you to almost any destination that can be reached on wheels. KTEL buses on the more idiosyncratic rural routes often have a distinct personal touch, their drivers decorating and treating the bus with great care.

In the larger cities there may be different KTEL stations for different destinations. Athens has two terminals, while Iráklio in Crete has three.

City buses With an influx of new, air-conditioned vehicles, travelling by the regular Athens blue-and-white buses is much less an ordeal than it used to be. They are still usually overcrowded, and the routes are a mystery even to residents. But they are eminently reasonable, at 45 cents per ticket, or €2.90 for an all-day pass. Tickets, valid on trolleys as well, are sold individually or in books of 10, from specific news kiosks and special booths at bus and metro stations, and at various points around the city. Most bus services run until nearly midnight.

Trolley buses, with an overhead pantograph, are marginally faster and more frequent, and serve points of tourist interest; number 1 links the centre of Athens with the railway stations, number 5 passes the Archaelogical Museum, and number 7 does a circuit of the central districts.

The most useful suburban services for tourists are the orange and white KTEL Attica buses going from 14 Mavromatéon Street, Pédhio toú Áreos Park, to Rafína (an alternative ferry port for the Cyclades and northeast Aegean) and Soúnio (for the famous Poseidon temple there).

Rural buses On the islands buses may be converted school buses, modern coaches, or even pick-up trucks with seats installed in the payload space to transport tourists. Some drivers ricochet through mountain roads at death-defying speeds; accidents, however, are rare. Stow your luggage carefully to be on the safe side.

A bus of some description will usually meet arriving ferries (even if a boat is delayed) to transport passengers up the hill to the island's *hóra*, or capital. Bus stops are usually in main squares or by the waterfront in harbours and vehicles may or may not run to schedule. A conductor dispenses tickets on the bus itself; often the fare required and the ticket will not show the same price, with the lower old price over-stamped. This isn't a con, but merely a practice – bus companies use pre-printed tickets until the supply is gone, which may take several years.

By metro

The Athens metro system opened in January 2000, halving travel times around the city and making a visible reduction in surface traffic. The stations themselves are palatial and squeaky-clean, with advertising placards kept to a minimum. The old

Airport At Level 0 of Arrivals at Eleftherios Venizelos airport, Pacific Left Luggage offers service (tel: 210 353 0160)

Hotels Most hotels in Greece are willing to store locked suitcases for up to a week if you want to take any short excursions. This is usually a free service, provided you've stayed a night or two, but the hotel accepts no responsibility in the highly unlikely event of theft.

Commercial offices On the islands there are left-luggage offices in many harbour towns. For a small charge space can be hired by the hour, day, week or longer. Although contents will probably be safe, take small valuables with you.

ISAP electric line, in existence since the 1930s, has been refurbished and designated line M1 (green on maps); it links Piraeus with Kifissiá via the city centre. Line M2 (red) links Ághios Dhimítrios in the south with Ághios Andónios in the northwest of town, with extensions planned all the way down to Glyfáda and up to Thivón. Line M3 (blue) joins Monastiráki with Dhoukíssis Plakendías in the far east, with a light rail connection to the airport. The main junction stations of the various lines are Omónia, Sýndagma and Monastiráki.

The best strategy for visitors is to buy a day pass for €2.90, which includes one journey to or from the airport; the ISAP line M1 and lines M2/M3 have separate pricing structures, with M1 tickets not valid on M2/M3, and if you're caught by the ubiquitous plainclothes inspectors with the wrong ticket, or no ticket, you get a spot fine of 20 times the standard fare.

By train

The best thing about rail travel in Greece is the price – even cheaper than the bus. Otherwise, the Greek rail service, known as OSE, is quite limited, both in the areas it reaches and frequency of departures. Trains are also fairly slow and, unless you are doing the Athens–Pátra run (where the station is virtually opposite the docks), you will probably find the bus more convenient.

You can speed things up by taking an Intercity express train for a considerable surcharge. If you're on a tight budget you can really cut costs by taking the train round-trip, in which case there is a 20 percent reduction. Students and people under 26 are usually eligible for certain discounts.

Ferry/Catamaran/Hydrofoil Timetables

Since 1997, the GNTO and GTP (Greek Travel Pages) have co-produced a comprehensive, fairly impartial, printed sea transport timetable, *Greek Travel Routes*. Alas, it appeared only sporadically and usually fairly late in the season, though it may revive again after the Olympic year. The best resource at present is the GTP'S websites, www.gtp.gr and www.gtpweb.com, which are fairly accurate, with updates at least every few weeks.

Alternatively, major tourist information offices (Rhodes, Iráklio, etc) supply a weekly schedule, and most offices hang a timetable in a conspicuous place so you can look up times even if the branch is closed. This should, however, not be relied on implicitly – you may miss your boat. In general, for the most complete and up-to-date information on each port's sailings the best source is the Port Police (in Piraeus and most other ports), known as the *limenarhío*.

Be aware that when you enquire about ferries at a travel agent, they will sometimes inform you only of the lines with which they are affiliated.

By sea

Ferries Piraeus is the nerve centre of the Greek ferry network, and chances are you will pass through it at least once; in diminishing order of importance, Rafína, Thessaloníki, Pátra and Kavála are also used. In high season, routes vary from "milk runs" stopping at five islands en route to your destination, to "express" direct ones, so it is worth shopping around before purchasing your ticket. It is also advisable not to purchase your ticket too far in advance: very rarely do tickets for the boat ride actually sell out, but there are frequent changes to schedules which may leave you trying to get a refund.

Personalised ticketing for all boats has been the rule since 2001, so it is no longer possible to purchase tickets on board as in the past. The only exceptions seem to be a few of the ro-ro short-haul ferries (eg Igoumenítsa-Lefkími).

When you buy your ticket, get detailed instructions on how to find its berth – the Piraeus quays are long and convoluted; the staff who take your ticket should make sure you are on the right boat.

Above all, be flexible when travelling the Greek seas. Apart from schedule changes, a bad stretch of weather can keep you island-bound for as long as the wind blows. Strikes too are often called during the summer, and usually last for a few days. Out on the islands in particular, the best way to secure accurate, up-to-the-minute information on the erratic ways of ferries is to contact the Port Authority (*limenarhío*), which monitors the movements of individual boats. Port Authority offices

All the common railpasses are honoured in Greece, though you may still have to pay certain supplements and queue for seat reservations.

are usually located on the waterfront of each island's principal harbour, away from the cafés.

If you are travelling by car, especially during the high season, you will have to plan much further ahead because during the peak season car space is sometimes booked many weeks in advance. The same applies to booking a cabin for an overnight trip during summer.

Gamma class – also known as deck, tourist or third – is the classic, cheap way to voyage the Greek seas. There is usually a seat of one sort or another – in community with an international multitude, singing with a guitar, passing a bottle around under the stars. And if the weather turns bad you can always go inside to the "low-class" lounge or the snack bar.

Catamarans/"high speeds"
Fleets of sleek new "high speed" ferries or true catamarans, made in France or Scandanavia, are steadily edging out most ordinary craft (as a stroll around the quays at Piraeus will confirm). They have some advantages over hydrofoils (see below) – they can be even faster, most of them carry lots of cars, and they're permitted to sail in wind conditions of up to Force 7, whereas "dolphins" are confined to port at 6. The bad news: there are no cabins (because they mostly finish their runs before midnight), food service is even worse than on the old ferries and there are no exterior decks. The aeroplane-seating salons are ruthlessly air-conditioned and subject to a steady, unavoidable barrage of banal Greek TV on overhead monitors (even in *dhiakikriméni* or "distinguished" class). Cars cost roughly the same to convey as on the old-style boats, but seats are priced at hydrofoil levels. Catamarans come in all shapes and sizes, from the 300-car-carrying behemoths of NEL Lines in the northeast Aegean, Cyclades and central Dodecanese, to

the tiny *Sea Star* in the Dodecanese. The useful Dodekanisos Express serves more of the Dodecanese, and can take five cars.

Hydrofoils Though catamarans are undoubtedly the wave of the future, there is still a network of scheduled hydrofoil services to many islands. Like catamarans, hydrofoils are more than twice as fast as the ferries and about twice as expensive, but as ex-Polish or ex-Russian river craft, are not really designed for the Aegean, and prone to cancellation in conditions above wind Force 6.

Hydrofoils (nicknamed *dhelfínia* or "dolphins" in Greek) connect Piraeus with most of the Argo-Saronic region (Éghina, Póros, Ýdra, Spétses and Peloponnese mainland ports as far as Monemvasía), as well as Vólos and the three northerly Sporades (Alónissos, Skiáthos, Skópelos). In the Ionian archipelago, there are hydrofoil services from Igoumenítsa to Paxí. In the northeast Aegean, there are local, peak-season services between Thássos or Samothráki and the mainland, while in the Dodecanese all the islands between Sámos and Rhodes, inclusive, are well served.

Phone numbers for the few surviving hydrofoil companies are constantly engaged, or spew out only pre-recorded information in rapid-fire Greek, so the best strategy is to approach the embarkation booths in person. In Piraeus these are on Aktí Miaoúli quay (for Saronic Dolphins and Hellas Dolphins); despite what you may read elsewhere, no services depart any longer from Zéa marina. At Vólos, apply to the gatehouse for the harbour precinct; elsewhere tickets are best obtained from in-town travel agents.

PORT AUTHORITY NUMBERS

The Ionian Islands
Corfu, tel: 26610 32655
Itháki, tel: 26740 32909
Kefalloniá (Argostóli), tel: 26710 22224
Lefkádha, tel: 26450 92509
Paxí, tel: 26620 32259
Zákynthos, tel: 26950 28117

The Saronic Gulf Islands
Aegina, tel: 22970 22328
Hydra, tel: 22980 52279
Póros, tel: 22980 22274
Salamína, tel: 467 7277
Spétses, tel: 22980 72245

The Cyclades
Andhros, tel: 22820 71213
Íos, tel: 22860 91264
Kéa, tel: 22870 21344

Kýthnos, tel: 22810 21290
Mílos, tel: 22870 22968
Mýkonos, tel: 22890 22218
Náxos, tel: 22850 22300
Páros, tel: 22840 21240
Santoríni, tel: 22860 22239
Sérifos, tel: 22810 51470
Sífnos, tel: 22840 33617
Sýros, tel: 22810 82690
Tínos, tel: 22830 22348

The Sporades
Alónissos, tel: 24240 65595
Skiáthos, tel: 24270 22017
Skópelos, tel: 24240 22180
Skýros, tel: 22220 93475

The NE Aegean Islands
Foúrni, tel: 22750 51207
Híos, tel: 22710 44433
Ikaría (Ághios Kírykos), tel: 22750 22207
Ikaría (Évdhilos), tel: 22750 31007
Lésvos (Mytilíni), tel: 22510 24515
Lésvos (Sígri), tel: 22530 54433
Límnos, tel: 22540 22225
Psará, tel: 22720 61252
Sámos (Vathý), tel: 22730 27318
Sámos (Karlóvassi), tel: 22730 30888
Sámos (Pythagório), tel: 22730 61225
Samothráki, tel: 25510 41305
Thássos (Liménas), tel: 25930 22106
Thássos (Prínos), tel: 25930 71290

The Dodecanese Islands
Astypálea, tel: 22420 61208
Hálki, tel: 22460 45220
Kálymnos, tel: 22430 29304

Kárpathos (Pigádhia), tel: 22450 22227
Kássos, tel: 22450 41288
Kastellórizo, tel: 22460 49270
Kós, tel: 22420 26594
Léros (Lakkí), tel: 22470 22334
Níssyros, tel: 22420 31222
Pátmos, tel: 22470 31231
Rhodes, tel: 22410 22220
Sými, tel: 22460 71205
Tílos, tel: 22460 44350

Crete
Ághios Nikólaos, tel: 28400 22312
Haniá, tel: 28210 98888
Iráklion, tel: 2810 244956
Kastélli, tel: 28220 22024
Réthymnon, tel: 28310 22276
Sitía, tel: 28430 27117

● Piraeus Port Authority, tel: 210 451 1311/210 422 6000; or 210 419 9000 (Zéa Marina).
● For more on island hopping by ferry, see *Island Hopping (page 75)*, and *Coping with Piraeus (page 115)*.

Private Transport

Taxis
Taxis in Greece, especially in Athens, merit a guidebook to themselves. There are three stages to the experience.

First: getting a taxi. It's almost impossible at certain times of the day in Athens, and probably worst before the early afternoon meal. When you hail a taxi, try to get in before stating your destination. The drivers are very picky and often won't let you in unless you're

Cruises

Apparently one in six of all visitors to Greece embarks on an Aegean cruise. These cruises can range from simple one-day trips to the Saronic Gulf islands close to Athens and Piraeus, to luxury four-day journeys taking in the part of the Turkish coast, Rhodes and Crete. Many people opt for a seven-day excursion, which offers an opportunity to see a couple of islands in the Cyclades, a few of the Dodecanese islands, and a foray over to Istanbul for good measure.

Accommodation, prices and standards on board ship vary widely and it would be a very good idea to shop around for a good price.

Ticket agencies in Athens are the places to visit, with cruise opportunities prominently displayed in windows. (However, if you have ever been at Mýkonos harbour

when the ships arrive and watched the frantic preparations of shop managers adjusting their prices upwards, it may change your mind about a cruise entirely.)

The most comprehensive company is **Royal Olympic Cruises**; it is accustomed to dealing with foreigners, and offers a variety of cruise durations. Details can be found from most Greek travel agents or from Royal Olympic's headquarters: 87 Aktí Miaoúli, 185 38, Piraeus, tel: 210 429 1000.

London-based **Swan Hellenic Cruises** offer more upmarket, all-inclusive holidays on large luxury liners, with guest speakers instructing passengers on anything from archaelogy to marine biology. Swan Hellenic are at Lynnem House, 1 Victoria Way, Burgess Hill, West Sussex, RH15 9NF; tel: 01444 462 170; www.swanhellenic.com.

Athens' Rush Hours

Drive at your peril in Athens during its multiple rush hours (8–10am, 2–3pm, 4.30–5.30pm, 8–10pm). The twin perils of traffic jams and pollution reached such heights in the capital that a law was introduced during the 1980s: on even days of the month only cars with even-numbered licence plates are allowed in the centre; on odd days only those with odd-numbered plates. This has done little to improve the congestion, noise and smog in Athens, as many families have two cars (one of each type of number plate) and alternate according to the day of the week.

going in their direction. If you see an empty taxi, run for it, be aggressive – otherwise you'll find that some quick Athenian has beaten you to it.

Second: the ride. Make sure the taxi meter is on "1" when you start out, and not on "2" – that's the double fare, which is only permitted from midnight to 5am, or outside designated city limits. Once inside, you may find yourself with company. Don't be alarmed. It is traditional practice for drivers to pick up two, three, even four individual riders, provided they're going roughly in the same direction. In these cases, make a note of the meter count when you get in. In fact, because taxis are so cheap, they can end up functioning as minibus services.

Third: paying up. If you've travelled with other passengers, make sure you aren't paying for the part of the trip that happened before you got in. You should pay the difference in meter reading between embarking and alighting, plus the €0.74 minimum. Otherwise, the meter will tell you the straight price, which may be adjusted according to the tariff that should be on a laminated placard clipped to the dashboard. There are extra charges for each piece of luggage in the boot, for leaving or entering an airport or seaport, plus bonuses around Christmas and Easter.

Some drivers will quote you the correct price, but many others will try to rip you off, especially if it seems that you're a novice. If the fare you're charged is clearly above the correct price, don't hesitate to argue your way, in whichever language, back down to a normal price.

These rules apply more to Athens than to the islands, although it's still necessary to be pretty assertive on Crete and Rhodes. On the smaller islands, expect to share your taxi, not

Car Hire (Rental)

Hiring a car in Greece is not as cheap as you might hope, owing to high insurance premiums and import duties. Prices vary according to the type of car, season and length of rental and should include CDW (collision damage waiver) and VAT at 18 percent. Payment can, and often must, be made with a major credit card. A full home-country driving licence (for EU/EEA residents) or an International Driving Permit (for all others) is required and you must be at least 21 years old.

In the UK and North America, you can book a car in advance through major international chains such as Hertz, Avis, Budget or Sixt – their websites have all-inclusive quotes and booking/payment facilities. But there are many reputable, smaller chains, some particular to Greece, that offer a comparable service at lower rates. In Athens most are on, or just off, Syngroú Avenue in the district known as Makrigiánni.

Antena
Syngroú 52, tel: 210 922 4000
Autorent
Syngroú 11, tel: 210 923 2514
Just
Syngroú 43, tel: 210 923 9104
Kosmos
Syngroú 9, tel: 210 923 4695
Reliable
Syngroú 3, tel: 210 924 9000

only with other passengers, but also with an animal or two.

In recent years various radio taxi services have started up in Athens and most other larger towns. They can pick you up within a short time of your call to a central booking number.

Cars

Having a car in rural Greece enables you to reach a lot of otherwise inaccessible corners of the country; however, driving a car in Athens is unpleasant and confusing. Tempers run short, while road signs, or warnings of mandatory turning lanes, are practically non-existent.

EU-registered cars are no longer stamped into your passport on entry to the country, can circulate freely for up to six months, and are exempt from road tax as long as this has been paid in the home country – however, you are not allowed to sell the vehicle. Non-EU/EEA nationals will find that a bizarre litany of rules apply to importing cars, chief among them that you must re-export the car when you depart, or have it sealed by

Breakdowns

The Greek Automobile Association (ELPA) offers a breakdown service for motorists, which is free to AA/RAC members (on production of their membership cards). Phone 104 for assistance nationwide. Some car-hire companies have agreements instead with competitors Hellas Service (dial 1057) or Express Service (dial 154), but these call centres can be slow to dispatch aid. Always ring a local garage number if this is what the hire company instructs you to do.

Customs in an off-road facility of your choosing.

Driving in Greece All EU/EEA licences, and licences held by returning diaspora Greeks irrespective of issuing country, are honoured in Greece. Conversely, all other licences – this includes North American and Australian ones – are not valid, as many tourists from those nations attempting to hire cars have discovered to their cost. These motorists must obtain an International Driving Permit before departure (issued by the AAA or CAA in North America on the spot for a nominal cost); the Greek Automobile and Touring Club (ELPA) no longer issues them to foreign nationals in Greece. Similarly, with the advent of the single European market, insurance Green Cards are no longer required, though you should check with your home insurer about the need for any supplementary premiums – many policies now include pan-European cover anyway.

Greek traffic control and signals are basically the same as in the rest of continental Europe, though roundabouts are handled bizarrely by French or English standards – in most cases the traffic entering from the slip road, not that already in the circle, has the right of way.

Motorways speeds are routinely in excess of the nominal 100–120kph (62–75 mph) limits, and drivers overtake with abandon. A red light is often considered not so much an obligation as a suggestion, and oncoming drivers flashing lights at you on one-lane roads means the opposite of what it does in the UK. Here, it means: "I'm coming through." Greece has the highest accident rate in Europe after Portugal, so drive defensively.

Greece has a mandatory seatbelt law, and children under 10 are not allowed to sit in the front seat. It is an offence to drive without your licence on your person (€83 fine). Every car must also carry a first-aid kit in the boot (though hire companies tend to skimp on this). Police checkpoints at major (and minor) junctions are frequent, and in addition to the above offences you can be done for not having evidence of insurance, paid road tax or registration papers in/on the vehicle.

Super and normal unleaded petrol, as well as lead-substitute super, are readily available throughout Greece, though filling up after dark can be difficult. Most garages close around 8pm and, although a rota system operates in larger towns, it is often difficult to find out which station is open. International petrol stations operated by companies like BP and Shell usually take credit cards, but Greek ones often don't.

Road maps Gone are the days when visitors had to suffer with mendacious or comical maps which seemed based more on wishful thinking (especially projected but unbuilt roads) than facts on the ground. There are now three commercial Greek companies producing largely accurate maps: Road Editions, Emvelia and Anavasis. They can be found country-wide, in tourist-shop racks and better bookshop chains like Newsstand or Papasotiriou.

Motorcycles and bicycles

On most Greek islands you'll find agencies that hire small motorcycles, various types of scooters, 50cc and under, and even mountain bikes. These give you the freedom to wander where you will, and weekly rates are reasonable.

For any bike of over 50cc, helmets and a motorcycle driving licence are both theoretically required, and increasingly these rules are enforced. The ill-fitting helmets offered are a bit of a joke, but if you refuse them you may have to sign a waiver absolving the dealer of criminal/civil liability – and police checkpoints (see above) can be zealous, levying €88 fines on locals and visitors alike.

Before you set off, make sure the bike of whichever sort works by taking it for a test spin down the street. Brakes in particular are badly set, lights may need new fuses or bulbs, and spark-plugs get fouled – ask for a spare and the small spanner (wrench) to change them. Otherwise, you may get stuck with a lemon, and be held responsible for its malfunctioning when you return it.

Reputable agencies now often furnish you with a phone number for a breakdown pickup service.

Above all, don't take unnecessary chances, like riding two on a bike designed for one. More than one holiday in Greece has been ruined by a serious scooter accident. It is strongly suggested that where possible you stick with the traditional, manual-transmission Honda/Yamaha/Suzuki scooters of 50–100cc, with skinny, large-radius, well-treaded tyres. The new generation of automatic, button-start *mihanákia/papákia* (as they're called in Greek slang), with their sexy fairings and tiny, fat, no-tread tyres, look the business but are unstable and unsafe once off level asphalt. In particular, if you hit a gravel-strewn curve on one of these you will go for a spill, and at the very least lose most of the skin on your hands and knees.

Yacht charter

Chartering a yacht is one of the more exotic ways of island-hopping in Greece. It is by no means cheap, although hiring a boat with a group of friends may not far exceed the price of renting rooms every night for the came number of people

Depending on your nautical qualifications and your taste for autonomy, you can either take the helm yourself or let a hired crew do so for you. There are over a thousand yachts available for charter in Greece, all of which are registered and inspected by the Ministry of the Merchant Marine. For more information about chartering contact:
The Hellenic Professional Yacht Owners' Association
43 Freattýdhos Street, Zéa Marina, Piraeus; tel: 210 45 26 335.
The Greek Yacht Brokers and Consultants Association
36 Alkyónis Street, Paleó Fáliron, Athens; tel: 210 98 16 582.

Kaïkia

Apart from conventional ferries, most of which carry cars, there are swarms of small *kaïkia* (caiques) which in season offer inter-island excursions pitched mostly at day-trippers. Since they are chartered by travel agencies, they are exempt from Ministry of Transport fare controls – as well as the 30-year-old, scrap-it rule now enforced in Greece for scheduled ferries – and can be very pricey if used as a one-way ticket from, say, Sámos to Pátmos. The stereotypical emergency transfer by friendly fisherman is, alas, largely a thing of the past; never comfortable at the best of times, it is now highly illegal – knowing this, skippers quote exorbitant prices if approached, and must undertake the journey when the port policeman's gaze is averted.

Where to Stay

How to Choose

There is a broad range of accommodation in Greece, from deluxe hotels to student hostels. Listed are a sample of different categories across the country.

On the islands the main type of affordable lodging is private rented rooms (*domátia*) and, increasingly common these days, self-catering studios or apartments (*dhiamerís-mata*). These are classified separately from hotels, but also subject to official regulation.

In general, when looking for any kind of accommodation, local tourist offices or the Tourist Police, can be of help if you're in a fix – most obviously if no rooms are on offer when you disembark at the dock. The best system, though, increasingly used even by backpackers equipped with mobile phones, is booking a room yourself a few days (or weeks) in advance.

Athens

Andromeda Athens
T. Vássou 22, Ambelókipi
Tel: 210 641 5000
Fax: 210 646 6361

Hotel Categories

The Greek authorities have six categories for hotels, this is currently expressed as letters but is due to be replaced by a star system (no-star=E, five-star=deluxe), although this is being resisted by hoteliers. Although the current letters are supposed to accurately reflect the hotels' amenities, a swimming pool or tennis court could place an establishment in the A or B bracket even though in every other respect it has indifferent facilities. Also, the number of rooms can limit one's maximum rating, so you commonly encounter 14-room C-class hotels which are superior in every respect to a nearby 50-room B-class.

The following general principles apply, though: Luxury, A-, B- and C-

www.andromedahotels.gr
A little out of the way, just beyond the Mégaro Mousikís, but small and chic, and very expensive. The well designed rooms and suites have Persian carpets, rather generic bits of art, and modern furnishings. There is a nice swimming pool and the well-regarded Etrusco restaurant. €€€
Athens Hilton
Vas. Sofías 46
Tel: 210 728 1000
Fax: 210 728 1111
www.athens.hilton.com
The new-look Hilton is both extremely plush and hideously expensive. Now open after a €96-million refit, everything is glitzy, from the grand lobby, to the luxuriously carpeted hallways, to the rooms with their marbles bathrooms. Four restaurants, including the rooftop Galaxy with stupendous views. €€€
Grande Bretagne
Sýndagma Square
Tel: 210 333 0000
Fax: 210 332 8034
www.grandebretagne.gr
Almost as expensive and just as plush in its own special way, the Grande Bretagne is the doyen of Athenian hotels. Also just emerged from a refit, this historic building oozes class, from its luxurious rooms, to its beautiful spa, to its highly recommended restaurant. €€€
St George Lycabettus
Kleoménous 2, Kolonáki
Tel: 210 729 0711
Fax: 210 729 0439
www.sglycabettus.gr
In a pre-Olympic fit of enthusiasm, the St George also underwent a renovation. Now styling itself a "boutique hotel", the external (more expensive) rooms have one of the

class hotels all have private bathrooms. Most D-class hotels have en-suite bathrooms, while the dwindling number of E-class hotels don't.

Luxury and A-class hotels must have a bar and restaurant and offer a full choice of breakfasts. B- and C-class should provide a buffet breakfast in a separate dining room, but classes below that will often offer little better than a bread roll, jam and coffee, if even that.

Luxury and A-class hotels should have some or all of these auxiliary facilities: a swimming pool, fitness centre, "private" beach, conference hall, internet access from the rooms, 24-hour desk attendance, "tamed" taxi service.

Price Guide

Price categories are based on the cost of a double room for one night in the high season:
€€€ Expensive over €100
€€ Moderate €50–100
€ Inexpensive under €50
For details of the Greek Tourist Authority's hotel classification system see Hotel Categories on page 317.

best views in the city. The cool, comfortable rooms and suites are elegant and subdued, and the rooftop swimming pool is a delight. There are also two good restaurants, one with a superb view over the Acropolis. €€€

Museum
Bouboulínas 16 and Tosítsa
Tel: 210 380 5611
Fax: 210 380 0507
www.bestwestern.com
Perhaps the best thing about this well-run hotel, is its location close to the Archaeological Museum. The rooms are plain and comfortable, but a little over-priced. There is no restaurant (good ones nearby) but breakfast is included. €€€

NJV Athens Plaza
Sýndagma Square
Tel: 210 335 2400
Fax: 210 323 5856
www.classicalhotels.com
Modern, swish, and just a bit corporate, the Plaza does, however, kit out its rooms with fabrics by Ralph Lauren and Versace and tries hard to pander to your every whim. The lobby café is a good retreat from the heat or cold. €€€

Royal Olympic
Ath. Dhiákou 28–34
Tel: 210 928 8400
Fax: 210 923 3317
www.royalolympic.com
A long-standing hotel, now spruced up, with comfortable, if slightly anonymous rooms. The 1960s lobby with a huge chandelier is quite amusing, as is the equally dated dining room, but this is due to period charm rather than it beng run-down. €€€

Acropolis View
Webster 10 and Robértou Gáli
Tel: 210 921 7303
Fax: 210 923 0705
www.acropolisview.gr
The implied view of the Acropolis is available from only a few of the 32 rooms, but also from the roof terrace. The rooms themselves are small but clean and well-cared-for, and the hotel has had the inevitable pre-Olympic makeover. The location is excellent with nearby metro. €€

Attalos
Athinás 29
Tel: 210 321 2801–3
Fax: 210 324 3124
www.attalos.gr
Fairly standard but comfortable rooms close to Monastiráki Square (noisy during the day but quietens down at night). The staff are attentive and friendly, and there is a fine view of the city and the Acropolis from the roof terrace. €€

Austria
Moúson 7, Filopáppou
Tel: 210 923 5151
Fax: 210 924 7350
www.austriahotel.com
Well-placed, clean and quiet, and for all its name very Greek, though it is popular with German-speaking visitors. The air-conditioned rooms are plain with small en-suite bathrooms and balconies.A good buffet breakfast included in the price. €€

Cecil
Athinás 39
Tel/fax: 210 321 7079
www.cecil.gr
Close by the Attalos, and almost identical in price, the rooms in this hotel are a little more spartan than in its neighbour, but clean, with wooden floors. Breakfast is included in the cost of your stay and the price reflects the hotel's location rather than its facilities. €€

Aphrodite
Einárdhou 12 and M. Vódha 65
Tel: 210 881 0589
Fax: 210 881 6574
www.hostelaphrodite.com
Clean, unpretentious and friendly, this small, basic hotel is a good deal. Slightly off the beaten track but midway between Viktoria and Stathmos Lárisas metro stations. There is a pleasant basement bar and an excellent deal on the inter-island pass. €

Marble House
A. Zínni 35, Koukáki
Tel: 210 922 8294/923 4058
Fax: 210 922 6461
www.marblehouse.gr
This inexpensive, clean and friendly hotel is probably the best deal in Athens. Close to the Syngroú-Fix metro. Some rooms now have air-conditioning (the others have powerful ceiling fans) and breakfast is available for an extra charge. It has been done up recently and the prices remain low for the city. €

Athens International YHA
Victor Hugo 16
Tel/Fax: 210 523 2540
www.hihostels.com
A very cheap and well-maintained (the hostel was renovated in 2002) place to stay close to Omónia Square, the

railway stations and the National Museum. The four- or twin- bedded rooms are clean, and the in-house travel service offers discount tickets. Other facilities include a kitchen and luggage store. €

XEN/YWCA
Amerikís 11
Tel: 210 362 4291
Fax: 210 362 2400
xene7@hol.gr
This central, women-only hostel is a clean, safe place to stay. Very good value and some of the rooms (shared triples or doubles) have attached baths. All of them have ceiling fans. There is also a basic restaurant. €

Saronic Gulf

Salamína

Gabriel
Eándio
Tel: 210 466 2275
Not plush but the best hotel on the island, in the seaside village of Eándhio, right by the water. Standard facilities and comfortable enough should you stay on Salamína. €€

Aegina

Apollo
Aghía Marína
Tel: 22970 32271
Fax: 22970 32688
apolo@otenet.gr
On the east side of the island in Éghina's main resort. Apollo is a large, somewhat ageing but still comfortable choice if you want to be near a decent beach. Good facilities and a restaurant. €€

Hotel Brown
Éghina Town
Tel: 22970 22271
Fax: 22970 25838
www.hotelbrown.gr
Right on the southern waterfront a five-minute walk from the ferry quay is this converted sponge factory, now a hotel still owned by the original family whose ancestry was partly English (hence the name). Rooms are spacious and tidy and there's a large leafy garden. €€

To Petrino Spiti
Éghina Town
Tel: 22970 23837
A three-floored stone house (pétrino spíti) a 10-minute walk from the harbour. Very comfortable and distinctive. There are nine studios all done out in different styles – a couple of them in antique style. €

Póros

Hotel Manessi
Póros Town
Tel: 22980 22273
Fax: 22980 24345

www.manessi.com
A very pleasant waterfront choice right in the middle of the action. Housed in a neo-classical building all rooms are well equipped with central heating and air-conditioning, TV and fridge and most have balconies looking over the port. €

Sto Roloi
Hatzopoúlou & Karrá 13,
Póros Town
Tel: 22980 25808
Fax: 210 963 3705
www.storoloi-poros.gr
Sto Roloi (At the Clock) is located near the prominent clock tower on top of the hill behind Poros town, in a 200-year-old house converted into three apartments, with two more next door at Anemone House and the Little Tower. All decorated with traditional furnishings. €€€

Seven Brothers Hotel
Platía Iróön, Póros Town
Tel: 22980 23412
Fax: 22980 23413
www.7brothers.gr
A small family-run hotel with a restaurant. Rooms are large and very comfortable, with TV and air-conditioning. Very handy for the centre of Póros Town and the ferry and hydrofoil quay. €€

Ýdhra

Orloff
Ýdhra Town
Tel: 22980 52564
www.orloff.gr
A very comfortable mansion turned hotel with all creature comforts. All rooms are individual, in different shapes and sizes. Some look out over the town, others onto the flower-filled garden, where a large buffet breakfast is served. €€€

Leto
Ýdhra Town
Tel: 22980 53385
Fax: 22980 53806
www.letohydra.gr
A traditional style Hydriot house turned boutique hotel. All rooms are tastefully designed in Hydriot naval style and all are air-conditioned. Facilities include an attractive breakfast room and a separate area for smokers – unusual in Greece. €€

Miranda
Ýdhra Town
Tel: 22980 52230
Fax: 22980 53510
www.mirandahotel.gr
Set in a mansion built in 1810 Miranda is a traditional style hotel with 14 differently decorated rooms, some traditional, others art deco. The classy atmosphere is enhanced by the in-house art gallery. Breakfast is served in the garden. €€

Spétses

Nissia Hotel
Spétses Town
Tel: 22980 75000
Fax: 22980 75012
Perhaps the classiest hotel on the island, the Nissia is 500 metres (550 yds) west of the main ferry quay, overlooking the promenade. Consists of 31 comfortable single-floor and two-floored apartments built in traditional island style, all with sea views. An extensive buffet breakfast is included. €€€

Spetses
Spétses Town
Tel: 22980 72602
Fax: 22980 72494
www.spetses-hotel.gr
Located on its own beach 800 metres (½ mile) west of the ferry quay. Rooms are large and amply furnished, and all have balconies overlooking the sea, TV, music system, air-conditioning and minibar. There is an in-house restaurant. €€€

Lefka Palace
Spétses Town
Tel: 22980 72311
Fax: 22980 72161
www.lefkapalacehotel.gr
The Lefka Palace is in a class of its own with large airy rooms and ample verandas. Close to the sea, there is also a large swimming pool, tennis courts and extensive gardens. €€

Cyclades

Ándhros

Paradisos
Ándhros town
Tel: 22820 22187
An elegant neo-classical mansion near the centre of town, 700 metres (760 yds) from the beach. Airy rooms with superb views from the balconies. €€€

Andhros Holiday Hotel
Gávrio
Tel: 22820 71384/71443
Fax: 22820 71097
www.androsholidayhotel.com
Close to the sea with panoramic views of the Aegean. Attractive rooms, all with sea-view terraces; swimming pool, tennis courts, restaurant. €€

Mare e Vista – Epaminondas
Batsí
Tel: 22820 41682 (summer); 21060 22247, (winter)
Fax: 21060 20542
www.mare-vista.com
The island's best hotel, with big rooms and terraces, a big pool, gardens and a garage; 15 minutes' walk from the town, 200m/yds from the beach. €€

Niki
Ándhros town
Tel/fax: 22820 29155
Opened in 2002, this renovated main street mansion is convenient, elegant and inexpensive. All rooms have balconies, some facing the main street, some the sea. €

Kéa

Ioulis
Ioulís (Hóra)
Tel: 22880 22177
Delightfully quiet spot in the kástro, with lovely views from the terrace. Basic but serviceable. €€

Kéa Beach
Koúndhouros Bay
Tel: 22880 31230
Fax: 22880 31234
Luxury bungalow complex 5 km (3 miles) south of Písses, built in traditional Cycladic style, with all facilities from a nightclub to watersports. €€

Tínos

Alonia
Hóra (3 km/1½ miles towards Pórto)
Tel: 22830 23541–3
Fax: 22280 23544
www.aloniahotel.gr
Externally unprepossessing, this is Tínos' most welcoming hotel. The pool is large and surrounded by greenery, the rooms' balconies have beautiful views, and the food is good. €€

Tinion
Hóra
Tel: 22830 22261
Fax: 22830 24754
www.tinionhotel.gr
Charming old-world hotel in the centre of town, with tiled floors, lace curtains and a large balcony. €€

Kýthnos

Kythnos Bay Hotel
Mérihas Bay
Tel: 22810 32247
Fax: 22810 32092
kythnoshotel@in.gr
Basic but friendly hotel right on the waterfront. Rooms at the front have balconies overlooking the sea. €

Sýros

Dolphin Bay Hotel
Galissás
Tel: 22810 42924
Fax: 22810 42843
www.dolphin-bay.gr
The largest, most modern resort-hotel on the island. Attractive building, large swimming pool, restaurant, and beautiful views over the bay. €€€

Hotel Faros Village
Azólimnos
Tel: 22810 61661
Fax: 22810 61660

www.faros-hotel.com
This large hotel by the beach is five minutes' drive away from the capital. It has all the usual facilities, including two pools and restaurant. All rooms in the hotel and the bungalows have balconies or terraces with either sea or garden views. €€€

Omiros
Ermoúpoli
Tel: 22810 24910
Fax: 22810 86266
omirosho@otenet.gr
Mid-19th-century neo-classical mansion restored to a high standard. Rooms furnished in traditional style, with views of the lively harbour. €€

Mýkonos

Cavo Tagoo
Hóra
Tel: 22890 23692
Fax: 22890 24923
www.cavotagoo.gr
Jet-set luxurious, set on a hillside 500 metre/yds) north of Hóra. Prize-winning Cycladic architecture, cool, modern decor, impeccable service, friendly atmosphere, good views, pool, and Mýkonos' best restaurant. €€€

Deliades
Ornós
Tel: 22890 79430
Fax: 22890 26996
www.hoteldeliadesmykonos.com
Built in 2001 with quiet good taste, a short walk up the hill from Ornós beach. Every room has a big terrace with sea view. Relaxed atmosphere, pool, port and airport transfer. €€€

Villa Konstantin
Ághios Vasílios
Tel: 22890 26204
Fax: 22890 26205
www.villakonstantin-mykonos.gr
700 metres/yds from the town, in authentic island style but with all the luxuries. All rooms have terraces or balconies, most with sea views, and some have kitchens. €€

Myconian Inn
Hóra
Tel: 22890 23420/22663
Fax: 22890 27269
mycinn@hotmail.com
Right on the upper edge of town, this hotel is convenient, quiet, unpretentious and tasteful. Balconies overlook the port. €

Sérifos

Areti
Livádhi
Tel: 22810) 51 47 9
Fax: 22810) 51 54 7
Family-run hotel built on a hill with superb views, 400 metres/yds from beach and 200 metres/yds from port. Rooms and studios; peaceful terraced garden overlooking the sea. €€

Sífnos

Platis Yialos Hotel
Platýs Yialós
Tel: 22840 71324
Fax: 22840 31325
Large, Cycladic-style hotel at the far end of the beach. Well furnished and tastefully decorated with wood-carvings and wall paintings. The flagstone terrace reaches to the sea. All amenities, including a restaurant with the same great view. €€€

Artemon Hotel
Artemónas
Tel: 22840 31303
Fax: 22840 32385
www.hotel-artemon.com
Simple, attractive family hotel with rooms that overlook fields rolling towards the sea. €€

Apollonia
Apollonía
Tel: 22840 31490
Charming small hotel (only 9 rooms) with traditional island architecture and friendly service. €

Moní Hrysopighí
Apókofto
Tel: 22840 31255
This 17th-century monastery, situated on an islet reached by footbridge, rents out simple cells in summer. Book well in advance. €

Andíparos

Hryssi Akti
near Kástro
Tel: 222840 61206
Fax: 22840 61105
Elegant hotel with good rooms right on the beach on the east coast. €€

Mantalena
Kástro
Tel: 22840 61206
Fax: 22840 61550
Clean but simple rooms on the waterfront, with good views of the harbour and across to Páros. €

Páros

Anemomylos
Náoussa
Tel: 2840 51482/51632
Fax: 2840 51989
anemomyl@otenet.gr
A fully-equipped apartment complex built in traditional Cycladic style around a courtyard and pool. €€

Astir of Paros
Náoussa
Tel: 22840 51986
Fax: 22840 51985
www.ila-chateau.com/astir/index.htm
One of Greece's finest deluxe hotels, right on the beach, across the bay from the town. Spacious rooms with balconies, and bathrooms lined with Parian marble. Large pool, golf course, extensive gardens.
€€€

Pandrossos Hotel
Parikía
Tel: 22840 22903
Fax: 22840 22904
www.pandrossoshotel.gr
On a pretty hill at Parikia's edge, yet in town. Beautiful views of the bay, pool, good restaurant, marble lobby. €€

Dina
Parikía
Tel: 22840 21325/21345
Fax: 22840 23525
Friendly hotel in the heart of the old town. Spotlessly clean rooms set around a lovely flowered courtyard. Only 8 rooms, so book early. €

Náxos

Apollon
Hóra
Tel. 22850 22468/26801
Fax: 22850 25200
apollon-hotel@naxos-island.com
An efficient, convenient place to stay in town with parking, on the picturesque pedestrian museum square by the cathedral. €€

Chateau Zevgoli
Hóra
Tel: 22850 26123/25201
Fax: 22850 25200
chateau-zevgoli@nax.forthnet.gr
Quiet, plush and exclusive, high up in the old town. A Venetian mansion with only 10 rooms, each lovingly decorated. One has a four-poster bed, most have great views. €€

Mílos

Kapetan Tassos
Apollónia
Tel: 22870 41287
Fax: 22870 41322
Modern apartments in traditional blue-and-white island architecture, with good sea views. 11 km (7 miles) from Adamás, so you need transport. €€

Popi's Windmill
Trypití
Tel: 22870 22286
A pleasant converted windmill with beautiful views towards Adamás port. Two bedrooms, kitchen and bathroom. €€

Panorama
Klíma
Tel: 22870 21623
Fax: 22870 22112
Small seafront hotel, family-run with friendly service. €

Folégandros
Fani-Vevis
Hóra
Tel: 22860 41237
Fax: 22860 41282
Comfortable hotel in a traditional
house with pleasant courtyard; 11
rooms, some overlooking the sea.
€€
Kastro
Hóra
Tel/fax: 22860 41230
A 500-year-old traditional house that
is actually part of the ancient Kástro
walls. Quaint rooms have pebble
mosaic floors, barrel ceilings and
spectacular views down sheer cliffs to
the sea. €

Síkinos
Kamares
Aloprónia
Tel: 22860 51234
Fax: 22860 51205
Traditional-style, affordable hotel with
average but comfortable rooms. €€
Porto Sikinos
Aloprónia
Tel: 22860 51220
Fax: 22860 51247
The best accommodation on the
island: a complex of 18 Cycladic-style
buildings right on the beach. Pool, bar
and restaurant. €€
Flora
Aloprónia
Tel: 22860 51214
Simple rooms built round courtyards
on the hillside above the port. Great
sea views and a 10-minute walk from
the beach. Most rooms face the sea.
€

Íos
Íos Palace
Mylopótas
Tel: 22860 91269/91204
Fax: 22860 91082
www.iospalacehotel.com
Modern hotel designed and decorated
in the traditional style. Near the
beach, with very comfortable rooms,
marble-lined bathrooms and balconies
overlooking the sea. €€€
Philippou
Hóra
Tel/fax: 22860 91230
Small, comfortable hotel in the centre
of Íos's hectic nightlife. Great location
if you plan to party all night.
Otherwise, bring earplugs or choose
somewhere out of town. €€
Acropolis
Mylopótas
Tel/fax: 22860 91303
info@hotelacropolis.gr
Clean, simple rooms with balconies in
traditional blue and white building
overlooking the beach below, which is
5 minutes' walk away. €

Amórgos
Aegialis
Órmos Eghiális
Summer: tel: 22850 73393
Fax : 22850 73395
Winter: tel: 210 689 0410
Fax: 210 683 1858
www.amorgos-aegialis.com
Smart modern hotel complex with
good facilities, including a taverna and
large swimming pool. Lovely views
over the bay from the veranda.
€€
Minoa
Katápola
Tel: 22850 71480
Fax: 22850 74168
Traditional-style hotel on the harbour
square. Can be noisy. €

Santoríni
Aigialos Houses
Firá
Tel: 22860 25191
Fax: 22860 22856
www.aigialos.gr
Every house is different in this
complex; all are tastefully luxurious,
quiet and convenient, and have
spectacular views, with balconies or
terraces overlooking the caldera. A fine
restaurant (residents only). €€€
Atlantis Villas
Ía
Tel: 22860 71214
Fax: 22860 71312
www.atlantisvillas-santorini.com
These traditionally furnished cave-
apartments are many white steps
down the Ía cliffside. Very friendly,
with all services, and caldera views
from terrace and pool. €€€
Fanari Villas
Ía
Tel: 22860 71007–8
Fax: 22860 71235
www.fanarivillas.com
Traditional skaftá cave houses
converted into luxury accommodation.
Pool, breakfast terrace, bar and 240
steps down to Ammoudiá Bay.
Attentive, friendly service. €€€
Katikies
Ía
Tel: 22860 71401
Fax: 22860 71129
www.katikies.com
One of the best on the island. Lovely
new apartments built on a clifftop in
traditional style, spectacular views and
a wonderful pool. Excellent service.
€€€
Theoxenia Hotel
Firá
Tel: 22860 22740
Fax: 22860 22950
www.theoxenia.net
Right on the main cliffside street, this
attractive small hotel is friendly and
efficient, and has all amenities,

including a pool. Upstairs rooms have
caldera views. €€€
Hermes
Kamári
Tel: 22860 31664
Fax: 22860 33240
Friendly, family-run hotel set in
beautiful gardens not far from the
town centre and the black beach.
Pool, comfortable rooms, and all the
amenities. €€

Rhodes
Marco Polo Mansion
Aghíou Fanouríou 42, Rhodes
Old Town
Tel/fax: 22410 25562
www.marcopolomansion.gr
Superb conversion of an old Turkish
mansion; all rooms are en-suite and
furnished with antiques from the
nearby eponymous gallery. Large
buffet breakfasts included, one-week
minimum stay, advance booking
required. €€€
Miramare Wonderland
Ixiá
Tel: 22410 96251
Fax: 22410 95954
Fake-vernacular bungalows painted in
traditional colours, in a landscaped
setting just behind the beach. Tasteful
mock-antique furnishings and jacuzzis
in some tubs. A private mini-railway
salvaged from a Welsh mine shuttles
guests around the huge grounds.
€€€
Andreas
Omírou 28D, Rhodes Old Town
Tel: 22410 34156
Fax: 22410 74285
www.hotelandreas.com
An old favourite under dynamic new
management, this pension in an old
Turkish mansion was thoroughly
refurbished in 2003. En-suite rooms
are in a variety of formats (including
family-size, and a spectacular tower
unit for two). A terrace bar serves
evening drinks and excellent
breakfasts. Two-night minimum stay.
Open late March–end October. €€
Ganymedes
Perikléous 68, Rhodes Old Town
Tel: 22410 33545
Fax: 22410 31937
www.ganymedeshotel.com
Just four rooms at this 2003-built
boutique hotel, three of them large
and airy, one best as a single, all
exquisitely furnished. There's a roof
terrace for evenings, and a genuine
French patisserie on the ground floor
for breakfast and cakes. €€
S. Nikolis
Ippodámou 61, Rhodes Old Town
Tel: 22410 34561
Fax: 22410 32034
www.s-nikolis.gr

Price Guide

Price categories are based on the cost of a double room for one night in the high season:
€€€ Expensive over €100
€€ Moderate €50–100
€ Inexpensive under €50
For details of the Greek Tourist Authority's hotel classification system see Hotel Categories on page 333.

A variety of restoration premises, of which the "honeymoon suites" are the best executed, while self-catering apartments are excellent value for groups or families. Open April–November, booking essential. €€

Niki's
Sofokléous 39, Rhodes Old Town
Tel: 22410 25115
Fax: 22410 36033
www.nikishotel.gr
An excellent budget hotel, most rooms having balconies and air-con. Helpful management and credit-card acceptance are other bonuses. €

Spot
Perikléous 21, Rhodes Old Town
Tel/fax: 22410 34737
www.spothotelrhodes.gr
Another good budget/backpacker hotel, a modern building containing cheerful en-suite rooms with air-con and private bath/shower. Internet facilities, free luggage storage; open March–November. €

Dodecanese

Kássos

Anagenessis
Frý
Tel: 22450 41495
Fax: 22450 41036
Comfortable rooms, some with sea views. Slightly more expensive than the Anessis hotel below, but not all rooms are en suite. €

Anessis
Mavrikaki 9, Frý
Tel: 22450 041201
Fax: 22450 041730
Exceedingly modest though they are, this and the Anagenessis represent nearly half the beds available in Frý, the port town. Fairly small rooms, but all en suite. €

Kárpathos

Atlantis
Pighádhia (by the Italian "palace")
Tel: 22450 22777
Fax: 22450 22780
www.atlantishotelkarpathos.gr
Helpful, well-appointed hotel with quiet setting, easy parking, and a small pool . €€

Akrogiali Studios
Potáli bay, Paralía Lefkoú
Tel/fax: 22450 71178
Just eight, spacious units, all with views towards the pebble beach; friendly management and minimarket downstairs for restocking. €

Astro
Ólympos
Tel: 22450 51421
A good, relatively comfortable en-suite "hotel" in this traditional village, kept by the two sisters who manage the Café Restaurant Zefiros where breakfast is served. €

Glaros
Dhiafáni
Tel: 22450 51501
Fax: 22450 51259
www.hotel-glaros.gr
The most comfortable lodgings here, 16 tiered studio units on the south hillside, some with four beds. €

Pine Tree
Ádhia hamlet, west coast
Tel: 697 73 69 948
www.pinetree-karpathos.gr
Ideal place to hide away, in a lovely oasis setting, but you must have your own transport. Units are basic but serviceable. €

Vardes Studios
Amopí beach
Tel/fax: 22450 811111
www.hotelvardes.gr
The best standard here among outfits accepting walk-in trade, with huge units (they can fit two adults and two children at a pinch) overlooking well-tended gardens some way inland. €

Sými

Aliki
Haráni quay, Yialós
Tel: 22460 71665
A 1895 waterfront mansion, and Sými's poshest hotel: tasteful rooms with wood floors and some antique furnishings, plus air-con and large bathrooms, though few sea views. €€

Les Catherinettes
north quay, Yialós
Tel: 22460 71671
Fax: 22460 72698
hotels@symi-island.com
Creaky but spotless en-suite pension above the restaurant of the same name, in a historic building with painted ceilings and sea-view balconies for most rooms. €€

Fiona
Top of Kalí Stráta, Horió
Tel: 22460 72755
symi-vis@otenet.gr
Mock-traditional hotel building, large airy rooms with double beds and stunning views; breakfast in mid-air on the communal terrace. Run by a friendly couple. Also two studio apartments to rent. €€

Albatros
Yialós marketplace
Tel: 22460 71707/71829
www.albatrosymi.gr
Partial sea views from this exquisite, small hotel with French co-management; pleasant second-floor breakfast salon, air-con. Families should ask also about their more expensive Villa Symeria. €

Kastellórizo

Mediterraneo Pension
North end of the west quay
Tel: 22460 49007
www.mediterraneo-megisti.com
Another architect-executed refurbishment, this offers simple but well-appointed rooms with mosquito nets and wall art, half with sea views, plus an arcaded ground-floor suite and optional breakfast with proprietress Marie's homemade marmalade. Unusually, open all year. €€

Karnayo
Platía at west end of the south quay
Tel: 22460 49225
Fax: 22460 49266
www.kastellorizokarnayo.gr
The best restoration accommodation on the island, designed by a trained architect. Rooms, studios and a four-bed apartment occupy two separate buildings, with wood-and-stone interiors. €€

Kastellorizo Hotel Apartments
West quay
Tel: 22460 49044
Fax: 22460 49279
www.kastellorizohotel.gr
These air-conditioned, quality-fitted studios or galleried maisonettes, some with sea view, offer the best facilities on the island. Tiny plunge pool, and its own lido in the bay. €€

Hálki

Most accommodation is block-booked by package companies from April to October; here are two exceptions.

Captain's House
North of the church and inland
Tel: 22460 45201
Five-room, en-suite pension in a converted mansion with garden bar and helpful management. €

Pension Keanthi
Inland near the school
Tel: 22460 45334
Bland, pine-furnished rooms with high ceilings, plus a few galleried studios. €

Tílos

Eleni Beach
Livadia, about halfway around the bay
Tel: 22460 44062
Fax: 22460 44063
www.elenihoteltilos.gr
Obliging management for large, airy,

white-decor hotel rooms right on the beach. Advance booking required. €€

Blue Sky Apartments
ferry dock, above Blue Sky taverna
Tel: 22460 44294
Fax: 22460 44184
www.tilostravel.co.uk
Nine well-appointed, galleried apartments above a popular taverna, with great views of Livadia Bay. €

Irini
Livadia
Tel: 22460 44293
Fax: 22460 44238
www.tilosholidays.gr
Long the top hotel on Tílos, Irini still wins points for its beautiful grounds and common areas, including large pool, and only 5 minutes' walk from the beach. Package patronage is heaviest in May and September; otherwise individual travellers can usually find a vacancy. The same management keeps the hillside **Ilidi Studios**, with both 2- and 4-person units. €€

Miliou Studios
Megálo Horió
Tel/fax: 22460 44204
The best-value accommodation this end of the island, in a leafy setting near the base of the village. A variety of units, from basic rooms to two-room apartments, fill quickly during July–August. €

Níssyros

Porfyris
Mandhráki centre
Tel/fax: 22420 31376
By default, the best hotel here; in 2001 fridges and air-conditioning were added to the 1980s rooms, which overlook either orchards and the sea or the large pool. €

Xenon Polyvotis
Mandhráki port
Tel: 22420 31011
Fax: 22420 31204
This municipally-run inn offers the best standard on the harbour, with biggish, neutral-decor rooms and knockout sea views. €

Kós

Grecotel Royal Park
Marmári
Tel: 22420 41488
Fax: 22420 41373
www.ellada.net/grecotel/royalpark
Garden- or sea-view bungalow units are a maximum 300 metres/yds from the beach, with fridges, air-conditioning, bathtubs. €€

Afendoulis
Evrypýlou 1, Kós Town
Tel: 22420 25321
Fax: 22420 25797
afendoulishotel@kos.forthnet.gr
Welcoming, family-run C-class hotel:

cheerful en-suite rooms with fans, most with balconies, plus some cooler basement "caves" much sought after in summer. Open April–late October. €

Alexis
Irodhótou 9, Kós Town
Tel: 22420 25594
A backpackers' home-from-home in a villa overlooking the Hellenistic baths. Rooms large, though most not en-suite. Self-catering kitchen and terrace; open late March to early November. €

Fenareti
Mastihári
Tel: 22420 59028
Fax: 22420 59129
www.fenareti.kosweb.com
Hillside hotel in the least packaged of Kós's coastal settlements, overlooking the widest part of the beach; rooms and studios in a peaceful garden environment. €

Kamelia
Artemisías 3, Kós Town
Tel/fax: 22420 28983
Friendly, well-placed, family-run hotel, which the Afendoulis refers to when full; rear rooms have an orchard view. Open April–October, with heating. €

Astypálea

Kilindra Studios
west slope of Hóra
Tel/fax: 22430 61131
www.astipalea.com.gr
Units built in traditional style in 2000 in the shadow of the castle, offering all luxury amenities including a swimming pool; open all year. €€€

Australia
Skála
Tel: 22430 61067
Fax: 22430 59812
2002-upgraded rooms and studios in separate blocks, with phones, fans, air con; good affiliated restaurant. €€

Maltezana Beach
Análipsi (Maltezána)
Summer: Tel: 22430 61558
Fax: 22430 61669
Winter: Tel: 0030 210 5624823,
Fax: 0030 210 5624823
www.maltezanabeach.gr
A state-of-the-art bungalow hotel, the island's newest and largest, with spacious, well-appointed standard rooms and even bigger suites arrayed around gardens and a pool. On-site restaurant; open Easter–end September. €€

Venetos Studios
base of west hillside, Livádhia
Tel: 22430 61490/61150
Fax: 22430 61423
venetos@otenet.gr
Units in several buildings scattered across an orchard; facilities range from basic rooms to four-person apartments. €

Kálymnos

Maria's Studios
Above Melitsahás cove
Tel: 22430 48135
Spacious units with proper kitchens fit three, don't get packages, and overlook one of the better beaches on the west coast. €

Pension Plati Gialos
Platý-Yialós
Tel/fax: 22430 47029
Ever-popular family-run backpacker haven overlooks Linária cove, and beyond to Kandhoúni. Units are basic but everything works (including wall fans and American-style showers); extended balconies, mosquito nets and breakfast terrace. €

Villa Themelina
Evangelístria district, Póthia
Tel: 22430 22682
Fax: 22430 23920
The town's top choice: en-suite rooms in a 19th-century mansion, plus an annexe of modern studios behind the pool and gardens. No air-con, but very good breakfasts served on the patio; open all year. €

Télendos

On the Rocks
Tel: 2243 48260
Fax: 2243 48261
www.telendos.com/otr
Just four smartly appointed rooms with double glazing, mosquito nets etc, above amiable Greek-Australian-run bar of the same name. €

Monastery Stays

Monasteries and convents can occasionally provide lodging for travellers, though their *xenónes* (guest lodges) are intended primarily for Orthodox pilgrims. Mount Áthos, of course, has a long tradition of this hospitality (for men only). If you have found a monastery that does accept overnight guests, you will have to dress appropriately and behave accordingly. The doors may close as early as sunset and some kind of donation may be expected.

Porto Potha
Tel: 22430 47321
Fax: 22430 48108
portopotha@hotmail.com
At the very edge of things, but this
hotel has a large pool and friendly
managing family. €

Léros
Castle Vigla
Vromólithos
Tel: 22470 24083
Fax: 22470 24744
www.castlevigla.gr
Cottage and studio complex with
some of the island's best views (vígla
means "watchpoint"). €€
Crithoni Paradise
Krithóni
Tel: 22470 25120
Fax: 227470 24680
cparadise@12net.gr
Léros' top-rated accommodation, a
low-rise complex with a pool, disabled
access and smallish but sea-view
rooms (go for the suites if money
permits). Buffet breakfast; open all
year. €€
Tony's Beach Studios
Vromólithos
Tel: 22470 24742
Fax: 22470 24743
www.tonybeach.gr
Spacious, simply appointed units
behind the best beach on the island;
handicapped access, ample parking,
very quiet. Open June–September
only. €€
Archontiko Angelou
Álynda
Tel: 22470 22749
Fax: 22470 24403
info@hotel-angelou-leros.com
An attractive and well-run hotel in a
late 19th-century mansion, in a rural
setting, close to the beach. €€
Rodon
4 Markopoulou Street (between
Pandhéli and Vromólithos in Spiliá
district)
Tel: 22470 22075
Small but well-kept, mostly balconied
rooms, better than you would expect
from this hotel's official E-class rating,
all en suite and with air-con. Also

ground-floor 3-person studios, with
less of a sea view. €

Lipsí
Aphrodite
behind Liendhoú beach
Tel: 22470 4100
A 1997-built, attractive studio
bungalow-hotel complex, with large
units; tends to get booked up by
package clients but usually there's a
vacancy. €
Galini Apartments
By the ferry jetty
Tel: 22470 41212
Fax: 22470 41012
Well-appointed rooms with balconies
and fridges, and a very welcoming
family who will take you fishing. €
Studios Kalymnos
Inland side of town on way to
Monodhéndri beach
Tel: 22470 41141
Fax: 22470 41343
studios_kalymnos@lipsi-island.gr
Fairly spartan but quiet rooms with
cooking facilities, in a garden setting.
€

Pátmos
Porto Scoutari
hillside above Melóï beach
Tel: 22470 33125/6940 827927
Fax: 22470 33175
www.portoscoutari.com
The island's top accommodation:
enormous self-catering suites, arrayed
around the pool area, have sea views
and air-con/heating, as well as mock-
antique furnishings and original wall
art. Elina the proprietress is a font of
island knowledge. €€€
Blue Bay
Skála, Konsoláto district
Tel: 22470 31165
Fax: 22470 32303
www.bluebay.50g.com
The last building on the way out of
town towards Gríkou, and spared the
late-night ferry noise that plagues
most hotels here. Rooms were
refurnished in 2001. Friendly
Australian-Greek management, on-site
internet café. €€
Effie
Skála, Kastélli hillside
Tel: 22470 32500/31298
Fax: 22470 32700
www.effiehotel.gr
Bland, blonde-pine-and-tile rooms
spread over two hotel wings, but with
balconies and air-conditioning they're
good value in a quiet setting. Open all
year. €€
Galini
Skála
Tel: 22470 31240
Fax: 22740 31705
www.travelinfo.gr/galini
In a quiet cul-de-sac near the ferry

quay, this C-class hotel offers B-class
standards in furnishings and
bathrooms, and excellent value. €€
Golden Sun
Gríkou
Tel: 22470 32318
Fax: 22470 34019
Hillside setting with most rooms
facing water; stays open into autumn
(unusual here) and not monopolised
by packages (though there are
"special interest" groups). €€
Maria
Hóhlakas Bay, near Skála
Tel: 22470 31201
Fax: 22470 32018
Very quiet, garden-set small hotel with
all air-con, balconied rooms facing the
sea (bathrooms are tiny though). €€

Northeastern Aegean

Sámos
Arion
1km (½ mile) west of Kokkári
Tel: 22370 92020
Fax: 22370 92006
www.arion-hotel.gr
The best accommodation on Sámos'
north coast, a well-designed hotel-
wing and bungalow complex on a
hillside. Famously good breakfasts.
€€€
Doryssa Bay Hotel-Village
Pythagorion, near airport
Tel: 22730 88300
Fax: 22730 61463
www.doryssa-bay.gr
One of the few actual beachfront
resorts on Sámos, with a saltwater pool
just in from the sand if the sea's too
cold. If budget permits, skip the dull
1970s hotel wing in favour of the
meticulously constructed fake "village",
no two houses alike and incorporating
all the vernacular styles of Greece.
€€€
Kerveli Village
approach to Kérveli beach
Tel: 22730 23631/22334
Fax: 22730 23006
www.kerveli-village.gr
This is a well-executed, smallish
bungalow hotel set among olive trees
and cypresses, with superb views
across to Turkey and over Kérveli Bay.
A good selection of beaches and
tavernas within walking distance.
€€€
Aïdonokastro
Platanáki/Aïdhónia district, near
Ághios Konstandínos
Tel: 22730 94686
Fax: 22730 94404
About half the abandoned hillside
hamlet of Valeondádhes has been
renovated as a unique cottage-hotel,
each former house now a pair of two-
or four-person units with traditional
touches. €€

Híos Houses

Omiros Travel in Volissós is a little booking office that handles 16 old village houses restored in the early 1990s. Units, all with period features, usually accommodate two people, prices €–€€. Tel: 22740 21413; fax: 22740 21521.

Amfilisos
Bállos beach, near Órmos
Marathókambos
Tel: 22730 31669
Fax: 22730 31668
The hotel itself is nothing extraordinary, but Bállos is a deliciously sleepy place for doing very little except exploring the coast to the southeast and sampling some good local tavernas. €€

Avli Pension
Áreos 2, Sámos Town
Tel: 22730 22939
Housed in the former convent school of French nuns who staffed the local Catholic church until 1973, this is the best budget choice in town. Just over half of the rooms round the courtyard (avlí) are en-suite. Affable owner Spyros is a reliable source of information on local tavernas and nightspots. €

Ikaría

Erofili Beach
Armenistís
Tel: 22750 71058
Fax: 22750 71483
www.erofili.gr
Considered the best-standard hotel on the island, with designer rooms and ample common areas. A small saltwater pool perches dramatically over Livádhi beach. €€

Messakhti Village
Messakhtí beach, Armenistís
Tel: 22750 71331
Fax: 22750 71330
www.messakti-village.com
Imposing common areas, large private terraces and equally spacious studios (fit 3 to 6), but the breakfast is rather poor and furnishings somewhat plain at this architect-designed hillside complex. The large pool is a necessity in August, when the sea here can be dangerously rough. €€

Akti
On a knoll east of the hydrofoil and kaïki quay, Ághios Kírykos
Tel: 22750 22694
A simple hotel, and not a place for a long stay, but ideal if waiting for an early ferry or hydrofoil; friendly, basic spotless, with rooms both en-suite and not, most with a balcony or terrace and good views. €

Híos

Kyma
East end of Evghenías Handrí
Tel: 22710 44500
Fax: 22710 44600
B-class hotel in a converted neoclassical mansion (plus less attractive modern extension); helpful management, good breakfasts in the original salon with painted ceiling. €€

Mavrokordatiko
Kámbos district, 1.5 km (1 mile) south of the airport on Mitaráki lane
Tel: 22710 32900
Fax: 22710 32902
www.mavrokordatiko.com
Best and most popular restoration project in the Kámbos, with heated, wood-panelled rooms and breakfast (included) served by the courtyard with its mánganos (waterwheel). €€

Spitakia
Avghónyma
Tel: 22710 20513–4
Fax: 22710 81202
kratisis@spitakia.gr
A cluster of small but well-restored houses taking up to five people, near the edge of this stunningly set west-coast village. €€

Chios Rooms
Eghéou 110, Híos Town
Tel: 22710 20198
chiosrooms@hotmail.com
Upstairs rooms with high ceilings and tile-and-wood floors, some en-suite, in lovingly restored building managed by a New Zealand/Greek couple. Best is the "penthouse", with a private terrace. €

Markos' Place
South hillside, Karfás beach
Tel: 22710 31990 or 697 32 39 706
www.marcos-place.gr
Inside a disused monastery, Markos Kostalas has created a uniquely peaceful, leafy environment. Guests are lodged in the former pilgrims' cells. Minimum stay 4 days; open April–November. €

Lésvos

Pyrgos
Eleftheríou Venizélou 49, Mytilíni
Tel: 22510 25069
Fax: 22510 47319
www.pyrgoshotel.gr
The town's premier restoration accommodation, with over-the-top kitsch decor in the common areas. Rooms, most with balcony, are perfectly acceptable, and there are three round units in the tower. €€€

Clara
Avláki, 2km south of Pétra
Tel: 22530 41532
Fax: 22530 41535
www.clarahotel.gr
The large, designer-furnished rooms of this pastel-coloured bungalow complex

look north to Pétra and Mólyvos; particularly renowned for its ample buffet breakfasts relying on local products. There are tennis courts and a pool. €€–€€€

Malemi
Skála Kallonís
Tel: 22530 22594
Fax: 22530 22838
www.malemi.com
Pleasant, family-run bungalow complex renovated in 2006, the most welcoming of half a dozen here, with units from doubles to family suites, attractive grounds, tennis court and a large pool. €€

Molyvos I
Mólyvos beach lane
Tel: 22530 71496
Fax: 22530 71460
Nominally B-class outfit on the pebble shore, behind the tamarisks. Large, tile-floored, 1980s rooms; reasonable buffet breakfast served on a stone-paved terrace. You get the use of (and a shuttle to) the pool and sports facilities at sister hotel **Molyvos II** at Eftaloú, though there is a "private" beach area here. €€

Vatera Beach
Vaterá
Tel: 22520 61212
Fax: 22520 61164
www.vaterabeach.gr
A rambling, Greek/American-run hotel set behind the best beach on the island. Rooms with air-con and minibar, free sunbeds, in-house restaurant relying on own-grown produce; free advice from proprietress Barbara. €€

Pension Lida
Plomári
Tel/fax: 22520 32507
A welcoming restored inn housed in two adjacent old mansions formerly belonging to a soap-manufacturing magnate. There are sea-view balconies in most units, enthusiastic management. €

Límnos

Porto Myrina Palace
Ávlonas beach, 2km N of Mýrina
Tel: 22540 24805
Fax: 22540 24858
Considered the best, and most easily bookable, luxury hotel on the island, with grounds incorporating a small Artemis temple. €€€

Price Guide

Price categories are based on the cost of a double room for one night in the high season:

€€€€ Expensive over €100
€€ Moderate €50–100
€ Inexpensive under €50

For details of the Greek Tourist Authority's hotel classification system see Hotel Categories on page 333.

Ifestos
Andróni district, Mýrina
Tel: 22540 24960
Fax: 22540 23623
Attractive small hotel whose rooms have a mix of seaward and hillside views, balconies, fridges, air-con. €€

Thássos

Thassos Inn
Panaghía village
Tel: 25930 61612
Fax: 25930 61027
Quiet except for the sound of water in runnels all around, this modern building in traditional style has most rooms facing the sea. €€

Alkyon
18 Octovriou Street
Tel: 25930 22148
Fax: 25930 23662
Spacious rooms, with harbour or garden view, plus gregarious Anglo-Greek management and afternoon tea, make this a firm favourite with English-speaking travellers. €

Samothráki

Eolos
Kamariótissa
Tel: 25510 41595
Fax: 25510 41810
Samothráki's port and capital is home to a few hotels including this decent budget to mid-range choice. Rooms are simple but clean and welcoming. Some have views overlooking the hills, others towards the sea. Continental breakfast is included. Cash only. €€

Mariva Bungalows
Loutrá Thermá
Tel: 25510 98230
Fax: 25510 98374
mariva@acn.gr
Situated in the island's resort centre, these lovely flower-shrouded bungalows are built on a gentle hillside. All units are self-contained, comfortable and reasonably spacious. Ideal for a longer stay. Cash only. €€

Sporades and Evvia

Skiáthos

Atrium
Plataniás
Tel: 24270 49345/49376
Fax: 24270 49444
www.atriumhotel.gr
Combines casual elegance with traditional architecture. It's chic, beautiful and enjoys a splendid view. Rooms are extremely comfortable, some have private balconies or patios. There's a pool and a poolside restaurant. €€€

Skiathos Palace
Koukounariés
Tel: 24270 49700
Fax: 24270 49666
www.skiathos-palace.gr
One the isand's largest resort hotels, overlooking the eastern end of Koukounariés beach. The standard rooms are average in size and all have balconies, the superior rooms and suites are worth the extra. Facilities include pool, sauna and in-house restaurant. €€€

Nostos Village
Tzanéria
Tel: 24270 22520
Fax: 24270 22525
www.center.gr/nostos
A large complex on the Kanapítsa peninsula midway between Skiáthos Town and Koukounariés. Built into a verdant hillside, one of the better and more popular resort choices for visitors to the island. Choose from simpler rooms or self-catering bungalows among pine trees. €€

Skópelos

Adrina Beach
Pánormos
Tel: 24240 23371/23373
Fax: 24240 23372
www.adrina.gr
This expansive hotel complex (42 standard rooms and 10 bungalows) occupies a large tract of hillside just to the north of Pánormos Bay, looking out onto its own virtually private beach. If you want to get married while on holiday, there is even a small on-site chapel. €€

Dionysos
Skópelos Town
Tel: 24240 23210
Fax: 24240 22954
www.dionyssoshotel.gr
The Dionysos is ideal for visitors wishing to stay as close as possible to town. The 52 rooms are furnished in traditional dark pine and have air-con, TV and balconies. The hotel also has a pool with a shallow end for children. €€

Skopelos Village Hotel
Skópelos Town
Tel: 24240 22517
Fax: 24240 22958
www.skopelosvillagehotel.com
A complex of self-catering bungalows about 500 m across the bay, with a large grassy area and a pool. Living areas are large and contain tasteful local furnishings. €€

Alónissos

Konstantina's Studios
Hóra (Old Alónissos)
Tel: 24240 66165/65900
www.konstantinastudios.gr
High up in the old renovated village this small traditionally renovated building houses eight studios and one apartment. All have exceptional sea views and wooden balconies with canvas deckchairs. €€

Liadromia
Patitíri
Tel: 24240 65160
Fax: 24240 65096
liadromia@alonnissos.com
One of the first hotels to open in Alónisos, it maintains an air of old-world charm with a dash of modernity. Rooms have stucco walls, stone floors and tasteful decoration. Overlooking the harbour at the north side of Patitíri Bay, handy for all island facilities. €€

Milia Bay
Miliá
Tel: 24240 66032/66035
Fax: 24240 66037
www.milia-bay.gr
Tucked away overlooking the sandy Miliá Bay, this quiet retreat consists of 12 ecologically constructed self-catering apartments, all very spacious and tastefully decorated. If you don't fancy the short walk to the beach there's a pool, as well as the in-house restaurant. €€

Skýros

Skyros Palace
Gyrísmata, Péra Kámbou
Tel: 22220 91994
Fax: 22220 92070
www.skiros-palace.gr
Tucked away at the northeastern end of the Magaziá-Mólos strip, down on the beach, the Skyros Palace is a fairly sumptuous place to stay, though its location may be a little inconvenient for some. Free bus shuttles ply between the hotel and Hóra. Open summer only. €€

Xenia
Magaziá
Tel: 22220 91209
Fax: 22220 92062
A rather obvious cement box on Magaziá beach. Aesthetics aside, the location is excellent and the hotel service is good, while the spacious rooms have been kept up to date with recent renovations. €€

Évvia

Thermai Sylla Spa Wellness Hotel
Loutrá Edhipsoú
Tel: 22260 60100

Fax: 22260 22055
www.thermaesylla.gr
Perhaps Greece's only official anti-stress hotel, this magnificent edifice at the northern end of the promenade is a turn-of-the-century experience brought up to date, offering beauty and therapy treatments based on the waters of the ancient spa. €€€

Hotel Karystion
Kriezótou 2, Kárystos
Tel: 22240 22391
Fax: 22240 22727
A busy foreigner-friendly hotel in the far south of Évvia, close to the fortress on the south side of town. Neat, air-conditioned rooms, all with balconies, TVs and phones. The town's best bathing spots are a few minutes' walk way. €€

Corfu

The official Greek Hotel guide lists over 400 licensed hotels on the island. Many of these remain in the firm grip of tour operators from May to October, closing in winter. The following are open off-season and/or to independent travellers. Additionally, if you have a car, you can usually find *dhomátia* or apartments on a walk-in basis at the less packaged resorts of Astrakerí, Kalamáki, Afiónas and Aríllas in the north, plus Paramónas and Boúkari in the southwest.

Kérkyra Town and around

Corfu Palace
Dhimokratías 2, north end of Gharítsa Bay
Tel: 26610 39485
www.corfupalace.com
The town's only "lux" class establishment, which enjoys a high level of repeat clientele, including VIPs and foreign dignitaries, especially in May and September. They come for the huge rooms with marble bathtubs, the big breakfasts and the assiduous level of service. Open all year. €€€€

Kontokali Bay
Kontokali
Tel: 26610 99000
Fax: 26610 91901
www.kontokalibay.com
Slightly more affordable and larger than the Corfu Palace, consisting of a hotel wing and bungalows in a leafy environment with two "private" beaches. Recently renovated, with lots of facilities for kids. €€€

Grecotel Corfu Imperial
Komméno
Tel: 26610 88400
Fax: 2661 91881
www.grecotel.com
Perhaps the best and most contemporarily decorated hotel on the island, and stratospherically

expensive. Three grades of accommodation: standard rooms, bungalows, and a few super-luxe villas with their own pool. All the facilities you'd expect for the price. €€€

Bella Venezia
Napoleóntos Zambéli 4
Tel: 26610 46500
Fax: 26610 20708
www.bellaveneziahotel.com
Neo-classical mansion well adapted as a hotel in a central yet quiet location at the south edge of town; no pool or extra amenities except a large patio garden with bar. €€

Kavalieri
Kapodhistriou 4, Kérkyra
Tel: 26610 39041
Fax: 26610 39283
A-class hotel in a 17th-century building overlooking the Spianádha. Frankly overpriced, with smallish rooms, but all have sea views, and the roof garden makes the place. €€

Konstantinoupolis
Zavitsiánou 11, Old Port
Tel: 26610 48716
Fax: 26610 80716
polis@ker.forthnet.gr.
1862 building, once a backpackers' dosshouse, now lovingly restored as a well-priced C-class hotel with sea and mountain views. Comfortable rooms and common areas, lift; open all year. €€

Nefeli
Komméno
Tel: 26610 91033
Fax: 26610 90290
www.hotelnefeli.com
This small inland hotel in mock neo-classical style, spread over three buildings among olive groves, has a loyal clientele, good service and air-conditioning in most units. Open May–October. €€

Palace Mon Repos
Anemómylos district, Gharítsa Bay
Tel: 26610 32783
Fax: 26610 23459
Renovated in the late 1990s, this hotel is the closest thing Kérkyra Town has to a beach resort. The lido opposite is of indifferent quality, but you've views to the sea, Old Fort and Mon Repos woods, and a small swimming pool. Open May–October. €€

Centre-west of Corfu

Pelekas Country Club
Km 8 of Kérkyra–Pélekas road
Tel: 210 664 0077 (Athens)
reservations@country-club.gr
Corfu's most exclusive rural hotel, just 26 units occupying an 18th-century mansion set in over 25 hectares (60 acres) of landscaped grounds. Outbuildings such as the stables and olive press are now self-

catering studios and suites, all different and antique-furnished. Stylish breakfasts in the central refectory, pool, tennis, helipad. Open January–November. €€€

Casa Lucia
Sgómbou hamlet, at Km 12 of Kérkyra–Paleokastrítsa road
Tel: 26610 91419
Fax: 26610 91732
www.casa-lucia-corfu.com
Peaceful setting at the very centre of the island. A restored olive-mill complex set among lovingly tended gardens comprises 11 units ranging from studios to family cottages. Most have kitchens, all share a large pool, though furnishings are resolutely 1980s. Open April–November; winter lets also available. €€

Fundana Villas
accessed by side road from Km 17 of Kérkyra–Paleokastrítsa highway
Tel: 26630 22532
Fax: 26630 22453,
www.fundanavillas.com
Another 1980s restoration inn, this time converted from a 17th-century manor, with a commanding ridgetop position in the middle of a gorgeous nowhere. Units from double studios to family apartments; most have brick-and-flagstone floors; several were added next to the pool in 2002. Open April–October. €€

Levant Hotel
above Pélekas, right beside "Kaiser's Throne"
Tel: 26610 94230
Fax: 26610 94115
www.levanthotel.com
A 1990s hotel in traditional style, with superb views both east and west over the island. Rooms are wood-floored, baths marble-trimmed, ground-floor common areas faux-rustic. There's a small pool, and some of the island's best beaches a few kilometres away. Open Apr–Oct. €€

Liapades Beach Hotel
Liapádhes
Tel: 06630 41370
Fax: 06630 41294
www.liapadesbeachhotel.gr
Two smallish wings make up this amiable C-class hotel at one of the quieter beach resorts on this coast. Open April–October. €€

The north of the island

Nisaki Beach
Krouzéri Bay, between Nissáki and Kalámi
Tel: 22630 91232
Fax: 22630 22079
www.nissakibeach.gr
A-class hotel with brutal 1970s architecture but popular for its open buffet restaurant, varied watersports and children's beach activities.

Northern Delights

Falcon Travel, a British-owned travel agency based in Nissáki, arranges stays in a dozen beach-side apartments and villas in the north of Corfu, or two sensitively restored houses which they own in the idyllic (and remote) Mt Pandokrátor hamlet of Tritsí. Car hire arranged for the latter; open April–October.
Apartments €, villas €€, houses €400–600 per week.
Tel: 26630 91318
Fax: 26630 91070
www.falcon-travel-corfu.com

Rooms, mostly with sea views, are large and recently redone. €€€
Villa de Loulia
Perouládes, 500m from beach
Tel: 26630 95394
Fax: 26630 95145
villadeloulia@yahoo.com
The third of Corfu's rural restoration inns, this 1803 mansion has been refurbished with high-standard furnishings and fittings in excellent taste. The bar, lounge and breakfast area are in a separate purpose-built structure flanking the large pool. Heating but only fans, no air-con. You're paying for the exclusivity – better value out of peak season. Open March–October. €€–€€€

The south of the island
Boukari Beach
Boúkari, 4km beyond Messongí
Tel: 26620 51791
Fax: 26620 51792
www.boukaribeach.gr
Two sets of sea-view A-class apart-ments sleeping up to four, with all amenities including coffee machines, a few paces from the excellent co-managed restaurant. Open April–October. €€

The Ionians

Paxí
Paxos Beach Hotel
Gáïos
Tel: 26620 31211
Fax: 26620 32695
www.paxosbeachhotel.gr
A hillside bungalow complex from where there is a path leading down through trees to its own small pebble beach about 2 km (1 mile) east of town. €€–€€€

Lefkádha
Olive Tree/Liodendro
north approach road, Ághios Nikítas
Tel: 26450 97453
olivetreehotel@hotmail.com

Halfway up the hill, with oblique sea views from most rooms, this C-class hotel has typical anodyne pine-and-white-tile decor, but no package allotment so good chance of vacancies. €€
Santa Maura/Ayia Mavra
Spyridhónos Viánda 2, Lefkádha Town
Tel: 26450 21308
Fax: 26450 26253
A pagoda-like period piece: pre-earthquake ground floor, wood and corrugated tin upstairs. Rooms have air-con, double glazing, traditional shutters, balconies; lovely breakfast salon and garden patio. €€
Ostria
north approach road, Ághios Nikítas
Tel: 26450 97483
Fax: 26450 97300
The 1970s-built rooms of this pension can be cell-like, but are enlivened by terracotta floor tiles, dried flowers and wall art. It's the unobstructed balcony views of the Ionian (save from four rooms) and the cool, trendy common areas (including a terrace bar open to all) that make the place a delight. The breakfast isn't always up to scratch. €–€€
Fantastiko Balkoni sto Ionio
Kalamítsi
Tel: 26450 99390
The name means: "Fantastic Overlook of the Ionian Sea" – and it certainly is. At the far west end of this quiet village, these state-of-the-art (mosquito screens, Italian tiling, tended garden) rooms with communal kitchen are idyllic, with friendly returned South African/Greek management. €
Nefeli
Agios Nikitas
Tel: 26450 97400
Fax: 26450 97402
www.nefelihotel.gr
An attractive small hotel, with just 20 rooms, of which four are studios with kitchenettes. Rooms have small verandahs with sea views. €€
Porto Lygia
Lyghiá
Tel: 26450 71441/72000
Fax: 26450 71900
www.portoligia.gr
Perched on promontory away from traffic, with a lawn leading down to its own pebble beach, this is a good choice for a seaside stay near (but not in) Lefkáda Town. €€

Ithákí
For rooms or villas across the island, contact one of these two travel agencies:
Delas
Tel: 26740 32104
Fax: 26740 33031
www.ithaca.com.gr

Polyctor
Tel: 26740 33120
Fax: 26740 33130
polyctor@otenet.gr
Captain Yiannis
East quay, Vathý
Tel: 26740 33173
Fax: 26740 32849
The closest thing to an exclusive resort on the island, with just 11 self-catering units set in walled grounds with a pool and tennis court. €€€
Perantzatha 1811 Art Hotel
Odyssea Androutsou, Vathý
Tel: 26740 33496
Fax: 26740 33493
www.arthotel.gr
Chic and fairly expensive but by far the loveliest hotel in Vathý. The 12 understated and tasteful rooms have been individually designed and are very comfortable. Not on the harbourfront itself (and so quieter than some other places), the rooms look out over pretty rooftops to the sea. Breakfasts are excellent. €€€
Nostos
about 200 metres (220 yds) inland from the quay, Fríkes
Tel: 26740 31644
Fax: 26740 31716
www.hotelnostos-ithaki.gr
Smallish but upmarket C-class hotel where all rooms look over a field towards the sunrise. €€
Kostas Raftopoulos
Last house on yacht quay opposite beacon, Kióni
Tel: 26740 31654 (summer)
Tel: 210 779 8539 (winter)
There are just four colonial-style rooms, with big beds and mosquito nets, upstairs at this imposing mansion built in 1894 for the niece of Lord Nelson's mistress Lady Hamilton. Returned South African Kostas, who bought it in 1965, is quite a raconteur. €–€€

Kefalloniá
Agnantia Apartments
28084 Tselendáta, Fiskárdho
Tel: 26740 51801–2
Fax: 26740 51803
www.agnantia.com
Very well maintained and beautifully located (although a little way out of Fiskárdho), these new rooms stacked up on a hillside are a lovely place to stay. As well as friendly and efficient service, the rooms are tasteful and comfortable with a small kitchen area, and most have a balcony with wonderful views over to Itháki. A good, and generous, breakfast is included. €€€
Emelisse Art Hotel
Émblisi, near Fiskárdho
Tel/fax: 26740 41200
www.arthotel.gr

Expensive and chic, this boutique hotel (one of the small Tsimaras chain that has several properties in this part of Greece) is set in a traditional building. The well designed rooms have luxurious bathrooms and the pool has a lovely view. For this sort of money you expect to be pampered and the service lives up to expectations. €€€

White Rocks Hotel and Bungalows
Platýs Yialós, Argostóli
Tel: 26710 28332–5
Fax: 26710 28755
www.whiterocks.gr
Large, A-class resort hotel and bungalow complex behind the closest good beach; well-kept and updated 1970s pile with a period charm. Obliging staff and decent restaurants complete the picture. €€€

The Architect's House
Ássos
Book through: Thomsons
Tel: 0870 165 0079
www.thomson.co.uk
This lovely traditional building, one of the few places to stay in Ássos itself, has three double bedrooms to rent and is down by the harbour. There is plenty of space – a separate living room and kitchen – and the beach and good places to eat are close by.
€€–€€€

Caretta's Nest
Kamínia Beach, near Skála
Book through:
Simply Travel
Tel: 0870 166 4979
www.simplytravel.co.uk
A cluster of modern, well furnished apartments by deserted Kamínia beach. This is a great place to get away from it all, but if you want to go into Skála or Kateliós to eat you will need your own transport or be prepared to walk. €€–€€€

Panas Hotel
Kilmatsia Beach, Spartiá
Tel: 26710 69506/69941
Fax: 26710 69505
www.panas-kefalonia.com
A largish but very pleasant B-class hotel south of Argostóli on Lourdháta Bay, close to a decent beach. The rooms, all with a balconies, are fine if a little plain. There are good facilities for children, including their own pool and play area. There are also a couple of restaurants and a poolside bar.
€€–€€€

Tara Beach
Skála
Tel: 26710 83341
Fax: 26710 83344
www.tarabeach.gr
Tara Beach is a large but unobstrusive hotel right on the excellent beach. The rooms are decent and if you feel too lazy to walk the few metres to the

sea, there is a good pool in the pleasant gardens, beside which is a handy bar. €€–€€€

Aenos Hotel
Platía Vallianoú, Argostóli
Tel: 26710 28013
Fax: 26710 27035
www.aenos.com
This, and the Ionian Plaza (below), are the two best places to stay on the town's central square. The uncluttered pastel-shaded rooms with large attached bathrooms probably give the Aenos the edge; it is also marginally quieter. €€

Belvedere Apartments
Póros
Tel: 26740 72493–4
Fax: 26740 72083
A small apartment complex in the centre of town. Although fairly simple – the standard small kitchenette, bedroom and bathroom – they are not without charm, and all have balconies looking over the sea. €€

Erissos
Fiskárdho
Tel: 26740 41055
One of the best hotels in town. Upstairs rooms in an old house a few steps back from the quay, next to the Alpha Bank. €€

Hotel Ionian Plaza
Platía Vallianoú, Argostóli
Tel: 26710 25581–4
Fax: 26710 25585
Open all year
Excellent value C-class designer hotel, with modern bathrooms and balconies overlooking the palm-studded square; the rooms are on the small side, but the staff are friendly. €€

Kastro Hotel
Sámi
Tel: 26740 22656/22282
Fax: 26740 23004
www.kastrohotel.com
A little way out of town, but close to the sea is this medium-sized, good value B class hotel. The good, if smallish, rooms either look out over the pool and sea or the mountains. Breakfast is provided and there is also a restaurant. €€

Le Mirage Apartments
Ioánnis Tzigánte, Argostóli
Tel: 26710 24312
Fax: 26710 22339
Simple but very clean, comfortable, three-room apartments, with limited cooking facilities. Each living room has a balcony and those facing east have a wonderful view over the bay and Mount Énos (compensation for the steep climb up from town); rooms on the west overlook the well-watered garden. €€

Moustakis Hotel
Aghía Effimía
Tel: 26740 61060/61030
Fax: 26740 61030

www.hotelmoustakis.agiaefimia.com
Smallish and tucked away behind the harbour front, this is the most pleasant of the hotels in town. All the rooms have air-con and balconies. Breakfast is available for an extra charge. Discounts are available for long stays. €€

Odysseus Palace
Póros
Tel: 26740 72036/72492
Fax: 26740 72148
This modern, newish hotel is the most comfortable place to stay in town. Good discounts may be available for the large and airy rooms (studios and apartments). Being away from the seafront, the hotel is quieter than most. Open all year. €€

Hotel Summery
Lixoúri
Tel: 26710 91771/91871
Fax: 26710 91062
www.hotelsummery.gr
A large but quiet hotel on Lixoúri's beach (to the south of town) that mainly caters to tour groups. The rooms are clean and unfussy, and some have balconies. For the amenities on offer (pool, plenty of sporty activities, and a shop) the prices are quite reasonable. €€

Zákynthos

Iberostar Plagos Beach
Amboúla Beach, Tsiliví
Tel: 26950 62800
Fax: 26950 62900
www.iberostar.com
Previously the Louis Plagos Beach, this is a large resort hotel with a huge range of facilities, particularly for children. The rooms are plain but large and have balconies, and there is the inevitable, but decent, hotel pool and restaurant. €€€

Nobelos Apartments
Ághios Nikólaos
Tel: 26950 27632/31400
Fax: 26950 31131/29277
nobelos@otenet.gr
These luxury apartments in the north of the island are hideously expensive but lovely. The four tastefully decorated suites are in a traditional stone-built house, each with an individual character. Along with excellent service, breakfast is provided and a secluded bay is close by. €€€

Hotel Palatino
Kolokotróni 10 and Kolivá, Zákynthos Town
Tel: 26950 27780
Fax: 26950 45400
www.palatinohotel.gr
Zákynthos Town's poshest option, refurbished in 1999 and well run. The rooms, designed for business travellers, are decent with all the trimmings, and the hotel as a whole has been well cared for. A buffet breakfast is provided and there is also a restaurant. €€€

Porto Koukla Beach Hotel
Lithakiá
Tel: 26950 52393/51577
Fax: 26950 52391/52392
www.pavlos.gr
A decent, large hotel at the western end of Laganás Bay. Popular with German and Austrian visitors, it is well away from the tawdriness further east. The gardens back onto a narrow beach which is overlooked by the hotel's excellent, and cheap, taverna. €€€

Villa Petunia
Lithakiá
Contact: Betty Andronikos
Tel: 6932 260534
androel@hol.gr
This huge, beautifully furnished villa is on a hill above the village. Surrounded by flowers with a fabulous view over Laganás Bay and the mountains, the villa sleeps 10 to 12 people and has every conceivable appliance from DVD player to *espresso* machine. There is a new swimming pool and organic eggs, oil and vegetables are available from the garden. €€€

Villa Contessa
Vasilikós
Tel: 26950 35161/210 281 9092
Fax: 210 645 2297
www.villacontessa.gr
Ten attractive studios (sleep four) with balconies in a traditional house set in landscaped gardens. €€

Ionian Star Hotel
Alykés
Tel: 26950 83416/83658
Fax: 26950 83173
www.ionian-star.gr
A smallish and very well kept hotel. The spotless rooms, recently refurbished, are excellent value (breakfast is included) and there is a restaurant which concentrates on Greek food. €€

Levantino Studio Apartments
9km (5 miles) from Vasilikós
Tel: 26950 35366
Fax: 210 747 4483 (Athens)
www.levantino.gr
Ten quiet and attractive apartments close to the sea at the far end of the Vasilikós Peninsula. All are equipped with a kitchen and some look out over the gardens and sea. Discounts available out of high season. €€

Montreal Hotel
Alykés
Tel: 26950 83241/83341
Fax: 26950 83342
A modern hotel block but attractive and covered in flowers. The plain, clean and well maintained rooms have balconies looking over the sea. There is also a restaurant dishing up the usual eclectic mix of food, from pizza to Greek salad. €€

Sirocco Hotel
Kalamáki
Tel: 26950 26083–6
Fax: 26950 26087
www.siroccohotel.gr
This is a good and reasonable quiet option for Kalamáki, the renovated and stylish standard rooms a bargain out of season. There is a large pool set in an attractive garden, though the beach is not too far away. €€

Hotel Strada Marina
Lombárdou 14, Zákynthos Town
Tel: 26950 42761–3
Fax: 26950 28733
stradamarina@aias.gr
The largest place in Zákynthos town with comfortable but not overly exciting rooms. A prominent, modern building close to Platía Solomoú, some of the rooms have a great view of the harbour. Breakfast is included and there is a rooftop pool. €€

Villa Katerina
Pórto Róma, Vasilikós
Summer: Tel: 26950 35456
Winter: Tel: 26950 27230
Fax: 26950 28205
www.villakaterina.com
These two buildings in pretty gardens have simple rooms with decent kitchenettes and attached bathrooms. Set back from the beach, the rooms are very quiet and the surrounding area is lovely. €€

Zante Palace
Tsiliví
Tel: 26950 490490
Fax: 26950 49092
www.zantepalace.com
This huge, newly built, hotel is on the bluff overlooking Tsiliví bay, giving great views across to Kefalloniá. For what's on offer the rooms (which look out over the bay) are good value and if you can't be bothered to walk down to the beach there is a nicely sited pool. €€

Kýthira

Kýthira has a short season, with most accommodation only open from May to October; advance booking is recommended.

Porto Delfino
Kapsáli
Tel: 27360 31940–1

Fax: 27360 31939
www.portodelfino.gr
A pleasant bungalow complex with views over the bay and Hóra. €€–€€€

Xenonas Keiti
Hóra
Tel: 27360 31318
Lovely accommodation in – for a change – non-smoking rooms, set in a rambling 18th-century mansion. The hotel has a remarkably distinguished guest-list. €€

Xenonas Porfyra
Pótamos
Tel: 27360 33329
Fax: 27360 33924
Nicely-furnished studios, arranged around a pretty, walled courtyard in characterful Pótamos. €€

Crete

Aghía Galíni

Rea Hotel
10 Marathonos
Tel: 28410 90330
Fax: 28410 90339
www.reahotel.com
One of the few decent options here. This is a small, newish hotel, with a garden restaurant and a rooftop bar. Half board available for only slightly more than the B&B price. €€

Aghía Rouméli

Agia Roumeli Hotel
Tel: 28250 9124/91232
Fax: Tel: 28250 9124/91232
One of the few good hotels among the more basic establishments here. Located to the west, near the main beach. The rooms have sea views. €

Ághios Nikólaos

Candia Park Village
Tel: 28410 26811
Fax: 28410 22367
info-candia@bluegr.com
A rather fanciful reconstruction of a Cretan village, sited between Ághios Nikólaos and Eloúnda. Expensive, there is a selection of discretely luxurious studios, rooms and suites. €€€

Minos Beach Art 'Otel
Aktí Ilía Sotírhou, Amoúdhi
Tel: 28410 22345
Fax: 28410 22548
info-minos@bluegr.com
An elegant, deluxe coastal resort set on a small peninsula, Minos Beach consists of a number of bungalows, all surrounded by mature gardens. The hotel is renowned for its collection of contemporary art. €€€

Minos Palace Hotel
Tel: 28410 23801
Fax: 28410 23816
minpal@otenet.gr
One of the area's many 5-star hotels, this one is built on a headland (30 minutes' walk from town) and was meant to resemble a Minoan palace. €€€

Crystal Hotel
Nissí
Tel: 28410 24407/24094
Fax: 28410 25394
www.ormos-crystal.gr
Set back from the main road, on the northern, Eloúnda, side of town, this pleasant small hotel (it has 37 rooms) is 1.5 km (1 mile) from the centre and 10–20 minutes' walk from the beach. €€

Lato Hotel
Amoúdhi
Tel: 28410 24581
Fax: 28410 23996
latohotel@uolservers.com
Right on the beach, about 1 km (½ mile) from Ághios Nikólaos, the Lato has 37 rooms set in lush gardens. They also manage the Karavostasi on the coast 8 km (5 miles) from town, where there are three self-catering studios. €€

Ormos Hotel
Nissí
Tel: 28410 24094/24533
Fax: 28410 25394
www.ormos-crystal.gr
The Ormos is a sister hotel to the Crystal (above). The accommodation consists of 47 comfortable rooms and two studios, and there's a swimming pool too. €€

Sgouros Hotel
Aktí Pangaloú, Kitroplatía Beach
Tel: 28410 28931
Fax: 28410 28914
www.sgourosgrouphotels.com
A decent, family-run hotel situated right by the sea and 300 metres (330 yds) from the centre of the town. €€

Ághios Yeórghios Lasithíou

Rea Hotel
Tel: 28440 31209
A modest but hospitable establishment. It is clean, nicely furnished and comfortable, and is very well sited for exploration of Lasíthi plateau. €

Almyrídha

Almirida Bay Hotel
Tel: 28250 31751
This decent medium-sized B-class hotel has a restaurant and pool. It is located in a small resort east of Haniá. €€

Balí

Bali Beach Hotel & Village
Tel: 28340 94210
Fax: 28340 94252
www.balibeach.gr
A large – 120-room – hotel with a pool and roof garden. The rooms have pleasant sea-views and all of them come with a fridge. €€

Eloúnda

Elounda Beach Hotel
Tel: 28410 63000
Fax: 28410 41373
www.eloundabeach.gr
One of the Leading Hotels of the World group, this hotel is regarded as one of the best on the island, and it's certainly the most comfortable. Fabulously expensive but exceptionally luxurious, it is a favourite of the European jet set – some of the suites have a private pool, sauna and gym, all watched over by your own butler and personal attendant. And, of course, helicopter transfer is laid on as well. €€€€

Elounda Mare Hotel
Tel: 28410 41102/41512
Fax: 28410 41307
www.eloundamare.gr
Competing with the Elounda Beach, this is the only Relais & Châteaux hotel in Greece. It comprises a deluxe complex offering bungalows with private pools. Very expensive and very swish. €€€

Akti Olous
Skhísma
Tel: 28410 41270
Fax: 28410 41425
Situated between the main road and the lagoon road, this hotel is very reasonable in both price and quality. €€

Aristea Hotel
Lassithi
Tel: 28410 41300
Fax: 28410 41302
This is a moderately priced hotel, with good facilities, located near to the sea. €€

Elounda Hill Apartments
Skhísma
Tel: 28410 41114
Set a short way uphill behind the village, these self-catering apartments are all available at good prices, making them a wise budget option – especially as the management is very friendly and helpful, encouraging lots of repeat visitors. €

Mountain Refuges

Mountain refuges are run by the various Greek mountaineering clubs and can range from a small 12-bed ski hut where you need to bring your own food and supplies to 100-bed lodges where all meals are provided. There are over 40 of them, but very few are permanently staffed – most conspicuously in Crete's White Mountains – and getting the key for the others from the controlling club is generally more trouble than it's worth.

Yeorghioúpoli

Mare Monte Hotel
Tel: 28250 61390
Fax: 28250 61274
maremonte@otenet.gr
A pleasant beach hotel, with pool, east of town towards Kavrós. €€€

Egeon Studios
Tel: 28250 61161
Fax: 28250 61171
Hospitable American-Greek management, and rooms right next to the river bridge. Good sea- and harbour-views from the front rooms. €€

Marika Studios & Apartments
Exópoli
Tel: 28250 61500
Very comfortable self-catering rooms set in the hills 3 km (2 miles) northwest of Yeorghioúpoli; friendly management. €€

Haniá

A number of the Venetian period townhouses in the old town on either side of the harbour have been converted into luxurious pensions and apartments.

Casa Delfino Suites
Theofánous 9, near Zambelíou
Tel: 28210 93098/87400
Fax: 28210 96500
www.casadelfino.com
Beautifully restored 17th-century Venetian house in the old harbour area; 20 luxury apartments surrounding a courtyard. €€€

Contessa
Theofánous 15, near Zambelíou
Tel/Fax: 28210 98565
Spacious rooms in a fine Venetian building, with expensive furniture, wooden floors and ceilings. €€

Elena-Beach Hotel Apartments
Aktí Papanikóli 27, Néa Hóra
Tel: 28210 97633
Fax: 28210 96606
One of the smaller, quieter hotels to be found in Néa Hóra, a western suburb 15 minutes' walk from the centre. €€

Kriti Hotel
Nikifórou Foká 10 & Kýprou
Tel: 28210 51881–3
Fax: 28210 41000
www.kriti-hotel.gr
A large, modern hotel to the east of
the centre, between the beach and
the town market; open all year.
€€

Nostos
Zambelíou 46
Tel: 28210 94743
Fax: 28210 94740
A superbly renovated building
(probably a 17th-century church) on
the harbour front; 12 studios and a
roof garden; open all year.
€€

Pension Eva
Theofánous 1 & Zambelíou
Tel: 28210 76706
Fax: 28210 50985
A six-bedroom pension in a renovated
Venetian/Turkish house with wooden
ceilings and brass beds. €€

Porto del Colombo Hotel
Theofánous & Muskhón
Tel: 28210 98466
Fax: 28210 98467
colompo@otenet.gr
Impressively restored Venetian/Turkish
house in the picturesque back streets
of the old town. €€

Porto Veneziano
Aktí Énosseos
Tel: 28210 27100
Fax: 28210 27105
www.portoveneziano.gr
Situated some distance east of the
bustle of the main harbour, near the
yacht marina and fishing harbour.
Spacious rooms and refreshing decor;
open all year. €€

Ifigenia Hotel & Apartments
Angélou & Gambá 21
Tel: 28210 94537
Fax: 28210 36104
www.ifigeniastudios.gr
Rooms and studios in the Venetian
quarter of the old town, overlooking
the harbour. €

Hóra Sfakíon

Vritomartis Hotel
Tel: 28970 91112
Fax: 28970 91222
www.vritomartis.gr
A large hotel and naturist resort,
about 1 km (½ mile) from the village.
Swimming pool and tennis courts
available. Open March to October.
€€

Ierápetra

Lyktos Beach Resort Hotel
Tel: 28420 61280
Fax: 28420 61318
A superior beach hotel, with sports
facilities, 7km (4½ miles) east of
town. €€€

Astron Hotel
Kóthri 56
Tel: 28420 25114
Fax: 28420 25917
This is a good hotel with comfortable
rooms, towards the eastern end of
town. Seaviews, and beach nearby.
€€

Iráklio

It may not be easy to find a quiet
room in the centre of town: light
sleepers should ask for a room at the
back.

Amirandes Hotel
Gouves
Tel: 28970 41113
Fax: 28970 41103
www.grecotel.com
This pleasant, comfortable and
expensive hotel is close to the beach,
and has all the facilities you would
expect. Part of the small Grechotel
chain. €€€

Astoria Capsis Hotel
Platía Elevtherías 5
Tel: 2810 229002
Fax: 2810 229078
www.astoriacapsis.gr
In the main square and a very short
walk from the Archaelogical Museum.
A large hotel with comfortable rooms
and suites; open all year. €€€

Candia Maris Hotel
Papandréou 72, Ammoudhára
Tel: 2810 377000
Fax: 2810 250669
www.maris.gr/candia
Large deluxe hotel with parking,
restaurant, pool, and a
thalassotherapy centre; on the
seafront to the west of the city. €€€

Galaxy Hotel
Dhimokratías 67
Tel: 2810 238812
Fax: 2810 211211
www.galaxy-hotels.gr
A large, superior hotel, renovated
2002, in the centre of the city, with
deluxe rooms, suites and a pool; open
all year. €€€

Atrion Hotel
Hronáki 9
Tel: 2810 246000
Fax: 2810 223292
www.atrion.gr
A quiet, superior B-class hotel, with
70 rooms, in the heart of the town;
open all year. €€

Daedalos Hotel
Dhedhálou 15
Tel: 2810 244812/244834
Fax: 2810 224391
A relatively quiet hotel, in the
pedestrianised centre of town; open
all year. €€

Kastro Hotel
Theotokopoúlou 22
Tel: 2810 284185
Fax: 2810 223622

www.kastro-hotel.gr
A comfortable, medium-sized hotel
with a great roof-terrace for
sunbathing; rooms spacious; open all
year. €€

Lato Hotel
Epimenídhou 15
Tel: 2810 228103
Fax: 2810 240350
www.lato.gr
Family-run hotel overlooking the
Venetian fortress on the old harbour;
open all year. €€

Irini Hotel
Idhomenéos 4
Tel: 2810 229703
Fax: 2810 226407
Quietly situated between the museum
and the Venetian harbour; open all
year. €

Olympic Hotel
Platía Kornárou
Tel: 2810 288861
Fax: 2810 222512
Standard rooms, located near the
southern end of market street; open
all year. €

Kastéli-Kissámou (Kíssamos)

Galini Beach Hotel
Tel: 28220 23288
Fax: 28220 23388
www.galinibeach.com
A friendly, well-run pension next to the
beach, between the Kamára river and
the football pitch. €

Liménas Hersonísou

Knossos Royal Village Hotel
Anísaras
Tel: 210 623 6150 (Athens)
Fax: 210 801 7451
www.aldemarhotels.com
The hotel has created a deluxe
version of a Minoan settlement, on
the beachfront at Anísaras. €€€

Loútro

Porto Loutro Hotel
Tel: 28250 91433/91444
Fax: 28250 91091
www.hotelportoloutro.com
A comfortable hotel, beautifully
situated overlooking the bay in this
tiny traffic-free resort; hospitable
Anglo-Greek management. €€

Mátala

Eva Marina Hotel
Tel: 28920 45125

Fax: 28920 45769
www.evamarina.com
C-class hotel in verdant gardens only 100 metres/yds from Mátala's sandy beach. Most of the rooms have a sea view. €
Matala Bay Hotel
Tel: 28920 45300
Fax: 28920 45301
www.matalabay.gr
A good and long-established hotel, not far from the sea. €
Orion Hotel
Tel: 28920 42129
Fax: 28920 45329
Modest but smart hotel, set in a secluded position just outside the village; large pool and good beaches nearby. €

Mýrtos
Esperides Hotel
Tel: 28420 51207
Fax: 28420 51298
www.esperides-hotel.gr
One of the better hotels in town, with a pool; open all year. €€
Myrtos Hotel
Tel: 28420 51227/51209
Fax: 28420 51215
www.mirtoshotel.com
Family-run hotel situated in the middle of the village; bookable on the internet. €

Ómalos
Exari Hotel
Tel: 28210 67180
Fax: 28210 67124
A cosy hotel, recently refurbished; of a higher standard than many other establishments here, with proper baths and a restaurant. €

Paleohóra
Polydoros Hotel
Tel: 28230 41150
Fax: 28230 41578
In a cul-de-sac near the beach; small but well-appointed. €€
Rea Hotel
Tel: 28230 41307
Fax: 28230 41605
A small, hospitable, family hotel, not far from the sand beach. Clean rooms, with bath. €€

Plakiás
Morpheas Rooms & Apartments
Tel:/Fax: 28320 31583/31642
www.morpheas-apartments-plakias-crete-greece.com
Older seafront rooms plus beautifully appointed new studios and apartments set back from the seafront. €€
Kyriakos Rooms
Tel: 28320 31307
Fax: 28320 31631
A quietly situated hotel with clean rooms, watched over by *rakí* connoisseur Kyriakos ever willing to share a glass with his guests. Next door to the recommended Medhoúsa Taverna. €
Phoenix Hotel
Tel: 28320 31331
Fax: 28320 31831
Located about 3 km (2miles) west of Plakiás, in the direction of Soúdha (Sweetwater) Beach. €

Réthymno
Fortezza Hotel
Melissinoú 16
Tel: 28310 55551/55552
Fax: 28310 54073
A modern, quiet hotel, named after the Venetian fortress just behind it. 5–10 minutes' walk from the beach. €€€
Aquila Rithymna Beach Hotel
Adhelianós Kámbos
Tel: 28310 71002/29491
Fax: 28310 71668
www.aquilahotels.com
One of Crete's finest hotels, combining discreet luxury, impeccable service and warm hospitality. On the beach, 8 km (5 miles) east of the town centre. €€€
Theartemis Palace Hotel
M. Portáliou 30
Tel: 28310 53991–5
Fax: 28310 23785
www.theartemis.gr
A comfortable A-class hotel with pool, to the east of the centre. It has recently been refurbished, but lies on a busy road. €€€
Veneto Hotel
Epimenídhou 4
Tel: 28310 56634
Fax: 28310 56635
www.veneto.gr
Ten suites and studios in a beautifully renovated building that is part 14th-century monastery, part 15th-century Venetian/Turkish townhouse. Garden courtyard and recommended restaurant. €€€
Brascos Hotel
Dhaskaláki 1 & Moátsou
Tel: 28310 23721–4
Fax: 28310 23725
www.brascos.com
Three-star hotel in the town centre, opposite the public gardens, 450 metres (¼ mile) from the beach. Rooms over six floors, but there's a lift. Pool; open all year. €€
Ideon Hotel
Platía N. Plastíra 10
Tel: 28310 28667/22346
Fax: 28310 28670
ideon@otenet.gr
Very convenient for the historical old town and fortress, with pool and good sea-views from the front rooms. €€
Kyma Beach Hotel
Agnostou Stratioti (Platía Iróön)
Tel: 28310 55503
Fax: 28310 27746
www.ok-rethymno.gr/kyma
Modern hotel at the edge of the old town, and opposite the beach. Open all year. €€
Palazzo Rimondi
Xanthoudhídhi 21
Tel: 28310 51289
Fax: 28310 51013
www.greekhotel.com/crete/rethymno/palazzo
Twenty luxury air-conditioned studios and apartments in a small complex of 15th-century buildings, with a small pool, in a quiet street in the heart of the old town. €€
Pearl Beach Hotel
Paraliakí Leofóros, Perivólia
Tel: 28310 51513
Fax: 28310 54891
www.pearlbeach.gr
Situated a 2.5-km (1½-mile) stroll along the beach promenade from the centre and old town. A stylish, high-quality, well-priced hotel, moments from the sea. €€

Sitía
Arhontiko Hotel
Kondyláki 16
Tel: 28430 28172
A lovely place set in an old mansion, kept very clean by the friendly management. €€
Crystal Hotel
Kapetán Sýfi 17
Tel: 28410 22284
Fax: 28410 28644
A good choice from the bunch of C-category hotels in the area behind the harbour; open all year. €€

Spíli
Tzermiádho
Kourites Hotel
Tel: 28440 22194
A pension with a good taverna a short distance down the street. €€
Heracles Rooms
Tel: 28320 22111
Fax: 28320 22411
www.heracles-spili.com
Well-furnished rooms on the main street of inland Spíli, a great area for walking. Host Heracles Papadakis can give good advice on the best places to walk. Breakfasts available. €

Zarós
Idi Hotel
Tel: 28940 31301
Fax: 28940 31511
www.idi-hotel.com
An attractive and friendly mountain hotel at the mouth of Roúvas Gorge, with old but functioning watermill. The

Rental Agencies

Palmyra Travel
Kalisperidhón & Aghíou Dhimitríou, Iráklio, Crete
Tel: 2810 244429
Fax: 2810 282229
palmyra@her.forthnet.gr
Accommodation, conferences, small groups, throughout Crete.
Porfyra Travel
Livádhi, Kýthira
Tel: 27360 31888
Fax: 27360 31889
www.kythira.info
Accommodation, car-hire, ferry agent.

hotel's own pond supplies fresh trout for the good restaurant, and visitors can learn how to cook Cretan specialities, and help pick olives if their stay coincides with harvest time. €€

Youth Hostels

Greece has a limited (and steadily dwindling) number of official, YHA-affiliated youth hostels for which you theoretically need a youth hostel card *(see preceeding listings for decent examples)*. However, you can often buy a card on the spot or just pay an additional charge for the night, so it's not worth buying a YHA card in advance.

There are surviving hostels in Athens, Santoríni, and Crete at Iráklio, Sitía, Réthymno, and Plakiás. There is also private, unaffiliated hostel-type accommodation of varying quality and repute in Athens and on numbers of islands such as Náxos, Rhodes and Corfu.

Traditional Settlements

The traditional settlements *(paradhosiakí ikismí)* are villages that have been recognised by the Greek government as forming an important part of the national heritage. they have been protected from modern intrusions and constructions by law. Buildings in these villages were variably restored under NTOG initiaitve as tourist inns back in the 1970s and 1980s.

All of these inns have been sold off and are now in private hands, although still protected by law, and private renovators have moreover brought other, generally higher-quality inns into service. Such houses and villages are, in their different ways, strikingly beautiful, and highly recommended for a long retreat in rural Greece.

Restoration inns are known to exist in the following locations, and more are appearing all the time:
Ýdhra (Hydra) Town (several sponge-captains' mansions, done as hotels)
Ía, Santoríni (interlinked village houses)
Mestá, Híos (several restored houses, as room-only or entire apartments)
Kámbos region, Híos (several restored mansions, usually with restaurant on-site)
Mytilíni and **Plomári**, Lésvos (several restored-house inns, from basic to luxurious)
Psará island (basic accommodation in a restored prison)
Rhodes Old Town (several high quality, and expensive, restoration inns)
Haniá, Crete (many fine restoration inns around the old harbour)
Valeondádhes, Sámos (six houses of an abandoned hamlet, restored)
Yialós and **Horió**, Sými (several old houses restored and divided into apartments)
Corfu (three restored olive mills or manor-houses in remote locations)
For a selection of the above, see the region under *Where to Stay*.

Camping

Large numbers of visitors to Greece rough it in one form or another. This can range from sleeping on the deck of ferries overnight to bringing a tent and setting up camp by a secluded beach.

Those who want to stay at organised campsites will find them all over Greece; these are all owned privately since the EOT divested itself of its last sites in 1998.

The most beautiful campsites in Greece, however, are usually the ones you find on your own. While in most places it is officially illegal just to lay out your sleeping bag or pitch a tent, if you're discreet you will rarely be bothered. That always means asking permission from the owners if you seem to be on private property, avoiding unofficial campsites set up in popular tourist areas (which can get pretty squalid), and always leaving the place looking better than it did when you came.

In the mountains camping is the rule as few alpine refuges are attended (see below), but even here you should get the local shepherds' consent if they're around, as you may be turfing down in the middle of a prime grazing site.

Where to Eat

What To Eat

Eating out in Greece is above all a social affair. Whether it be with your family or *paréa*, that sacred circle of friends, a meal out is an occasion to celebrate.

This may have something to do with the fact that eating out in Greece continues to be affordable and common, not something restricted to those on expense accounts. And the predominance of the *tavérna*, that bastion of Greek cuisine, reflects this popularity.

These casual eating establishments have more or less the same style and set-up throughout Greece, and the menu is similar (indeed, often pre-printed by drinks companies in return for including their logo): no frills, no packaging that tries to convince the consumer that this *tavérna* is different from the others, special or distinct.

The place, and your being there, is somehow taken for granted: you eat the good food at Yiannis's or Yeorghios's, you enjoy yourself, and (usually) you don't end up paying an arm and a leg for it.

This is the general background for eating out in Greece against which we find, of course, considerable variation. The *tavérna* is by no means the only kind of establishment. You will also encounter the *estiatório*, the traditional urban restaurant, which ranges from the tradesman's lunch-hour hangout, with ready-cooked *(magirevtá)* food and bulk wine, up to pricey linen-tablecloth places with bow-tied staff.

The *psistariá* is a barbecue-style restaurant specialising in lamb, pork or chicken on a spit; the *psarotavérna* specialises in fish and shellfish; while the *yirádhiko* (*yíros* stall) and *souvlatzídhiko* purvey *yíros* and *souvláki* respectively, sometimes to a sit-down trade, garnished with salads. Although the best *souvlákia* are made from lamb, most are pork nowadays.

More popular of late among students and urban intelligentsia are the so-called *kultoúra* restaurants, nouvelle Greek cuisine based on updated traditional recipes, and *ouzerí* (or *tsipourádhika* in the north), where the local tipple serves as accompaniment to *mezédhes* or small plates of speciality dishes.

Vegetarians are not well catered for in Greek restaurants. Most main courses will include either fish or meat. Your best bet is mixing and matching from a selection of *mezédhes*.

There is considerable regional variety in Greek cuisine and you should keep an eye out for specialities of the house you haven't seen before. Another thing you'll quickly learn is how strikingly different the same dish can be when it is prepared well or badly. It is therefore worthwhile shopping around for your *tavérna* (especially in heavily visited areas), asking the locals what they suggest, walking into the kitchen to look at the food (still a customary practice), instead of getting stuck with a tourist trap that spoils your taste for *moussakás* for the rest of the trip. For experienced travellers, the term "tourist *moussakás*" is shorthand for an exploitative version of this standard dish, slathered with potatoes and poorly executed béchamel sauce, with nary a slice of aubergine or a crumb of mince.

Some *tavérnes*, especially in rural areas or on non-touristy islands, may not have menus, in which case it is essential to establish the price of at least the most expensive main courses, particularly seafood. Otherwise, prices are usually in two columns: the first without and the second with tax and service. The listings below mention some of the more popular foods you will find.

Athens

Athinaikon, Themistokéous 2, close to Omónia; tel: 210 383 8485.
An *ouzerí* established in 1932, with loyal lunchtime customers from the neighbouring offices. An extensive list of fresh fish and seafood, a few good Greek cheeses and some interesting offal, including *spléna yemistá* (stuffed spleen). Decent barreled wine.
Bakalarakia/O Damingos, Kydhathinéon 41, Pláka; tel: 210 322 5084. Excellent food dished up in a long-established cellar restaurant (look for the photograph of Josephine Baker being served by the present owner's grandfather). Good things to order include *fáva*, *loukánika* and *saganáki*; the house speciality is *bakaliáro skordhaliá* (salt cod with garlic). Excellent barreled wine.
Baïraktaris, Platía Monastiráki 2; tel: 210 321 3036. One of Athens' oldest extant restaurants dating back to

1879, known for its cheap and wholesome food, particularly *magirevtá*, with tasty *fasoládha* (bean soup), *dhomátes yemistés* (stuffed tomatoes) and *fáva*. Also *souvláki* and *yíros* takeaway service.
Benaki Museum Café, Koumbári 1 and V. Sofías; tel: 210 367 1030. Set on a lovely terrace on the second floor of the museum, this is a favourite with the more artistic Kolonáki crowd who "do lunch". As well as excellent coffee and *retsína* there are good salads and daily specials, as well as some sinful cakes and desserts. The Thursday evening buffet (when the museum is open until midnight) is well worth booking for.
Café Avyssinia, Kynéttou 72, Monastiráki; tel: 210 321 7047. A handy stop-off after a browse through the flea-market, with bags of atmosphere to boot. Hearty, Macedonian-inspired food is served against a backdrop of bohemian entertainment, courtesy of an accordionist and a singer.
Epirus/Monastiri/Papandreou. These three cheap, basic eateries are all close together in the Central Meat Market off Athinás. Open 24 hours a day, they specialise in cooking up the more *recherché* parts of animals, in particular *patsás*. This tripe soup is much vaunted as a hangover cure.
Frame, Kleoménous 2, Kolonáki; tel: 210 7290 711. A flash, trendy new restaurant in the refurbished St George Lycabettus hotel. Seating is either inside near the bar, on a mezzanine (where it becomes a fish restaurant), or outside in a designer tent. The food is Mediterranean (lots of tomato, olive oil and various grilled meat and fish), and of a high standard. Your fellow-diners are likely to be young and fashionable.
GB Corner, Platía Sýndagma; tel: 210 333 0000. The restaurant for the refurbished Grande Bretagne; expensive but well worth a splurge. The service is excellent and the warm breads that come as a prelim are lovely. The mains, which are filling and generous, include a good mushroom risotto, salads, grilled meats and some thoughtful fish dishes; there is also enough on the menu for vegetarians to get by. Fabulous desserts, too.
Iy Klimataria, Platía Theátrou 2, Omónia; tel: 210 321 6629. A touch more sophisticated since its 2006 refit, Iy Klimataría remains an excellent source of robust cooking, as the row of stew pots used by mountain shepherds testify on your way in. Of note is the authentic live acoustic music, a world away from 'Greek Night' travesties, that justifies the slightly higher prices.

When to Eat

For Greeks the main meal of the day is eaten between 2pm and 3.30pm and, even in the cities, is usually followed by a siesta break lasting until 5.30 or 6pm. The evening meal can either be another full meal, or an assortment of *mezédhes*. This is usually eaten between 9pm and 11pm.

Breakfast in Greece is traditionally small, usually bread and coffee. There are, however, wonderful *píta* and turnover options available from bakeries, for snacking on the hoof.

Kafeneio, Epiharmoú 1, Pláka; tel: 210 324 6916. Set in an attractive neo-classical building with some outside tables, this Pláka restaurant serves excellent food while being relaxed and quite intimate. The menu here concentrates on *mezédhes*, with good *keftedhákia*, *fáva* and unusual cheeses, as well as good cheap bulk wine.
Kioupi, Platía Kolonáki 4; tel: 210 361 4033. A surprising find amid these posh surroundings, a cheap, friendly and spotless cellar restaurant that turns out good *magirevtá* from lunchtime onwards. Order from the trays displayed in front of the tiny kitchen. There is usually a fine selection of *bámies*, green beans stewed in oil, *hórta*, and chicken in various guises.
Noodle Bar, Apóllonos 11, Pláka; tel: 210 331 8585. The tables at the flagship franchise of this small local chain are hotly contested thanks to its wok-tossed noodles, rice dishes running the gamut from Indonesia to Thailand, chicken satay or sweet and sour, and imaginative salads. They also do a bumping trade in take-away.
Ouzadiko, Karneádou 25–29, Kolonáki; tel: 210 729 5484. The area's most established *ouzerí*, crowded and convivial, reputedly offers more varieties of *oúzo* and *tsípouro* than anywhere else in Athens. There's a host of platters to accompany the drinks, such as *lakérda* (white-fleshed marinated bonito) and *revythokeftédes* (chickpea croquettes), not forgetting the daily specials.
Papadakis, Voukourestíou 47, corner Fokylídou, Kolonáki; tel: 210 360 8621. You can expect creative renditions of monkfish, crayfish and *astakomakaronáda* (pasta flaked with lobster) from Papadakis, whose reputation for fresh, well-executed seafood has followed them here from Páros island. The dining area is minimalist with linen-covered tables.

Platanos, Dhiogénous 4, Pláka; tel: 210 322 0666. A *tavérna* founded 1932 close to the Roman Agora. Although not that cheap, it has a pleasant interior, and in summer tables spill out onto the small *platía* in front. It serves good, basic food, including a number of good vegetable dishes as well as lots of grilled and baked meats.

Thanasis, Mitropóleous 69, Monastiráki; tel: 210 324 4705. This Athenian institution is the place to eat *souvláki*. Essentially the food consists of grilled meat, salad and chips; all best washed down with chilled beer.

Tristrato, Dhedálou34 and A. Géronda, Pláka; tel: 210 324 4472. A lovely 1920s building on a corner, with an original interior, now a charming *galaktopolío*-cum-café popular with intellectuals and students. A good place for breakfast as well as a place to sit and read after dark. There is a large range of teas, as well as excellent cakes and homemade liqueurs.

Vasilenas, Etolikoú 72, Piraeus; tel: 210 461 2457. Justly famous for its enormous list of *mezédhes*, this plain looking *tavérna*, one of the best in the Athens area, has had its interior overhauled without the loss of original charming touches (such as the marble serving counter). Open evenings only, the set menu of some 16 dishes is good value, and challenging in quantity. It is very popular and booking is essential.

Saronic Gulf

Aegina

Agora, Éghina Town; tel: 22970 27308. This no-nonsense fish taverna has been around for over 40 years so it's doing something right. There's nothing flash about the ambience: the fish is as fresh as it can be and that's what counts. Wash it down with *oúzo* or draft wine.

Greek Salad

"Greek" salad is a staple of Greek cuisine. *Horiátiki*, the full monty with tomatoes, cucumber, green pepper, *féta* cheese and olives, is a lunch in itself with bread – and this is what you'll probably get if you ask for "salad". Some restaurateurs omit one or two of the vegetable ingredients – not all are available all summer – but by law *horiátiki* must contain a generous chunk of *féta*. If all you want is a small side salad, ask for *angourodhomáta* (just tomatoes and cucumber).

To Steki, Éghina Town; tel: 22970 23910. A similar establishment to Agora and it's also close by. It's always busy so come early if you want a table. Grilled octopus is the speciality, though you can choose your fish from those on display and have it grilled as you sip your retsina or *oúzo* and ice.

Póros

Taverna Karavolos, Póros Town; tel: 22980 26158. Meaning a type of snail in Greek, Karavolos is a very popular taverna in the back streets of Póros town. Yes, the restaurant does serve snails, served with a rich sauce. There's a selection of readymade *magirevtá* (home cooked) dishes as well as grills. Dine indoors or on a leafy patio. Reservations recommended.

Taverna Platanos, Póros Town; tel: 22980 25409. High up in the back streets of Póros town under a plane tree (*plátanos*). The speciality here is grills ranging from regular steaks to *kokorétsi*, mixed offal grilled on a long skewer. The atmosphere is relaxed and laid-back; evening dining is the best time to enjoy this place.

Ýdhra

Moita, Ýdhra Town; tel: 22980 52020. Perhaps the best restaurant on the island. The cuisine is generic Mediterranean and the dishes constructed with care and attention, combining the best ingredients into imaginative creations. Seafood predominates with prawns delicately cooked in spinach worth a mention. Reservations suggested.

To Steki, Ýdhra Town; tel: 22980 53517. A simple taverna-cum-*ouzerí* just a short step back from the harbour front. Locals come here to sip wine and gossip. The food is simple and unadorned and consists in the main of ready-cooked dishes with a smattering of grills and fries. The lamb fricassée is worth tasting as are the tasty *píttes* (small triangular pastry turnovers).

Taverna Gitoniko, Ýdhra Town; tel: 22980 53615. Popular with locals and foreigners alike, the Taverna Gitoniko (aka Kristina's) offers discreet rooftop dining as well as indoor dining downstairs. Good-value dishes range from simple island vegetarian fare to hearty grilled meats and fish. Veal in quince or red wine sauce is a house speciality. Excellent draft wine.

Spétses

Exedra, Old Harbour; tel: 22980 73497. One of several classy tavernas in the Old Harbour, Exedra is a fish taverna, and you can virtually see them as you dine on a platform extending into the harbour. The house speciality is fish cooked in garlic and tomato and baked in the oven. You'll also find prawns and lobster, both prepared either with cheese or with spaghetti.

Liotrivi, Old Harbour; tel: 22980 72269. Close to the Exedra is a restaurant in an old olive press (*liotrívi*). This is also a fish taverna in a very attractive location near the old boatyards. Mainly Greek clientele enjoy all kinds of variations on fish and other seafood. Best for evening dining.

Orlof, Old Harbour; tel: 22980 75255. Before you reach the Old Harbour proper you'll come across this long-established *ouzerí* inside a large white building overlooking the waterfront. There's a huge range of creative *mezédhes* to choose from. It's also a people-watching joint and gets very busy at night with people constantly dropping in and out.

Cyclades

Santorini

1800, Ía; tel: 22860 71485. In an old captain's mansion on main street, 1800 is one of Greece's best for elegant Mediterranean cuisine. Expensive. Reservations essential.

Aktaion, Firostéfani. This traditional taverna, on the caldera edge, has served traditional Greek food for 60 years. This is how moussaka is supposed to taste – Mum's recipes are still in use. Inexpensive.

Camille Stefani, Kamári. This restaurant, right on the black beach, has been serving seafood and Greek cuisine for 25 years. Locals favour it even in summer. A good choice is *laháno dolmádhes* (stuffed cabbage). Reasonable prices.

Kastro, Ía; tel: 22860 71045. Many customers come here for the famous sunset view, and eat grilled fruit with honey with their drink. The wise ones stay for a reasonably-priced dinner.

Restaurant Nicholas, Firá. On Stavros Street, parallel to the caldera road, Nikolas is Firá's oldest taverna. It serves all the usual Greek dishes. Open year round, lunch and dinner. Inexpensive.

Selene, Firá; tel: 22860 22249. Go to Selene for the quiet terrace with its caldera view, its fine cuisine based on local recipes, its unobtrusively elegant service, or even to take cooking classes in summer. Fairly pricey.

Sphinx, Firá; tel: 22860 23823. Everything here is homemade, from the bread to the noodles. Try squid in basil sauce, and don't forget the chocolate soufflé. Expensive, but worth it for the food and the caldera view. Advance booking suggested.

Taverna Katina, Ammoúdi, Ía; tel: 22860 71280.On the right at the bottom of the steps leading down from Ía. In many people's eyes, the fresh, grilled fish, prawns and Santoríni specialities make this the island's best taverna, all helped along by the excellent, friendly service. Easter–October; from lunch until late.
Taverna Pyrgos, Pýrgos Village; tel: 22860 31346. An elegant, moderate-priced restaurant with an unusual view. Order a table-full of their excellent *mezédhes*, or starters, especially the smoky aubergine salad.

For after-hours tippling, you can't beat the **Kira Thira Jazzbar**, a barrel-vaulted jazz and blues haunt in central Firá. Dimítris Tsavdharídhes mixes a mean sangria. Alternatively, **Franco's Bar**, on the caldera in Firá, was rated one of the world's best by no less than *Newsweek International*. The tall drinks it serves are works of art; so is the wonderful view; the music is classical. For youthful nightlife, **Koo Club** and **Enigma** are next to each other, and rock all night on Firá's caldera path.

Mýkonos

L'Angolo Bar, Láka district, Hóra. Italians make the best espresso. Breakfast and packed lunches are also good.
La Bussola, Láka district, Hóra. Chef Giovanni Marale serves up excellent Genovese dishes, but the pizza is also delicious. Whatever your main course, be sure to finish with the pannacotta.
Cavo Tagoo, Hóra, a 15-minute walk out towards Ághios Stéfanos; tel: 22890 23692. In the Cavo Tagoo Hotel restaurant, contemporary Mediterranean cuisine makes the most of seasonal Greek produce, while a sushi corner provides an alternative taste sensation. Expensive.
Efthimios' Patisserie, Fl. Zouganeli, Hóra. Efthimios has sold his famed *kalathakiá* ("little baskets") and almond milk from this immaculate sweet shop for over 40 years. (Takeaway only.)
Katrin's, Ághios Yerásimos district, Hóra; tel: 22890 22169.
For more than two decades, Katrin's Greek cuisine with a French accent has made this restaurant, on a back alley, world famous. Order the seafood starters and finish with chocolate mousse. Fairly expensive, reservations recommended.
Matthew Taverna, Tourlós (on Ágh. Stéfanos road). This is a polished *tavérna*, and the service on the cool terrace is friendly and quick. Try *bekrí mezé* – lamb wrapped in vine leaves. Open summer noon–1am.
Nikola's Taverna, Aghía Ánna Beach (after Platýs Yialós). A locals'

favourite: an authentic Greek taverna on a pretty, tiny beach.
Sea Satin Market – Caprice, Alevhándra quarter, directly below the windmills, Hóra. Unique waveside restaurant, where Greeks often party after a baptism or wedding. Eat fish and shellfish. Easter–Oct.
Taverna Niko's, just off the harbour, Hóra. For a quarter-century, Niko's has made fresh fish and lobster a speciality. Try homemade moussaka, salads with capers and rocket. Great service, moderate prices.

Náxos

Gorgona, Aghía Ánna. This longtime beach taverna has grown more elaborate, but the prices are still good, as is the traditional Greek food. The fresh fish is bought at the dock out front. Try the *kakaviá* (fish stew). Locals eat here year-round.
Meltemi Restaurant, Extreme southern end of Hóra's waterfront. The Meltemi has been here for 50 years, serving inexpensive traditional Greek cuisine, including fresh fish. It's authentic and popular with locals. Easter till end October, all day till midnight.
The Old Inn, Boúrgos, Hóra; tel: 22850 26093. In a charming garden, Berlin chef Dieter von Ranizewski, who has spent most of his life on Náxos, serves Greek and international cuisine. He makes everything, even the smoked ham.

Páros

Boudaraki, harbour road, Parikía. This is a typical Greek *ouzerí* with drinks and *mezédes* such as grilled octopus and fresh sea urchins. Open Easter–early Oct.
O Christos, opposite the Church of the Panaghía Pantanássa, Naoússa; tel: 22840 51442. Páros' most elegant restaurant (and one of the more expensive) has Mediterranean food, perfect service and great attention to detail. The menu changes, but not the excellence.
Levantis, Market Street, Parikía; tel: 22840 23613. Inventive Mediterranean cuisine in a pretty, quiet garden. Daily specials. Try sesame-coated marinated pork with wild mushrooms and Chinese noodles. Moderate to expensive.
Porphyra, Parikía; tel: 22840 22693. Serves the fresh fish and shellfish, including oysters, the owners have caught themselves. And there are daily specialities, such as sea-urchin salad. Open Mar–Dec.
Tamarisko Garden Restaurant, Néos Drómos, Parikía. Located in the Old Agora marketplace. Order pork stew *tamariskó*, mushrooms in sauce, and

the dreamy chocolate mousse. March till end-Oct from 7pm. Closed Mon.

Rhodes

L'Auberge Bistrot, Praxitélous 21, Rhodes Old Town; tel: 22410 34292. Genuine, popular bistro run by a couple from Lyon; for about €20 you'll get three hefty courses, (wine from a well-selected Greek list extra), jazz soundtrack included. Summer seating in the courtyard of this restored medieval inn; inside under the arches during cooler months. Open for dinner daily except Mon, late Mar–late Dec; reservations suggested.
Fotis, Menekléous 8, Rhodes Old Town; tel: 22410 27359. The affiliate of Fotis Melathron (below) serves only fish, plus the odd green salad. Somewhat pricey at about €70 for two with wine, but fresh catch of the day guaranteed.
Fotis Melathron, Dinokrátous, off Apéllou, Rhodes Old Town; tel: 22410 24272. The town's top *koultoúra* taverna, lodged in a lovely old Turkish mansion, with upstairs "snugs" for private functions and plush terrace seating. The fare is generally successful nouvelle Greek, featuring fish/seafood starters (eg filleted crayfish nuggets), meaty mains, and decadent desserts.
O Giannis, Vassíleos Yeorghíou tou Deftérou 23, Koskinoú. The stock in trade here is abundant *mezédhes* with a Cypriot/Turkish/Middle Eastern flair, washed down with Émbona wine or *oúzo*; it's extremely reasonable, especially for a group, and is open daily for dinner all year.
Ta Marasia, Aghíou Ioánnou 155, southwest of Rhodes Old Town; tel: 22410 34529. Currently the best *ouzerí* in Rhodes, occupying the patio and interior of a 1923 house. The food's excellent if not very traditional – red cabbage, yoghurt with nuts, grilled oyster mushrooms – plus more ordinary seafood (urchins, herring salad). Don't over-order as portions tend to be big.
Mavrikos, Líndos; tel: 22440 31232. Founded in 1933 in the fig-tree square, and in the same family ever since, Mavrikos has been nominated one of the five best Greek eateries outside of Athens. *Mezédhes* like manoúri cheese with basil and pine-nuts are accomplished, as are quasi-French main courses such as cuttlefish in wine sauce; dipping into the excellent (and expensive) Greek wine list will double a basic bill of about €25 each.
To Petrino, Váti; tel: 22440 61138. The central *kafenío* in this far-south

village is liveliest at weekends when Greeks come to enjoy the local speciality of *gourounópoulo* (suckling pig), but there's lots else – including spicy *revíthia*, real *hórta* and chocolate cake.

Pigi Fasouli, Psínthos; tel: 22410 50071. This is the best and friendliest of several tavernas here, serving excellent grills (goat, *soúvla*, etc) and appetisers as well as a few *magirevtá* of the day. In a lovely position with tables overlooking plane trees and the namesake spring.

To Steki tou Heila, Kodhringtónos/Dendrinoú, near Zéfyros beach; tel: 22410 29337. Considered the best seafood *ouzerí* in Rhodes New Town. It's wise to check prices beforehand on the more exotic shellfish like *kydhónia* (cockles) and *yialisterés* (smooth venus).

To Steki tou Tsima, Peloponnísou 22, 400 m (¼ mile) south of Old Town; tel: 22410 74390. A good alternative for moderately-priced shellfish delicacies and a wide selection of *oúzo*. Open daily, supper only.

To Steno, Aghíon Anarghíron 29, 400 m (¼ mile) southwest of Old Town walls. A small and genuinely welcoming *ouzerí*. The menu is limited (sausages, chickpea soup, *pitaroúdhia* or courgette croquettes, salads with caper sprigs), but superbly executed and eminently reasonable in price.

Dodecanese

Kárpathos

L'Angolo-ly Gorgona, south end of quay, Dhiafáni. A versatile café run by a couple from Genoa, with offerings including real Italian-standard coffees, *soumádha* (almond drink), lovely pies and limoncello liqueur.

Blue Sea, main bay, Paralía Lefkoú; tel: 22450 71074. Reasonable, if basic, fare served up by kindly management in a resort rather given to poor value. Strengths are *magirevtá* and pizzas; also pancake breakfasts.

Dramoundana, Mesohóri. Remarkably reasonably priced for Kárpathos, this features local caper greens, village sausages and marinated fish.

To Ellinikon, one block inland from quay, Pigádhia; tel: 22450 23932. A *mezedhopolío* that caters all year to a local clientele with hot and cold *orektiká*, meat and good desserts.

Iy Orea Karpathos, southeast end of main quay, Pigádhia; tel: 22450 22501. The best all-round taverna, with palatable local bulk wine, *trahanádhes* soup and great spinach pie. The locals treat it as an *ouzerí*,

so it's okay to order just a few *orektiká* (eg, marinated artichokes, spicy sausages) to accompany a *karafáki*.

Kostas', Kamarákia beach, 1 km (½ mile) north of Finíki. Much-loved *stéki* under two tamarisk trees; excellent value fare includes expertly grilled swordfish and courgette chips. Vegetables come from the adjacent patch. Open all day until about 10pm, depending on the weather and crowd.

Pine Tree, Ádhia, 7 km (4 miles) north of Finíki; tel: 69 77 369 948. Sustaining, reasonable rural taverna with country fare like lentils and *htapodhomakaronádha* (octopus in pasta), washed down by sweet Óthos wine. Sea-view terrace under the trees of the name, plus a few rooms to rent.

Hálki

Houvardas, near the north end of Emborió quay. Consistent quality *magirevtá* over the years.

Remezzo (Takis), Emborió waterfront; tel: 22460 45061. Excellent for *magirevtá* and pizzas.

Kastellórizo

Akrothalassi, southwest corner of quay; tel: 22460 49052. The most consistently salubrious fish and meat grills, reliably open at lunch too (unusual here), owing to shade from its arbour.

Little Paris, central waterfront; tel: 22460 49282. The longest-established taverna on the island. Quality can vary, but it's certainly better value than certain nearby fish tavernas which take advantage of a not-too-discriminating yachtie clientele.

Ta Platania, Horáfia district; tel: 22460 49206. This was the canteen for the crew of the film *Mediterraneo*; competent *magirevtá*, dips and usually a daily dessert served on an atmospheric little square.

Sými

Dimitris, south quay near ferry dock, Gialós; tel: 22460 72207. Excellent, family-run, seafood-strong *ouzerí* with exotic items such as *hohlióalo* (sea snails), *foúskes* (mock oysters), *spinóalo* (pinna-shell flesh) and the indigenous miniature shrimps, as well as more usual platters. Lunch and supper.

Georgios, top of Kalí Stráta, Horió; tel: 22460 71984. An island institution, over 30 years old and still very good; nouvelle Greek cuisine in large, non-nouvelle portions, served on the pebbled courtyard. Informal live music some nights.

Haritomeni, south hillside above petrol station, Yialós; tel: 22460 71686. A superb *ouzerí* with a good mix of meat, fish and veggie platters such as pork cheeks, *mydhopílafo*, sea-snails, artichokes in egg-lemon sauce and mushroom-stuffed aubergine – plus a superb view. Open most of the year.

Meraklis, rear of bazaar, Yialós; tel: 22460 71003. Reliable, long-running bet for good fish grills, *magirevtá* and *mezédhes*. Lunch and supper; seating out on the cobbles.

Mythos, south quay, Yialós; tel: 22460 71488. A supper-only *ouzerí* that is reckoned among the best-value cooking on the island. Ignore the menu and let chef Stavros deliver a Frenchified medley which may well include salad, seafood starters (squid in basil sauce), duck with juniper berries, lamb medallions, and own-made desserts. Open Easter–November.

Tílos

To Armenon (Nikos'), on the shore road, Livádhia; tel: 22460 44134. Excellent and salubrious beach-taverna-cum-*ouzerí*, with octopus salad, white bean salad and the like, as well as pricier scaly fish.

Delfini, Ághios Andónios port, Megálo Horió; tel: 22460 44252. This is the place for well-priced, freshly landed fish served under the tamarisks. A good sign is the numerous locals in attendance at weekends.

Joanna's Café, Livádhia village centre; tel: 22460 44145. Italian-English couple offer full breakfasts

Fruits of the Sea

Seafood is now one of the most expensive dishes on the Greek menu (except for frozen squid and fresh octopus, which are widely available). Fish are usually in a tray of ice for you to choose from, and your dish is priced by the weight of the fish of your choice. It is strongly suggested that you watch the (uncleaned) fish being weighed, and reiterate the price you are quoted, as "fingers on the scales" and later misunderstandings are not unknown.

There is so much farmed and frozen seafood (often marked only in Greek with a "*k*" or "*kat.*", for *katapsygméno*) lying in ambush for the inexperienced these days that the best strategy is to eat humbly and seasonally: far better a platter of grilled fresh sardines in August than a slab of swordfish frozen since June.

(9am–1pm) and decadent desserts, novelty coffees and excellent pizzas (7pm–1am). Open Mar–Nov.

Kalypso, uphill from the ferry dock; tel: 694 7213278. A French-Vietnamese family resident since 1987 offers something different: creative appetisers, Antillean- or southeast Asian-tinged mains. The Martiniquois shimp acras and Uncle Ho's vermicelli (with oyster mushrooms and pork) are tops.

Omonia (Mihalis'), just above the harbour square; tel: 22460 44287. Sit under the trees strung with fairy lights and enjoy the closest thing to an authentic *ouzerí* on the island by night; filling breakfasts in the morning.

Níssyros

Aphroditi, Pálli fishing port; tel: 22420 31242. The yachts habitually at anchor here have pushed prices predictably upward, but this is still a good bet for *magirevtá*, seafood, homemade desserts and bulk Cretan wine.

Iy Porta, Nikiá. Installed in an imposing structure built in 1926 to house a pharmacy, this café-taverna on one of the Aegean's most picturesque *platíes* does just a handful of simple but salubrious dishes daily – eg salad with local goat-cheese, own-made *tzatzíki*, *pittiés* – at attractive prices. Lunch and supper Jun–Sep, sporadically otherwise.

Iy Fabrika, Mandráki; tel: 22420 31552. This was once a *patitíri* (wine press) and *kapílio* (tippling shop), and the staff have returned it to something like its original function: an evening-only, musical *ouzerí* with a few local specialities and plenty for vegetarians.

Panorama, near Hotel Porphyris, Mandráki; tel: 22420 31485. Sea views, despite the inland setting, and good-quality fare (especially suckling pig and fish of the day), though portions could be larger. Tends to keep rather short hours by Greek standards.

Taverna Irini, Platía Ilikioméni, Mandráki; tel: 22420 31365. The place for more complicated *magirevtá* and vegetable dishes that the more touristy spots on the water can't be bothered with; also fish in season.

Kós

Ambavris, Ambávris hamlet, 800 metres (½ mile) south of Kós Town; tel: 22420 25696. Ignore the perfunctory English-language menu in favour of the constantly changing *mezédhes pikilía* or house medley – six platters for about €22 can encompass such delights as *pihtí* (brawn), stuffed squash blossoms,

fáva dip, little fish. Courtyard seating. Open for supper Apr–Oct .

Ambeli, 1 km (½ mile) east of Tingáki resort; tel: 22420 69682. Best policy here is to avoid mains and order a variety of excellent starters such as *pinigoúri* (cracked wheat), *bekrí mezé* (pork chunks in spicy pepper sauce), *hórta*, sausages and *yiaprákia* (the local variant of *dolmádhes*). Plates are fair priced and deceptively large, so don't over-order. Pleasant seating indoors and out in the vineyard; open daily lunch/dinner Easter–Oct, winter Fri & Sat eve, Sun lunch.

Ekatse iy Varka, Platía Dhiagóra, Kós Town; tel: 22420 23605. An amazing find in a generally touristy area: a reasonable fish taverna, with remarkably fresh, unusual seasonal species like *zargánes* (garfish) and *filipákia* (particular to Kós), washed down by good bulk wine. Outdoor seating with views past the minaret to the ridge beyond Ambávris.

Iy Palea Pigi, Pylí village; tel: 22420 41510. Inexpensive, basic (*loukánika*, fried vegetables, marinated sardines, *bakaliáros* with mashed potatoes) but nourishing fare at this taverna hidden away beside the giant cistern fountain with lion-headed spouts. Open lunch and supper, may close Dec–Mar.

Makis, one lane in from front, Mastihári; tel: 22420 51592. Currently the best – and best-priced – fish on the island outside of Kós Town, and an excellent spot to wait for the ro-ro ferry to Kálymnos. No *magirevtá*, a few salads and dips, and oblique sea views at best mean relatively few tourists.

Olympiada, Ziá village; tel: 22420 69121. Perhaps the only one of a dozen *tavérnes* here without a sunset view, so the food – lots of stews with *pinigoúri* (bulgur wheat) on the side – has to be good. Open most of the year.

Platáni village, central junction. Ethnic Turkish management at several clustered establishments dish out tasty Anatolian-style *mezédhes* and kebabs; best go in a group so that you can pass the little platters around. The most popular, if the most touristy, is **Arap** (tel: 22420 28442); if you can't get in, head across the way to **Asklipios** or **Serif** (tel: 22420 23784), which fills with locals later in the evening. Between November and April these close, leaving **Gin's Place** a few steps further inland (tel: 22420 25166) – where the food is often even better – as the sole option. At any season, finish off with an Anatolian ice cream, best on the island, at **Zaharoplastio Iy Paradosi** opposite the three summer restaurants.

Pote tin Kyriaki, Pissándrou 9, Kós Town; tel: 22420 27872. The island's only genuine *ouzerí*, with fair prices and patio seating in summer, indoors in the converted old house otherwise. Supper only, closed Sunday.

Psaropoula, Avérof 17, Kós Town; tel: 22420 21909. The most genuine and reasonable of three fish tavernas grouped here, with good *orektiká* preceding fair-priced seafood; sidewalk terrace, but also indoor area and thus open all year.

Astypálea

Australia, just inland from the head of the bay, Skála; tel: 22430 61275. Kyria Maria presides over the oldest and most wholesome taverna here, with fresh seafood, island wine and masterfully prepared own-grown vegetables. Open most of the year.

Barbarosa, Hóra, next to town hall; tel: 22430 61577. Greek and "continental" standards, with careful cooking and ingredients selection justifying somewhat bumped-up prices. Open most of the year for supper, and lunch Jul–Aug.

Ovelix, Maltezána (Análipsi), inland road; tel: 22430 61260. Grilled lobster specialists, but also scaly fish, vegetables and soft island cheese. Open most of the year for supper, Jul–Aug also for lunch.

To Yerani, in the streambed just behind Livádhia beach; tel: 22430 61484. The most consistently good, and consistently open (May–Oct) taverna here, renowned for its excellent *magirevtá*.

Kálymnos

Iy Drossia (Andonis), fishing anchorage, Melitsahás; tel: 22430 48745. Tops for oysters, lobster and shrimp as well as scaly fish at affordable prices. Open all year.

Pandelis, cul-de-sac behind the water-front, Póthia; tel: 22430 51508. Daily, fresh-gathered shellfish like miniature oysters, *foúskes* and *kalógnomes*, plus scaly fish at reasonable prices. Also a fair selection of grills for non-fish-eaters.

Pizza Porto Kalymnos (tel: 22430 23761) and **Pizza Imia** (tel: 22430 50809), near each other at mid-quay, Póthia, both offer excellent wood-fired pizzas.

Léros

Iy Thea Artemis, Blefoúti beach, beyond airport; tel: 22470 24253. Better-than-average beach taverna in the middle of nowhere; the usual *marídhes* and *kalamária* with chips.

Mezedopolio Dimitris, Spiliá district, on road between Pandélli and Vromólithos; tel: 22470 25626. The best food on the island, hands down, and the best view of Vromólithos. Stars include chunky, herby Lerian sausages, potato salad, *hanoúm bórek* (stuffed with cheese and *pastourmás* or cured meat). Moderate prices and large portions. Open most of the year.

Mezedopolio tou Kapaniri, Agía Marína seafront; tel: 22470 22750. Standards here aren't quite up to Dimitris or Neromylos, and portions on the small side, but still a contender. Best at night, with plenty for vegetarians – bean soup, Cypriot *halloúmi* cheese, *hórta* – as well as pizzas and seafood; open all year.

Osteria Da Giusi e Marcello, Álynda; tel: 22470 24888. Genuine Italian-run spot for pizzas, pasta dishes, a few antipasti and salads, plus top-notch desserts like sorbet and tiramisu, washed down by good Italian bulk or bottled wine. Supper only; open late Mar–early Jan.

Ouzeri Neromylos, out by the sea-marooned windmill, Aghía Marína; tel: 22470 24894. The most romantic setting on the island, whether for lunch or supper. Specialities include *garidhopílafo* (shrimp-rice), baked four-cheese casserole and *kolokythokeftédhes* (courgette patties). Open mid-Mar–late Oct; reservations mandatory Jul-Aug.

Psaropoula (Apostolis), Pandélli beach; tel: 22470 25200/24671. A good balance of fresh seafood and *magirevtá*, especially popular with locals at weekends. Open and enclosed sea-view terraces, so open most of the year.

Lipsí

O Giannis, mid-quay; tel: 22470 41395. Excellent all-rounder, with meat and seafood grills but plenty of salads and *ladherá* dishes for vegetarians too. The only taverna open for lunch as well as supper all season long. Early May–early Oct

La Nave da Massimo/The Boat, village centre. Italo-Greek run place that's tops for meat and seafood grills, a few pasta dishes and oddities such as *glystrídha* (purslane) salad. Open May–Sep.

Pátmos

Benetos, Sápsila cove, 2 km (1 mile) southeast of Skála; tel: 22470 33089. Since 1998, this eatery has earned a reputation as one of the best spots on the island for Mediterranean/Pacific Rim fusion cuisine, with a stress on seafood. Count on €30 for drink and three courses, which may include roast vegetable terrine with balsamic vinegar and raisins, baked fish fillet with

risotto and Hubbard squash, and lemon sorbet. Open Jun–early Oct, Tues–Sun, supper only; reservations needed in summer.

Hiliomodi, just off the Hóra road, Skála; tel: 22470 34080. Vegetarian *mezédhes* and seafood delicacies such as limpets (served live), grilled octopus and salted anchovies served at this *ouzerí* with summertime tables on a quiet pedestrian lane. Supper only; open all year.

Ktima Petra, Pétra beach, south of Gríkou; tel: 22470 33207. Hands down the best beach taverna on an island blessed with many such places. Chunky *melitzanosaláta*, lush rocket salad, and pork *yiovétsi* are typical of lunchtime offerings, with excellent retsina from Thebes; at sunset the grill is lit for delicious meat and fish, and still later the place becomes a full-on bar, with a long list of mixed drinks. Open Easter–Oct.

To Kyma, Áspri cove, opposite Skála; tel: 22470 31192. Fish specialists in perhaps the most romantic setting on the island: a little waterside platform, with views of the floodlit Hóra fortifications across the bay. Supper only; Jun–early Sep.

Leonidas, Lámbi beach, north end of island; tel: 22470 31490. Yet another reliable beach taverna; the food is fairly simple, emphasising grilled meat and fish. Open lunch and supper, Easter–Oct

Livadi Geranou, above eponymous beach; tel: 697 24 97 426. Doesn't look like much, but this taverna has a cult following for the sake of its coarse-cut *hórta*, *keftédhes* and seafood dishes – plus views over the entire island.

To Marathi, southeast end of Maráthi beach; tel: 22470 31580. The more welcoming of two establishments here, with simple fish and free-range goat served up by piratically garbed Mihalis Kavouras, at attractive prices and to the accompaniment of Greek music. Open all day according to Mihalis' whim.

Vengera, opposite marina, Skála; tel: 22470 32988. Opened in 2002, this has quickly established itself as a worthy rival to Benetos, with top-drawer generic French/ Mediterranean cooking and polished service. €35 and up per head. Supper only, May–early Sep. Must reserve in high season.

Agathonísi

O Glaros, Ághios Yeórghios, mid-bay; tel: 22470 29062. The most authentic taverna here, the one the locals favour; mostly grills and a few house specialities.

Northeastern Aegean

Samothráki

Fengari Restaurant, Loutrá Thermá; tel: 25510 98321. Using an outside wood oven to cook most of the dishes, the Fengari (named after the island's mountain) serves a range of traditional island dishes as well as meat and fish grills. Very pleasant ambience and very good value for money.

I Klimataria, Kamariótissa; tel: 25510 41535. On the waterfront some 100 m north of the ferry quay, this unassuming taverna puts out a range of good *magirevtá* (ready-cooked) dishes and grills to order. Twice a week the chef makes *yianniótiko* – a rich dish of pork, egg, potatoes, onions and garlic. Worth sampling.

Thássos

O Glaros, south end of the beach, Alykí hamlet; tel: 25930 53047/ 31547. Oldest, least expensive and most authentic of several tavernas here; usually has a modest breed of local fresh fish. Open late May–Sep.

O Platanos, under the central tree, Sotíros village; tel: 25930 71234. Summer-only taverna run by a sympathetic young couple from nearby Rahóni village. Elaborate *magirevtá* when trade justifies it, otherwise simple grills and powerful homemade *tsípouro* if you ask.

Iy Pigi, central platía, Liménas; tel: 25930 22941. Old standby dishing out dependable *magirevtá* next to the spring of the name; best at supper.

Symi, east waterfront, Liménas; tel: 25930 22517. Despite the touristy cadre, this makes a decent fist of fish and *mezédhes*. Seating, weather permitting, under trees on a raised terrace. Open all year.

Límnos

To Korali, Kótsinas. About the best place on the island for fresh, affordable fish.

Ostria, town end of Toúrkikos Yialós beach, Mýrina; tel: 22540 25245. Grills, fish and *mezédhes* from noon to midnight, at rather less than the prices charged by tavernas around the fishing harbour.

Platanos, Mýrina bazaar; tel: 22540 22070. Traditional, long-established purveyor of *magirevtá* under two plane trees; best at lunch on weekdays.

O Sozos, main square, Platý; tel: 22540 25085. The best and oldest *tsipourá-dhiko* grill here, with steamed mussels, chops, *orektiká*. Fight for a table

Lésvos

Anemoessa, Skála Sykaminiás, closest to the harbour chapel; tel:

22530 55360. Tops for fresh fish, and good *mezédhes* like stuffed squash blossoms. Open all year (weekends only Nov–Apr).

Balouhanas, Yéra Gulf seafront, Pérama; tel: 22510 51948. Seafood *ouzerí* with wood-kiosk seating overhanging the water; interesting *mezédhes* and own-made desserts too. Open all year.

Captain's Table, fishing harbour, Mólyvos; tel: 22530 71241 . As the name suggests, a strong line in seafood but also meat and vegetable specialities such as their "Ukrainian" aubergine dip, as well as excellent own-label wine (both white and red). Open May–late Oct.

Ermis, Kornárou 2, corner Ermoú, Mytilíni Town; tel: 22510 26232. The best and most atmospheric *ouzerí* of a cluster in Páno Skálo district, with two centuries of claimed operation and indoor/outdoor seating. Special strengths: sardines, sausages, Smyrna-style meatballs.

Iy Eftalou, by Eftaloú thermal baths, 4 km (2½ miles)from Mólyvos; tel: 22530 71049. Well-executed, reasonably priced grills (fish on par with meat), and salads. Seating under the trees or inside by the fireplace according to season. Open all year except Nov–mid-Dec.

To Petri, Petrí village, in the hills above Pétra/Mólyvos; tel: 22530 41239. Salubrious *magirevtá*, a few grills and unbeatable terrace seating. Open May–mid-Oct.

Taverna tou Panaï, Ághios Isídoros, north edge of village; tel: 22520 31920. Plainly presented but tasty food: vegetarian *mezédhes*, grills, cheese and so on. Mostly Greek clientele; open all year.

Una Faccia Una Razza, Sígri; tel: 22530 54565. Italian-run and ultra-hygienic, with lovely garlicky vegetable appetisers, pizza, pasta, carefully grilled fish or meat and an Italian wine list – the bulk wine is fine. Open Apr–mid-Oct.

Women's Agricultural Tourism Co-op, central *platía*, Pétra; tel: 22530 41238. Upstairs restaurant with lots of simple grills – including seafood – *mezédhes* and rather fewer *magirevtá*. Indoor and (weather permitting) outdoor terrace seating. Open May–Oct.

Híos

Fakiris Taverna, inland between Thymianá and Neohóri. Home-marinated aubergine and artichokes, goat baked in tomato sauce and excellent wood-fired pizzas along with well-executed seafood and pork-based *bekrí mezé* in big portions.

O Hotzas, Yeorghíou Kondýli 3, Híos Town; tel: 22710 42787. Oldest and

arguably best taverna in the city. Fare varies seasonally, but expect a mix of vegetarian dishes (*mavromátika*, cauliflower, stuffed red peppers) and sausages, baby fish and *mydhopílafo* (rice and mussels) with own-brand *oúzo* or retsina. Open all year, supper only (not Sun).

Inomayerio Iakovos, Aghíou Yeorghíou Frouríou 20, Kástro, Híos Town; tel: 22710 23858. Well-executed fishy dishes, grilled titbits, cheese-based recipes and vegetables; local white wine or *oúzo*. Atmospheric garden seating in a vine-cloaked ruin opposite, or inside during winter. All year, supper only; closed Sun.

Iy Petrini Platia, Kipouriés village A superb *psistariá* set in a fountain-nourished oasis, well placed for a meal stop while touring. It's open daily June to mid-September, but weekends only off-season.

Makellos, Pityós tel: 22720 23364. on the west edge of the village, this is a shrine of local creative cuisine; daily Jun–Sep, Fri–Sun eve Oct–May.

Mylarakia, Tambákika district, by three restored windmills; tel: 22710 41412. Every brand of Hiot *oúzo* accompanies a wide selection of seafood served at waterfront tables. Supper all year; lunch when they feel like it.

Tavernaki tou Tassou, Stávrou Livanoú 8, Bella Vista district, Híos Town. Superb all-rounder with creative salads, better-than-average bean dishes, *dolmádhes*, snails and a strong line in seafood; a little bit pricier than usual but worth it. Open lunch and supper most of the year, seaview garden seating in summer.

Yiamos, Karfás beach; tel: 22710 31202. Classic, 1970s-vintage beachfront taverna under new management. The fare – *magirevtá*, fried seafood, dips – is decent, the outdoor terrace seating even more so. Open most of the year.

Sámos

Aeolos, west end of quay, Ághios Konstandínos. Best-value fish and grills here, plus a few oven dishes of the day; unbeatable seating by the pebble shore.

Artemis, Kefalopoúlou 4, near the ferry dock, Vathý; tel: 22730 23639. Good all-rounder, with curiosities like *foúskes* for *mezédhes*, good *hórta* and *fáva*, plus the usual meat grills; best avoid the *magirevtá*, at supper time anyway.

Iy Psarades, Ágios Nikólaos Kondakeïkon; tel: 22730 32489. Long reckoned the best fish taverna on the island, at surprisingly reasonable prices, plus the usual *orektiká*. In

season you have to book. Open Easter–Oct.

Iy Psili Ammos, Psilí Ámmos; tel: 22730 28301. The one on the far right as you face the water; gives Kalypso (below) a good run for its money, though fare's restricted to seafood, meat grills and salad. Limited table space, so booking advised for large parties.

Kalypso, Mykáli beach; tel: 22730 25198. Arguably the best beachfront taverna in the east of the island, with a good balance of seafood, salads and *magirevtá*. Open all day May–mid-Oct.

To Kyma, east end of quay, Ághios Konstandínos. Good fried *mezédes*, bulk wine and various *magirevtá* make this a winner. Apr–Oct.

To Kyma, harbour road, Karlóvassi; tel: 22730 34017. Long-running *ouzerí*, the island's most genuine, where an Ethiopian proprietress gives a welcome spicy flair to traditional dishes. Open Apr–Oct.

Lekatis, Órmos Marathokámbou, east end of front; tel: 22730 37343. Unassuming little place, but it's where the fishermen tie up, unload and congregate, so the seafood's excellent, and reasonable. Open all year.

To Ostrako, Themistoklí Sofoúli 141, seafront, Vathý; tel: 22730 27070. As the name says (Greek for "shell"), the place for shellfish as well as scaly fish, plus a long line of *mezédhes*. Open all year; garden seating in summer.

Ikaría

Delfini, Armenistís; tel: 22750 71254. Across the way from Paskhalia; more traditional, less polished, even more popular than its neighbour for the sake of the waves lapping the terrace – and the sustaining cooking.

Leonidas, Fáros. Well-loved, quick-serving fish taverna at this beach community 10 km (6 miles) northeast of Ághios Kírykos. Grilled or fried seafood washed down by good bulk wine; many locals make the trip out from the port town.

Paskhalia, Armenistís; tel: 22750 71226. Ground-floor diner of a small pension that does good breakfasts (for all comers) plus reasonable fish with good bulk wine later in the day. May–Oct.

Foúrni

Rementzo (Nikos'), tel: 22750 51253. Best and longest-lived of several full-service waterfront tavernas; here you'll almost certainly find *astakós* (Aegean lobster), except during Aug–Dec closed season, and the succulent *skathári* or black bream.

Sporades and Évvia

Skiáthos

Agnantio, 1 km (½ mile) from Skiáthos Town; tel: 24270 22016.
It's worth the walk out of town to reach this place. The view over Skiáthos is great and you dine on genuine Greek cooking on a wooden deck. The menu is a mixture of ready-made and to-order but it's guaranteed to be top class.

1901 En Skiatho, Skiáthos Town; tel: 24270 21828. Right in the middle of town. Apart from the good live music, the food is excellent, mixing Greek and Mediterranean elements to produce original dishes. There's an extensive wine list, but the draft wine is good, too.

Sklithri, Kalamáki; tel: 24270 21494. Blink and you'll miss this tiny eatery almost hidden by the roadside a few kilometres from Skiáthos town. Most tourists do, so you'll find mainly locals dining on sardines or other fish dishes. It's cheap, unassuming and genuine. Best of all, it's right in the beach.

Skópelos

O Kipos tou Kalou, Skópelos Town; tel: 24240 22349. Signposts point down a narrow side street at the southern end of town to this quiet, flower-garlanded haven where classic Greek and Mediterranean cuisine reigns supreme. Sample charcoal grills as well as ready-made dishes. Stuffed pork in cheese sauce with couscous is highly recommended.

Taverna Finikas, Skópelos Town; tel: 24240 23247. *Finikas* means palm tree – and there is a big one right in the middle of this popular restaurant, well signposted in the back streets of Skópelos. There's a range of rather unusual menu items featuring various fruits combined with classic Greek meats.

Taverna Perivoli, Skópelos Town; tel: 24240 23758. Dine in an enormous shady garden (*perivóli*) in an atmosphere of cool and calm. The menu is a mixture of classic Greek-Mediterranean with Southeast Asian elements, such as the chicken in a wine and soya sauce.

Alónissos

Astrofengia, Hóra (Old Alónissos); tel: 24240 65182. High up in the former capital are a clutch of good quality tavernas. This one enjoys a superb view over the south of the island from its streetside tables. The cuisine combines classic Greek with Middle East elements such as couscous, humus and tahini.

To Kamaki, Patitíri; tel: 24240 65245. Down in the port and along the east main street you'll find this busy *ouzerí* with its wide range of carefully prepared *mezédhes*. Order several to your taste, a small carafe of *oúzo* and tuck in. Great place for people-watching.

Paraport, Hóra (Old Alónissos); tel: 24240 65608. On the far south side of Hóra and also enjoying a fine view, the Paraport is in an old house and one of the island's better tavernas. Features fish and a good range of ready-made dishes, plus some enticing *mezédhes* such as the aubergine salad or pepper cheese with capers.

Skýros

Anatolikos Anemos, Platía Brooke, Hóra; tel: 22220 92822. A small café-style dining venue in a two-storey building of wood and stone at the far north end of Hóra. The food is Mediterranean with a few inventive variations. There is a good wine list from small producers not commonly seen elsewhere.

O Antonis, Atsítsa; tel: 22220 92990. This is about as unassuming as you can get: a few rickety tables under a shaded patio overlooking a crumbling boat quay – but the food is far from rickety. Simple and unadorned, fish predominates and there are always a few ready-made dishes on offer.

O Pappous ki Ego, Hóra; tel: 22220 93200. It's the eclectic music that first grabs your attention here: good quality *éntehno* (artistic) Greek sounds. The food follows suit – a quality mixture of *mezédhes* and mains served up in a rather small dining area. Get there early for an outside table.

Ordering Drinks

býra	beer
krasí	wine
áspro	white wine
kokkinélli	rosé wine
mávro	red wine
me to kiló	wine by the kilo
hýma	bulk, from the barrel
neró	water
retsína	resin-flavoured wine
oúzo	aniseed-flavoured grape-pressing distillate
rakí	another distilled spirit from vintage crushings
tsípouro	north-mainland version of *rakí*
tsikoudhiá	Cretan version of *rakí*, flavoured with terebinth
portokaládha	orange juice
lemonádha	lemon juice

Évvia

Astron, Katoúnia, Límni; tel: 22270 31487. It's a 3-km (2-mile) drive south out to this seaside tavern, open all year round, with an open fireplace for the winter chills, and a large leaf-shaded veranda for summer. Food is classic Greek with no surprises but it is consistently good. The meat and fish is all locally raised and caught.

Cavo d'Oro, Kárystos; tel: 22240 22326. There's nothing flash about this old-style *magírío* (diner or cook-house) in a narrow street close to the main square in Kárystos. Just look at the dishes on display, point and dine on home-cooked food. Cheap and simple, just as it used to be.

Mesogios, Loutrá Edhipsoú; tel: 22260 60100. Redolent of old-world elegance – down to the carefully manicured table settings – this is a classy, rather expensive, but undeniably quality dining venue. The menu is Greek haute cuisine with a light touch.

Corfu

Kérkyra Town

La Famiglia, Maniarízi & Arlióti 30, Campiello district; tel: 26610 30270. Greek/Italian-run bistro specialising in salads, pasta, lasagne and Italian puddings. Excellent value and efficient service; limited seating both indoors and out, so reservations always mandatory. Open evenings only, Mon–Sat.

Hryssomallis (Babis), Nikifórou Theotókou 6, Kérkyra; tel: 26610 30342. The sign says it's a *zythopsitopolío* ("beer-hall-grill"), but it's also about the last traditional oven-food place in the old town: stews, *hórta*, *moussakás*, lamb offal and so forth. A typical bill won't be more than €10–13 each. The Durrells ate here during their 1930s stay, but the restaurant has been around a lot longer.

Mouragia, Arseníou 15, north quay, Kérkyra Town; tel: 26610 33815. A good mix of seafood (with fresh and frozen items clearly indicated) and Corfiot *magirevtá* such as *sofríto* and *pastitsádha*. Inexpensive for any island, let alone Corfu, and great sea views in the bargain. Open daily noon–12.30am.

Tenedos, alley off Solomóu, Spiliá district; tel: 26610 36277. French-Corfiot cooking with ample seafood choice and Lefkímmi bulk wine. Locals go especially for the *kandádhes* in the evening. Open lunch and dinner.

Theotoki Brothers (Kerkyraïki Paradosiaki Taverna), Alkiviádi Dhári 69, Gharítsa Bay. By far the best of half-a-dozen tavernas with tables out in the eucalyptus park here. A full range of *magirevtá* dishes and grills, plus some seafood, at very reasonable prices. Service can be leisurely, even by Corfu standards. Open lunch and dinner.

Venetian Well, Platía Kremastí, northwest of Cathedral, Kérkyra Town; tel: 26610 44761. Tucked away through an arch, with tables around the well, is some of the town's most innovative and expensive cooking, generic Aegean with interesting twists. Recipes change seasonally, depending on the proprietor's winter travels and inspiration, but past dishes have included duck in plum sauce or *dolmádhes* with wild rice. Excellent (and pricey) wine list. Supper only Mon–Sat, all year.

Around the Island

Agni, Agní cove, between Nissáki and Kassiópi; tel: 26630 91142. The romance of the proprietors – she's Greek, he's English – has been the basis of newspaper features and a BBC documentary, but, beyond the media hype, the food is very good, and reflects the meeting of cultures: stuffed sardines, garlic prawns, mussels in wine and herbs. Open for lunch and dinner Apr–Oct.

Akrogiali, Ághios Yeórghios Págon; tel: 697 7334278. A bumpy track leads 1,500 metres (1 mile) south from the beach to this little eyrie (marked by a windmill) run by a local lad and his Dutch partner. The fish is

excellent, as are the *mezédhes*. Open daily Jun–Oct.

Alonaki Bay, Paralía Alonáki, near Korissíon lagoon; tel: 26610 75872. Good country recipes, strong on vegetables and seafood – beans, greens, scorpion-fish soup – at shady tables on a terrace overlooking the sea.

Boukari Beach, Boúkari; tel: 26620 51791. The less commercial of two seafood tavernas at this seashore hamlet, in an idyllic setting, with patently fresh fare at some of the most attractive prices on the island. Open all day Apr–Oct.

Cavo Barbaro (Fotis), Avláki; tel: 26630 81905. An unusually good beach taverna, with welcoming service. A few *magirevtá* dishes at lunch, more grills after dark, plus homemade *glyká koutalioú* (candied fruit). Seating on the lawn, and plenty of parking. The only thing "barbarous" here can be the wind, as there's no shelter.

Etrusco, just outside Káto Korakiána village, on the Dhassiá road; tel: 26610 93342. Top-calibre nouvelle Italian cooking purveyed by father, son and spouses, served at a carefully restored country manor. Specialties like *timpano parpadellas* (pasta with duck and truffles) and a 200-label wine list don't come cheap – budget a minimum €30 each before drink – but this has been ranked one of the best five Greek tavernas outside of Athens. Early booking essential. Open Apr–Oct, supper only.

Foros, Paleá Períthia; tel: 26630 98373. The less commercial and friendlier of two tavernas in this rather melancholy village, operating in a restored house. Fare is basic – grills, salads, local cheese, *píttes*, a dish of the day – but so are the prices. Open daily May–Oct.

Ftelia (Elm Tree), Strinýlas village; tel: 26630 71454. An almost mandatory stop on the way to or from the summit of Mt Pandokrátor, this taverna specialises in game (venison, wild boar), unusual starters like snails or artichoke pie, and apple pie with proper Dutch coffee. Open lunch and dinner May–Oct, weekends only in winter.

Kouloura, Kouloúra cove; tel: 26630 91253. Fairly priced seafood or fish, large selection of *mezédhes* and salads, plus unusually elaborate pies at this taverna overlooking one of the most photogenic anchorages on Corfu. Open daily all day Apr–Oct; reservations needed at peak season.

Little Italy, Kassiopí, opposite Grivas supermarket; tel: 26630 81749. Jolly *trattoria* in an old stone house run by Italian brothers; fare includes salmon in pastry parcels, pizza, pastas smothered in made-from-scratch sauces. Reservations suggested.

Maria, riverbank, Lefkímmi; tel: 26620 22150. Ideal for an inexpensive lunch of *magirevtá* (baked pork chops, baked fish, green beans, good bulk wine); seating under the trees overlooking the river. Maria is a colourful granny

The Wines of Greece

While Greek wines have yet to obtain the status of their French counterparts, young oenologists trained abroad are definitely having a go at it, and there is a growing number of micro-wineries on the mainland. Nico Manessis' *The Illustrated Greek Wine Book* (Olive Press Publications, Corfu; www.greekwineguide.gr) is the definitive guide to what's new in the field.

All this wonderful wine, however, costs as much as anywhere else: €6–10 in a bottle shop, easily double that in a taverna.

Island wines

Many islands produce excellent vintages that they can't or won't export, and which are sold only locally. Although barreled/bulk (*me to kiló, hýma*) wines tend to be rough and ready, they're cheap (€3–8 per litre) and certainly authentic.

In Corfu, **Theotoki** is the local wine (red or white); the speciality of the island is a very sweet liqueur called

Kumquat, based on the tiny citrus fruit of that name. In Kefalloniá **Robola** is a delicate expensive white; **Gentilini** is reckoned the best label.

The lush green vineyards of Zákynthos produce **Comouto** rosé or the white **Verdea**. The grapes of Andípaxi are much appreciated; ask for wine from the barrel.

CAIR, the Rhodes cooperative originally founded in the 1920s by the Italians, has the ubiquitous white **Ilios** and red **Chevalier du Rhodes**, but the private Émbonas winery Emery is more esteemed for its **Mythiko** and **Villaré** red and white.

Sámos in the northeastern Aegean is one of the few islands to export wine, not only to the mainland but also abroad. The fortified Samos dessert wines **Anthemis** and **Vin de Liqueur** are esteemed world-wide. On Híos, particularly around Mestá, a heavy, sherry-like but very palatable wine is made here too – try Tetteris brand.

Lésvos is the undisputed *oúzo*

capital of Greece, producing at least 15 varieties. **Varvagiannis** is the most celebrated, and expensive, but some prefer **Arvanitis**. EPOM is the principal cooperative, marketing among others the "Mini" brand, a staple of *ouzerí* across the country.

Like most volcanic islands, Límnos produces excellent whites (especially the oak-aged **Dryiino**), as well as a few good reds and rosés.

Thássos specialises in *tsípouro* – often flavoured with exotic spices or pear extract rather than the anise of *oúzo*. Homemade firewater gets lethally strong; anything over 50 percent alcohol must be barreled, not bottled, lest it explode.

Santoríni, a volcanic island like Límnos, is known for its upscale whites like **Boutari Nyhteri** and **Ktima Argyrou**.

In Crete, **Logado** plonk has been the delight of backpackers for years, but superior labels such as **Economou** (Sitía province) and **Lyrarakis** (Iráklio) have made an appearance.

Corfu Takeaways

Invisible Kitchen, based in Aharávi, is not a restaurant per se, but a catering service: young British chefs Ben and Claudia will deliver ready meals for your villa party or *kaïki* day out. Nouvelle Italian, French, Thai, Indian, Chinese or Greek menus (€20 each, minimum 4 diners) or boat picnics at about €10 each – and the food is to die for. Operates late Apr–mid-Oct.
Tel: 26630 64864, 697 6652933;
www.theinvisiblekitchen.co.uk

who will give you a crash course in elaborate Greek swearing.
Mitsos, Nissáki; tel: 26630 91240. On the little rock-outcrop "islet" of the name, this ordinary-looking beachside taverna stands out for the cheerful service from the two partners, and high turnover and thus freshness of the inexpensive fare, which includes fried local fish and well-executed *sofríto*.
7th Heaven Bar/Panorama Restaurant, Longás Beach cliff, Perouládhes; tel: 26630 95035. The place to watch Corfu's most majestic sunset; by half an hour before the event, it's standing-room only and ambient music from staff doubling as DJs. The restaurant part, if you elect to linger after dark, is better than you'd think. Open all day May–Oct.
Toula, Agní cove; tel: 26630 91350. Worth a special mention for its professional demeanour, nice line in hot *mezédhes* and the house special *garídhes* (prawns, shrimp) grilled with spicy mixed-rice pilaff. Excellent bulk white wine; budget about €23 each; lunch and supper.

The Ionians

Paxí

Alexandros, Platía Edward Kennedy, Lákka; tel: 26620 30045. The most authentic *nisiótiko* cooking and most atmospheric setting in town; own-produced grilled meat and chicken, specialities like rabbit *sofríto* and mushroom pie, a few seafood dishes, but avoid the barrel wine.
Diogenis, opposite the Kafenio Spyros, Lákka; tel: 26620 31442. Honest, fresh meat grills purveyed by a welcoming family; recently introduced *magirevtá* recipes are not always as successful.
Lilas, Magaziá; tel: 26620 31102. Inexpensive little meat grill with good bulk wine in an ex-grocery shop at the

centre of the island; usually live accordeon or stringed music at weekends.
Vassilis, Longós quay; tel: 26620 31587. Now often known as Kostakis after the son who's taken it over, this has grown from a grilled fish specialist to an all-round taverna with imaginative recipes for *magirevtá*, like stuffed mushrooms and peppers, baked meat dishes and various oven pies.

Levkádha

T'Agnandio, west hillside, Ághios Nikítas; tel: 26450 97383. Tucked away up a lane with views to rival Sapfo's, one of the friendliest, least expensive home-style tavernas on the west coast; stress on *magirevtá* and fresh seafood such as *garídhes* from the Amvrákikos gulf. Creditable barrel wine; supper only low season.
Panorama, Atháni; tel: 26450 33291. A classic village grill serving assorted simple starters, local lamb chops, fish and bulk wine from vineyards out on Cape Lefkátas. Inexpensive.
Pantazis, Nikiána; tel: 26450 71211. Appealingly set at the far end of the yacht harbour, this locally patronised taverna does fresh seafood at very reasonable prices – though salad trimmings could sometimes be fresher. *Magirevtá* in high-season evenings; open all day.
Ta Platania, central platía, Karyá. Seating under the giant plane trees of the name, and fresh wholesome grills, salads and beers at budget prices. Tables for two other eateries share the square.
Regantos, Dhimárhou Verrióti 17, Levkádha Town; tel: 26450 22855. Supper-only taverna with a good balance of grills (especially spit-roasted chicken), oven food and fish; inexpensive and colourful.
Sapfo, on the beach, Ághios Nikítas; tel: 26450 97497. Innovative, deftly executed recipes such as seafood lasagne and cheese-and-courgette pie, decent bulk wine; not over-priced for the quality and arguably the best view in the resort.

Itháki

Nikos, inland near the National Bank, Vathý; tel: 26740 33039. A good all-rounder, with grills, a few *magirevtá* dishes daily, and fish; inexpensive bulk wine. Tourists go 8–9pm, then locals hold forth until closing time.
Kalypso, Kióni; tel: 26740 31066. Specialities here include onion pie and artichoke soufflé with ham and cheese; not too inflated price-wise considering that yachts tie up nearby. Remarkably full Greek beer list.
Kandouni, Vathý quay; tel: 26740 32918. Strong on *magirevtá* such as

stuffed squash blossoms and stuffed peppers; if you want well-grilled fish, select it next door from the fishmonger. Good Kefalloniá bulk wine, homemade dessert of the day, does breakfast too.
Rementzo, Fríkes; tel: 26740 31719. This taverna features local recipes like *savóro* (cold fish in raisin and rosemary sauce) and chunky *astakomakaronádha* (lobster on pasta), and supports local producers, such as the suppliers of their bulk wine and sticky sweets. Portions on the small side, but so are prices; uniquely here, open all year.
Sirines/Sirens, inland from square, Vathý; tel: 26740 33001. The capital's only genuine (and very reasonable) *mezedhopolío*, with a stress on *saganáki* (cheese sauce) items, chicken, seafood and own-grown organic vegetables. Normally open Easter–end Sep.

Kefalloniá

Akrogiali, Lixoúri quay, towards south end; tel: 26710 92613. An enduring, budget-priced institution, with largely local clientele. Wholesome and tasty food with a stress on oven-casserole food (including *yiouvétsi*, *kreatópita* and great *hórta*), but also fish and grills in the evening, plus excellent bulk wine.
Blue Sea (Spyros'), Káto Katélios; tel: 26710 81353. Speciality is pricey but clearly fresh and superbly grilled fish from the little anchorage adjacent. Budget about €30 each for a large portion with a share of *mezédhes* and their bulk wine.
Ta Delfina, Sámi waterfront. A basic but pleasant waterfront place with daily *magirevtá* such as *briám* (similar to ratatouille), *yiouvétsi* and good *hórta*. There is also some fresh fish, usually sardines. The best in a line of rather touristy places.
To Foki, at the head of Fóki Bay. This is a very pleasant taverna, friendly and just opposite the beach. It serves simple but tasty food – *fáva*, *souvláki* and salads – and lovely *milópita* (apple pie). Much better, and far cheaper, than anything to be found in Fiskárdho.

Lukewarm Food

Many Greek specialities are cooked in the morning and left to stand, so food can be lukewarm (occasionally downright cold), but the Greeks believe this is better for the digestion and steeping of the flavours. For some vegetarian dishes, they are right; for dishes containing meat, this is a downright dodgy practice.

Ionio Psisteria, Mánganos, just after the turn off to Matsoukáta. A pleasant, unpretentious roadside restaurant about 10 km (6 miles) before Fiskárdho. Very reasonable, the food is honest and tasty, especially the *moussakás*, and the service is friendly. On Saturdays they spit-roast a whole pig.

To Kafenio tis Kabanas, Lithóstroto 52B, Argostóli; tel: 26710 24456. Housed in a reconstructed Venetian tower, with seating in the square opposite, is a pleasant café serving light snacks. As well as the usual coffees, local specialities include *soumádha* (an orgeat drink) and *amyghdhalópita* (almond pie).

Kyani Akti, A. Trítsi 1, far end of the quay; tel: 26710 26680. A superb, if pricey, *psarotavérna* built out over the sea. The speciality is fresh fish and seafood, often with unusual things to try (like the delicious *dháktylia* – "fingers" – akin to razor clams). All the fish and seafood is sold by weight. There is also a range of *mezédhes* and salads, and some tasty house wine.

Maïstralo, far north end of quay, Argostóli; tel: 26710 26563. Set yourself up at this genuine *ouzerí* with a seafood *pikilía* (medley), some of their abundant hot/cold *mezédhes* and *oúzo* by the 200-ml carafe. Pleasant waterside seating beside a pine grove; Apr–Oct only.

Mr Grillo, A. Trítsi 135, Argostóli. A *psistariá*, not far from the port authority building, very popular with locals for Sunday lunch. The grilled meats are tasty and accompanying *mezédhes* fine. All reasonably priced.

Nirides, Ássos, the far end of the harbour; tel: 26740 51467. This little *estiatório* in a great spot overlooking the harbour has the usual range of salads and a few grilled and oven dishes, as well as fresh fish by the kilo. It is all well cooked – especially the fried peppers with cheese and *melitzánes imám*.

Paradisenia Akti (Stavros Dendrinos), far east corner of Agía Effimía resort; tel: 26740 61392. Fair-priced savoury dishes such as *hortópita* and local sausage, though seafood portions could be bigger; lovely terrace seating under pines and vines overlooking the sea.

Patsouras, A. Trítsi 32 (north quay), Argostóli; tel: 26710 22779. Popular *magirevtá* specialist just along from the Lixoúri ferry. Good rib-sticking food with especially tasty *bámies* (okra), a few grills, big portions and a velvety red house wine. Open all year and inexpensive.

To Pevko, Andipáta Erísou, by the turn for Dhafnoúdhi beach; tel: 26740

41360. A serious contender for the best place to eat on the island, with seating outside under a huge pine tree. A mouthwatering selection of *mezédhes*, oven-cooked dishes and some grilled meat and fish. Particularly good are the tomato, mint and *féta keftédhes*, the *gígandes* (butter beans) and aubergine with garlic.

Romantza, Póros; tel: 26740 72294. This *estiatório* is in a charming position, built into the headland at the end of the town beach. You eat on a first-storey balcony which has views over the sea to Itháki. The focus of the menu is on a large range of fresh fish (priced by weight), but there are also good *mezédhes* and salads.

Vasso's, southeast end of quay, Fiskárdho; tel: 06740 41276. *Magirevtá* with a difference: olive tapenade for your bread, dill and other herbs flavouring many dishes, seafood pasta, creative desserts. Reasonable (for Fiskárdho anyway) at about €25 each.

Zákynthos

Agnadi Taverna, beyond Argási, 8 km (5 miles) from Zákynthos Town; tel: 26950 35183. A modern but attactive wooden building on a steep slope overlooking the sea. It is slightly touristy, but the home cooking is authentic and tasty.

Akrotiri Taverna, Akrotíri, 4 km (2½ miles) north of Zákynthos Town; tel: 26950 45712. A pleasant summer-only taverna with a large garden. Grilled meats are a speciality here, but they also bring round large trays of very tempting *mezédhes* from which you pick and choose. The house wine is very acceptable.

Alitzerini, entrance to Kilioméno; tel: 26950 48552. Housed in one of the few surviving 17th-century Venetian village houses, this little *inomagerío* offers hearty, meat-based country cooking and its own wine; *kandádhes* some evenings. Evenings only: Fri–Sun Oct–May, daily Jun–Sep. Reservations essential.

Andreas, Paralía Beloúsi, near Dhrossiá; tel 26950 61604. A no-nonsense fish taverna serving fresh catch at fair prices. During summer there is terrace seating by the sea. To go with the fish there is good bread, wonderful *kolokythákia* (boiled courgettes) and decent wine.

Andreas Zontas, Pórto Limniónas, Ághios Léon. Location can count for a lot. The food here is relatively expensive, standard taverna fare, but it is served on a promontory overlooking an idyllic rocky bay and facing west to the sunset.

Arekia, Dhionysíou Romá, Zákynthos Town; tel: 26950 26346. A smoky

Olive Oil

The Greeks are more generous with oil in food, especially olive oil, than most northern European palates are used to. Although you can ask for no oil on a salad, for instance (*hóris ládhi*), most waiters will think this an odd request as Greeks generally regard oil as good for the digestion. A whole category of slow-cooked, casserole-tray vegetable stews are bluntly referred to as *ladherá* or oil-cooked dishes.

and unpretentious hole-in-the-wall, fitting perhaps 70 diners cosily on bench seats; open evenings only all year round. The food's decent but incidental to the main event: *kandádhes* and *arékia* singing after 10pm.

To Fanari tou Keriou, 1.5 km (1 mile) beyond Kerí village; tel: 26950 43384/697 26 76 302. Watch the moon rise over the Myzíthres sea-stacks below the Kerí cliffs. The food's on the expensive side, but portions are fair size and quality is high – try the daily *mode galaktoboúreko* or vegetable-stuffed *pantsétta*, redolent of nutmeg. Reservations essential.

Kalas, Kambí. By far the best taverna in Kambí, Kalas is set in a pretty garden, shaded by large trees, and serves up all the usual favourites (*fáva*, *loukánika*, *horiátiki* and *patátes*), all tasty and freshly cooked. Good bulk wine as well.

Komis, Bastoúni tou Aghíou, Zákynthos Town; tel: 26950 26915. A lovely *psarotavérna* tucked into a rather unlikely spot behind the port authority building. The emphasis is on slightly pricey but fresh and inventive fish and seafood dishes, but there is a good list of *mezédhes*, decent wine and tempting desserts.

Malanos, Aghíou Athanasíou 38, Kípi district, Zákynthos Town; tel: 26950 45936. Deservedly popular and inexpensive all-year shrine of *magirevtá*: mince-rich *yiouvarlákia* and *fasolákia yiahní* are typical offerings. Unusually good bread as well as the expected barrel wine.

Mikrinisi, Kokkínou, 1 km (½ mile) beyond Makrýs Yialós. Standard, but reasonable, *tavérna* food – *horiátiki*, *kalamarákia*, *souvláki* and other such offerings – but the situation is lovely, on the edge of a headland overlooking a tiny harbour.

Roulis, Kypséli Beach, near Dhrossiá; tel: 26950 61628. This is a friendly place overlooking the sea. Popular with islanders, Roulis gets very fresh fish – one of its main attractions – but also does the usual salads and vegetables well. The house wine is drinkable and the freshness of all the ingredients make it worth the detour from the main coast road.

Theatro Avouri Estiatorio, north of Limodhaíka near Tragáki. A peaceful, stone-built open-air theatre complex set in lovely countryside. Local food (including excellent bread) is cooked in a traditional oven, and you can also catch one of the story-telling performances. Open every night from around 7pm.

Theodoritsis, just past Arghássi in Vassilikós municipal territory; tel: 26950 48500/694 41 35 560. Where the beautiful people of Zákynthos go at weekends; there is a stress on *magirevtá* but there are also grills and *mezédhes*. Moderately pricey with a summer terrace overlooking town, there is also a tasteful interior; open all year.

Crete

Ághios Nikólaos

Du Lac, 28-Oktovríou; tel: 28410 22414. Greek and international food served in picturesque surroundings of Lake Voulisméni. Inflated prices but high quality and popular with the locals.

Pórtes, Anapávseos 3; tel: 28410 28489. Located to the southwest of the town centre, this decent eatery serves up a large selection of tasty *mezédhes*.

Stámna, 200 metres/yds from Hotel Mirabello, Havánia; tel: 28410 25817. A well-established restaurant which dishes up superb Italian and Greek food.

Arghyroúpoli

Paleós Mylos; tel: 28310 81209. A lovely eatery set in a stunning location. The grilled meats are a particular speciality here.

Arhánes

Diktamos, Pérkolo 3 (side street in town centre). Pleasant surroundings, friendly service, high quality Cretan food at reasonable prices.

Eloúndha

Akrohoriá; tel: 28410 42091. Overlooking the bay; this place serves good charcoal-grilled fish, lobster and seafood.

Myli, Káto Pinés; tel: 28410 41961. In the hills above Eloúndha; traditional, tasty, well-prepared Cretan food, very reasonable prices

Vritómartis; tel: 28410 41325. On its own little island, moored in the centre of the harbour. Excellent fish, caught by the owner.

Haniá

Anaplous, Sífaka 34, Maherádhika; tel: 28210 41320. Modishly set in a restored ruin; traditional Cretan specialities including pork baked in a clay pot, and vegetarian dishes. Live music sometimes.

Karnagio, Platía Kateháki 8; tel: 28210 53366. Set back from the harbour, and set in an old *hamám* (steam-baths), this is a superb restaurant. Beloved by the locals, it serves up quality Cretan and vegetarian dishes and tries to use organic products.

Karyatis, Platía Kateháki 12; tel: 28210 55600. Good reputation for its Italian dishes: pasta and pizzas.

Kormoranos, Theotokopoúlou 46; tel: 28210 86910. A *mezedádhiko* with barrel wine and *tsikoudhiá*. Also snacks and sandwiches during the day. Very good value.

Pigadi tou Tourkou, Sarpáki 1-3, Splántzia; tel: 28210 54547. Run by Jenny, an Englishwoman who specialises in Middle Eastern dishes. Long-established.

Rudi's Bierhaus, Sífaka 26, Maherádhika, tel: 28210 50824. An Austrian-owned bar, with over 100 different international beers. As well as the booze there are excellent *mezédhes* and great jazz.

Tamam, Zambelíou 49, tel: 28210 96080. Squeezed into another old *hamám*, this is a good place to try out Cretan and also to find tasty vegetarian dishes.

Hersónisos

Georgios Place, Old Hersónisos, tel. 28970 21032. A haven of tasty traditional Cretan cooking, found 3 km (2 miles) up in the hills behind the touristy coastal resort.

Horafákia (Akrotíri Peninsula)

Irini, tel: 28210 39470. A busy taverna with good traditional Greek home-cooking.

Hóra Sfakíon (Sfakiá)

Lefka Ori, western end of the harbour front, tel: 28250 91209. Some of the best traditional dishes in the area.

Iráklio

China House, Papandhréou 20, just off Akadhamías, tel: 2810 333338. Surprisingly good Chinese food, and reasonable prices, make this the place to take a break from Greek dishes.

Coffee, Chocolate and Tea

Greeks generally drink their coffee with lots of sugar. Essential phrases for those who like it without are *horís záhari*, "without sugar", or *skéto*, "plain". If you like some sugar ask for *métrio*. If you love sugar say nothing and they'll probably dump a few teaspoons into whatever you're drinking. *Me gála* means "with milk".

Whole beans suitable for cafetière or percolator coffee only arrived in Greece in the early 1990s; they are making steady inroads among locals and tourists fed up with the ubiquitous "Nescafé", which has become the generic term for any instant coffee. The formula sold in Greece is far stronger than that made for northern European markets, and the most palatable use for it is in *frappé*, cold instant coffee

whipped up in a shaker, and an entirely Greek innovation despite its patently French name.

Espresso and cappuccino, when available, are exactly as in Italy, though not always so expertly made. You will often be given a little shaker of cinnamon (*kanélla*) to sprinkle on the froth. *Freddoccino*, another resourceful Greek invention, is a cold, double cappuccino for the summer months.

Gallikós ("French"), in other words percolated coffee, is usually quite acceptable. *Fíltros* means the same thing. *Ellenikós kafés* is Greek coffee, boiled and served with the grounds in the cup. If you want a large cup, ask for a *dhiplós*. *Ellenikó cafés* is also known as *turkikós cafés* but this sometimes

provokes patriotic objections.

Chocolate drinks (*tsokoláta*) can be very good indeed, served cold or hot according to season.

Tea (*tsái*) is the ragged stepsister of the hot-drinks triad; quality bulk (black) tea of Twinings or Whittard's standard is almost impossible to find, so you'll usually have to make do with bagged tea of obscure Ceylonese or Madagascan vintage, never seen elsewhere. It is served either with milk or with lemon (*me lemóni*).

Herbal teas are easy to find in shops, and at more traditional *kafenía*. *Hamomíli* is camomile tea, and *tsái (tou) vounoú* is "mountain tea", made with mountain sage leaves. It's called *alisfakiá* in some of the islands, especially in the Dodecanese and Cyclades.

Four Rooms (formerly Giovanni), Koráï 12, tel: 2810 289542. Set in a fine neo-classical building, this restaurant specialises in Greek and Italian cuisine.

Ionia, corner Évans and Yiánnari, tel: 2810 283213. This venerable eatery has been offering Greek meat, fish and vegetable dishes since 1923.

Ippokambos, Mitsotáki 2; tel: 2810 280240. A superb establishment overlooking the old harbour, famed for its meticulously prepared *mezédhes*. It is usually packed with locals so go early. Open lunch and evenings.

Kyriakos, Dhimokratías 51, tel. 2810 222464. An old restaurant with traditionally cooked Cretan meat, fish and vegetable dishes. You choose your food in the kitchen.

Loukoulos, Koráï; tel: 2810 224435. An elegant, upmarket and expensive Italian restaurant – but with good food. Vegetarians are also well catered for.

Vyzandio, Vyzándio 3; tel: 2810 244775. A typical modern taverna; it has Greek and international dishes at reasonable prices.

Ístro

El Greco, 10 km (6 miles) southeast of Ághios Nikólaos; tel: 28410 61637. This place has Greek specialities, concentrating on fish and lobster.

Kalýves

Alexis Zorbas; tel: 28250 31363. A family-run taverna; open all year. Large portions, tasty food.

Kastéli-Kissámou (Kíssamos)

Kelari, beachfront promenade; tel: 28220 23883. Stélios takes great pride in his local cuisine.

Káto Zákros

Akrogiáli, by the beach; tel: 28430 26896. Friendly service and a good reputation for fresh fish and meat make this a good place to eat.

Kournás

Kali Kardia, Kournás village, 3 km (2 miles) above the eponymous lake; tel: 28250 96278. Excellent local cooking and fresh meat. Aficionados travel a long way for the *galaktoboúreko*, a lemony egg-custard dessert.

Lassíthi Plateau

Andonis, between Psyhró and Pláti; tel: 28440 31581. Set in quiet and attractive surroundings, this taverna offers a good selection of charcoal grilled meats.

Lefkógia

Stelios; tel: 28320 31866. Run by the son of the local butcher; this predictably has fine meat dishes. The tasty home cooking and fresh orange juice come at very reasonable prices.

Margarítes

Vrysi, outskirts of Margarítes village (32 km/20 miles east of Réthymno). Very pleasant, with typical Cretan food.

Palékastro-Angathía-Hióna

Kakavia, on Hióna beach, just beyond Palékastro (20 km/12 miles east of Sitía); tel: 28430 61227. Named after its speciality, fish soup.

Nikolas O Psaras, Angathía village, 1 km (½ mile) from Palékastro; tel: 28430 61598. An excellent taverna: fresh fish and Cretan specialties; beautiful view.

Paleohóra

Christos, on the promenade; tel: 28230 41359. A vast array of meat and fish dishes.

Third Eye, between the centre and the beach; tel: 28230 41234. This excellent vegetarian restaurant also offers Asian and Indian dishes.

Pánormos

Sofoklis, Pánormos harbour (22 km/13 miles east of Réthymno); tel: 28340 51297. A good place to try Greek and Cretan cooking.

Plakiás

Lysseos, Plakiás seafront, tel: 28320 31479. Cypriot chef Louká's stylish cooking and the multilingual Litó's exemplary management make this one of Plakias' most popular tavernas. Evenings only – arrive early.

Medousa, Plakiás, inland from the pharmacy; tel: 28320 31521. Fine home cooking by Despina, accompanied by shots of Babis' excellent *rakí*.

Panorama, Mýrthios village, overlooking Plakiás Bay. Tasty food, with good vegetarian options, and fantastic views from the balcony.

Polyrrínia

Odysseas, 7 km (4 miles) south of Kastéli-Kissámou; tel: 28220 23331. A taste of the Cretan countryside, all made from very fresh home-grown ingredients.

Réthymno

Apostolis & Zambia, Stamathioudháki 20; tel: 28310 24561. Excellent, extremely reasonably priced fish, seafood and traditional *mezédhes*. One of Réthymno's best.

Fanari, Kefaloyiánnidhon 16; tel: 28310 54849. A taverna specialising in traditional Greek *mezédhes*, but with good main fish

and meat dishes, as well as decent wine.

Globe, E. Venizélou 33, opposite the promenade; tel: 28310 25465. A good selection of Cretan food, as well as pasta, pizza and some vegetarian dishes.

Koumbos, Akrotiríou 3, Koumbés; tel: 28310 52209. Located in a western suburb by the sea, this taverna serves up well-cooked and very fresh fish caught by the owner.

Kyria Maria, Moskhovíti 20 (behind the Rimondi Fountain); tel: 28310 29078. Good basic Cretan cooking. Some vegetarian dishes.

Othon, Platía Plátanos; tel: 28310 55500. An *estiatório* offering a wide variety of Greek and European dishes.

Veneto, Epimenídhou 4; tel: 28310 56634. An upmarket restaurant serving refined Greek and Mediterranean cuisine.

Rodhiá

Exostis, Rodhiá village overlooking the Gulf of Iráklio; tel: 2810 841206. Great views, excellent food, fair prices, friendly service from owner, Andréas.

Sitía–Agía Fotiá

Neromylos, 5 km (3 miles) east of Sitía; tel: 28430 25576. An eatery with simple grilled food. It has a wonderful view.

Stalós

Levendis, in Áno Stalós, 6 km (4 miles) west of Haniá; tel: 28210 68155. A village taverna excelling in home-cooked food.

Stavroménos

Alekos, 11 km (7 miles) east of Réthymno centre; tel: 28310 72234. A family-run taverna with typical Cretan food.

Zarós

Oasis, main street. A small, congenial place; *souvláki*, grilled meat and fish, oven bakes and an excellent homemade wine.

Culture

Music & Dance

Thanks to Greece's geographical position and the vast number of cultures that have called it home, there is astonishing regional variety in the various regional folk musics. Crete has one of the more vital traditions, characterised by the *lýra* (three-string spike fiddle) and *laoúto* (mandolin-like lute). In the Dodecanese, these are often joined by either *tsamboúna*, a goatskin bagpipe, *violí* (western *violin*) or *sandoúri*, the hammer dulcimer popularised in the islands by refugees from Asia Minor.

Nisiótika is the general name for island music; that of the Ionians is the most Italian-influenced and western in scale. Mainland music is also

Cultural Events

April–October Sound and Light performances on Corfu at the Páleo Froúrio; Rhodes at Grand Master's Palace.
May–September Folk dancing by the Dora Stratou Group in Athens, and Nelly Dimoglou Group in Rhodes Old Town.
June Jazz & Blues Festival, Lykavittós Theatre, Athens
June–September Athens Festival at the Herod Atticus Odeon, among other venues: events include ballet, opera, jazz, and experimental music, plus modern and classical plays performed by world-ranking artists.
July Music Festival on the island of Itháki (Ithaca).
July–August Réthymnon Renaissance Fair: cultural activities at the Venetian Fort.
August Iráklio Festival – concerts, theatre, opera and so on.
August Lefkáda Festival of Music, Folklore and Theatre, with overseas groups.
August–September Santorini Music Festival, mostly classical events
August–September Sými Festival; a mix of classical and Greek pop performances.
August–October Rhodes Festival

unmistakable, characterised by the extensive use of the *klaríno* (clarinet) and, in Epirus, an extraordinary, disappearing tradition of polyphonic singing.

Contemporary sounds include original syntheses or derivations of the traditional and rebetic traditions by such artists such as Thessalonian Dionysis Savvopoulos, who first challenged the supremacy of *bouzoúki* in the mid-1960s with his guitar and orchestral-based compositions, and who spawned a whole generation of disciples and protegés such as the rock-influenced Nikos Papazoglou, Nikos Xydakis and Heimerinoi Kolymvites.

Each region (and sometimes island) of Greece has its own particular folk dances. These ranges from the basic *sta tría* – three steps to one side, followed by a kick (growing gradually faster and faster) – to a frenzied combination of complicated footwork, jumps, slaps and kicks. Troupes, dressed in traditional Greek costume, are most likely to be performing on public holidays (you may also see them on TV). Probably the best-known professional group is Dora Stratou Greek Folk Dances, which holds regular shows from May to September at the Dora Stratou Theatre, Filopáppou Hill (southwest slope), Athens.

In Athens, outstanding Greek and foreign musicians often perform at the **Lykavittós Theatre** on Mount Lykavittós, not to mention the larger concerts that take place in the soccer stadiums. Opera can be seen at the Olympia Theatre, performed by the **Lyrikí Skiní** (the National Opera Company), while classical music, from national and international ensembles, is typically performed at the **Mégaron Musikís** near the American Embassy.

Theatre

Athens has an active theatre life but, as most productions are in Greek, options for English-speakers are limited. Most productions in English take place during festivals (*see Cultural Events, below*). One recent cultural initiative has provided some excellent productions of both modern and ancient drama in English at one of Greece's most striking open-air theatres – the Stone (Pétra) Theatre in Petropolis in the suburbs of Athens. In summer, plays are produced under the auspices of the Stones and Rocks Festival.

Cinema

Going to the cinema in Greece during the summer is a special pleasure not

to be missed. Nearly all the movie theatres that run in the summer (the others shut down unless they have air-conditioning) are open-air, sometimes tucked among apartment buildings (whose tenants watch the film from their balconies); in other areas, they are perched on a seaside promontory under the stars. Tickets, at €6–8, are slightly cheaper than indoor cinemas and soundtracks are in the original language (with Greek subtitles). On smaller islands there may be only one showing, at around 9.30pm, while elsewhere there will be two screenings, at 9 and 11pm.

Festivals

January 1 *Feast of Ághios Vasílios* (St Basil), this is celebrated all over Greece.
January 6 *Epiphany/Aghía Theofánia* – Blessing of the waters: all over Greece.
February–March *Carnival season* for three weeks before Lent: all over Greece. Some places with celebrations of special interest are: Náoussa, Zákynthos, Skýros, Híos (Mestá, Olýmbi), Lésvos (Agiássos), Agía Ánna (Évvia), Kefalloniá, Kárpathos, Iráklio, Réthymno and (best of all) Pátra.
"Clean" Monday Beginning of fast for Lent. Picnics in the countryside and kite-flying, all over Greece.
March 25 *Feast of Annunciation/ Independence Day:* military parades in all main towns, pilgrimage to Tínos.
Easter weekend *Good Friday, Holy Saturday* and *Easter Sunday* are celebrated throughout Greece.
April 23 *Feast of St George:* celebrated especially in Kaliópi (Límnos), Así Gonía (near Haniá) and Pylí (Kos).
May 1 *Workers' Day:* picnics in the countryside all over Greece.
August 15 *Assumption of the Virgin:* festivals all over Greece. Major pilgrimage to Tínos.
October 28 *Ohi (No) Day:* anniversary of Greek defeat of Italian army in 1940 and Metaxas' supposed one-word response to Italy's ultimatum. Military parades in major cities.
Christmas season All over Greece. In a dwindling number of places, children sing *kálenda* (carols) from door to door for a small gratuity.
December 31 *New Year's Eve.* Many Greeks play cards for money on this occasion, and cut the *vasilópitta* with a lucky coin hidden in it. Special celebration in the town of Híos.

Nightlife

Metropolitan nightlife in Greece (essentially Athens, Iráklio, Kérkyra, Ródos Town and Pátra) can be roughly divided into four categories: bars; live music clubs with jazz, Greek music (most likely *laïki*, or a watered-down version of *rebétika*) or rock; dance clubs, mostly with a techno, house or ambient soundtrack; and musical *tavérnes* where food prices reflect the live entertainment.

For most Greeks, however, the simple *tavérna* remains the most popular site for a night out spent eating, drinking and, sometimes, singing and dancing. In general, younger Greeks frequent the bars and dance clubs, while the locales for popular Greek music are more patronised by the older generations.

In Athens, the weekly *Athinorama* (in Greek) has an extensive listing of all the various venues and events. If you really want to find out what's going on in the city, ask a Greek friend to help you sort through the listings.

During the summer (late June–early September) many clubs and music halls close down, with musicians of all stripes touring the countryside for the summer festival season, or performing in the islands and coastal resorts.

Casinos

For a more sophisticated – and potentially more expensive – night out, there are casinos in numerous Greek cities and resorts, including Corfu, Rhodes and Ermoúpoli (Sýros).

Gay Life

Overt gay behaviour is not a feature of Greek society. Homosexuality is legal at the age of 17, and bisexual activity fairly common among younger men, but few couples (male or female) are openly gay. Mýkonos is famous as a gay Mecca, and Skála Eressoú on Lésvos (where the poetess Sappho was born) for lesbians. But elsewhere in Greece single-sex couples are liable to be regarded as odd, although usually as welcome as any other tourists. If discrete, you will attract no attention asking for a double room and will find most people tolerant.

Sport

Hiking & Mountaineering

Greece has long been a magnet for hikers and mountain climbers, with many surviving footpaths on certain islands threading through forested areas untouched by the tourist masses. Big-wall climbing is currently growing in popularity on islands such as Kálymnos. For information on trails, maps and excursions, consult one of the specialist guides in the booklist, or if you'd prefer an organised excursion, see the list of trekking operators on page 309.

Caving

Greece is honeycombed with caves, though many are locked to protect delicate formations or archaelogical artefacts, and are only opened to qualified potholers on an expedition. The following, however, have set hours

Sailing

Numerous companies offer sailing packages and cruises round the coast of Greece that can be booked from home – an internet search will be very productive. One useful website is:
www.sailingissues.com

Much of the sailing is in flotillas helmed by the hire companies, but experienced sailors can charter their own yacht. Alternatively, once you're in Greece you can hire boats by the day or week at many marinas. Either way, you can rely on the Port Authorty Harbour Police in your area for up-to-the-minute information on conditions.

The best times to sail are spring and autumn, as winds can be high through the summer months and prices are hiked up to many times that of the cooler seasons.

There are sailing schools, housed in the naval clubs of the following cities: Athens (Paleó Fáliro); Corfu; Rhodes; Sýros. Further information can be obtained from: Hellenic Yachting Federation, Marina Delta Falirou, Tzitzifies; tel: 210 940 4825; fax: 210 940 4829.

and facilities for public visits: Drongaráti and Melissáni, Kefalloniá; Andíparos, in the Cyclades; and the cave of Sykiás Olýmbon on Híos.

Scuba diving

Diving in Greece is tightly controlled, with the aim of preserving the nation's heritage of submerged antiquities. However, there is a growing number of authorised sites for diving – consult your nearest EOT/GNTO branch for an updated list. Those of long standing include Thérmes Kallithéas on Rhodes; Vlyhádhia Bay on Kálymnos; Ýdra island; Paleokastrítsa Bay, Corfu; most of the coast around Léros; and much of southern Mýkonos.

Although there is a lot to see around the coast, do not expect undersea fauna and flora of Caribbean splendour; free-diving with a mask, fins and snorkel is likely to be just as rewarding in Greek waters.

Horse Riding

Many small riding schools offer horse riding. For information, contact the **Hellenic Equestrian Federation** 37 Dimitríou Ralli Str, Maroussi, Athens, tel: 210 614 1986/614 1987, fax: 210 614 1859; email: press@equestrian.org.gr.

Tennis

Although there are tennis clubs in most larger cities, few are open to non-members/non-residents. Public courts are equally rare. But most island hotels and inclusive complexes of A or Luxury class have facilities, where you may be able to book court space by the hour.

Waterskiing

Waterskiing (and in some places parasailing as well) is far cheaper in Greece than in most Mediterranean resorts. You will find waterskiing facilities at: Vouliagméni (southeast of Athens); numerous locations on Corfu; Haniá, Crete; Eloúnda, Crete; Pórto Héli; Rhodes; and Skiáthos.

Windsurfing

Greece is ideal for windsurfing learners, with gentle breezes blowing around many small coves. Boards are available for rent, and lessons are available (at very reasonable rates), at many popular Greek beaches, and at most of the beaches maintained by the GNTO.

The premier resorts dedicated to the sport, where people come from overseas just to windsurf, are: Prasonísi, Rhodes; Paleohóra, Crete; Kokkári, Sámos; Náxos (Ághios Yeórgios); and Vasilikí, Lefkádha.

Language

The Greek Language

Modern Greek is the outcome of gradual evolution undergone by the Greek language since the Classical period (5th–4th centuries BC). The language is still relatively close to Ancient Greek: it uses the same alphabet and much of the same vocabulary, though the grammar – other than the retention of the three genders – is considerably streamlined and is less complicated. Many people speak English, some very well, but even just a few words in their native language will always be appreciated.

Pronunciation tips

Most of the sounds of Greek reasonably straightforward to pronounce for English speakers. There are only five vowel sounds: *a*, *e*, *i*, *o*, *u*, and *y* are consistently pronounced as shown in the table opposite. The letter *s* is usually pronounced "s", but "z" before an *m* or *g*. The sound represented here as *th* is always pronounced as in "thin", not "that"; the first sound in "that" is represented by *d*.

The only difficult sounds are *h*, which is pronounced like the "ch" in Scottish "loch" (we render this as *kh* before "s" so that you don't generate "sh"), and *g* before *a* or *o*, which has no equivalent in English – it's somewhere between the "y" in "yet" and the "g" in "get".

The position of the stress in words is of critical importance, as homonyms abound, and Greeks will often fail to understand you if you don't stress the right syllable (compare *psýllos*, "flea" with *psilós*, "tall"). In this guide, stress is marked by a simple accent mark (´).

Greek word order is flexible, so you may often hear phrases in a different order from the one in which they are given here. Like the French, the Greeks use the plural of the second person when addressing someone politely. We have used the polite (formal) form throughout this language section, except where an expression is specified as "informal".

Communication

Good morning	*kaliméra*
Good evening	*kalispéra*
Good night	*kaliníhta*
Hello/Goodbye	*yiásas*
(informal:)	*yiásou*
Pleased to meet you	*hárika polý*
Yes	*ne*
No	*óhi*
Thank you	*efharistó*
You're welcome	*parakaló*
Please	*parakaló*
Okay/All right	*endáxi*
Excuse me (to get attention)	*me synhoríte*
Excuse me (to	*syngnómi*

ask someone to get out of the way)

How are you?	*Ti kánete?*
(informal:)	*Ti kánis?*
Fine, and you?	*Kalá, esís?*
(informal:)	*Kalá, esí?*
Cheers/Your health! (when drinking)	*Yiámas!*
Could you help me?	*Boríte na me voithísete?*
Can you show me...	*Boríte na mou díxete...*
I want...	*Thélo...*
I don't know	*Dhen xéro*
I don't understand	*Dhen katálava*
Do you speak English?	*Xérete angliká?*
Can you please speak more slowly?	*Parakaló, miláte sigá-sigá*
Please say that again	*Parakaló, xanapésteto*
Here	*edhó*
There	*ekí*
What?	*ti?*
When?	*póte?*
Why?	*yiatí?*
Where?	*pou?*
How?	*pos?*

Telephone Calls

the telephone	*to tiléfono*
phone-card	*tilekárta*
May I use the phone please?	*Boró na tilefoníso, parakaló?*
Hello (on the phone)	*Embrós/Oríste*
My name is...	*Légome...*
Could I speak to...	*Boró na milíso me...*
Wait a moment	*Periménete mía stigmí*
I didn't hear	*Dhen ákousa*

Our Transliteration System

In Greece, all town and village names on road signs, as well as most street names, are written in Greek and the Roman alphabets. There's no universally accepted system of transliteration into Roman, and in any case the Greek authorities are gradually replacing old signs with new ones that use a slightly different system. This means you will have to get used to seeing different spellings of the same place on maps and signs and in this book.

Below is the transliteration scheme we have used in this book: beside each Greek letter or pair of letters is the Roman letter(s) we have used. Next to that is a rough approximation of the sound in an English word.

A α	a	father	M μ	m	man	AI αι (ai)	e	hay
B β	v	vote	N ν	n	no	AY αυ (au)	av/f	lava
Γ γ	g(h)/y	got *except before "e" or "i", when it is nearer to yacht, but rougher*	Ξ ξ	x	taxi	EI ει (ei)	i	ski
			O o	o	long	EY ευ (eu)	ev/f	ever
			Π π	p	pen	OI οι (oi)	i	ski
			P ρ	r	room	OY ου (ou)	ou	tourist
Δ δ	dh	then	Σ σ/ς	s	set	ΓΓ γγ (gg)	ng	long
E ε	e	egg			*or* charisma	ΓΚ γκ (gk)	ng	long
Z ζ	z	zoo	T τ	t	tea	ΓΞ γξ (gx)	nx	anxious
H η	i	ski	Y υ	y	ski	ΜΠ μπ (mp)	b	beg
Θ θ	th	thin	Φ φ	f	fish		*or* mb	limber
I ι	i	ski	X χ	h	loch	NT ντ (nt)	d	dog
K κ	k	kiss	Ψ ψ	ps	maps		*or* nd	under
Λ λ	l	long	Ω ω	o	cord	TZ τζ (tz)	tz	adze

In the Hotel

Do you have a vacant room?	Éhete dhomátio?
I've booked a a room	Ého kratísi éna domátio
I'd like...	Tha íthela...
a single/ double room	éna monóklino/ dhíklino
double bed	dhipló kreváti
a room with a bath/shower	éna domátio me bánio/dous
One night	éna vrádhi
Two nights	dýo vrádhia
How much is it?	Póso káni?
It's expensive	Íne akrivó
Do you have a room with a sea-view?	Éhete domátio me théa pros ti thálassa?
Is there a balcony?	Éhi balkóni?
Is the room heated/ air-conditioned?	To domátio éhi thérmansi/ klimatismós?
Is breakfast included?	Mazí me to proinó?
Can I see the room please?	Boró na do to domátio, parakaló?
The room is too hot/cold/small	To domátio íne polý zestó/ krýo/mikró
It's too noisy	Éhi polý thóryvo
Could you show me another room, please?	Boríte na mou díxete állo domátio, parakaló?
I'll take it	Tha to páro
Can I have the bill, please?	Na mou kánete to logariasmó, parakaló?
dining room	trapezaría
key	klidhí
towel	petséta
sheet	sedhóni
blanket	kouvérta
pillow	maxilári
soap	sapoúni
hot water	zestó neró
toilet paper	hartí toualéttas

At a Bar or Café

bar/café	bar/kafenío (or kafetéria)
patisserie	zaharoplastío
I'd like...	Tha íthela...
a coffee	éna kafé
Greek coffee	ellinikó kafé
filter coffee	gallikó kafé/ kafé fíltro
instant coffee	neskafé (or nes)
cappuccino	kapoutsíno
white (with milk)	me ghála
black (without milk)	horís ghála
with sugar	me záhari
without sugar	horís záhari
a cup of tea	éna tsái
tea with lemon	éna tsái me lemóni
orange/lemon	mía portokaládha/

soda	lemonáda
fresh orange juice	éna hymó portokáli
a glass/bottle of water	éna potíri/boukáli neró
with ice	me pagháki
an ouzo/brandy	éna oúzo/koniák
a beer (draught)	mía býra (apó varélli)
an ice-cream	éna paghotó
a pastry, cake	mía pásta
oriental pastries	baklavá/kataífi

In a Restaurant

Have you got a table for...	Éhete trapézi yiá...
There are (four) of us	ímaste (tésseres)
I'm a vegetarian	íme hortofághos
Can we see the menu?	Boroúme na doúme ton katálogho?
We would like to order	Théloume na parangíloume
Have you got wine by the carafe?	Éhete krasí hýma?
a litre/half-litre of white/red wine	éna kiló/ misó kilo áspro/kókkino krasí
Would you like anything else?	Thélete típot' állo?
No, thank you	óhi, efharistó
glass	potíri
knife/fork/ spoon	mahéri/piroúni/ koutáli
plate	piáto
napkin	hartopetséta
Where is the toilet?	Pou íne i toualétta?
The bill, please	to loghariasmó, parakaló

Food

Mezédes/Orektiká

taramosaláta	fish-roe dip
tzatzíki	yoghurt-garlic-cucumber dip
melitzánes	aubergines
kolokythákia	courgettes
loukánika	sausages
tyropitákia	cheese pies
antsoúyies	anchovies
eliés	olives
dolmádhes	vine-leaves stuffed with rice
saganáki	fried cheese
fáva	puréed fava beans
piperiés florínis	red sweet pickled peppers

Meat Dishes

kréas	any meat
arní	lamb
hirinó	pork
kotópoulo	chicken
moskhári	veal, beef

Emergencies

Help!	Voíthia!
Stop!	Stamatíste!
I've had an accident	Íha éna atíhima
Call a doctor	Fonáhte éna yiatró
Call an ambulance	Fonáhte éna asthenofóro
Call the police	Fonáhte tin astinomía
Call the fire brigade	Fonáhte tous pirozvéstes
Where's the telephone?	Pou íne to tiléfono?
Where's the nearest hospital?	Pou íne to pio kondinó nosokomío?
I would like to report a theft	Éghine mia klopí

psitó	roast or grilled
sto foúrno	roast
sta kárvouna	grilled
soúvlas	on the spit
souvláki	brochettes on skewers
kokinistó	stewed in tomato sauce
krasáto	stewed in wine sauce
avgolémono	egg-lemon sauce
tiganitó	fried
kapnistó	smoked
brizóla	(pork or veal) chop
païdákia	lamb chops
sykóti	liver
kymás	mince
biftéki	burger (without bun)
keftédhes	meat-balls
soutzoukákia	rissoles baked in red sauce
yiouvarlákia	mince-and-rice balls in egg-lemon sauce
makarónia	spaghetti
piláfi	rice
me kymá	with minced meat
me sáltsa	with tomato sauce
pastítsio	macaroni with minced meat
yíros me pítta	doner kebab
domátes yemistés	stuffed tomatoes
piperiés yemistés	stuffed peppers

Seafood

frésko	fresh
katapsygméno	frozen
psári	fish
óstraka	shellfish
glóssa	sole
xifías	swordfish
koliós	mackerel
barboúnia	red mullet
sardélles	sardines
ghávros	fresh anchovy
marídhes	picarel

Numbers

1	énas/mía/éna (masc/fem/neut)
2	dhýo
3	tris/tría
4	tésseres/téssera
5	pénde
6	éxi
7	eptá
8	októ
9	ennéa
10	déka
11	éndeka
12	dódeka
13	dekatrís/dekatría
14	dekatésseres/dekatéssera
15	dekapénde
16	dekaéxi
17	dekaeptá
18	dekaoktó
19	dekaennéa
20	íkosi
30	triánda
40	saránda
50	penínda
60	exínda
70	evdomínda
80	ogdónda
90	enenínda
100	ekató
200	dhyakósa
300	trakósies/trakósa
400	tetrakósies/tetrakósa
500	pendakósa
1,000	hílies/hília
2,000	dýo hiliádhes
1 million	éna ekatomírio

mýdhia	mussels
strýdhia	oysters
kydhónia	cockles
kalamarákia	squid
soupiés	cuttlefish
htapódhi	octopus
gharídhes	prawns
kavourákia	baby crabs
astakós	lobster

Vegetables

angináres	artichokes
arakádhes	peas
domátes	tomatoes
fakés	brown lentils
fasólia/fasoládha	stewed white beans
fasolákia (fréska)	green beans, in tomato sauce
hórta	various kinds of boiled greens
karóta	carrot
kolokythákia	courgettes
kounoupídhi	cauliflower
koukiá	broad beans
kremídhi	onion
láhano	cabbage
maroúli	lettuce
pandzária	beetroot
patátes	potatoes

(tighanités/sto foúrno)	(chips/roast)
radhíkia	dandelion leaves
revíthia	chickpeas
skórdho	garlic
spanáki	spinach
spanakópitta	spinach pie
vlíta	boiled greens
ghíghandhes	stewed butter-beans
saláta	salad
domatosaláta	tomato salad
angourodomáta	tomato and cucumber salad
horiátiki	Greek salad

Fruit

míla	apples
veríkoka	apricots
banánes	bananas
kerásia	cherries
sýka	figs
stafýlia	grapes
lemónia	lemons
pepónia	melons
portokália	oranges
rodhákina	peaches
ahládhia	pears
fráoules	strawberries
karpoúzi	watermelon

Basic Foods

psomí	bread
aláti	salt
pipéri	pepper
ládhi	(olive) oil
xýdhi	vinegar
moustárdha	mustard
voútyro	butter
tyrí	cheese
avgá (tiganitá)	(fried) eggs
omelétta	omelette
marmeládha	jam, marmelade
rýzi	rice
yiaoúrti	yoghurt
méli	honey
záhari	sugar

Sightseeing

information	pliroforíes
open/closed	anihtó/klistó
Is it possible to see the church/ archaeological site?	Boroúme na dhúme tin eklisía/ta arhéa?
Where can I find the custodian/key?	Pou boró na vro to fílaka/klidhí?

At the Shops

shop	magazí/ katástima
What time do you open/close?	ti óra aníyete/ klínete?
Are you being served?	exiperitíste?
What would	Oríste/ti

you like?	thélete?
I'm just looking	Aplós kitázo
How much is it?	Póso éhi?
Do you take credit cards?	Pérnete pistotikés kártes?
I'd like...	tha íthela...
this one	aftó
that one	ekíno
Have you got...?	éhete...?
size (for clothes)	número
Can I try it on?	Boró na to dhokimáso?
It's too expensive	Íne polí akrivó
Don't you have anything cheaper?	Dhen éhete típota pyo ftinó?
Please write it down for me	To gráfete parakaló?
It's too small/big	Íne polý mikró/ meghálo
No thank you, I don't like it	Óhi efharistó, dhen m'arési
I'll take it	Tha to páro
I don't want it	Dhen to thélo
This is faulty; can I have a replacement?	Aftó éhi éna elátoma; boró na to aláxo?
Can I have a refund?	Boró na páro píso ta leftá?
a kilo	éna kiló
half a kilo	misókilo
a quarter	éna tétarto
two kilos	dhío kilá
100 grams	ekató gramária
200 grams	dhyakósa gramária
more	perisótero
less	ligótero
a little	lígo
very little	polý lígo
with/without	me/horís
That's enough	ftáni
That's all	tipot'álo

Travelling

airport	aerodhrómio
boarding card	kárta epivívasis
boat	plío/karávi
bus	leoforío
bus station	stathmós leoforíon
bus stop	stási
coach	púlman
ferry	feribót
first/second class	próti/dhéfteri thési
flight	ptísi
hydrofoil	iptámeno
motorway	ethnikí odós
port	limáni
return ticket	isitírio me epistrofí
single ticket	aplo isitírio
station	stathmós
taxi	taxí
train	tréno

Public Transport

Can you help me, please?	Boríte na me voithísete, parakaló?
Where can I buy tickets?	Pou na kópso isitírio?
At the counter	sto tamío
Does it stop at...	Káni stási sto...
You need to change at...	Tha prépi n'aláxete sto...
When is the next train/bus/ ferry to...	Póte févyi to tréno/leoforío/ feribót yia...
How long does the journey take?	Pósi óra káni to taxídhi?
What time will we arrive?	Ti óra tha ftásume?
How much is the fare?	Póso íne to isitírio?
Next stop please	Stási parakaló
Can you tell me where to get off?	Tha mou píte pou na katévo?
Should I get off here?	Edhó na katévo?
delay	kathistérisi

At the airport

I'd like to book a seat to...	Tha íthela na kratíso mia thési yia...
When is the next flight to...	Póte tha íne i epómeni ptísi yia...
Are there any seats available?	Ipárhoun thésis?
Can I take this with me?	Boró na to páro avtó mazí mou?
My suitcase has got lost	Háthike i valítsa mou
The flight has been delayed	I ptísi éhi kathistérisi
The flight has been cancelled	I ptísi mateóthike

Directions

right/left	dhexiá/aristerá
Take the first/ second right	Párte ton próto/ dhéftero drómo dhexiá
Turn right/left	strípste dhexiá/ aristerá
Go straight on	Tha páte ísia/ efthía
after the traffic lights	metá ta fanária
Is it near/ far away?	Íne kondá/ makriá?
How far is it?	Póso makriá íne?
It's five minutes' walk	Íne pénde leptá me ta pódhia
It's ten minutes by car	Íne dhéka leptá me to avtokínito
100 metres	ekató métra
opposite/next to junction	apénandi/dhípla dhiastávrosi
Where is/are...	Pou íne...
Where can I find a petrol station a bank a bus stop	Pou boró na vro éna venzinádhiko mia trápeza mia stási

a hotel?	éna xenodohío?
How do I get there?	Pos na páo ekí?
Can you show me where I am on the map?	Boríte na mou díhete sto hárti pou íme?
Am I on the right road for...	Yia... kalá páo?
No, you're on the wrong road	Óhi, pírate láthos drómo

On the Road

Where can I hire a car?	Pou boró na nikiázo avtokínito?
What is it insured for?	Ti asfália éhi?
By what time must I return it?	Méhri ti óra prépi na to epistrépso?
driving licence	díploma
petrol	venzíni
unleaded	amólivdhi
oil	ládhi
Fill it up	Óso pérni
My car has broken down	Hálase to avtokinitó mou
I've had an accident	Íha éna atíhima
Can you check...	Boríte na elénhete...
the brakes	ta fréna
the clutch	to ambrayáz
the engine	i mihaní
the exhaust	i exátmisi
the fanbelt	i zóni
the gearbox	i tahítites
the headlights	ta fanárya
the radiator	to psiyío
the spark plugs	ta buzí
the tyre(s)	ta lástiha

Times and Dates

(in the) morning/ afternoon/ evening	to proí/ to apóghevma/ to vrádhi
(at) night	(ti) níhta
yesterday	htes
today	símera
tomorrow	ávrio
now	tóra
early	norís
late	arghá
a minute	éna leptó
five/ten minutes	pénde/dhéka leptá
an hour	mia óra
half an hour	misí óra
a quarter of an hour	éna tétarto
at one/ two (o'clock)	sti mia/ stis dhýo (i óra)
a day	mia méra
a week	mia evdomádha
(on) Monday	(ti) dheftéra
(on) Tuesday	(tin) tríti
(on) Wednesday	(tin) tetárti
(on) Thursday	(tin) pémpti
(on) Friday	(tin) paraskeví

(on) Saturday	(to) sávato
(on) Sunday	(tin) kyriakí

Health

Is there a chemist's nearby?	Ipárhi éna farmakío edó kondá?
Which chemist is open all night?	Pio farmakío dhianikterévi?
I don't feel well	Dhen esthánome kalá
I'm ill	Íme árostos (feminine árosti)
He/she's ill	Íne árostos/ árosti
Where does it hurt?	Pou ponái?
It hurts here	Ponái edhó
I suffer from...	Pás-ho apo...
I have a...	Éxo...
headache	ponokéfalo
sore throat	ponólemo
stomach ache	kiliópono
Have you got something for travel sickness?	Éhete típota yia ti navtía?
It's not serious	Dhen íne sovaró
Do I need a prescription?	Hriázete sindagí?
It bit me (of an animal)	Me dhángose
It stung me	Me kéntrise
bee	mélisa
wasp	sfíka
mosquito	kounoúpi
sticking plaster	lefkoplástis
diarrhoea pills	hápia yia ti dhiária

Notices

ΤΟΥΑΛΕΤΕΣ	toilets
ΑΝΔΡΩΝ	gentlemen
ΓΥΝΑΙΚΩΝ	ladies
ΑΝΟΙΚΤΟ	open
ΚΛΕΙΣΤΟ	closed
ΕΙΣΟΔΟΣ	entrance
ΕΞΟΔΟΣ	exit
ΑΠΑΓΟΡΕΥΤΑΙ	no entry
ΕΙΣΙΤΗΡΙΑ	tickets
ΑΠΑΓΟΡΕΥΤΑΙ ΤΟ ΚΑΠΝΙΣΜΑ	no smoking
ΠΛΗΡΟΦΟΡΙΕΣ	information
ΠΡΟΣΟΧΗ	caution
ΚΙΝΔΥΝΟΣ	danger
ΑΡΓΑ	slow
ΔΗΜΟΣΙΑ ΕΡΓΑ	road works
ΠΑΡΚΙΝΓ	parking
ΧΩΡΟΣ ΣΤΑΘΜΕΥΣΕΩΣ	car park
ΑΠΑΓΟΡΕΥΤΑΙ Η ΣΤΑΘΜΕΥΣΗ	no parking
ΤΑΞΙ	taxi
ΤΡΑΠΕΖΑ	bank
ΤΗΛΕΦΩΝΟ	telephone
ΤΗΛΕΚΑΡΤΕΣ	phone cards
ΕΚΤΟΣ ΛΕΙΤΟΥΡΓΙΑΣ	out of order

Further Reading

Ancient History & Culture

Burkert, Walter **Greek Religion: Archaic and Classical**. Excellent overview of the gods and goddesses, their attributes, worship and the meaning of major festivals.

Burn, A.R. **The Penguin History of Greece**. A good, single-volume introduction to ancient Greece.

Finley, M.I. **The World of Odysseus**. Recently reissued 1954 standard on just how well (or not) the Homeric sagas are borne out by archaelogical facts.

Grimal, Pierre, ed **Dictionary of Classical Mythology**. Still considered to be tops among a handful of available alphabetical gazetteers.

Hornblower, Simon **The Greek World, 479–323 BC**. The eventful period from the end of the Persian Wars to Alexander's demise; the standard university text.

Byzantine History & Culture

Norwich, John Julius Byzantium (3 vols): **The Early Centuries, The Apogee** and **The Decline**. The most readable and masterful popular history, by the noted Byzantinologist; also available as one massive volume, **A Short History of Byantium**.

Psellus, Michael **Fourteen Byzantine Rulers**. That many changes of rule in a single century (10th–11th), as told by a near-contemporary historian.

Rice, David Talbot **Art of the Byzantine Era**. Shows how Byzantine sacred craftsmanship extended from the Caucausus into northern Italy, in a variety of media.

Runciman, Steven **The Fall of Constantinople, 1453**. Still the definitive study of an event which continues to exercise modern Greek minds. His **Byzantine Style and Civilization** covers art, culture and monuments.

Ware, Archbishop Kallistos **The Orthodox Church**. Good introduction to what was, until recently, the de facto established religion of modern Greece.

Anthropology & Culture

Campbell, John **Honor, family and patronage: A study of institutions and moral values in a Greek mountain community** Classic study of Sarakatsáni shepherds in the Zagorian Píndos, with much wider application to Greece in general, which got the author banned from the area by touchy officialdom.

Danforth, Loring H. and Tsiaras, Alexander **The Death Rituals of Rural Greece**. Riveting, annotated photo essay on Greek funeral customs.

Du Boulay, Juliet **Portrait of a Greek Mountain Village**. Ambéli, a mountain village in Évvia, as it was in the mid-1960s.

Holst, Gail **Road to Rembetika : Songs of Love, Sorrow and Hashish** (Denise Harvey, Límni, Évvia). Introduction to the enduringly popular musical form; with translated lyrics and discographies.

Mackridge, Peter **The Modern Greek Language**. In-depth analysis by one of the foremost scholars of the tongue's evolution.

Cuisine

Dalby, Andrew **Siren Feasts**. Analysis of Classical and Byzantine texts shows just how little Greek food has changed in three millennia.

Davidson, Alan **Mediterranean Seafood**. 1972 classic that's still the standard reference, guaranteed to end every argument as to just what that fish is on your *tavérna* plate. Complete with recipes.

Manessis, Nico **The Illustrated Greek Wine Book** (Olive Press Publications, Corfu; order on www.greekwineguide.gr). Includes almost all Greek vintners, from mass-market to micro.

Modern History

Clogg, Richard **A Concise History of Greece**. Clear and lively account of Greece from Byzantine times to 2000, with helpful maps and well-captioned artwork. The best single-volume summary; be sure to get the second edition (2002).

Koliopoulos, John and Thanos Veremis **Greece, the Modern Sequel: From 1831 to the Present**. Thematic and psycho-history of the independent nation, tracing trends, first principles and setbacks.

Mercouri, Melina **I Was Born Greek**. The tumultuous life and times of Greece's most famous actress, written in 1971 while she was in exile from the junta.

Pettifer, James **The Greeks: the Land and People since the War**. Useful general introduction to politics, family life, food, tourism and other contemporary topics. Get the new, updated 2002 edition.

Woodouse, C.M. **Modern Greece: A Short History**. Spans the period from early Byzantium to the early 1980s. His classic **The Struggle for Greece, 1941–1949**, recently reissued by C Hurst (London), is perhaps the best overview of that turbulent decade.

Modern Greek Literature

Beaton, Roderick **An Introduction to Modern Greek**. Readable survey of Greek literature since independence.

Cavafy, C.P. **Collected Poems**, trans. by Edmund Keeley and Philip Sherrard or **The Complete Poems of Cavafy**, translated by Rae Dalven. Considered the two best versions available in English.

Elytis, Odysseus **The Axion Esti, Selected Poems** and **The Sovereign Sun**. Pretty much the complete works of the Nobel laureate, in translation.

Kazantzakis, Nikos. Nobel laureate, woolly Marxist and self-imposed exile, Kazantzakis embodies the old maxim that classics are books praised but generally unread. Whether in intricate, untranslatable Greek or wooden English, Kazantzakis can be hard going. **Zorba the Greek** is a surprisingly dark and nihilistic work, worlds away from the crude, two-dimensional character of the film; **The Last Temptation of Christ** provoked riots by Orthodox fanatics in Athens in 1989; **Report to Greco** explores his Cretanness/ Greekness; while **Christ Recrucified** (published in the US as The Greek Passion) encompasses the Easter drama within Christian-Muslim dynamics on Crete.

Leontis, Artemis, ed **Greece: a Traveler's Literary Companion**. Various regions of the country as portrayed in very brief fiction or essays by modern Greek writers; an excellent corrective to the often condescending Grand Tourist accounts.

Mourselas, Kostas **Red Dyed Hair** (Kedros, Athens). Politically incorrect picaresque saga of urban life from the 1950s to the 1970s among a particularly feckless *paréa*; the Greek original still sells well, and formed the basis of popular TV series.

Papandreou, Nick **Father Dancing**. Thinly disguised, page-turning roman-à-clef by the late prime minister's younger son; Papandreou *père* comes across as an egotistical monster.

Ritsos, Yannis **Exile and Return, Selected Poems 1967–1974**. The outcome of junta-era internal exile on Sámos for Greece's foremost communist poet.

Papadiamantis, Alexandros; trans. Peter Levi **The Murderess**. Landmark novel written in an early form of demotic Greek, set on Skiáthos at the turn of the 19th/20th centuries.

Seferis, George; trans. Edmund Keeley **Collected Poems 1924-1955**; **Complete Poems**. The former has Greek-English texts on facing pages and is preferable to the so-called "complete" works of Greece's other Nobel literary laureate.

Sotiriou, Dido **Farewell Anatolia** (Kedros, Athens). A best-selling classic since its appearance in 1962, this traces the end of the Greeks in Asia Minor from 1914 to 1922, using a character based on the author's father.

Tsirkas, Stratis; trans. Kay Cicellis **Drifting Cities**. (Kedros, Athens). Welcome paperback re-issue of this epic novel on wartime leftist intrigue in Alexandria, Cairo and Jerusalem.

Vassilikos, Vassilis. **Z**. Based closely enough on the assassination of leftist MP Grigoris Lambrakis in 1963 by royalist thugs to get the book – and author – banned by the colonels' junta.

Foreign Writers in/on Greece

Andrews, Kevin **The Flight of Ikaros**. An educated, sensitive, Anglo-American archaeologist wanders the back-country in surprising freedom as the civil war winds down. Despite the massive changes since, still one of the best books on the country.

Bouras, Gillian **A Foreign Wife**, **A Fair Exchange** and **Aphrodite and the Others**. Scottish-Australian marries Greek-Australian, then consents to return to the "mother" country; the resulting trilogy is about the best of many chronicles of the acculturation experience.

De Bernières, Louis **Captain Corelli's Mandolin**. Heart-rending tragicomedy set on occupied Kefalloniá during World War II which has acquired cult status and long-term best-seller-list tenancy since its appearance in 1994.

Durrell, Lawrence **Prospero's Cell** and **Reflections on a Marine Venus**. Corfu in the 1930s, and Rhodes in 1945–47, now looking rather old-fashioned, alcohol-fogged and patronising of the "natives", but still entertaining enough.

Fowles, John **The Magus**. Best-seller, inspired by author's spell teaching on Spétses during the 1950s, of post-adolescent manipulation, conspiracy and cock-teasing (ie, the usual Fowles obsessions).

Gage, Nicholas **Eleni**. Epirus-born American correspondent returns to Greece to avenge the death of his mother at the hands of an ELAS firing squad in 1948.

Leigh Fermor, Patrick. **Roumeli: Travels in Northern Greece and Mani**. Written during the late 1950s and early 1960s, before the advent of mass tourism, these remain some of the best compendia of the then already-vanishing customs and relict communities of the mainland. Manus, Willard **This Way to Paradise: Dancing on the Tables** (Lycabettus Press, Athens). An American expatriate's affectionate summing-up of 40-plus years living in Líndos, from its innocence to its corruption. Wonderful anecdotes of the hippie days, and walk-on parts for the famous and infamous.

Miller, Henry **The Colossus of Maroussi**. Miller takes to Corfu, the Argolid, Athens and Crete of 1939 with the enthusiasm of a first-timer in Greece who's found his element; deserted archaeological sites and larger-than-life personalities.

Salmon, Tim **The Unwritten Places** (Lycabettus Press, Athens). Veteran Hellenophile describes his love affair with the Greek mountains, and the Vlach pastoral communities of Epirus in particular.

Stone, Tom **The Summer of my Greek Taverna**. Set in a thinly disguised Kámbos of early-1980s Pátmos, this is a poignant cautionary tale for all who've ever fantasised about leasing a taverna (or buying a property) in the islands.

Storace, Patricia **Dinner with Persephone**. New York poet resident a year in Athens successfully takes the pulse of modern Greece, with all its shibboleths, foundation myths, carefully nurtured self-image and rampant misogyny. Very funny, and spot-on.

Regional and Archaeological Guides

Burn, A. R. and Mary **The Living Past of Greece**. Worth toting its oversized format around for the sake of lively text and clear plans; covers most major sites from Minoan to medieval.

Hetherington, Paul **Byzantine and Medieval Greece**. Erudite and authoritative dissection of the castles and churches of the mainland.

Chilton, Lance **Various walking guides** Short but detailed guidelets to the best walks around various mainland and island charter destinations, accompanied by maps. See the full list and order from: www.marengowalks.com

Wilson, Loraine **The White Mountains of Crete**. The best of several guides to the range, with nearly 60 hikes of all levels, described by the most experienced foreign guide.

Botanical Field Guides

Baumann, Helmut **Greek Wildflowers and Plant Lore in Ancient Greece**. As the title says: lots of interesting ethnobotanical trivia, useful photos.

Huxley, Anthony, and William Taylor **Flowers of Greece and the Aegean**. The only volume dedicated to both islands and mainland, with good photos, though taxonomy is now a bit obsolete.

Polunin, Oleg **Flowers of Greece and the Balkans**. This book is also showing its age, but again has lots of colour photos to aid identification.

Polunin, Oleg and Anthony Huxley **Flowers of the Mediterranean**. Lots of colour plates to aid in identification, and includes flowering shrubs; recent printings have a table of taxonomic changes.

Feedback

We do our best to ensure the information in our books is as accurate and up-to-date as possible. The books are updated on a regular basis, using local contacts, who painstakingly add, amend and correct as required. However, some mistakes and omissions are inevitable and we are ultimately reliant on our readers to put us in the picture.

We would welcome your feedback on any details related to your experiences using the book "on the road". Maybe we recommended a hotel that you liked (or another that you didn't), as well as interesting new attractions, or facts and figures you have found out about the country itself. The more details you can give us (particularly with regard to addresses, e-mails and telephone numbers), the better. We will acknowledge all contributions, and we'll offer an Insight Guide to writers of the best letters received.

Please write to us at:
  Insight Guides
  PO Box 7910
  London SE1 1WE
  United Kingdom
Or send an e-mail to: insight@apaguide.demon.co.uk

ART & PHOTO CREDITS

4 Corners/Johanna Huber 281
B. & E. Anderson 91R
Heather Angel 88
Archiv Gerner 296
Ashmolean Museum 22
axiom/J. Sparshatt 175
axiom/Peter M. Wilson 280
David Beatty 40/41, 42/43, 54/55, 104, 127, 171, 180, 225, 236, 247, 250/251, 252, 253, 255, 252R, 269, 270, 272, 273, 274, 275
Benaki Museum 23, 26, 27, 28, 29, 30, 32,33, 34, 35, 36, 37
Pete Bennett/Apa front flap top, 39, 68/69, 81, 98/99, 161, 208/209, 220, 227, 231, 245L
Marcus Brooke 71, 72, 79, 153, 199, 224, 246, 239L, 239R, 259L, 282, 283, 286
J. Allan Cash Ltd 45, 74
Lance Chilton 300T
circa/Bip Mistry 166
Bruce Coleman 90L, 90R, 91L
Pierre Couteau 6/7, 8/9, 12/13, 16, 14, 18, 44, 50, 60, 84/85, 86/87, 94, 100/101, 142/143, 154/155, 160, 165, 228, 304
Marc Dubin 46, 138, 151, 167, 176, 179, 181, 202, 234/235, 214, 217,249, 293, 295
Faltaïts Museum 203
Guglielmo Galvin/Apa front flap bottom, 61, 149T, 239, 240, 240T, 241, 242T, 243, 245T, 245R, 248, 248T, 259R, 259T, 260, 261
Glyn Genin/Apa back cover left/spine, 78, 108, 114B, 114T, 185, 280, 284, 285, 287, 287T, 288, 289, 290T, 292, 293T, 294T, 298T, 300
getty/Walter Bibikow 212
robert harding/Angelo Cavalli 294
robert harding/Riccardo Lombardo 188
Blaine Harrington 169, 201
Terry Harris/Just Greece 47, 58, 77, 80, 95, 120, 165T, 170, 171T, 178T, 215, 256T

Markos G. Hionos 57, 63, 75, 97, 102/103, 122, 123, 135, 158, 198, 205, 238, 299
Ideal Photo 114T
Michael Jenner 148, 265, 266L, 266T
Ann Jousiffe 147, 221, 223, 257L, 257R
Michele Macrakis 16, 17, 48, 59, 82, 83, 134, 187, 210/211
John Miller/Corbis 133
Emil Moriannidis 1, 152, 219
Susan Muhlauser 226
Museum of Cycladic Art 24
National Tourist Organisation of Greece 19, 263
Richard T. Nowitz 109, 111, 112B, 113, 115,
Steve Outram 118/119, 139
A. Pappas/Ideal Photo 172T, 178, 224T
Anita Peltonen 144, 218, 210
M. Pharmaki/Ideal Photo 256
Photoshot/Wojtek Buss 267
Pictures Colour Library/Terry Harris 194/195
Planet Earth Pictures 137
Princeton University Library 20/21
Brian Rogers/Biofotos 89
Spectrum Colour Library 186
Karen Van Dyke 38, 48
C.Vergas/Ideal Photo 70, 132, 172, 173, 174, 202T, 297
Bill Wassman 2/3, 4/5, 10/11, 56, 73, 76, 168, 169T, 177, 189, 192/193, 232/233, 242, 262, 268, 271
Marcus Wilson Smith 25, 33
Phil Wood/Apa back cover centre, back cover right, back cover bottom, 62, 112T, 125T, 126, 126T, 128, 131, 131T, 133T, 134T, 136, 140/141, 146, 149, 175T, 184, 185T, 188T, 196, 197, 223T, 226T, 230T, 230
Gregory Wrona/Apa 15, 17, 51, 52/53, 116/117, 125, 129, 150, 156/157, 164, 183, 204, 206, 258, 276/277, 290, 291, 298, 301

Maps Polyglott Kartographie
© 2003 Apa Publications GmbH & Co. Verlag KG (Singapore branch)

Picture Spreads

Pages 64/65
Top row, left to right: Terry Harris, C. Vergas/Ideal Photo, Terry Harris, Steve Outram. Centre row: both by C. Vergas/Ideal Photo. Bottom row, left to right: Terry Harris, C. Vergas/Ideal Photo, Terry Harris, Steve Outram.

Pages 92/93
Top row, left to right: Terry Harris, Steve Outram, Terry Harris, B. & E. Anderson. Centre: Steve Outram. Bottom row: G. Sfikas/Ideal Photo, G. Sfikas/Ideal Photo, Terry Harris, Terry Harris.

Pages 190/191
Top row, left to right: Terry Harris, C. Vergas/Ideal Photo, C. Vergas/Ideal Photo, Terry Harris. Centre row, left to right: Terry Harris, Terry Harris, C. Vergas/Ideal Photo. Bottom row, left to right: Steve Outram, Natasha/Ideal Photo, Terry Harris.

Pages 302/303
Top row, left to right: Steve Outram, C. Vergas/Ideal Photo, Steve Outram, AKG Berlin. Dolphin fresco: Glyn Genin. Centre, left to right: Steve Outram, D. Ball/Ideal Photo. Bottom row: all by Steve Outram.

INSIGHT GUIDE
GREEK ISLANDS

Cartographic Editor Zoë Goodwin
Design Consultants
Carlotta Junger, Graham Mitchener
Picture Research Hilary Genin

Index

*Numbers in italics refer to
photographs*

A
B
C
D
E
F
G
H
J
a
c
d
e
f
g
h
i
j
k
l

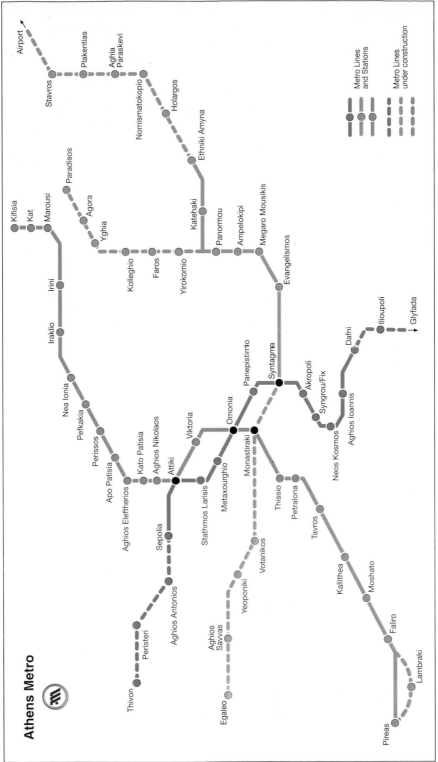

Athens Metro

INSIGHT GUIDES

The classic series that puts you in the picture

INSIGHT GUIDES
www.insightguides.com